INDIAN GOVERNMENT AND POLITICS

Indian Government and Politics

[For UGC-NET, M.A., UPSC and State Public Service Commission Examinations]

By

MANOJ SHARMA

ANMOL PUBLICATIONS PVT. LTD.

NEW DELHI - 110 002 (INDIA)

ANMOL PUBLICATIONS PVT. LTD.
4374/4B, Ansari Road, Daryaganj
New Delhi - 110 002
Ph.: 23261597, 23278000
Visit us at: www.anmolpublications.com

Indian Government and Politics

First Published, 2004

ISBN 81-261-2012-6

PRINTED IN INDIA

Published by J.L. Kumar for Anmol Publications Pvt. Ltd., New Delhi - 110 002 and Printed at Mehra Offset Press, Delhi.

Contents

Preface

Indian Government and Politics as a paper is being taught at the graduate and post graduate level in Political Science syllabus in almost all the Indian Universities. The various courses conducted by various institutions at the Central and State level too have been considered in respect of their syllabus, course contents and requirements. Thus the material presented here would be of interest as well as great use to the students of Political Science. This book has been especially designed for UGC-NET Examination, M.A. (Political Science) Students and other competitive examinations by UPSC and Public Service Commission of various States.

The major topics dealt in this book are—Making of Constitution and Development; Bases of Indian Constitution; Constitution and Amendments; Structure and Process; Panchayati Raj Institutions; Federalism : Theory and Practice in India; Emerging Trends in Centre-State Relations; Judiciary; Political Parties and Pressure Groups; Elections and Electoral Behaviour etc.

Manoj Sharma

1

Making of Constitution and Development

East India Company set its foot on Indian soil in the year 1600 A.D. when Mughals were at the height of their power and glory. Within a century of their stay in our beautiful rich country. Mughal empire began to decay and disintegrate, after the death of last Great Mughal Emperor, Aurangzeb in 1707 A.D. There were rebellions against Mughal authorities in all parts of the country and Rajputs, Marathas, Scindias, Holkars and many other declared themselves independent. Almost none of these powers was militarily well-equipped, financially sound and with any scientific spy system and with well developed means of transportation and communication to face any powerful enemy.

Socially, the society was sharply divided into castes and sub-castes. Both the Hindus and the Muslims were suffering from their own social evils. Era of mutual understanding that had been opened by Great Mughal Emperor Akbar, was a thing of the past. Hatred, jealousy and spirit of revenge between the two communities was to be seen almost every where.

There was lack of political leadership and the whole country had no leader under whose banner and at whose call all Indians could unite and face any calamity. On the whole Indian society was completely degenerated one. The society suffered from superstitions and was full of orthodoxy. There was also large scale poverty and illiteracy. The division of society into caste and sub-castes very adversely affected even our political unity. The country badly lacked national feelings. As pointed out by Dr. R.C. Mazumdar the people knew of Bengal, Maharashtra and Madras but not of India. For a

Bengali a Maratha was not a foreigner but a hated foreigner. India badly lacked sense of social and political unity.

We can devide the constitutional history of India into five phases:

(i)	I Phase	-	1600 to 1772
(ii)	II Phase	-	1773 to 1832
(iii)	III Phase	-	1833 to 1857
(iv)	IV Phase	-	1858 to 1909
(v)	V Phase	-	1909 to 1947

REGULATING ACT OF 1773

1t was this social, economic and political background which prevailed in India during first half of 18th century. Real matter of regret was that situation was deteriorating day-by-day. The whole country was lying exposed before any victor, whose coveted eyes could grab it any moment, without much difficulty, though not without resistance. East India Company which had come to India merely for trading could not resist this temptation of converting India into a part of British empire. But it was not the only power which dreamt for mastery over India. France and Portugal were other contenders which challenged British traders in India. Several factors combined together ultimately resulted in the victory of East India Company and defeat of other European powers.

Each victory of East India Company, both against the Indian princes as well as western powers, created both a sense of superiority and arrogances. Military strength of the Company went on increasing and with that the number of forts, ports and territories too. Revenues of the Company rose many-folds and even beyond the expectations of the servants of the Company.

Unfortunately, however, the servants of the Great Company in India, did not follow policy of enlightened rulers. They did not give justice to the people of India. Both the princes as well as the masses were ruthlessly exploited. They were even forced to sell their utensils to pay off the revenues of the Company. Respected rulers and people were disgraced and humiliated in the public. In fact, most inhuman and unfair means were used to collect money from the people. The result was that poverty, misery, unemployment and insecurity in the country increased beyond all proportions. Even the conscience of civilised world shocked to know the brutalities of traders. When India was being exploited, the shareholders of the Company were being in no way profited, the Company revenues were always in the red. It was primarily because servants of the Company were engaged in their private trade. They were the neo-rich who polluted not only India's social and economic system, but also political system of their own country. With the help of their illegally earned money, they purchased voters and themselves returned to House of Commons, thus, upsetting the whole political system. This was increasingly becoming cause of serious concern for politicians, feudal lords and even monarchy itself. Though East India Company was expanding itself in India, yet there was no written law to govern and guide either the administration or the subjects. It was because India was never governed by a written constitution and secondly, in England there was also no written constitution. For want of written constitution, British Parliament also could not excrcise any effective control over East India Company.

Requests for Finances. Both for the Directors as well as servants of East India Company interference from any corner in their internal affairs was not at all a welcome. But when due to regular and expensive wars with Indian princes and large-scale private trade of servants of the Company, it reached a point of financial bankruptcy, there was no other alternative but to approach the British Parliament to come to the rescue of Company Bahadur. Horrifying news of economic exploitation, and stories of mis-deeds of Company's servants were heart-rendering for British people, who were awaiting an opportunity to set the house of the Company in order. This first opportunity was, therefore, not missed, more particularly because it was felt that it will help in checking political pollution in England engineered by neo Nawabs in the shape of Company's servants. The Parliament agreed to advance funds to the Company provided it agreed to accept its control in its working. Since there was no other alternative, the Company willy-nilly agreed to the controls, which were exercised through the instrument of Acts passed from time to time, more or less at 20 years intervid till 1857, when first war of Indian independence broke out and subsequently Company's administration was transferred from the Company to the Crown.

With the passing of each Act, British government tried to have more and effective control over the working of East India Company, but unfortunately the situation could not be contained till the control of Indian administration was transferred from the Company to the Crown. One salient feature of these Acts remained that no effective masures were taken to find out Indian opinion on the performance of East India Company. It can, therefore, appropriately be said that the whole law making process was just a trial and error method and more like duping in the dark, rather than based on public estimation or on any scientific or rational principles.

British government in India was much concerned about the poor administration of East India Company in India, which was based on naked exploitation of the masses. It was an administration which claimed from people only rights without itself performing corresponding duties. By this time it had become de facto sovereign of Bengal, Bihar and Orissa. The system of double government introduced by Lord Clive in Bengal in 1765, had resulted utter administrative confusion. All the three organs of the government vied each other in mis-management. There was so much of exploitation of masses that in the words of G.N. Singh, "Never before had the natives experienced a tyranny which was at once of skilfull, so searching and so strong that on appearance of party of English merchants, the villages were at once deserted and the shops shut and the roads thronged with panic stricken fugitives." But in spite of all economic exploitation of Indians, East India Company was facing financial crisis. In 1772, it approached British Parliament for a loan for meeting, financial crisis. The Parliamant agreed to this and decided to regulate the affairs of the Company. It passed Regulating Act of 1773.

Main Provisions of Act, 1773. Main provisions of the Act of 1773, were that only those proprietors were allowed to vote for the appointment of Directors of Company who held a stock of £ 1000.

The Directors were required to submit copies of all correspondence about Indian revenues to the treasury. Provision was made for the appointment of a Governor-General and for Councillors for the Presidency of Fort William in Bengal. The Governor of Bengal was to be known as the Governor-General. In case of differences, the Governor-General was to go by majority decision. He was, however, given a casting vote. He was also to look after and control the administration of Presidencies of Bengal, Bihar and Orissa.

Governor-General and members of the Council were to hold office for a period of 5 years but could be removed earlier as well. He was also required to supervise the working of Presidencies of Bombay and Madras. No hostilities against any Indian prince could' start or end without prior permission of the Governor-General. He, in his Council could, also issue orders and rules as well as ordinances for the good government of territories under Company's control. No such law which was, however, to be repugnant to any law of England and was considered valid only after that had been registered and published by the Supreme Court. The Crown was also empowered to disapprove any law, rule or ordinance issued by the Governor-General in Council.

Provision was also made for the establishment of a Supreme Court of judicature at Fort William in Bengal. The Court was equipped with civil, criminal, admirality and ecclesiastical jurisdictions. Its jurisdictions were to. extend to all British subjects in India. The Supreme Court was to try all cases by a jury of British subjects residing in India. It was to consist of a Chief Justice and two other judges. It was empowered to hear all complaints against any of the Majesty's subjects for any crime. The Governor-General and members of his Council were, however, kept out of its jurisdictions. It was given both original and appellate jurisdictions.

The servants of the Company were forbidden to either directly or indirectly receive any presents. They were also not allowed to do any private business nor lend money at higher rate of interest. The salaries of servans of the Company were also increased to check their temptation of accepting bribery.

Critical Evaluation of the Act. Soon the operation of the Act showed that it had certain inherent defects. Some of its defects as Punniah makes us beheve were due to in experience of the authors. But on the whole the defects were so serious that it was good luck of the British government that these did not prove fatal. According to the provisions of the constitution the Governor-General was completely placed at the mercy of his Council. Thus, he was reduced to a cipher. There was no clear cut division of powers of the Governor-General-in-Council and the Supreme Court, which obviously resulted in very serious problems. It was also not specified, which type of law the courts were to administer, *i.e.* British or Indian; Voting conditions and qualifications for Directors', appointment were raised, resulting in disfranchisement of many. Roberts is of the view that this did not serve the object and purpose for which it was enacted. Though the Company was required to send copies of the correspondence to the Parliament, yet there was no machinery to scrutinise these and thus, Parliament's control remained ineffective.

The Act made the Governor-General responsible for the preservation of peace throughout India but it did not confer adequate powers on him for discharging this responsibility. Initiative for declaring war and concluding peace still remained with Presidency governments. The Act also did not clearly specify the relationship of Supreme Court with the existing courts and as such jurisdictional conflicts very much arose. The Act also did not specify as to who was servant of the Company and what entitled one of be a as servant of the Company.

Thus, the Act had certain basic defects which came to light soon after it was but in to operation. But at the same time it cannot be denied that it was a significant measure. With the passing of this Act it was accepted that East India Company was a political organisation. It curtailed the powers of the Company and was in fact a step forward to end its scandalous mis-rule. Then with this Act British government, as a nation accepted responsibility of Indian administration. In the Words of Lyall, the Act gave a definite and recognizable form, to the vague and arbitrary powers of sovereignty, that had devolved upon the Company.

The Act is important because it was first step towards unification of India. All the three presidencies were combined into a unified whole. The Governor-General-in-Council was made responsible for peace and good government of company's possessions in India. In the words of G.N. Singh, "The Act of 1773.... asserted for the first time the right of Parliament to dictate the form of government in what were considered till then the private possessions of the company and because it is the first of a long series of parliamentary statutes that altered the form of government in India."

THE AMENDING ACT OF 1781

In a bid to rectify the defects of the Regulating Act, before it was a complete break down, a Committee was appointed in 1781 to look into its working. It was on the basis of recommendations of this committee that Amending Act was passed. By provisions of this Act public servants of the Company, while performing their duties, were exempted from the jurisdictions of the Supreme Court. The court was to administer personal law of the defendant and show reverence to religious laws and practices of Indians. The Governor-General-in-Council was empowered to make regulations for provincial courts and Councils and these were now need not be necessarily registered with the Surpreme Court.

It was now provided that the Supreme Court shall not have powers in revenue matters and acts done in revenue collection. The Act also recognised appellate jurisdictions of Governor-General-in-Council and provided that henceforth appeals from the Privincial Councils would lie before the Governor-General-in-Council and not in the Supreme Court. The decision of the Governor-General-in-Council was to be final. He was also to act as a revenue court. He was also given powers to frame regulations for provincial courts and Councils from time to time. The King-in-Council, however, could disallow any such regulation.

In this way the Act tried to clarify the relationship between the Governor-General and the Supreme Court. It recognised as well as legalised legislative powers of the Governor-General-in-Council over Bengal, Bihar and Orissa. A.B. Keith is of the view that the Act asserted the necessity of supporting the government, the importance of regular collection of revenues and the maintenance of people in their ancient laws.

DUNDA'S BILL

In April 1783, Dunda introduced a bill in the House of Commons in which he proposed that the King should be given powers to recall principal servants of the Company and that the Governor-General should be given powers to over-ride the decisions of his Council, if need be. He should be given more powers in his dealings with Presidencies. But Dunda's bill could not be carried out, because he was in the opposition.

FOX'S BILL

Dunda's Bill had its own importance and was significant in the sense that it focused nation's attention towards introducing reforms. In November of the same year Fox interoduced East India Bill. It provided for marking a distinction between commercial and non-commercial interests of the Company and also replacement of existing Court of Directors and propritors by a Board of Commissioners. The Board was to sit in London and its minutes could be inspected by the British Parliament. But the Bill was vehemently opposed. It was felt that the proposed Bill aimed at destroying, chartered rights of the Company. It was also felt that, "It seemed to shift a vast patronage not from the company to the Crown but to the political party, who it was asserted would use it to debauch Parliament and gild the chains of new political slavery." The bill was defeated in the House of Lords with the personal-intervention of George III. It must, however, be acccepted that, "It was sincere and statesman like effort to deal with a great problem on comprehensive lines" and undoubtedly a vigorous effort to reform the whole constitution. It undoubtly set the ball in motion for more control over company affairs and to examine deeply the problems which were hollowing down whole of its super-structure.

PITTS INDIA ACT, 1784

Early in 1784, Pitt introduced his own Bill to mend the affairs of the Company, but the Bill was defeated in the initial stages. Pitt dissolved the House but was voted back to power. In August of the same year he introduced his Bill again which was passed into an Act. Some of the main provisions of the Act were as under:

It provided for a Board of Control of six members which included both a Secretary of State and Chancellor of Exchequre. They were all to be appointed by the King and to hold office during his pleasure. They were honorary members and not vested with any power of making appointments. They had access to all papers of the Company and Court of Directors were bound by their orders. They were to ensure prompt disposal of business. They could also send secret letters to the Court of Directors on any important matter. In future all the appointments of servants of the Company were to be made by the Court of Directors but the Crown was given powers to retain any person so appointed. All commercial transactions were to be done by the Court of Directors.

It was provided that only covenanted servants of the Company could be appointed as Councillors of the Governor-General. Council of Governor-General was in future to consist of only three and not four members. The Governor-General was to be appointed by the Court of Directors. The control of the Governor-General over the presidencies was strengthened the former was given the power of superintendence over the latter. It was specifically provided that the Presidency Governors were duty bound to carry out the instructions of the Governor-General-in-Council. The Council of Governors of the Presidencies was also to consist of 3 and not of 4 members. These were placed under the control of Bengal Presidency and thus, a step forward was taken towards India's unification. The Governor and his councillors could be removed by the King. Provision was also made for trial of Company's servants in England for the offences committed by them in India. Servants of the Company were not to deal with money matters with native princes. Commander-in-Chief of armed forces of the Presidency was to be a member of the Governor's Council.

Critical Assessment of the Act. The Act was really important and remained baste structure of Indian administration till 1858. In the words of Prof. S.R. Sharma. "The directors now payed second fiddle to the British Government who possessed almost unlimited powers of issuing such orders which the Directors were bound to obey. It established centralised control of Governor-General-in-Council in India over Indian Affairs. The position of the Governor-General and Governor was very much strengthened and they became executive heads of their respective administration. Powers of the Court of Proprietor considerably got reduced. Rose J. Holland, in his 'Life of William Pitt' has said that the Bill was Pitt's highest achievement because he combined the two ideal of Government, namely, oriental and occidental.

The Act established dual government. On the one hand was Board of Control whereas on the other was Board of Directors. The former was made much more powerful as compared with the latter because it was givin extensive powers about superintendence, direction and control of British possessions in India. It could also give orders in a way to the Board of Directors. According to some, the control of Board of Control was so extensive that for all practical purposes, the Board of Director became a non-entity. But in actual working of the Act, it was found that the system was not based on very sound principles, because the control was both remote and territories very extensive. The Act made an attempt by which government was divided into two halves and it proved to be unworkable. In fact, it resulted in weak and inefficient administration. The relations in such matters as appointment, and control of troops between the Board of Control and Board of Directors were not defined in much detail. The Governor-General's position was very awkward because he was to serve two masters; on the one hand was the Board of Control and on the other Board of Directors. Since all correspondence was to pass through Board of Control and its approval was necessary in all matters, therefore, whole administrative machinery of the Company became slow, sluggish and cumbersome. Directors of the Company were still not well paid and always felt tempted to accept bribes and use other illegal means to make money. The Act also came under heavy pressures because it gave the Board of Control all authority without any responsibility.

THE ACT OF 1786

The Regulating Act made the Governor-General powerless before his Council. In its actual working this provision of the Act created many problems. The Act of 1786, empowered the Governor-General to over-rid his Council, whenever he felt that, that was absolutely necessary. He was however, bound to consult his Council but it was left to him to accept or not to accept Council's advice. It was provided that in future no one shall be appointed as a member of the Council unless he had atleast 12 years service. The Court of Directors could combine the office of the Governor-General and Commander-in-Chief.

THE CHARTER ACT OF 1793

According to one of the provisions of the Act of 1773, the Charter of the Company was confirmed only for 20 years. Accordingly it fell due for renewal in 1793, when country was busy in dealing with France. Accordingly the Act was passed without much noise. According to Dr. A.C. Banerjee, the Act was merely a statute of consolidation.

According to this Act Company's privileges were extended for another period of 20 years. The members of Board of Control who were hitherto honorary were paid salaries out of Indian funds. Some amount was earmarked for the liquidation of Company's debt and increased dividends. It was now not compulsory that the Commander-in-Chief must be member of Governor-General or Governor's Council. The Governor-General could also appoint a Vice-President. The Governor-General and the Governors were given powers to over-ride their Council in cases involving safety, tranquility and interests of British possessions. The servants of the Company were forbidden to accept any gifts/presents, etc. and each servant of the company was to be accorded some rank.

It was now not necessary to have the approval of the king for the appointment of Governor-General, Governor and Commander-in-Chief. It was once again made clear that the Company should not interfere in the affairs of Indian princely states.

Each Presidency was to be governed by a Governor and three members of Council who must have resided in India for a period of 12 years. Their departure from India without permission was to be considered as resignation from service. Governor-General and the Governors were empowered to over-ride their Councils, if need be. When visiting a Presidency the Governor-General was to supersede the Governor. In such cases he was also authorised to issue orders and directions to subordinate Presidencies. Promotions of civil servants was based on seniority and it was made clear that policy of conquests and expansion should be abondoned.

Since the Act did not introduce any important changes, therefore, it did not attract much attention of the people. Constitutionally not much significance is, however, attached to it.

THE CHARTER ACT OF 1813

The Act of 1793, was passed without much noise and did not draw much attention of the nation because of England's involvement in France. In 1813, when Charter of the Company came up again for renewal, there was a demand that it should not be renewed. There were several reasons for this. It was a time when theory of laissez faire as expounded by Adam Smith, had become popular. Many British exporters had suffered on account of blockade of Napolean and wanted new avenues for trade. Since Company's territories had expanded very much it was pleaded that commercial mercial interests of the Company should be clearly separated from non-commercial interests. It was also pleaded that Company in India was following a costly policy of wars and conquests and as such it need be checked. Thus, when the Charter came for renewal, the Parliament was under heavy pressure not to renew that. But ultimately it decided to continue the Company in India for another 20 years and Charter was renewed. The main provisions of the Act were:

Main Provisions of the Act. The Charter of the Company was renewed for another 20 years but trade in India was thrown open to all British subjects. British merchants and missionaries were permitted to go and settle in India. The Justices of Peace were empowered to try British subjects in India. A sum of Rs. one lakh annually was earnmarked for the spread of education, science and literature in India. Vacancies in the offices of Governor-General and Commander-in-Chief were to be filled by the Directors, subject to the approval of His Majesty. Number of troops paid out of Company's revenues was fixed at 20,000. Board's power of superintendence and direction was clearly defined. The Company was to keep apart a fixed sum of amount for meeting eventualities and provision was made from reduction of Company's debts.

Christian missionaries were also allowed to be settled down in India. The Company was also now required to maintain two separate accounts one for commercial transactions and the other for territorial possessions. The Company was authorised to hold court martial and the Board of Control was empowered to make regulations for civil and military servants of the Company. Its powers of superintendence were considerably increased. Local governments were empowered to impose taxes on those who were within the jurisdictions of the Supreme Court. The Act also made a provision for the administration of justice in cases in which Indians and Britishers were involved.

The Act was important because it abolished Company's trade monopoly in India and thus, was reduced to the position of a competitor. It accepted in principle that the Company had responsibility to morally and intellectually lift the people of India. But with the free flow of British capital in India, there was exploitation of Indians and indigenous industries received a great set-back. The Act also permitted the coming of Charistion missionaries to India and thus, in the religious field a new chapter was opened.

THE CHARTER ACT OF 1833

In 1833, Company's Charter again came for revision before the British Parliament. It was a time when the people of England were thinking in terms of liberalism, humanitarianism and free trade. Slave trade had been abolished and there was talk of human rights. The people like Bentham, Macaulay, Grey and Mill were at that time at the helm of affairs Grant, Lansdowne and Buckingham very vehemently criticised Company's administration and the ways in which it was conducting itself in India. The Company came under severe criticism and a demand was made that Indians should be associated in the running of their own administration. It was also pleaded that British Parliament should take more interest in Indian affairs. Keith went to the extent of saying that, "A broken head in Cold Bath field produces a greater sensation among us than three pitched battles in India." Macaulay very forcefully defended the Company in the face of bitter opposition. The Charter Act, 1833 was however ultimately passed.

Main Provisions of the Act. The Company's Charter this time was not renewed for a period of 20 years but it was asked to retain India's administration and political powers in trust for His Majesty till April, 1854. The Company's trade monopoly with China came to an end. The constitution of Board of Control was modified and restrictions on immigration and acquisition of landed property by European in India were removed. The Act aimed at centralising all powers and authority in the hands of the Governor-General. All Powers of superintendence and control were vested in the hands of Governor-General-in-Council. A fourth member, *i.e.* a Law Member was added to his Council. For the codification of law he was authorised to appoint an Indian Law Commission.

Administration of Presidencies was to be run by the Governor-General-in-Council and each Governor could suggest to the Governor-General-in-Council drafts for the enactment of laws. Each Presidency government could correspond directly, with the Board of Directors. In all financial matters Presidencies were made subordinate to the Supreme Government.

Several senior Ministers of the government were made ex-officio members of the Board of Control. The President of the Board was given a casting vote, if the Board was equally divided on any issue. The President of the Board was to be assisted by two assistant Commissioners. He was made Minister for Indian affairs. The Presidencies of Bombay and Madras were deprived of all legislative powers. These powers were now vested in the Governor-General. The laws passed by the Governor-General-in-Council had jurisdictions over all British subjects, but he could not make any changes in the Charter of the Company.

It was said that in future fitness shall be the sole criteria for holding all job in Company's service. Steps were to be taken for the abolition of slavery in India and also that facilities were to be provided for training of civil servants for India at Company's college at Hailesbury.

Presidency Governors were deprived of legislative and financial powers. They were now to get approval of Governor-General-in-Council for all expenses. Except in urgent cases they could not enact any regulation. Presidencies could maintain armies but these were subject to the control of Governor-General. All natural born subjects of Crown could now reside in any part of India without procuring any licence.

The Act was significant in several ways. It declared that henceforth all posts shall be filled up on the basis of fitness and not on the considerations of birth or religion of the person. Then another significance of the Act was that it suggested codification and simplification of laws. Again it was this Act which did not renew Company's Charter for another twenty years and ended Company's trade monopoly with China. It made a provision for the training of Company's civil servants and as such a step forward for efficient administration of Company's affairs was taken.

THE CHARTER ACT, 1853

The Charter Act, 1853 had made very high sounding promises. Indians had hoped to get some share in the running of their own administration. But during 1833—53 not even a single native got any important job. Company's mis-management continued and nothing substantial came out as was hoped by the authors of the Act. There was an increasing demand that Company's Charter should not be renewed. The government accordingly appointed a select committee to examine the whole issue. On the basis of the recommendations of the Committee, the Act of 1853, was enacted. It was the last Charter Act which was passed by the Parliament for the Company.

The Act did not renew Charter for 20 years and reduced the number of Directors from 24 to 18, six of whom were to be appointed by the Crown. A provision was made for a separate

Govemor of Bengal. The Directors were empowered to create one more Presidency. Law member was made regular member of Governor-General's Council. Executive and legislative functions of the Governor-General's Council were separated from each other.

The Court of Directors was deprived of all its patronage power as all services were thrown open for competitive examinations. The Government was to fix the salaries of members of Board of Control, which were however, to be paid out of company funds. Provision was also made for the appointment of Lt. Governor of Bengal and appointment of Law Commission in England. The Commission was to review the draft laws proposed by Indian Law Commission. Ordinary member of Governor-General's Council was given the status of regular member with voting right in the meetings of the executive Council.

The Act also enlarged the Council of the Governor-General for legislative purposes by adding 6 new legislative members, thus raising Council's strength to 12. It introduced local representative in the Indian legislature for the first time. The laws passed by the Councils of Madras, Bombay and Bengal were subject to the approval of the Governor-General.

Evalution of the Act. The Act of 1853, was important in its own way. By providing separate Governor of Bengal interests of that Presidency were protected. The Directors were denied their power of patronage. The prestige of the President of Board of Control increased. It marked the beginning of parliamentary system of government in India. It provided separate legislative council which meant realisation about good legislation In the arrangement of things. It stressed the need of merit in recruitment to services than appointment on patronage basis. But the Act did not associate any Indian in law making process. It also did not abolish the system of double government.

From the brief account given above it becomes clear that the British government wanted to have some control over the affairs of East India Company, but it was not capable of doing so. Firstly, the Directors of the Company were not interested in parting with their powers and did everything possible to create hurdles. Most of the members of Parliament were not aware of the real conditions of the people of India. In fact, they were not interested in knowing these as well. They were guided by the servants of the Company who were always keen to give a wrong one-sided picture. In addition, those at the helm of affairs legislated on the basis of paper reports and thus laws were not based on practical experience. The areas governed were also vast. Combined together British Parliament was unable to have any effective control over Company's affairs.

One characteristic of feature of these Acts was that no efforts were made to know Indian public opinion for getting the co-operation of Indians in running their own administration. In this way whole Administration was run without caring for the needs of the people of India and this ultimately bursted in the rising of 1857.

CAUSES RESPONSIBLE FOR THE RISING OF 1857

Though British Parliament had been passing Acts renewing the Charters of the Company, from time to time, yet no Indian was associated in the whole process. Accordingly there was no mechanism by which indian opinion or aspirations could be known to the Governor-General or his Council. Thus, many Act were passed and steps taken which were much, against the wishes of the people of India and highly resented by the masses.

Then the British Parliament had been on record that Indians will be given increasing share in the running their own administration. The people of India had also been assured that in recruitment to all services ability and not religion or birth of the candidate will be the sole criteria. But this remained a wishful thinking. Indians remained where they were in the services and they were practically allowed no entry to services. No Indian was ever appointed on any high job. It was taken for granted that Indians had no administrative ability or merit.

The Charter Acts had provided for the entry of Christian Missionaries to India. They had government support. Soon they spread their activities all over the country. There was a wide-spread feeling among Indians that these missionaries were converting them to their own religion and disgracing and disreputing their culture and civilisation for which we had maximum regard.

Then was the policy of annexation which was followed by Lord Dalhousie. His doctrine of lapse was a constant threat for the prices and they found that the only solution to the problem was end of East India Company rule. East India Company had followed policy of dumping in Indian market goods manufactured in their own country. These were cheap, good and beautiful. The result was that Indian manufacturers and handicraft workers lost their jobs and they became unemployed. Thus, in the country on the one hand was exploitation whereas on the other was ever increasing poverty and unemployment. This created great discontentment among the masses.

The intelligentsia in India was also greatly upset and brewing with discontentment because their worth was not being apperciated and they were not being given due respect and recognition. They had been denied higher jobs in company's services. Not only this but the East India Company in India followed a policy of racial discrimination in which Indians were always considered an inferior race. Indian Culture and civilisation was seen with great contempt and the rulers believed that a everything that was Indian must be hated. This created popular resentment against the rulers.

East India Company in India followed policy of conquests and as such Indians were always at war in one part of the country or the other. The whole nations had become sick of these wars and wanted to decide its fate in one way or the other. Indian army was not at all satisfied with East India Company. The soliders were very low paid. Indians were not allowed to occupy high positions in the army even though they very much deserved these. The Company also annoyed the last of the Mughals, Bahadur Shah by refusing him the title of the 'King'. As the time passed Indian cottage and small-scale industries which provided employment to millions were killed. There was large-scale poverty and unemployment both among the educated, uneducated, skilled and unskilled masses. Indians were groaning under the pangs of poverty and unemployment.

East India Company did nothing for the welfare of Indian masses. It only ruthlessly, economically exploited Indians. The servants of the Company suffered from superiority complex and injured self-respect of Indians at each stage.

In this way there was no section of Indian society, which was happy with the policies which the Company was following in India. There was sufficient discontentment in the country which could engulf the nation on little pretext and this came out when soldiers in the army were asked to use greased cartridges. It proved a signal and Rising began on January 23,1857. It spread in several parts of the country. The leaders of the Rising were Rani Laxmi Bai of Jhansi Tantia Tope and host of othcrs who held the banner of the Rising and tried to make it a mass movement. The Rising spread to Delhi, Meerut, Kanpur, Calcutta and many other parts of the country.

The Company of course could suppress the Rising With the help of its superior armed strength and active co-operation of some native princes yet it was an eye awakening for the British government. In the words of G.N. Singh, "In restoring order, however, the British committed great atrocities, the memory of which rankled in Indian mind long after the rising was suppressed and produced consequences whose significance escaped recognition till only recently."

Nature of Rising. What was the real nature of rising? The British historians and supporters of the East India Company have tried to establish that it was not arrising but only a sepoy revolt which had the backing of some dispossessed and disgrantled native princes who extended their support to the soldiers. It was thus, according to them, not at all a rising. According to some others it was a rising which had been engineered by intelligentsia to air their grievances and to focus Company's attention to meet their demand of additional share in their administration. Still others come with the argument that it was an engineered movement of landlords of the country. It is also claimed that it was not national because it simply spread in some pockets of the country. But this does not appear to be true. It was real rising in the sense that in its spread the landlords, the princes; the soldiers, the intelligentsia, and even common people, including artisans and agriculturists actively contributed. The movement could not spread throughout the country, because Indians had no quick means of transportation and communication at their disposal. They also did not have the requisite military strength and training to face the East India Company. There was also lack of leadership. There was serious shortage of finances as well.

Abolition of the East India Company. The rising established beyond doubt that Indians wanted a new political system, in which they should have their own share. They proved that they were politically conscious and thus could not be manhandled by their rulers. Then as Keith has pointed out, "Inevitably the blame for the debacle fell on Company and its rule was doomed." The British government, therefore, decided to take over India's administration in its own hands and give the country a new political system. In February 1858, Lord Palmerston introduced a bill for the abolition of East India Company. This was ably opposed by J.S. Mill, who supported the cause of the Company. According to him the affairs of East India Company were being regularly reviewed by the Parliament since 1783. The Company had all along submitted its reports to the Board of Control. It had created an empire in India by making all sacrifices. But Palmerston pleaded, "I see no reason either on the score of principle or on the score of augmentation of patronage or on the score of time or constitutional danger, why we should not at once pass the measure." On March 26, 1858, Bill was introduced in the House of Commons to take over the administration of India by the British government from the Company. There were many changes in the proposed Bill and ultimately it became an Act on August 2, 1958.

THE GOVERNMENT OF INDIA ACT OF 1858

Military and Naval Forces of the Company were transferred from the Company to the Queen and Government of India was to be carried on by the Viceroy on behalf of the Queen. Both the Board Directors and Board of Control were abolished. All the revenues were to be received and spent by the Government of India. A separate Secretary of State was to be appointed to look after Indian affairs and to be paid out of Indian revenues. All communications and orders for the commencement of hostilities in India were to be placed before both the Houses of Parliament within a period of 3 months.

Secretary of State for India was to superintend and control Indian affairs. He was to have his Council and was to be a member of the British cabinet. His Council was to consist of 35 members out of which eight were to be appointed by the Crown and remaining seven to be elected by Court of Directors. At least 50% of the members were to be those who would have lived in India for at least ten years and not left the country for more than 10 years at the time of their appointment.

Secretary of State was given casting vote in case of differences of opinion, but ordinarily all the decisions were to be taken by a majority of votes. Appointments to all covenated services were to be made on the basis of open competitions. Governor-General and Governors were to be appointed by the Crown.

Queen's Proclamation. While taking over Indian administration, the Queen however made it amply clear that, "We shall respect the right, the dignity and honour of native princes as our own." It was also decided that there will be no policy of annexation and conquest of territories and the British government will adhere to the principles of secularism and religious neutrality and had a desire to admit all the subjects of Her Majesty to public services without distinction of race or creed.

It was also proclaimed that all treaties obligations of the Company already given to Indian princes will be honoured. It assured complete freedom of religion and worship and that while enacting laws due regard will be shown to ancient customs and wages. The works of public utility for the benefit of all subjects will be undertaken.

Significance of the Act. Both Queen's Proclamation as well as Act of 1858, have great constitutional significance. It was accepted that in future ability and not religion or colour will govern recruitments in public services. India's revenues were henceforth to be invested in India and era of annexations and conquests was to come to an end. The Council of Secretary of State was to have at least 50% such members who were aware of Indian conditions and the people of the country. India was no more to be governed by traders and as such it could be reasonably hoped that the period of exploitation had come to an end. The system of double government, *i.e.* that of Board of Directors and Board of Control came to an end. Healthy relations were established between the native princes and the British government once it was clear that there would be no conquests or annexations. Dr. Ishwari Parsad is of the view that, "The Act of 1858, was the culmination of the process begun by Pitt in 1784, and merely dressed the seat of power and responsibility with the outward semblance of authority.

According to some thinkers the assumption of Government of India by the Crown was formality because the crown was already exercising a lot of control over the Company. Gradually and slowly the Company's powers had been reduced and it was made obligatory for it to accept the decisions of the Parliament. It had lost much of its authority and power long before the Act was passed.

The change was, however, real and effective and as such it is difficult to agree with Sir H.S. Cunningham who has tried to establish that assumption of Government of India by the Crown was rather a formal than a substantial change.

But major defect of the Act still remained that neither any political rights were given to Indians nor they were given any share in the running or their own affairs. The power and authority of permanent civil servants for India appointed in England was very much increased. They were virtually not amendable to control of any superior authority in india.

THE INDIAN COUNCILS ACT, 1861

The Act of 1858, was passed in a great hurry as there was no time to think over the details. All that was wanted was that administration of India should come in the hands of British government and the people of India should be kept satisfied. But still the Act made no provision by which Indians could be associated in the running of their own administration. Both in India and England it was crystal clear that had there been a mechanism by which Indian public opinion could authentically be known to the rulers perhaps there would have been no outburst. It was felt that, "Voice of people alone can check error in the bud and warn us of dangers before they burst upon and destroy us. It was also felt that though the Company had done some good to the country, but the greatest mischief lay in this that the people mis-understood the views and intentions of the government." Therefore, there was strong desire that if the blunder was not to be repeated it was essential that Indians should be associated with the working of the Councils.

It was realised that the present arrangement in which one Council enacted laws for the whole country was inadequate and there was every possibility that most of the laws could be passed in ignorance. Provincial governments were feeling unhappy because there was growing feeling among them that these were being unnecessarily dominated by Bengal Council and the Governor-Gernreal. Moreover there was an increasing demand in India that they should be associated in legislative and other decision-making processes.

To overcome these difficulties Sir Charles Wood introduced a Bill on June 6, 1861 to incorporate necessary changes in the Act of 1858, to make it more representative in nature and character. The Bill subsequently came to be known as the Indian Council Act, 1861.

Main Provisions of the Act. The number of ordinary members of executive council of Governor-General was raised to five, the fifth being the one who possessed legal qualifications. The Governor-General was empowered to frame rules and regulations for the transaction of business in his Council. Secretary of State was empowered to appoint Commander in-Chief as extraordinary member of his Council.

It was provided that the Council of Governor-General would be expanded for law making purposes by the addition of not less than 6 and not more than 12 members and 1/2 of these would be non-official members. Legislative Council was invested with the power of making laws for the whole country, but in certain cases previous sanction of the Governor-General was necessary before introducing a legislative measure. A bill could become an Act only when Governor-General had assented to it, but Her Majesty could invalidate any measure on the recommendations of Secretary of State.

The Governor-General could revoke any measure approved by Provincial Council. He was also authorised to constitute new provinces and appoint Lt. Governors for them.

At least three members of the executive council of the Governor-General were to be those who would have been in the service of the Crown in India for at least 10 years. The Governor-General was empowered to make rules and orders for the more convenient transaction of the business in the Council. Legislative council was assigned purely legislative function. Governor-General was given the powers of promulgating ordinances.

Some changes were also introduced in the provinces as well. Legislative powers of Presidencies of Bombay and Madras were restored. The Governers of these presidencies were also empowered to nominate to their legislative councils, the Advocate General of Presidency and between 4 and 8 other additional members less than one-half of whom were to be non-officials for the purposes of making laws, rules and regulations. Provincial governments were authorised to make laws on such matters which did not effect an act of Parliament of such other subjects as army, currency, coinage, post and telegraphs, etc. In certain cases previous approval of the Governor was necessary for introduction of a Bill.

Legislative Councils were set-up in Punjab, NWFP and Presidency of Fort William in Bengal.

Critical Evaluation of the Act. The Act was of great constitutiunal significance, though not without its limitations as well. In the words of G.N. Singh, the Act was important because, "It enabled the Governor-General to associate the people of the land with the work of legislation." In the words of Sir Bartle Frere, a member of Governor-General Council, "The Act indeed provided opportunities for our alien masters to appraise themselves of the minds of the natives and thus avoid mis-understanding and suspicion against the activities of the government of the day." The Act made a beginning in representative institutions and legislative devolution. The people got an opportunity to put forward their grievances and government got an opportunity to defend its policies and programmes. According to some thinkers and constitutionalists, the frame-work provided by this Act lasted till the British rule in India. Its significance also lies in the fact that it introduced portfolio system.

Non-official members were of course added to the Councils but they were not elected by the people but nominated by the Governor-General or the Governors. They took no interest in the work in of the country. They were in no hurry to come, but always in a hurry to go. Non-official members had practically no say in the matter and remained always disinterested. On the other hand, they were always keen to side, with the Governor-General. According to Punniah, "The Act did not attempt in any but cursory manner to demarcate the respective spheres of the Central and Provincial legislatures in matters of provincial or local concerns.'' By empowering Governor-General to promulgate ordinances the Governor-General was made very powerful and thus scope was made for enacting such laws which suited his personal interests. The Councils remained merely debating bodies as these were not given power to call for information. This, however, appears to be quite one-sided picture and a pessimistic view. Undoubtedly, the Act made a beginning of representative government in India.

INDIAN COUNCIL ACT, 1892

Indian Council Act, 1862 of course was a great landmark and a step forward towards new political system, but as already pointed out it was not without its defects too. Non-official members even indirectly did not represent views and wishes of the people. They were not made to feel their responsibility and were reluctant to accept membership. It was because as Sir Subramainen lyer, a member of the Madras Legislative Council pointed out was, because, "The functions for these Councils are limited to registering the decrees of executive government and stamp them with legislatures which were legislatures neither in their organisation nor in their functions but mere committees for making laws. The Councils could not enquire into the grievances, call for information or examine the conduct of the executive." In the words of Coupland, "These Councils were akin to the darbars which Indian rulers had traditionally held in order to sound their subjects of their opinion." These powers were further 'reduced and position of fire. Council weakened because the Governor-General had been empowered to issue ordinances for the good Government of British India in an emergency.

In this way the Act had its own defects. The people of India got very much frustrated because practically they had not been given any share in the share in the running of their own administration for which there had been much talk since 1858.

In 1885, Indian National Congress was founded. It was making regular representations to the government to associate Indians in the running their own administration. Poverty of the people was on the increase and in fact nothing had been done to end that. Unemployment was increasing every year and indigenous industries had been ruined. Enlightened classes in India were demanding not only expansion of the Councils but increase in their powers.

The government was, however, not favourably inclined to accept the demands of the Congress. In 1888, Lord Dufferin declared, "How could any reasonable man imagine that the British government would be content to allow this microscopic minority to control the administration of that majestic and multi-form empire for whose safety and welfare, they are responsible in the eyes of God and before face of civilisation?" Though Lord Dufferin had given a rebuff to the Indian National Congress, yet he also accepted that for pupularising the Acts of government both association and co-operation of Indians was unavoidable. In 1890, Charles Bradlaugh, a member of House of Commons introduced a bill in the House to amend the Act of 1861. The Bill could not be immediately passed but it saw the light of day after several wrangles and amendments in 1892.

Main Provisions of the Act. According to the provisions of the Act, the number of additional members of Supreme Council was fixed at not less than ten and not more than sixteen. Similarly number of Bombay and Madras Councils was also fixed at not less than 8 and not more than 20. The Governor-General was empowered to make rules for the nomination of additional members. Governor-General-in-Council, Governor-in-Council and Lt. Governor-in-Council were empowered to make rules for the discussion of financial statements in their respective Councils. The members were allowed to give free and frank criticism of government policies and financial measures though not to vote these item by item. They were also authorised to put questions on matters of urgent public importance, but President of the Council could disallow any question. Certain non-official members were to be nominated by the head of the government on the recommendations of District Boards. Chamber of Commerce, etc. In the case of Imperial Legislative Council, the composition was :

Officials:	6
Nominated non-officials:	5
Calcutta Chamber of Commerce: (Non-official)	1
One each non-official member from four provincial councils	4

Critical Evaluation of the Act. The Act, however, was not without its defects, Indians still did not have much of representation. Their representatives did not represent any body. The Council had no substantial control over the budget and the members had no right to put supplementary questions. The representation given to various communities was unscientific. If some communities had over-representation, the others did not get any representation at all. The Councils were so composed that non-official members had practically no chance to get a bill, as introduced by the government, amended. Moreover the size of the provincial councils was so small that it was impossible to give proper representation to any shade or opinion. The rules framed by the Governor-General for the nomination of additional members were highly defective and defeated the very purpose for which nominations were made. The power to ask questions was hedged by numerous restrictions. The President could disallow any question without assigning any reason. It failled to come up to the expectations of educated Indians who were clamouring more share in running their own administration. According to Gokhale, actual working of the Act manifested its hollowness. In the words of Pheroze Shah Mehta the Act may be described as a "most superb steam engine in which the necessary material to generate steam were carefully excluded, substituting in its place coloured shams to look like it." S.N. Banerjee believed that, "the restrictions seem to me to defeat the purpose of a beneficial legislation." According to Punniah, "While no efforts were made to enlarge the boundaries of educated class, to provide them with any training in responsible government, or to lay the foundations of a future electorate to control them, the Act deliberately attempted to dally with the elective idea."

But in spite of some of it defects the Act of 1892, was not without its advantages. The indians got an Opportunity to enter the Councils and they undoubtedly influenced the course of proceeding, trend of thinking and line of debates. It was accepted in principle that the legislatures should have ultimate control over the executive and that is why the members were allowed to put questions. In addition, constituting of legislative bodies on electoral basis was also accepted. It can rightly be said that the Act laid the foundations of representative form of government. Functons of legislative councils were considerably enlarged and non-offcial members got an opportunity to have free and full discussion on financial policies of the government. Thus, also provided an opportunity to the government to remove many apprehensions of people. The authors of the report on constitutional reforms confessed that those in the legislature were much benefited by the advice of Indian representatives. It has rather been very appropriatly said that, "It was an attempt to compromise between the official view of the Councils as pocket legislatures and an educated Indian view of them as embroy Parliament."

THE INDIAN COUNCIL ACT, 1909 (MORLEY-MINTO REFORMS)

The Act is also commonly known as Minto-Morley Reforms. This Act sowed the seeds of reservation of seats and occupies considerable significance in the process of advancement towards new political system. There is no doubt about it that the Act of 1892, was of considerable significance, but as already pointed out, it was also not without its limitations. It was much below the expectations of the people of India, particularly the extremists. It was being increasingly felt all over the country that Councils were merely debating societies and elective system was most unsatisfactory.

Indian National Congress which came into being in 1885, had considerable influence on the minds of the people and had also awakened them to demand more rights. The people felt that they were being hood-winked.

In 1896-97, there was plague in India which was one of its worst kind in the country and the masses were worst hit by it. In 1899, there was famine again in the country. Unfortunately relief measures adopted by the government were inadequate and the way in which relief operations were executed created so much hatred among the people against the government that Plague Commissioner Rand was shot dead.

In those days Lokmanya Tilak had become very popular. Through his speeches and writings in Kesari he awakened the people. His writings had deep influence on the minds of the people. Unfortunately he was arrested on account of murder of Rand. This also created resentment among the people.

Lord Curzon became Viceroy of India in 1898. He was high neck stiffed person. He followed the policy of deliberately crushing the aspirations of educated Indians. He made it clear that all high posts in India should undoubtedly and invariably be held by the Britishers and not by Indians.

In 1905, he decided for the partition of Bengal much against the wishes of the people of India. There were widespread agitations and resentments in the country and even the Moderates felt that no useful purpose would be served in having constitutional agitation against an alien government, if that gave us the partition of Bengal. The partition of Bengal was one single important action which awakened masses to an extent to which many consistent efforts on the part of Indian would not have.

It was in the same year 1905, that tiny Japan won a high sounding victory on mighty Russia. This created strong feelings of confidence among the nationalists in India. Party felt that if tiny Japan could defeat mighty Russia, then why could not we throw Britishers out of our soil. This defeat exploded the myth of superiority of Europeans and the idea of their invincibility. Pardhan has said that this defeat heralded, "the dawn of a new era for the whole of Asia." In this way a new sense of sacrifice and feelings of hard work were created among the people of India against British regime.

Unfortunately when in India there was a lot of discontentment, Indians abroad were being humiliated. Toll tax was imposed on them in Africa from where several thousand Indians were expelled in a disgracing manner. They were subjected to intolerable humiliation in rail-road carriages. In 1907, Transval Government passed the Asiatic Registration Act which required Indians to be registered by means of finger prints. All these humiliations were brought to the notice of Indians by Tilak and other extremist leaders. But Indians were very much indignant because British government was taking no steps to save Indians from this humiliation, abroad, even in a colony which was under their thumb and control.

In the economic field the people were suffering from groaning poverty. Their economic standard was very low and day-by-day it was lowering. The prices of necessities of life were much going up and indigenous industries had been ruined much. The high-handedness of the Britishers and poor economic conditions of the people of India were exposed in the writings of many Indian nationalists and in fact in those day vernacular press played a very important role.

It was on account of these activities that people's faith in the Moderates and constitutional struggle against the Britishers began to disappear. There was spread of violent activities. There were also revolutionary and terrorist activities in which several Britishers were killed. There were incidents of bomb throwing.

In constitutional struggle and towards a new system in India, there was rise of Muslim communalism in the country. British government in India encouraged the Muslims to put forth their demands and on December 30, 1906, Muslim League was founded. In the same year H.H. Aga Khan waited on the Governor-General Lord Minto and demanded separate representation for the Muslims. A demand was made by the Muslims and accepted by the government for separate electorate. It was this Muslim communalism which ultimately resulted in the partition of the country.

It was under these circumstances that the British government was compelled to satisfy the aspirations of Indians and meet their demand for an increased share in the running their own administration. It was amply clear that unless constitutional reforms were introduced in the country, there was every likelihood of violence and the situation in the country might go out of control. It was at this stage that the Liberals came to power in England and they realised the magnitude of the problem, Lord Morley, who was Secretary of State for India realised the need of changes and set-up a Committee to suggest constitutional reforms. Accordingly several proposals were considered by the Government of India and the Home Government in England to find a way out and solution to the problem in such a way that the people of India got satisfied and at the same time the grip of British government in India did not in any way get loose. Ultimately in 1909, was passed, what is today known as Indian Council Act of 1909 or Morley-Minto Reforms.

Main Provisions of Act. By this Act the strength of additional members of Governor-General's Council was increased to 60 whereas those of the Provinces was fixed as under:

Bombay, Madras, UP, Bihar and Orissa	50
Punjab, Burma and Assam	30

This number, however, did not include ex-officio members. Each Council was however, to consist of nominated members both officials and non-officials, as well as elected ones. The strength of Imperial Legislative Councils was:

Officials 37	: (28 to be nominated by the Governor-General, One was the Governor-General himself; 6 ordinary members of his Council; 2 extraordinary members: namely, Commender-in-Chief and the head of the Province where Council happened to meet.)
Non-official 32	: (27 elected. 5 to be nominated by the Governor-General)

It was ensured that in the Imperial Legislative Council, there was official majority. As regards elected element it was made clear that territorial representation was unsuited to India and that only class and interest based electoral system was possible in a vast country like India. Therefore, 27 elected representatives were distributed to be as follows:

Landlords	6
Muslims	5
Muslim Landlords	1
Chamber of Commerce, Bengal	1
Chamber of Commerce, Bombay	1
Non-official members of non-provincial Councils	13

In the provincial councils still more tighter control was maintained and there was absolute official majority. We, for example, take the case of Madras Legislative Council. In it there were 26 non-officials and 21 official members who were composed of:

21 officials :	Governor	1
	Governor's Executive Councillors	3
	Advocate General	1
	Other nominated	16

GOVERNMENT OF INDIA ACT, 1919

In and after 1914, Great Britain became involved in a war with Germany and Austria-Hungary, and the need for India's aid and support was strongly felt. In order to ensure that those could be enlisted the policy-makers in London began to re-examine the issue of constitutional reforms to be introduced in India after the war. Lionel Curtis studied the question deeply, and expressed the view that Indians would possibly be satisfied if the governmental powers were divided between the existing executives responsible to the Secretary of State, and through him to parliament, and new executives to be made and unmade by representative bodies in India. Similarly, Lord Chelmsford, who succeeded Hardinge as the Viceroy of India in

1916, expressed the view that the institution of the responsible government alone would evoke effective cooperation from the Indian people to the war efforts of Great Britain and its Allies. In February-March 1917, Germany restarted the hostilities with utmost ferocity, and England was confronted with a grave military situation. At about the same time alarming developments took place on the Indian political scene. In January 1916, the extremists had rejoined the parent body (the Congress), and in December of the same year the Muslim League had joined hands with Congress. Under the leadership of the Home Rule Leagues of Tilak and Annie Besant the national movement was becoming stronger.

Realizing that India's cooperation and support was vital to British survival, the new Secretary of State, Montagu, who succeeded Chamber-lain issued, on 20th August, 1917, a statement on British policy towards India. On the lines of this statement, an Act, known as the Government of India Act, 191) was passed by Parliament on 23, December.

This Act was described as, "An Act to make further provision with respect to the Government of India." It was divided into six parts and forty-seven articles. Part first dealt with Local Governments; part second, with Government of India; part third, with Secretary of State in Council; part fourth, with the Civil Services in India; part fifth, with Statutory Commission, and part sixth covered miscellaneous provisions. Let us discuss each one of them in details:

PREAMBLE TO THE ACT, 1919

The Preamble to the Act laid down a few significant points in respect of the Government of India. Those were:

(1) The declared policy of Parliament was to provide for the increasing association of Indians in every branch of Indian administration and to develop gradually the self-governing institutions, "with a view to the progressive realization of responsible government in British India as an integral part of the empire."

(2) Progress in giving effect to this policy could only be achieved by successive stages; and

(3) The development in that direction was to commence from the provinces of India, and as such those provinces should be given in provincial matters, "the largest measure of independence of the Government of India," This was, however, to be, "compatible with" the due discharge by the Government of India of its own responsibilities.

ORGANIZATION

Part II of the Government of India Act, 1919 provided for the reorganization, powers and functions of the Government of India. The Imperial Legislative Council was abolished, and Article 17 provided for a bicameral legislature composed of the Legislative Assembly and the Council of State, The Governor-General remained, as before, a part of the Legislature, The Council of State consisted of not more than sixty members nominated or elected and not more than twenty of them could be official members. The Council when constituted had 34 elected members, 19 nominated officials and 6 nominated non-officials. The Governor-General appointed from among the members of the Council a President.

The total number of the members of the Legislative Assembly was, as laid down in the Act, one hundred and forty. The number of elected members was fixed at one hundred, and that of the non-elected at forty, of whom twenty-six were to be official members. Provision was also made in the Act for increasing the number of members, and the proportion which the classes of members should bear one to another was determined. At least five-sevenths of the members were to be elected members, and at least one-third of the other members were to be non-official members.

Every member of the Governor-General's Executive Council was nominated as a member of one chamber of the Legislature, and had the right of attending and addressing in the other chamber, but he could not be a member of both chambers.

An official was not qualified for election as a member of either of the two chambers, and, if any non-official member of either chamber accepted any office in the service of the Crown in India his seat in that chamber became vacant. If an elected member of either chamber became a member of the other chamber, his seat in such first mentioned chamber thereupon became vacant. If any person was elected a member of both chambers he, before taking seat in either chamber, was required to signify in writing the chamber of which he desired to be a member, and thereupon his seat in the other chamber became vacant.

Provision in the Act was made for the election of a President and Deputy President by the Legislative Assembly. The Deputy President presided over the Assembly meetings when the President was absent. Both of them held office for a term of four years, but they could resign their office and could be removed by a vote of the Assembly with the concurrence of the Governor-General. An elected President and Deputy President ceased to hold office if they ceased to be members of the Assembly. Members of both the chambers enjoyed freedom of speech on the floor thereof, and were not liable to any proceedings in any Court by reason of their speech or vote. All questions in either chamber were decided by a majority of votes of members present other than the presiding officer who had, and exercised, a casting vote in the case of an equality of votes.

POWERS AND FUNCTIONS

The Indian Legislature could legislate:

(a) For all persons, for all courts, and for all places and things, within British India;

(b) For all subjects of His Majesty and servants of the Crown within other parts of India;

(c) For all native Indian subjects of His Majesty without and beyond as well as within British India;

(d) For all persons employed or serving in or belonging to the Royal Indian Marine Service; and

(e) For repealing or altering any laws which for the time being were in force in any part of British India.

The restrictions imposed upon the law-making powers of the Governor-General in Legislative Council during the period. before 1919, were reimposed upon the Indian Legislature. Unless so authorized by Act of Parliament, it could not make any law repealing or affecting: *(1)* any Act of Parliament passed after 1860 and extending to British India, or *(2)* any Act of Parliament enabling the Secretary of State in Council to raise money in the United Kingdom for the Government of India.

The Indian legislature was denied power to make any law affecting the authority of Parliament in so far as that authority affected the sovereignty or dominion of the Crown over any part of British India. Without the previous approval of the Secretary of State in Council, the Indian Legislature could not make any law empowering any Court other than a High Court to sentence to death any of His Majesty's subjects born in Europe or the Children of such subjects. Likewise, it could not make any law abolishing any High Court.

The Indian Legislature was given more powers than hitherto in the passing of the Budget. The estimated annual expenditure and revenue were laid in the form of a statement before both chambers of the legislature in each year. The proposals for the appropriation of revenue or moneys relating to the various heads of expenditure were submitted to the vote of the Assembly in the form of demands for grants. The Assembly might assent or refuse its assent to any demand or might reduce the amount referred to in any demand by a reduction of the whole grant. But the following heads of expenditure were not submitted to the vote of the Legislative Assembly nor were they open to discussion by either chamber at the time when the annual statement was under consideration:

(i) Interest and sinking fund charges on loans;

(ii) Expenditure of which the amount was prescribed by or under any law;

(iii) Salaries and pensions of persons appointed by or with the approval of His Majesty or by the Secretary of State in Council;

(iv) Salaries of Chief Commissioners and Judicial Commissioners;

(v) Expenditure classified by the order of the Governor-General in Council as:

(a) ecclesiastical, (b) political, (c) defence.

If at any time a question arose whether any proposed appropriation of revenue or moneys did or did not relate to the above heads, the decision of the Governor-General on the question was final.

The Act gave co-equal powers to the Assembly and the Council with regard to law-making. In order to become an Act of the Indian Legislature, a Bill needed to passed by both the Chambers. Article 24 (3) laid down that if any Bill that had been passed by one chamber was not, within six months after the passage of the Bill by the chamber, passed by the other chamber either without amendments or with such amendments as might be agreed to by the two chambers, the Governor-General might in his discretion refer the matter for decision to a joint sitting of both chambers. Decision in such a sitting was made by the majority of votes of the members present.

August Declaration. In order to win the sympathies of Indians in their war efforts, Montague made a declaration on 20th August, 1917 that policy of British government in India was that of increasing association of Indians in every branch of administration. But the government was the exclusive judge to decide about the time at which step towards advancement may be taken. This statement was important in the sense that it underlined the policy of British government in India. It was implicit in the statement that some day India will get the right of self-government. In fact in constitutional development in India this declaration occupies a very significant place and position.

The usual procedure of appointing commissions was not adopted now and Lord Montague himself toured the whole of India to find for himself how far Indians were keen to have new system of government. He found the people quite keen to participate in legislative process. In fact he tried his best to find out a formula by which he could satisfy Indians and also get the approval of House of Commons. He stayed in India for about 4½ months and met leaders of various shades of Indian public opinion. On his return to England he declared that three cordinal principles of reforms were:

(a) The provinces are the domain in which the earlier steps towards the progressive realisation of responsible government should be taken.

(b) The Indian Legislative Council should be enlarged and made more representative and its opportunities of influencing government should be increased.

(c) The control of Parliament and the Secretary of State over the government of India and provincial governments must be relaxed.

These basic principles were accepted by the British government and the scheme was introduced in the House of Commons in June 1919, and the Bill became an Act on December 23, 1919. It was, however, in February 1921, that the provisions of the Act were actually enforced.

The Act of 1919, basically introduced diarchy in the provinces. By the provisions of the Act provincial activities were divided into two parts. One part was called 'reserved' part with which elected representatives of the people bad nothing to do, whereas other part was called 'transferred' part. Subjects listed in this part were brought to some extent, under the control of the elected Ministers, though hold of the governor over these subjects was in no way less tight. But on the whole as Coupland says, "It crossed the line between legislative and executive authority. Now Indians were to govern so to speak, on their own. They were to take charge of great departments of provincial administration not as official nominees but as leaders of elected majorities in their legislature and responsible to them."

The Act was, however, introduced at a time when climate in the country had been considerably tensed on account of Jallianwala Bagh tragedy at Amritsar in which thousands innocent Indians were massacred and Punjab had been placed under martial law. The massacre had shocked the whole civilised world from its very foundations and the people of India completely lost faith both in words and sincerity of British people towards India. The horrors of the massacre were thus in the minds of Indians when the Act was introduced in the House of Commons.

The scheme, as introduced in 1919, had some novel features and relaxed the control of central government over the provinces. It also introduced a type of government in which provincial administration was divided into two halves, which was hitherto unknown to India. The hold of the Home Government was relaxed to some extent on the one hand and that of the central government over the provinces on the other. It was for the first time that central and state subjects were separated from each other and for administrative, financial and legislative purposes these were specifically enumerated. In the provinces diarchy was introduced and to some extent democratic element was also introduced and it was to be experimented that India was fit for democracy or not. In the words of RK. Bombwall the Act, 'blazed a new trial' and laid the foundation of Indian federalism, which has been called by Whyte as 'federalism in embryo'. A sort of element of responsibility was Introduced in Indian provinces. It injected a doze of autonomy in Indian political system and created an appetite for more doses of autonomy in administration. To quote Bombwall again, "The Act reveals fist major breach in the constitutional monolithism of a unitary system of government and shows the provinces throwing off a part of Centre's tutelage."

THE GOVERNMENT OF INDIA ACT, 1919

Preamble of the Act. Spirit in which Act was enacted and given to the people is reflected in its Preamble. According to it main aim of British policy in India was to increasingly associate Indians in the running their own administration. Then it was also said that the British government will try to gradually develop self-governing institutions so that there is progressive realization of responsible government in British India as integral part of the empire. It was also said in the Preamble that the task of associating Indians in the task of administration will be realised by successive stages and the time and manner of each advance will be determined only by the British Parliament. It was also made clear that British government was responsible for the welfare and advancement of Indian people. But in determining the time for giving next step and share in administration it will very much depend upon the people in which confidence and responsibility is reposed, which in effect meant Indian leadership. In this way Preamble of the Act specified the goal of British government's stay in India and sought the co-operation of Indian leadership in this task so that Indian nation could go forward and achieve the goal of self-government without loss of time. But it kept the lever with it by providing that ultimate decision whether the time was appropriate and opportunate ultimately rested with the British Parliament. In this way, Indians were to struggle and British government was to sit on judgment about the maturity of their soundness and extent of political participation in running Indian administration. It ruled out the possibility of self-government even in the provinces in the near future.

PROVISIONS OF THE ACT

The Act of 1919, was a very comprehensive documents. By and large it did not touch central administration which remained as autocratic as it was in the past. The Governor-General was still the head of the whole a administration in India. His grip over the administration was very tight. He had of course his Council, which had limited powers and no effective check over him but some changes were introduced in the provinces. The system was known as diarchy. The Governors still enjoyed very extensive powers and control even over transferred subjects. The control of Secretary of State over Indian administration was somewhat relaxed. According to G.N. Singh, "The Central proposal of Montford Reform then was an important beginning in the provincial autonomy, in both senses of the terms, *i.e.* in the sense of freedom from above and also in the sense of transfer of power to the people." Since the Act introduced major changes in the provinces it is, therefore, better to discuss this part of the Act in the first instance.

PROVINCIAL GOVERNMENTS

The authors of the Act claimed that in the provinces they had introduced democratic system. In order to give the provinces some sort of independence, subjects between the provinces and the centre were clearly demarcated. Those subjects which were of uniform nature and required a type of legislation which applied to whole of India or concerned more than one province were kept with the centre, while such subjects which concerned provinces were kept in the provincial list. Provincial list contained such subjects as local self-government, land revenue, famine relief, co-operative society and agriculture, etc., the central list included defence, foreign and political relations, customs, currency, posts and telegraphs, etc. Residuary powers were of course left to the centre, which made that really more powerful and broadened the scope of its activities.

Not only this that there was division of subjects between the centre and the provinces, but subject enumerated under provincial list were further sub-divided into two categories; namely, reserved subjects and the transferred subjects. Whereas the former were placed under official control the latter under popular control. Broadly speaking, reserved subjects were land revenue, irrigation, law and order, industrial disputes whereas local self-government, public health, education, medical administration were transferred subjects. In case there was any dispute as to whether a particular subject was reserved or transferred, the decision of the Governor-General was final to be and binding. Reserved subjects were to be administered by the Governor, with or without the help of his Executive Council and in his personal judgment, whereas transferred subjects were to be administered by the Governor with the help of his Ministers. The Ministers were to be chosen from amongst the members of the legislature, whereas he could nominate the members of his own Executive Council.

Finance Department was kept as a reserved subject and under the control of the Governor, who was to run it with the help of his executive council. It was this department which was to provide funds for the running of the transferred subjects. The advise tendered by the Finance Department was more or less binding because a Minister could not turn that down without referring that to the Governor, whose decision was to be final. Not only this, but division of finances between reserved and transferred subjects was to be ultimately made by the Governor.

Though provincial subjects were divided into reserved and transferred ones, yet no separate staff was provided for the administration of transferred subjects, All superior posts were to be controlled by All India Service personnel who were to be controlled by the Secretary of State and the Governor-General. Their salaries, allowances; conditions of services and all other matters, including their grievances, were to be looked after by them. Ministers even could not transfer them or sit as judges on the quality of their work. Administratively they were not under their control. Thus, in matters of running administration, the Ministers had all responsibilities but in no way control over the service personnel from whom they were to get work. In the words of Punniah, "A complete and logical system of diarchy would have involved the establishment of two in the same area, with separate legislatures, separate foods and separate executive-staff. But this was not aimed at by the authors of the Reforms."

The Provincial Executive. In the Provinces the executives was to be headed by a Governor, who was appointed by the Secretary of State and in doing so he might consult the Governor-General. The Governor was responsible to the Secretary of State for acts of omission and commission. He was to maintain law and order in the province and also to ensure that provincial administration worked smoothly. In respect of transferred subjects he was to be assisted by his Ministers, whereas reserved subjects were to be administered by him with the help of his Executive Council. The councillors were to be appointed by the Secretary of State and were responsible to him in all matters. There were certain subjects which he was to administer in his own discretion. In such matters he was responsible to the Secretary of State. Each Executive, Councillor was to remain in office for a period of 5 years. Their, salaries and service conditions were not subject to the vote of the provincial legislature. All decisions in the Council were to be taken by a majority of votes and in case of need the Governor could use his casting vote. He was also to preside over the meetings of the Council. The Governor could also over-ride the majority decision of his Council, if he was satisfied that implementation of such a decision was likely to disturb peace and tranquility of India.

Administration of Transferred Subjects. Pivot of 1919, Reforms was division of subjects into reserved and transferred subjects. As already said reserved subjects were to be administered by the Governor with the help of elected Ministers. It was here that element of responsibility and democratisation was introduced. Though no upper limit on the strength of. Ministers was fixed, yet usually it was kept at three only. Each Minister must belong to the legislature Minister was to be appointed by the Governor and held office during his pleasure. No official, therefore, could be a Minister. The Ministers were made responsible to the Legislative Council and their salaries were also voteable. Though the Governor was appointing and dismissing authority of Ministers, yet it was hoped that he would act as constitutional head and would not dismiss a Minister as long as he enjoyed confidence of the Council. It was expected of the Governor that with regard to transferred subjects he would be guided by the advice of his ministers unless there were serious reasons to believe that the advice tendered should be turned down. It was hoped that with regard to transferred subjects the Governor would try to act as constitutional head of the state. Each Governor was issued an Instrument of Instructions making clear to him that while not agreeing with the advice of his Council of Ministers he should take into consideration his relations with the Legislative Council on the one hand and wishes of the people of the province on the other.

Special Responsibilities of the Governors. Some of the subjects, in the provinces were to be administered by the Governor with the help of his Executive Council, while others with the help of his Council of Ministers, but each Governor had certain special responsibilities as well. For the administration of these matters and discharge of these responsibilities he was to use his discertion and mayor may not consult the Council of his Ministers or Executive Councillors. Some of the important matters which were covered in this category included:

(i) Maintenance of safety and tranquility of all parts of the province;

(ii) Avoiding of religious and racial conflicts;

(iii) Ensuring compliance of orders issued by the Secretary of State and/or Governor-General;

(iv) Promoting of the welfare of those who could not as yet fully rely for their welfare upon joint political action;

(v) Ensuring that no order of his government and no Act of his Legislative Council should be so framed that any of the diverse interests of/or arising from race, religion, social conditions or any other circumstances, might receive unfair advantage or might be unfairly deprived of advantages which they had hither to enjoyed;

(vi) Safeguarding of all members of the public services employed in the provinces in the legitimate exercise of their functions;

(vii) Taking care that no monopoly or special privilege which was against the common interest should be established;

(viii) Ensuring that no unfair discrimination was made in matters affecting commercial or industrial interests.

Principle of Joint Ministerial Responsibility. Provincial administration was divided into reserved and transferred subjects. The latter part of the administration was to be looked after by the Ministers who were members of Legislative Council. This obviously raised the question of joint or collective responsibility. It was the intention of the framers of the Act that the principle of joint and collective responsibility should be encouraged but that was not incorporated in the Instrument of Instructions issued to the Governors. It was on the other hand provided that in the administration of transferred subjects the Governor will consult the Minister concerned. Therefore, the Act in spirit did not promote the principle of joint and collective responsibility.

DIARCY IN GOVERNOR'S PROVINCES

The Act of 1919, marked the beginning of responsible government in Governor's Provinces. The Provinces had been divided into three categories—Governor's Province, Lt. Governor's Province, and Chief Commissioner's Province. The Governor's Provinces were the three Presidencies of Bombay, Madras and Bengal; the Lt. Governor's Provinces were Bihar and Orissa, the United Provinces of Agra and Oudh and the Punjab; and the Chief Commissioner's Provinces were Assam, the Central Provinces, the N.W.F.P., British Baluchistan, Delhi, Ajmer-Merwara, Coorg and the Andaman and Nicobar Islands. Article 52 of the 1915, Act contained a proviso that if the Secretary of State thought fit he might direct that U.P. be constituted a Presidency under a Governor. Article 59 of the same Act, stipulated that the Governor-General in Council might, with the approval of the Secretary of State, take any part of British India under the immediate authority and management of the Governor-General in Council, place it under a Chief Commissioner and give him all necessary orders and directions respecting its administration. Article 60 authorized the Governor-General in Council to alter the boundaries of any of the Provinces into which British India was then divided.

Leaving the three-tier classification of Provinces undisturbed the Government of India Act, 1919 sought to introduce responsible government in 'some of them. The Provinces chosen for this were listed in Article 3 and those were, the Presidencies of Bombay, Madras and Bengal, U.P., the C.P., Assam, the Punjab, Bihar and Orissa, the latter ones having been raised to the status of "Governor's Provinces." In these Provinces a system of double government—diarchy—was introduced. The first Article of the 1919, Act provided for the classification of subjects of administration into two categories, Central and Provincial, for the purpose of distinguishing the functions of local governments and local legislatures from the functions of the Governor-General in Council and the Indian Legislature. The Central subjects determined subsequently were defence, external relations, relations with Native states, communications, currency and coinage, customs. All-India Services, public debt and civil and criminal law and procedure, post and telegraph and patents and copyrights. The subjects assigned to the Provinces were divided into two categories—"transferred subjects" and "reserved subjects." The "transferred subjects" were local self-government, education, sanitation and public health, hospitals, public works, such as roads and buildings, excise, agriculture, development of industries and cooperative societies.

The "reserved subjects" were land laws and land revenue administration, famine relief, irrigation, forests, administration of justice, police and prisons and factory and labour matters, and local self-government. The "transferred subjects" were administered by the Governor "acting with ministers appointed under this Act" and the "reserved subjects" were to be administered by the Governor in

Council. The Governor of a Governor's Province might, Article 4(1) said, appoint ministers, not being members of his Executive Council or other officials, to administer "transferred subjects," and any minister so appointed held office during his pleasure, No minister shall hold office; it was laid down, for a longer period than six months unless he was or became an elected member of the provincial Legislature. In relation to the "transferred subjects" the Governor was required to be guided by the advise of his ministers unless he saw "sufficient cause to dissent from their opinion." In which case he might require action to be taken otherwise than in accordance with that advice. Provision in the Act was also made for the framing of rules for the temporary administration of a "transferred subjects" where, in cases of emergency owing to a vacancy there was no minister in charge of the subject by such authority and in such manner as might be prescribed by the rules.'

Paragraph (4) of Article 4 also authorized the Governor of a Governor's Province to appoint, at his discretion, from among the non-official members of the Provincial Legislative Council, Secretaries who held office during his pleasure, and discharged such duties in assisting members of the Executive Council and Minister as he might assign to them. A Council Secretary ceased to hold office if he ceased for more than six months to be a member of the Legislative Council.

No minimum or maximum number of Ministers or Secretaries was laid down in the Act, and the Governors were left free to determine it in each Province.

GOVERNOR'S EXECUTIVE COUNCIL

The constitutional provision upto 1919, was that the number of members of the Governor's Executive Council should not exceed four. This remained as it was. The earlier provision that two of those members must have been for at least twelve years in the service of the Crown in India was changed and the number of such members was reduced from two to one. The earlier rule that the Commander-in-Chief of His Majesty's forces in India if resident at Calcutta, Madras or Bombay, should, during his continuance there be a member of the Governor's Council ceased to operate. The members of the Governor's Executive Council continued to be appointed by His Majesty on the advice of the Secretary of State. They were ex-officio members of the Legislative Council, but were not responsible to it. The Governor was not bound by the advice of the Executive Councillors, but if a decision were taken by the Executive Council by a majority of votes, that decision had a binding effect.

POWERS OF THE GOVERNOR

(a) Executive Powers. The Governor enjoyed almost the same powers in his Province as the Governor-General did in British India. While that position changed with respect to the administration of "transferred subjects," it remained unaffected in respect to the "reserved subjects." All proceedings of the Government of a Governor's province were expressed to be made by the Governor in Council and were authenticated by the Governor.

The Governor made rules and orders for the more convenient transaction of business in his Executive Council and with his Ministers, and all acts done and business transacted in accordance with those rules and orders were treated as being the order or the Act of the Government of the Province. The Governor also regulated the relations between his Executive Council and his Ministers for the purpose of the transaction of the business of the Provincial Government, and for that purpose made the necessary rules and regulations. The Governor had a domineering position in his Executive Council. Although normally he was bound by the majority decision, he could, on his own authority and responsibility, adopt, suspend or reject any such measure as "affected the safety, tranquility or interests of his Presidency or any part thereof."

(b) Legislative Powers. The more extensive powers of the Governor were in the legislative field. Here he was central to the birth, central to the life and central to the death of the Legislative Council. Article 7 laid down that Governor shall not be a member of the Legislative Council, but he shall have the right of addressing the Council, and might for that purpose require the attendance of its members. The term of office of the Legislative Council was fixed for three years from its first meeting, but the Governor could dissolve it sooner. He could also extend that period for a period not exceeding one year if he thought special circumstances existed to justify such an extension. After the dissolution of the Council the Governor appointed a date not more than six months or with the sanction of the Secretary of State, not more than nine months from the date of dissolution for the next session of the Council. He appointed such times and places for holding the sessions of his Legislative Council as he thought fit. He prorogued the Council also by notification or otherwise. The first President of the Legislative Council, as constituted under the Act of 1919, was appointed by the Governor for a period of four years from the first meeting of the Council, and thereafter, he was to be a member of the Council elected by the Council and approved by the Governor. The appointed President could be removed from office by the Governor, and the vacancy so caused was filled by him. An elected President and a Deputy President could be removed from office by a vote of the Council with the concurrence of the Governor.

The Governor played almost a decisive role in law-making by the Legislative Council. Article 11 (4) laid down that if any Bill had been introduced, or any amendment to a Bill was moved or proposed to be moved, the Governor was empowered to "certify" that the Bill or any clause thereof or the amendments affected the "safety or tranquility of his Province or any part of it or of another province," and he could direct that no proceedings shall be taken by the Council in relation to the Bill, clause or amendment, and effect shall be given to any such direction.

Article 12 of the Act dealt with 'return and reservation of Bills'. After a Bill had been passed by a Legislative Council, the Governor, (Lt. Governor or Chief Commissioner) had four options. He could give his assent, withhold his assent return the Bill to the Council for reconsideration, either in whole or in part, together with any amendments which he might recommend, and reserve the Bill for the consideration of the Governor-General. A Bill returned to the Legislative Council for reconsideration, if reaffirmed with or without amendments, was again presented to the Governor (Lt. Governor or Chief

Commissioner). Any Bill reserved for the consideration of the Governor-General would, if assented to by the Governor-General within a period of six months from the date of such reservation, become law in the same way as a Bill assented to by the Governor (Lt. Governor or Chief Commissioner). But if the assent was not accorded by the Governor-General within such period of six months the Bill lapsed and was of no effect unless before the expiration of that period either *(a)* the Bill had been returned for further consideration of the Legislative Council; or *(b)* in the case of the Council not being in session a notification had been published of an intention so to return the Bill at the commencement of the next session. Instead of assenting to or withholding his assent from any Bill passed by a Provincial Legislative Council, the Governor-General might declare that he reserved the Bill for the significance of His Majesty's pleasure thereon, and in such case the Act would not have validity until His Majesty in Council had signified his assent.

If a Legislative Council had refused leave to introduce or had failed to pass in a form recommended by a Governor any Bill relating to a "reserved subject" the Governor might "certify" that the passage of that Bill was essential for the discharge of his responsibility for the subject and on signature by the Governor it became an Act of the Council. Every such Act was sent to the Governor-General who reserved the Act for the significance of His Majesty's pleasure, and upon the signification of such assent, the Act had the same force and effect as an Act passed by the Legislative Council and duly assented to.

(c) Financial Powers. The Governor's control extended to the finances of his Province. Article 11(2) laid down that the estimated annual expenditure and revenue of the Province shall be laid before the Legislative Council in each year in the form of a statement, and the proposals of the Provincial Government for the appropriation of provincial revenues and other moneys in any year shall be submitted to the vote of the Council in the form of demands for grants. The Council was empowered to assent or refuse its assent to a demand or to reduce the amount therein or to omit any of the items of expenditure. But if any such demand related to a "reserved subject" and the Governor certified that the expenditure provided for by the demand was essential to the discharge of his responsibility for the subject, the Provincial Government would have power, in relation to any such demand, to act as if it had been assented to notwithstanding the withholding of such assent or the reduction of the amount therein referred to.

The Governor was empowered, in cases of emergency, to authorize such expenditure as in his opinion was necessary for the safety or tranquility of the province or for the carrying on of any department. Moreover, no proposal for the appropriation of any such revenues or other moneys for any purpose could be made except when recommended to the Council by the Governor. There were certain heads of expenditure which did not require to be submitted to the Legislative Council for its assent. These were:

(i) Contributions payable by the provincial Government to the Governor-General in Council;

(ii) Interest and sinking fund charges on loans;

(iii) Expenditure of which the amount was prescribed by or under any law;

(iv) Salaries and pensions of persons appointed by or with the approval of His Majesty or by the Secretary of State in Council; and

(v) Salaries of Judges of the High Court of the province and of the Advocate-General.

ROUND TABLE CONFERENCE

British government in India was under heavy strains and quite confident that unless the present Act was modified to the satisfaction of Indians, the situation was not likely to improve. Under the Act of 1919, it had been provided that the British government will set-up a Commission in 1931, to decide about the extent by modifying the existing system. But it was forced by the circumstances to set-up such a Commission in 1927. It was known as Simon Commission.

As already pointed out it was boycotted everywhere and at most of the places the demonstrators were mercilessly lathi charged. This all whiteman Commission came to the conclusion that dyarchy should be abolished from the provinces and entire provincial administration should be given to elected Ministers responsible to the legislature. The government should continue to look after rights of the minorities and that the Central Government should not be made responsible to the legislature.

It also recommended enlargement of provincial Legislative Councils and Constitution of a Provincial fund to ensure adequate financial resources for the provinces without infringing their autonomy. At the centre there should be bicameral legislature consisting of Federal Assembly and Council of States. It was of the view that Federal Assembly should be enlarged and should include elected members of provincial Councils. It preferred federal rather than unitary system for India. It also proposed Council of Greater India to discuss matters of common interest. The Commander-in-Chief need not be a member of Viceroy's Executive Council.

It was of the opinion that the High Courts should be placed under the administrative Control of Government of India. Sindh should be separated from Bombay and Burma from India. It also favoured Indianisation of army and extension of franchise.

The report did not find favour with Indian leaders. It failed to accept the demand of Indian public for introduction of responsible government at the centre. Indirect election to central legislature and retention of communal representation too was disliked by Indians. A.B. Keith is of the view that Indian leadership should not have rejected this report out and out. "If it had been accepted, the British government could hardly have failed to work on it and, responsible government in the provinces would have been achieved much earlier than it could be under any other later scheme."

Nehru Report. British government had all along been challenging Indian leadership that if they felt dissatisfied with what was being given to them; they should come out with a scheme which should be acceptable to all the sections of Indian public opinion. When India rejected Simon Commission recommendations, this challenge became still more meaningful. In order to meet the challenge an All Parties Conference was convened in Bombay on 19th May, 1928 which appointed a sub-committee with Pandit Motilal Nehru as its chairman to frame a constitution for India. The Committee pleaded for immediate Dominion Status for India, felt dire necessity for provincial autonomy, abolition of communal representation and a federal polity for India. It also, recommended a bicameral system of legislature and also a Supreme Court, at the court of appeal in India. It also recommended that the Governor-General should act on the recommendations of the executive government. The report was accepted by almost all the sections of Indian public opinion except by the .Indian princes and extremist Muslims. It recommended same constitutional status for India in British empire as was enjoyed by the Dominions of Canada and Australia. In the bicameral legislature senate was to consist of two hundred members to be elected by provincial councils for 7 years. The House of Representatives was to consist of 500 representatives elected on the basis of universal adult franchise. Its normal life was fixed at 5 years. The Governor-General was to appoint Prime Ministers while other Ministers were to be appointed by him on the recommendations of Prime Minister. Defence budget was to be subject to the vote of House of Representatives. Governor-General was also to appoint a Public Service Commission. The judges of the Supreme Court were to be appointed by the Governor-General in Council and could be removed only on the recommendations of both the Houses.

The report had mixed reception but on the whole it proved to be a comprehensive document which contained aspirations of people of India.

Jinnah's Fourteen Point Programme. In order to protect the Muslim interest Mt. Muhammad Ali Jinnah gave his own fourteen point programme. He also suggested federal system of government and autonomy for provinces. He, however, stressed that all legislatures should have adequate representation for minorities and in central legislature Muslim representation should not be less than 1/3 of its total strength. There should be adequate share for the Muslims in the constitution of all services and there should be adequate safeguards for projection and promotion of Muslim culture. In every cabinet at least 1/3 should be Muslim Ministers.

Both Nehru Report and Jinnah's fourteen point programme provided sufficient input to British government. No less importance can be attached to Simon Commission, in so far input to the system is concerned.

In 1929, Gandhiji, along with some other leaders met the then Viceroy, but all were disillusioned and found that the British government was in no mood to give Dominion status to India. Accordingly it decided at its Lahore Session, held in that year, that complete independence of India would be the goal of national struggle in India. Tri-colour was hoisted on the midnight of December 31,1929 and January 26 was fixed as the day for the celebration of independence.

Disobedience Movement. In order to check violence in national struggle, Gandhiji started civil Disobedience Movement in 1930-31, in which the people were persuaded not to pay taxes. He also undertook his famous Dandi March on March 12, 1930. As expected the government followed repressive measures to check the spread of the movement. National leaders of the Congress party and others were arrested and their number rose to about 60,000. Some of the main demands at the time of Disobedience Movement included reduction of land revenue by 50%, abolition of sales tax, reduction in military expenses by at least 50%, reduction in the salaries of British officers, abolition of CID Department and protective tariff against foreign cloth.

Dandi March which started on 12th March, 1930 under Gandhiji from Sabarmati Ashram covered a distance of 241 miles and reached Dandi to break Salt Law. On April 5, 1930 it reached Dandi where Salt Law was defied. The programme included picketing of liquor shops, and leaving of governments schools, colleges and services, etc. The response was very favourable. The Muslim attitude towards the movement was however not very co-operative. In the words of Coupland Mr. Jinnah believed that, "We refuse to join Mr. Gandhi because his movement is not a movement for the complete independence of India but for making the seventy millions of Indian Musalmans dependent on Hindu Maha Sabha." There was, however, complete confusion in the country and movement created serious law and other problem for the administrators and executive authorities.

In between George Solocombe, Dr. Jayakar and Sir Tej Bahadur Sapru tried to bring about a solution to the problem, but failed. Ultimately the British Government decided to convene a Round Table Conference in 1930, to find a solution to Indian political problem. Indian National Congress decided to boycott the same. Obviously such a conference which had no representative from a national organisation could achieve nothing. While discussing the nature of the Conference Brailsford once said, "In St. James Palace there did assemble princes and untouchables, Sikhs, Muslims, Hindus and Christians, spokesman of landowners, trade union and Chamber of Commerce, but Mother India was not there." Though the Conference went on deliberating for quite some time, yet as expected nothing substantial came out of it.

Gandhi-Irwin Pact and After. With the co-operation of Dr. Jayakar and Sir Tej Bahadur Sapru, Gandhi-Irwin Pact was signed in 1931, by which all political prisoners were released and Congress agreed to withdraw Civil Disobedience Movement, to pave way for the Congress to participate in Second Round Table Conference, which was convened next year to find a solution to India's political problem.

In the conference communal and vested interest were given upper most prominance. In the words of Jawahar Lal Nehru, at the conference Gandhiji was the only representative who thought in terms of nation as a whole. This conference too failed, with the result that Civil Disobedience Movement was again started. To deal with situation government issued several ordinances to get extraordinary powers and the press was gagged. There were repressions and so on.

Since no solution to the political problem in India was insight, therefore, Lord McDonald gave his Communal Award on August 16, 1932 with which separate electorates for special interests and minorities and the Muslims were retained. Depressed classes were also given recognition as minorities. Weightage was given to the Muslims in Muslim majority provinces. Three per cent seats were reserved for women and separate electorate was provided for Indian Christians and Anglo-Indians. Seats were also reserved for labour, commerce, landlords and planters. This Award was protested all over the country because it was unfair to the Hindus and gave over representation to Christians and Europeans. It was also detrimental to national unity and aimed at perpetuation of dissensions among the Hindus. In order to undo the mischief of McDonald Award Gandhiji decided to go on fast unto death. His health badly deteriorated and in a bid to save Gandhiji's life Poona Pact was signed on September 20, 1932, with which much of the harm done on account of the Award was undone.

In order to solve India's political problem a Third Round Table Conference was convened on November 17, 1932, but again nothing came out of it and the British government issued a White Paper in March, 1933. It was on the basis of this White Paper that a Bill was introduced in the House of Commons in 1935, which subsequently came to be known as the Government of India Act, 1935.

It will thus be seen that sufficient inputs were given to the act from all sources. Indian National Congress, All India Muslim League, Indian Princes, Chambers of Commerce and Industries, Indian Christians, religious minorities and vested interests all gave sufficient inputs and feed-backs for the new system that was likely to replace to the old one.

GOVERNMENT OF INDIA ACT, 1935

The years after 1920-21, were a period of great political turmoil and intense activity. The British authorities started a long series of discussions and investigations. On 31, October 1929, the Viceroy, Lord Irwin, announced that Dominion Status was "the natural issue" of the Declaration of 1917, and that the British Government would soon hold Round Table discussions with representatives of Indian political parties to finalize the next scheme of constitutional reforms. Three such conferences were held, and in March 1933, a White Paper, outlining the new scheme of reforms, was published by the British Government. Shortly after, a joint Select Committee of Parliament was set-up to prepare a draft constitution, The report of this committee, made public on 11 November 1934, served as the basis of a Bill which received the Royal assent on 2 August 1935. It was called the Government of India Act, 1935. Like the 1919 Act, this Act made further provisions with respect to the Government of India. It did not contain any Preamble to describe the intention of Parliament in passing it. Article 321(a) however, laid down that nothing in this Act shall affect the Preamble to the Government of India Act, 1919. This showed that Parliament was sticking to the intentions expressed in 1919, *viz.*, "to provide for the increasing association of Indians in every branch of Indian administration, and for the gradual development of self-governing institution, with a view to the progressive realisation of responsible government in British India as an integral part of the Empire."

SALIENT FEATURES OF THE ACT

The new Act was a marked improvement upon all the earlier measures of constitutional reforms. Its salient features were: All India Federation, Dyarchy at the Federal level, Provincial Autonomy, restrictions on the Federal and Provincial Legislatures, safeguards and special responsibilities of the Governor-General and Governors. Let us examine each of them in detail.

ALL INDIA FEDERATION

Up to 1935, the governmental system in India was unitary, an the Provincial Government derived their powers and authority by devolution from Central Government, and "discharged their functions," as. C.L. Anand has put it, "subject to the authority of their respective legislatures, under 'superintendence, direction and control,'" of the Governor-General in Council and ultimately the Secretary of State. After 1919, these Governments had however, begun to enjoy some measures of autonomy in respect of the administration of "transferred subjects." Through the 1935 Act, Parliament decided to put the governmental system of British India on a federal basis, and the Central Government and the Provincial Governments began to drive their power and authority directly from the Crown and Parliament.

The Act, it might be noted, did not set-up the federation; it only provided for the establishment of a federation. The federation was to be constituted by His Majesty, and His Majesty could do so only if an address in that behalf was 'presented to him by each House of Parliament. And Parliament could present such address only if the conditions laid down in Article 5 of the Act were fulfilled. Those conditions were that the Rulers of as many States as were entitled to choose not less than half of the 104 members of the Council of State and whose population was not less than at least one half of the total population of the States should sign the "Instrument of Accession" and express willingness to accede to the federation. The rest of the Rulers might accede subsequently if they, so wished. The accession of State was to be effected by the King's acceptance of an "Instrument of Accession" executed by the Ruler personally and the authority of the King, the Governor-General, the federal legislature, the federal court and any other federal authority extended in relation to his state only to such function as might be fested in them by or under the Instrument. The extent of federal authority could be enlarged, but not diminished, by a subsequent Instrument duly accepted. The Governors' Provinces were included in the federation automatically 'but the Chief Commissioners' Provinces were to be included after the federation had been set-up.

The tribal areas, such as the frontier lands of India and Bluchistan, which were not parts of British India or of any Indian or foreign state but over which the Crown exercised protection were also to form part of the federation. His Majesty in Council could, after ascertaining the views of the federal executive and federal legislature; declare any other territory as part of the Indian federation.

(a) Written and Rigid Constitution. A written and rigid constitution was essential for a federation so that the central and provincial governments knew precisely and definitely the scope and limitations of their power and authority and might not seek to so enhance that power as to subvert or diminish that of the other. The Constitution consisted of 321 Articles, and all the possible details relating to the three organs of federal and provincial governments had been laid down. The Indian Legislatures both federal and provincial—could not empower, alter or amend the constitution except as regards extension of the jurisdiction' of the federal Court. These were only subordinate law-making bodies and operated only within the frame-work of limitations laid down by British Parliament under the Act

(1935). The power of amending and altering the Constitution continued to vest in Parliament, although after the expiration of ten years from the commencement of the federation or the provincial autonomy, the federal or provincial legislatures, as the case might be, could adopt resolutions asking for amendment of the Constitution in a few minor matters. These matters related to the size or composition of the federal or provincial legislatures. Even in these matters the procedure laid down in the Act for carrying through the amendments was very cumbersome.

(b) Division of Powers. In a federal polity, the legislative and administrative powers of government were exercised by the Federal government on the one side and the governments of the federating units on the other. In order that there was no ambiguity about the scope and extent of those powers, the Act of 1935 made a clear distribution of legislative powers between them, and also determined their administrative relationship in all possible details. Article 99 laid down that the Federal Legislature could make laws of the whole or any part of British India or for any federated State, and a Provincial legislature could make laws for the Province or for any part thereof.

All possible subjects on which legislation might be required were classified into three lists—Federal Legislative List, Provincial Legislative List and Concurrent Legislative List. The Federal List consisted of 59 subjects, more important of which were foreign affairs, foreign trade, railways, posts and telegraphs, banking, currency, broadcasting, the Federal Public Service Commission, duties, taxes on income other than agricultural income, arms, fire-arms and ammunition and so on. The Provincial list comprised 54 subjects and more important of them were law and order, education, health, police, prisons, agriculture and land revenue, local self-government, forests, Provincial Public Services and Provincial Public Service Commission, trade and commerce within the Province, taxes on agricultural income, tolls, intoxicating liquors and narotic drugs, and so on. The Concurrent List included 36 subjects, some of which were criminal law, criminal and civil procedure, marriage and divorce, legal, medical and other professions, poisons and dangerous drugs, factories, welfare of labour, trade unions, electricity etc. etc.

Article 100 laid down that the Federal Legislature had, and a Provincial Legislature had not power to make laws with respect to any of the matters enumerated in the Federal List, that Provincial Legislature had, and the Federal Legislature had not, power to make laws with respect to any of the matters enumerated in the Provincial List, and that both the Federal and Provincial Legislatures had power to make laws with respect to subjects of the Concurrent List.

Notwithstanding that the law-making competence of the Federal and Provincial Legislatures had been demarcated, the Act made the Federal Legislature predominant in that sphere. It could make law for a Province or any part thereof with respect to any subject of the Provincial list if the Governor-General had, in his discretion, issued a "Proclamation of Emergency" under Article 45 of the 1935 Act. Such a Proclamation did not restrict the law-making power of the Provincial Legislature, but if any provision of a Provincial law was repugnant to any provision of a Federal law made by the Federal Legislature under this proviso, the Federal law, whether passed before or after the Provincial law, prevailed and the Provincial law was, to the extent of repugnancy, void, but only so long as that Federal law was in effect. Such a Federal law ceased to have effect on the expiration of a period of six months after the proclamation had ceased to operate.

Similarly, if some provisions of a Provincial law on a subject of the Concurrent List were repugnant to some provisions of a Federal law on the same subject, the provisions of the Provincial law were void.

As provided in Article 103, the Federal Legislature could make a law on any subject of the Provincial List if resolutions authorising the Federal Legislature to do so were passed by the Chamber of Chambers of those Provincial Legislatures. Any Act so passed could, as respects any Province to which it applied, be amended or repealed by an Act of the Legislature of the Province.

The Federal Legislature could make a law to implement treaties and agreements with other countries even if that law related to a subject of the Provincial List.

The Governor-General could in his discretion, empower either the Federal Legislature or a Provincial Legislature to enact a law with respect to any matter not enumerated in any of the three Legislative Lists, and the executive authority of the Federation or of the Province, as the case might be, extended to the administration of any law so made.

(c) Independent Judiciary. Although the powers and extent of authority of the federation and the federting units had been clearly demarcated the possibility of conflict as to the interpretation of the constitution was always there. The very nature of a federal constitution involved such conflicts. In order that those conflicts were resolved impartially and without prejudice the framers of the Act provided for the setting-up of a Federal Court.

PROPOSED INDIAN FEDERATION

Under the Act of 1935, India was to be a federation. Accordingly there was distribution of subjects between the centre and the provinces. There was much controversy as to whether residuary powers should be left with the centre or with provinces. The authors of the Act did not wish to see a weak centre and at the same time also did not wish to give many powers to the provinces. Accordingly they divided the subjects with considerable details. These were divided as 'Central Subjects', 'Provincial Subjects', 'Concurrent Subjects' and residuary powers were left with the Governor-General himself, who was to decide which legislature should be loaded with the responsibility of enacting on subject(s) not mentioned in the three lists. There were as many as 59 subjects which were included in the federal list. These included armed forces, foreign affairs, railways, posts and telegraphs departments, customs, etc. In the provincial list there were 54 subjects and included justice, police, education, land revenue, local self-government, etc. In the concurrent list were included subjects like marriage and divorce, arbitration, news-papers, trade union, electricity, etc.

Then another characteristic of Indian federation was that it was made a bicameral legislature consisting of the Council of States and Legislative Assembly. Indian States were to send 104 members to the

Council of States and 125 to the federal Assembly. This federation was to consist of eleven Governors provinces and six Chief Commissioner's provinces. Their joining the proposed federation was absolutely compulsory. In so far as princes, *i.e.* Indian States were concerned, it was left to them to decide whether they wanted to join the proposed federation or not. Each prince who agreed to join the federation was to sign an Instrument of Accession, which was final and irrevocable. It was proposed that the proposed federation will come into being only when half of the total number of Indian states agreed to join the federation or those princes who wanted to be an integral part of the federal system, had half of the total population of Indian states.

A Supreme Court was also created to decide disputes if any, which arose between the centre and the provinces or between the provinces themselves or for the interpretation of any part of the Act or any order in Council made thereunder.

A Peculiar Federation. In spite of the fact that the Act of 1935, created the structure of a federation in India, yet the whole system was unlike many other federations which made it a peculiar federation. It may however be remembered that Indian federation did not come into being because Indian States and their princes who had been given the option of joining the federation did not come forward in requisite number. Some of the important deviations from a usual federal pattern were as under.

Deviations From Federal Pattern. Usually in a federation residuary powers are left either with the Central Government or with the federating units. In the case of proposed Indian federation the subjects to be dealt with by federal government and provincial governments were specified and clearly defined. A, concurrent list was also prepared on which both the centre and the provincial governments could enact laws. Residuary powers were, however, left with the Governor-General. This never happens in the case of federation, where such powers are left either with 'the centre or the provinces.

The another salient feature of a federation is that the federating units willingly come together. They decide the subject matters which are to be surrendered to the Central Government and which are to be retained by them. The constitution which is to specify the terms and conditions of bringing them together is accepted by them. There is no super imposition in any manner from any quarter. In other words, it is just friendly and co-operative coming together. In the words of R.P. Dutt, "A federation is a voluntary union of independent sovereign units impelled by common political aims, ideals or external needs, to establish a sovereign centrol organ based on the units and responsible to them or to their populations and establishing a restricted measure of common organisation, falling short of full centralisation but such as to institute within the voluntarily agreed limitations a single federal laws for all the citizens of the union."

But in India proposed units of proposed federation never desired to come nearer to closer to each other. They never drafted a constitution for themselves and in fact never agreed to the constitution which was given to them. The Act which was to bring them closer was prepared by the British Parliament and passed by that body. Both the provinces and the states, for all practical purposes, were told to join the federation. In this regard it was also a peculiar federation.

Then another peculiar feature of the federation was the way in which federation was brought into being. Usually in a federation, there are certain independent states, which desire to come together. In other words, from disunity there is unity and from disintegration, there is integration. But in the case of Indian federation just reverse was the case. India was first divided into provinces and then these provinces were asked to join themselves into a federation.

Still another important deviation in India from usual federal system was non-supremacy of the Constitution. In a federation a constitution is allways supreme. If there is any difference between the federating units or between a federating unit and the Central Government, it is the constitution which is referred and considered final. But in Indian federation British Parliament, the Secretary of State and even the Governor-General was above the Act and their decisions and words were final rather than the Act which created federation.

Then a federation is usually created when federating units have almost similar type of political awakening and a mission to make the system a success. But this was not with India. In Indian federation the States had less political awakening and much less a desire to make the federation a success, as compared 'With the Indian provinces.

In a federation, upper chamber represents the States and lower chamber the will of the people and thus directly elected representatives of the people constitute it. On the other in the case of Indian federation Lower House was to consist of not directly elected but indirectly elected representatives, which, was of course peculiar in a federal set-up.

In a federation federating units as well as the Central Government enjoy full powers to amend the constitution in the way they like. But in the case of Indian federation power of amendment of the Act was not vested in Indian federation, but with the British Parliament.

In the proposed federation the States, which were a part of the federation, were given undue representation than what these deserved. In a good federation no unit is given any weightage over the other and both are equally well treated and kept at par.

In a federation it is hoped that federating units will enjoy perfect autonomy and shall be free to express their views and exert their rights without any hindrance whatsoever. But in the case of India this was not the case. The provinces were not autonomous, they could not act in the manner they liked. There were several subjects which were kept with the Governor who was empowered to deal with these in his own discretion. Not only this, but both Governor as well as Governor-General collaborated with each other to make the working of the provinces difficult and influence their right of free expression.

In a federation both at the Centre as well as in the federating units the legislature is supposed to exercise an effective control over the executive. The head of the State acts on the advice of the elected representatives of the people. But in the case of Indian federation neither the Governor-General nor the Governor was responsible to the elected representatives of the people. They were really not bound to act on their advise. They were responsible to the British Parliament through the Secretary of State and as such will and wishes of elected representatives of the people did not matter much for them.

Then in a federation centre has much more autonomy than the federating units. In the case of Indian federation reverse was the case. In the provinces there was the system of dyarchy before the introduction of Act of 1935. Under the Act the provinces were given more powers and the system of provincial autonomy was introduced. So technically the provinces were supposed to be autonomous. On the other hand, dyarchy, which had failed in the provinces, and which put many restrictions was introduced at the centre, and as such even technically centre was not made autonomous. Thus whereas provinces were autonomous, Centre was not. This peculiar situation does not prevail anywhere else.

One finds that Indian princes did not like the: idea of political awakening in their states. Once states became an integral part of Indian federation, the tide of nationalism was sure to touch Indian States and shake their autocratic authority. In this way, Indian princes and British master-mind created a federation with necessary, inherent confidence that was not going to work in any way. Samuel Hoarce once said about Indian fed ration that, "Compared with other federations, there will be inherent in this federation, many anomalies that we do not see elsewhere," In the words of Punniah Indian federation was, "a Priori, more unworkable federation could not have been devised by ingenuity of man," In the words of R.P. Dutt, "It should, therefore, be correctly termed as a scheme to give the despotic Indian princes responsible to nobody save the British masters, power to legislate for the 270 millions of British India," Thus, the whole scheme of federation as created by the Act of 1935, was deliberately made complex, difficult and unworkable, both intentionally as well as operationally.

It may, however, be remembered that Indian federation did not come into being because requisite number of Indian princes did not agree to join the federation. They decided to keep their own narrow state interest above collective national interests, Since Indian States formed an integral part of Indian federation and these were not agreeable to join it, therefore, Indian federation could not be inauguarated in terms of the Act.

THE FEDERAL EXECUTIVE

The Federal Executive comprised the Governor-General and his Council of Ministers, A system of dyarchy was proposed to be introduced at the federal level, and that has already been discussed. It would be desirable to mention here that the executive authority of the federation was to be exercised on behalf of His Majesty, by the Governor-General either directly or through officers subordinate to him. That authority extended *(a)* to the matters with respect to which the Federal Legislature had power to make laws; *(b)* to the raising in British India of naval, military and air forces and to the governance of His Majesty's forces borne on the Indian establishment; and *(c)* to the exercise of such rights, authority and jurisdiction as were exercisable by His Majesty by treaty, grant, usage, sufferance, or otherwise in and in relation to the Tribal Areas.

THE GOVERNOR-GENERAL—HIS EXTRAORDINARY POWER

In order to enable the Governor-General to administer the "reserved subjects" and to discharge his "special responsibilities," the Constitution gave him some extraordinary powers, Article 45 (1) laid down that if at any time the Governor-General was satisfied that the government of the federation could not be carried on in accordance with the provisions of the 1935 Act, he could by proclamation: *(a)* declare that his functions shall to such extent as may be specified in the Proclamation be exercised by him in his discretion; *(b)* assume to himself all or any of the powers vested in or exercisable by any federal body or authority. The Governor-General was however, not authorised to assume to himself any of the powers vested in exercisable by the Federal Court or to suspend, either in whole or in part, , the operation of any provision of the Act relating to the Federal Court. Any such Proclamation could be revoked or varied by a subsequent Proclamation. It ceased to operate at the expiration of six months unless a Proclamation was once promulgated to revoke a previous Proclamation.

Any Proclamation issued under Article 45(1) was to be communicated forthwith to the Secretary of State who was required to lay it before each House of Parliament. If, and so often as a resolution approving the continuance in force of such a Proclamation was passed by both Houses of Parliament the Proclamation, unless revoked, continued in force for a period of twelve months from the date on which it would otherwise have ceased to operate.

If at any time the government of the federation was carried on for a continuous period of three years under and by virtue of a proclamation, then, at the expiration of the period, the Proclamation ceased to have effect and the government of the federation was carried on in accordance with the Provisions of the Act, subject to any amendment thereof which Parliament might make. If the Governor-General, by a Proclamation made any law, that law continued to have effect until two years clapsed from the date on which the Proclamation ceased to have effect, unless sooner repealed or re-enacted by Act of the appropriate legislature. All functions by the Governor-General under this Section were exercised "in his discretion."

On the whole Governor-General remained autocratic as in the past. There was not much change in his powers and position. He was still responsible to the British Parliament. In India he was responsible to none. He enjoyed very vast and extensive powers and everyone looked towards him for patronage and favour. He was above his councillors and also the Council of Ministers on the one hand and legislature on the other.

As already pointed 'out there were certain subjects which the Governor-General was to deal in his discretion. These included:

(a) Subjects to be dealt with by the Governor-General in his Discretion:

1. Administration of such departments as Defence, Foreign Affairs, religious matters and trebles welfare.
2. Appointment and dismissal of Ministers.
3. Presiding over at the meetings of Council of Ministers.

4. Appointment of Councillors, Financial Adviser, Chief Commissioners of Delhi, Ajmer, Marwar, Coorg, Governors and Deputy Governors of Reserve Bank of India, etc.
5. Vetoing a bill passed by the Federal Legislature, if necessary.
6. Making Legislation on a Bill already disapproved by the Federal Legislature.
7. Prohibiting discussion on a matter pending before legislature for its consideration if necessary.
8. Distribution of work among the Ministers.
9. Framing of rules for convenient transaction of government business.
10. Authentication of orders.
11. Promulgation or revoking of an ordinance or ordinances.
12. Issuing order to provincial Governors to either revoke or promulgate an ordinance.
13. Vetoing a provincial legislation.
14. Summoning, proroguing or dissolving Lower House of a legislature.
15. Sending message about a bill lying before the legislature.
16. Summoning, Joint sessions of Legislature.
17. According approval to the introduction of certain bills.
18. Issuing of emergency proclamation and suspending the constitution.
19. Issuing of directions to the Governor(s) when the latter acted in their discretion.
20. Recommending proposals for taxation and expenditure.
21. Exercising of complete control on non-voteable items of expenditure.
22. Issuing of rules and regulations for police administration.
23. Control over the working of armed forces.
24. Appointing High Commissioner for India in England.

25. Recommending of introduction of budget and money bills in the federal legislature.

(b) Powers to be exercised by the Governor-General in his Individual Judgement. According to Instrument of Instructions there were certain matters which were to be dealt with by the Governor-General in his own discretion. These included:

1. Prevention of grave menace to the tranquility of India.
2. Safeguarding of financial stability of India.
3. Safeguarding of interests of minorities.
4. Preventing discremination against taxes on British goods.
5. Prevention of commercial discrimination.
6. Protection of rights and interests of Indian princes.
7. Safeguarding of rights and interests of public servants.

From the above it will be observed that the Governor-General enjoyed very vast and extensive powers. He was really himself to decide whether interpretation given to a particular term was in accordance with the spirit of the Act or not. He was to give any narrow or wide interpretation to any provision of the Act and sometimes narrow interpretation could be so narrowed down that it even destroyed the very basic principle of responsible government, which British government claimed to promote in India.

(c) Powers to be Exercised by the Governor-General on the Advise of Ministers. Governor-General in India, under the Act of 1935, was the most powerful authority in India towards whom all looked for favours. As already pointed out dyarchy had been introduced in the centre. Insofar as reserved subjects were concerned these of course were under the charge of Governor-General. According to Instruments of Instructions there were very many subjects which the Governor-General was supposed to administer in his own individual judgment or under his own discretion. The remaining subjects were however to be dealt with by the Governor-General on the advise of his Minister who, as already pointed out, could be to a maximum of ten.

A very important question which accordingly arose was as to what was covered under this category. Under this category was included what was not covered under Reserved Subjects or 'Subjects to be dealt with in his discretion' or individual judgment. Thus very little was covered under this category, particularly when what was covered in other categories was to be interpreted by the Governor-General himself. In the words of A.B. Keith, "To enable him to secure that none of his responsibilities are over-looked, he may after consulting Ministers make in his discretion rules as to the information given to his requiring not only Ministers but Secretaries to his notice any matter likely to involve a responsibility."

Critical Assessment of Powers of Governor-General. The Governor-General was not to have powers in theory but he was to exercise these in practice as well. Coupland has tried to defend the authors of the Act for their giving these vast powers by saying that, "These safeguard looked more formidable on paper than they were actually to prove in practice." But from the very beginning Keith was very sceptical about the system which had been introduced in the centre. He did not see any reason as to how could the system of dyarchy which had failed in the province could be a success in the centre. In his own words, "The difficulties of dyarchy were clearly exposed in the Provinces under the Act of 1919, and there is no reason to suppose that they will not be repeated in the federation." Beyond all doubt the experiment at the centre was not likely to succeed and the system of responsible government at the centre had very few chances to grow when Governor-General had very extensive powers. About his powers Pt. Jawahar Lal Nehru in his 'Discovery of India' has said, "No man in the world today has had or has such absolute authority over such large number of people as the British Viceroy of India. The Viceroy speaks in a manner such as no Prime Minister of England or the President of United States can adopt. The only possible parallel would be that of Hitler."

Governor-General in India was rightly compared with Hitler. He controlled 80% of the total budget. He could veto any bill passed by the legislature and directly or indirectly could kill any legislative measure. Services were working under his domination and control. Division of subjects was very defective. If law and order was a transferred subject then maintaining peace and tranquility was the special responsibility of the Governor-General. In fact examples of the type and kind can be multiplied. Prof. K.T. Shah said about the pitiable conditions of Ministers and powerful position of the Governor- General that, "it seems extremely doubtful if the popular Ministers of Federation of India will have any real opportunity to inaugurate constructive scheme of economic betterment or social reconstruction." The reason being quite obvious that the funds will not be made available for inaugurating such scheme. About the powers of the Governor-General in India Mr. Churchil once said, "the Viceroy or Governor-General was armed with all powers of Hitler or Mussolini by a stroke of pen he could scatter the constitution or decree any law to be passed.

INSTRUMENT OF INSTRUCTIONS

The Governor-General in India was of course given very extensive powers and many such powers he was to use in his individual judgment and in his discretion. Some of his powers he was to use on the advise of his Ministers. British Government, therefore, thought it better to issue certain guidelines to the Governor-General indicating the manner in which he should govern and exercise his powers. These were just like Directive Principles for the governance of the country. These had no legal force. Some of the important guidelines which were given to the Governor-General through the Instrument of Instructions included:

(a) In the Council of Ministers representatives of minority communities and Indian states should be included.

(b) Collective responsibility among the members should be encouraged.

(c) Choice of Ministers should be made on the advice of the leader of majority party in the Lower House of Legislature.

(d) Ministers should be consulted in matters relating to Defence of India, etc. etc.

CRIPPS MISSION

Cripps Mission was a failure. It ended in bad taste and the gulf between the Congress and the League on the one hand and between the Congress and the British rulers, on the other very much increased. Gandhiji demanded that the British should leave India and they themselves will take care of their own affairs without involving the Britishers. In a frustrated mood on June 9, 1942, Gandhiji declared that "There is no half way house between withdrawal and non-withdrawal". On July 14, 1942 Indian National Congress also passed a resolution demanding immediate withdrawal of Britain from Indian soil. Mr Jinnah, however, reacted to this resolution of the Congress by saying that such a demand was merely to establish Hindu Congress Raj on minorities and the Muslims and nothing else. A.I.C.C. on August 8, 1942, however, made it clear that after withdrawal the power will pass on the the Indians and not to the Congress party. It was also suggested that a provisional government should be set up with the responsibility of evolving a scheme for the setting up of the Constituent Assembly. Basically the constitution will be federal in nature and maximum autonomy will be given to the provinces.

Quit India Movement. Gandhiji declared that Congress was going to launch a mass movement to make the Britishers Quit India. This resolution technically came to be known as 'Quit India' resolution. The mass movement for quitting India, however, did not start all of a sudden. Mira Ben was deputed to meet Viceroy and convey the sense behind this resolution. She was refused interview and clearly told that such a resolution sensed rebellion and the government will not tolerate this when war was going on. As a first measure Gandhiji and other of Congress leaders were arrested, Congress was declared as an illegal organisation and offices and property of the organisation was seized. This in turn had its own reaction. The people rose in revolt. There were demonstrations thoughout the country. There were also conflicts between the people and police and even army. People in thousands were killed and many more arrested. There was complete dislocation of communication system. Men and women were mercilessly tortured. In the words of Michael Brecher, "To short every where government repression was very harsh and police state was established to deal with the danger which constituted the greatest threat to British rule since the rebellion of 1857." More or less similar views were expressed about repressions by Pt. Nehru when he said that, "All conventions and subterfuges that usually veil the activities of government were torn aside and only naked force remained as the symbol of authority."

Meanwhile British government tried to establish that Congress movement which believed in non-violence had become revolutionary in character and was in League with Japanese aggressors. Gandhiji, therefore, demanded that the charge that Congress organisation was in league with Japanese aggressors should be investigated. When this demand was not accepted he went on fast on February 10, 1944. His health day-by-day deteriorated. Meanwhile British government also thought it advisable to release him from jail so that he could control the movement and run it on non-violent lines. Accordingly Gandhiji was released on May 6, 1944. But by now his health had so much deteriorated that he could not undertake any major activity or launch any programme. After improving his health Gandhiji decided to make another attempt to find a solution of India's political problem with Muslim League. Maulana Azad, however, feels that this attempt was a blunder.

In his words, "Gandhiji's approach to Mr. Jinnah on the occasion was a great political blunder. It gave a new and added importance to Mr. Jinnah which the latter exploited to the full."

Rajaji Formula. In order to solve constitutional deadlock, C. Rajagopalachari, gave his own formula. Some of the important provisions of the formula were:

(a) Muslim League should accept India's demand for independence.

(b) It should co-operate with the Congress, in the formation of an interim government.

(c) As soon as the hostilities are over a Commission will be set up to demarcate Muslim majority contiguous districts in the North, West and East of India. Thereafter plebiscite will be held on the basis of adult franchise in these areas to decide the issue of separation from Hindustan.

(d) Before plebiscite every political party will be given the fullest opportunity to express its view point before the people.

(e) There will be no use of force in transfer of population if at all that became unavoidable and that will be on voluntary basis.

(f) In case some of the provinces wanted separation an agreement will be singed with them about defence, commerce and communication, etc.

(g) These terms will be binding only, if Britain transferred power to India into to.

Mr. Jinnah, however, did not agree to the formula and put forth such terms and conditions which were absolutely unacceptable to the Congress. He wanted the Congress to accept two nation theory and partition without plebiscite. He was not in favour of allowing the non-Muslim majority areas to take part in deciding the issue of a separate state for the Muslims. But effects of the formula were no less significant. Prestige of Mr. Jinnah went very high. The Hindus of Punjab and Bengal got demoralised to the idea of their being a part of an Islamic state. No less nervousness was among the Sikhs. In the words of Menon, "The offer was calculated only to strengthen Jinnah's hands and further the cause of Muslim League."

THE WAVELL PLAN

Lord Wavell came to India as Viceroy and Governor-General of the country. He had long association with India and had also worked with Cripps when he came to India. He gave his plan on July 19, 1945. There were several causes responsible for giving his plan to India. By 1945 it had become amply clear that Indians were by now sufficiently awakened and also that mere jugglary of words will not satisfy them. It was, therefore, very essential that they should be given something real and concrete. Moreover, by 1945 war situation had considerably changed to the advantage of the Allies and Nazis were being defeated on every front. There was every hope that war in Europe will soon come to an end. It was, however, expected that Japan would not surrender along with Hitler and might continue war for some time more. The best base from where Japan could be counter attacked was India and for this India's co-operation was unavoidable. In the country discontentment also got aggravated on account of the famines in which about 115 million persons perished and about 4.5 million people suffered.

When war came to an end in Europe, Churchill was not considered to be a suitable Prime Minister for post war reconstruction work. He was, therefore, replaced by non-conservative government. He, however, wanted to prove that the real problem which stood on the way of solving constitutional dead-lock in India was not lack of sincerity on the part of British government but mutual differences of two major religious communities, namely, the Hindus and the Muslims. It was under these circumstances that Wavell Plan was given to India. Some of the important provisions of the plan were:

(a) Executive Council of the Viceroy will be reconstituted and expanded in which all its members except the Viceroy and the Commander-in-Chief will be Indians.
(b) The Governor-General will sparingly use his veto power.
(c) In the Executive Council the Muslims and caste Hindus will have equal representation and all other communities will be given balanced representation.
(d) A British High Commissoner will be appointed to look after Indian commercial interests in other dominions.
(e) Secretary of State will interfere in Indian affairs only in the interest of India.
(f) Indians will frame their own constitution notwithstanding anything contained in this scheme.
(g) Section 93 of the Act of 1935 will be scrapped from the provinces, if India accepted this scheme.

Shimla Conference. Lord Wavell invited Indian leaders to Shimla to discuss the scheme. The discussions opened on June 29,

1945, and lasted till July 14 of the same year, but ultimately these failed. In spite of the fact that 70% of the Hindu population was placed on parity with 30% of the Muslim population, Mr. Jinnah turned down proposals on the plea that Muslim League should have the exclusive right to send Muslim representatives on the executive council of the Viceroy. He was not prepared to accept the idea that Congress should nominate any Muslim even from its own quota. Though this idea was not at all favoured by British government but Lord Wavell accepted that because he did not wish to annoy Muslim League. He instead of setting the matter right declared that, "This was a matter which should be decided between the Congress and the Muslim League and it would not be proper for either the government or for himself as an individual to enforce a decision on any party. About the failure of the talks Pattabhai Sitaramayya worte, "The years back in April 1942, it was the Congress that broke the Cripps Mission, if it was not Cripps himself who broke his own. In Shimla it was the League that broke the Wavell Plan although Lord Wavell took blame upon himself."

About the effects of the Wavell Plan it can be said that it exposed to the people of India strategy of Mr. Jinnah in no hidden terms. It was now clear that communal politics and not national interest was the main objective of the League. Similarly it also made it amply clear that British government in India was not quite keen to give self-government to the people of India but it was only killing time and postponing the problem on one pretext or the other. Maulana Azad writes, "The Shimla Conference marks a break down in Indian political history. This was for the first time that negotiations failed not on the basic political issues between India and Britain but on the communal issue dividing different Indian groups." Similarly K.P. Menon also wrote, "The Shimla Conference afforded last opportunity to the forces of nationalism to fight a rear guard action to preserve the integrity of the country, and when the battle was lost the waves of communalism quickly engulfed it. Only the Hobsons choice of partition was left." About the Plan Banerjee said, "The Cripps Plan had been rejected by the Congress as also by the Leagues. The Wavell Plan was rejected by the League alone. Less than a year later

Jinnah found himself in a much stronger position and the partition of India was in sight."

Cabinet Mission came to India at a very critical time of Indian history. The failure of Wavell plan had created an atmosphere of frustration, particularly among the majority community whose interests were sacrificed. Minority community was sitting as a veto on the will of the majority. It was amply clear that the British government was in league with the Muslim League and not at all interested in solving India's constitutional problem. This indifference of the government towards India had still more increased because Britain had won war in Europe.

INA Affairs. When Britain was adopting this indifferent attitude at that time came the trial of INA. Subhash Chandra Bose had suddenly left India because he felt that Gandhian way of solving constitutional problem would take a very long time and that India could not wait for that long. He, therefore, left India in disguise via Afganistan and reached Germany. After this he went to Japan and decided to organise Indian National Army. It mostly consisted of those Indians who had been fighting on British side but had been arrested by the Nazis. They were patriots and under the supreme command of Subhash Chandra Bose organised a separate independent government on Japanese soil. INA so well organised itself that soon invaded India and reached Burma border and Manipur. When INA was knocking Indian soil fortunately war in Europe turned in favour of Britain and Allied forces. After the fall of Hitler, position of Japan became very weak. She ultimately surrendered when the USA dropped two atom bombs on Japanese soil. When Japan surrendered, with that British forces were in a position to capture some INA soldiers. In India they were given by the people, thumping welcome. But for Britain they were war criminals. The government decided to try them as rebellious soldiers. This created great resentment among the people of India and thus strained relations between the government and the people. One serious effect of whole episode was that to the British government it became very clear that Indian soldiers were not with British government. This was really very alarming situation for the rulers.

Naval Mutiny. On the heels of INA come naval mutiny which took place in 1945-46. Royal Air Force revolted at Dum Dum and other air force stations. There was also hunger strike in the air force. On February 18, 1946 there was mutiny at Bombay at RIN air base which lasted for five days. Even officers resorted to direct action. There were also disturbances in the army and air force and by now it was amply clear that armed forces were not loyal to the British government. Maulana Azad wrote that, "All these developments convinced the British that they could no longer rely on the armed forces unless the political problem of India was satisfactorily solved."

British government on its part convened a conference of Provincial Governors on 1st August, 1945, where problem of ending Governor rule in the provinces was considered and it was decided to hold elections in the provinces. Elections were announced for Central and Provincial legislatures. But meanwhile situation in England changed and Conservative Party which had taken a rigid stand about India's independence was defeated at the polls and Labour Party came to power. On 19th September, 1945 on behalf of British government Lord Wavell declared that, "His Majesty's Government are determined to do their utmost to promote in conjunction with the leaders of Indian public opinion the early realisation of self-government in India." He also assured the people of India that His Majesty's government was quite keen for setting up a Constituent Assembly for India.

Since the elections had been announced Congress, after prolonged discussions, decided to participate in these. In Congress election manifesto it was made clear that it stood for equal rights for all citizens; fundamental rights and civil liberties for every Indian citizen, eradication of poverty and raising of living standard of the masses. It also stood for world federation of free nations. Congress wanted national freedom from which all other freedoms would automatically flow.

As a result of these elections Congress came to power in all Hindu majority provinces and also in NWFP. In Bengal and Sindh Muslim League was in a position to form government. In Punjab a coalition government in which Congress was a partner, came into being.

CABINET MISSION IN INDIA

After the elections were over Lord Attlee issued a statement on March 15, 1946 in which India's right of self-determination and framing her own constitution was clearly admitted. He also made it amply clear that it would be for India to decide, whether she wanted to remain a member of the Commonwealth or not. It was also stated that minority will not be allowed to veto the advance of majority. It was also stated that a Commission consisting of Cabinet Ministers will soon be sent to India to discuss Indian problem. Accordingly a Commission consisting of Lord Pathick Lawrence, Sir Stafford Cripps and A.V. Alexander arrived in India on March 23, 1946. During his stay in India the Commission interviewed 472 Indian leaders and held many formal and informal meetings. It tried to have an agreed formula for India's independence, but failed. During the course of his discussions Gandhiji made it clear that, "Pakistan which connotes the division of India will be a sin and the two nation theory propounded by Mr. Jinnah is absurd." On the other hand, Muslim League insisted that India should be partitioned.

Cabinet Mission gradually got convinced that the Hindus and the Muslims were nowhere coming nearer to each other. Even then it made it amply clear that the sovereign state of Pakistan was not feasible because creation of such a state was not likely to solve the problem of Muslim minorities left in remaining India. Such a state was not feasible even on economic, administrative and military point of view. This will also create problems for Indian states as well.

When it became clear that united India was only solution to India's political problems Congress gave its own scheme. In this it was provided that India should be united state in which provinces should be given maximum autonomy. These will be required to surrender only three subjects; namely, Defence, Foreign Affairs and Communications. There will be single Constituent Assembly for which members will be elected on the basis of single transferable vote system from the provinces. In the Assembly the representatives of the States will also be added. The Constitution was to be revised after every 10 years. Since this scheme was also not acceptable to the Muslim League, on May 16, Cabinet Mission released its own scheme.

PROPOSALS OF CABINET MISSION

Cabinet Mission scheme had the following characteristics:

(i) There will be Union of India, which will include Indian states.

(ii) The proposed Union will deal with subjects like Foreign Affairs, Defence, Communication and raise funds for running these subjects.

(iii) The Union will have an executive and a legislature which will be constituted from the British India and Indian states.

(iv) Every major communal issue will be decided by a majority vote of the representatives of both the major communities present and voting.

(v) The provinces will be free to form their own groups and each such group shall have a separate executive and legislature. Each group will be independent and decide the subjects to be taken in common.

(vi) There will be a provision for the revision of constitution after every ten years.

(vii) Cabinet Mission also made a provision for a Constituent Assembly for India. It was provided that in the proposed Constituent Assembly each province will be given representation on the basis of its population.

(viii) All subjects except those mentioned above, as well as residuary subjects will be vested in the provinces.

(ix) The states will themselves decide the subjects which they will like to surrender to the Union.

(x) Each province will send representatives on the basis of population of each community in that province.

(xi) There will be three classes of electorates, namely, General, the Muslims and the Sikhs.

(xii) It was hoped that India will continue to remain a member of the Commonwealth; but decision will be entirely her own.

(xiii) A treaty will be signed between the Constituent Assembly and the British government giving effect to the transfer of power.

(xiv) Since the Constituent Assembly was to take some time to complete its task, it was provided that there will be an interim government at the Centre and till then such a government shall have 14 members, out of which 6 will be of the Congress, 5 of the Muslim League and one each of the Indian Christians, the Sikhs and the Parsees. All the portfolios will be transferred to Indian leaders.

(xv) After the transfer of power paramountcy over Indian States will end and it was hoped that each state will negotiate with the new power and union government.

The scheme also provided that the representatives of the Indian provinces for the Constituent Assembly will be represented on the basis of proportional representation from the provincial Assemblies by transferable vote system. It will be ensured that each community gets proper representation. The representatives of the States were to be represented by a Negotiating Committee.

Critical Evaluation of the Plan. Cabinet Mission plan was, of course, not accepted by India, but the scheme had its very good point as well. In the words of Gandhiji, "It is best document the British Government could have produced in the circumstances." In the words of Maulana Azad, "The acceptance of Cabinet Mission Plan by both Congress and Muslim League was a glorious event in the history of freedom movement in India." The whole plan, by all means was a sincere effort on the part of British government to solve India's constitutional deadlock. The merit of the scheme also lies in the fact that it was made amply clear that partition of India was not a feasible solution to the problem of Indian minorities. Both Lord Pathick Lawrence and Sir Stafford Cripps repeatedly said that they could not see how a scheme of Pakistan, as envisaged by Muslim League, could be viable or stable. Grouping formula which the scheme proposed was to satisfy the Muslims of India because Groups 'B' and 'C' contained predominantly Muslim majority provinces. In this way to a large extent Muslim demand was also met. It was also a domocratic scheme because for the Constitution of Constituent Assembly the principle of proportional representation was accepted. In this way the old idea of giving weightage to the minorities was abandoned.

Then the merit of the scheme was that in the Assembly all the representatives were to be Indians. Similarly in the interim government all the portfolios were to be dealt with by Indians. The Constituent Assembly was made a sovereign body and Indian states were to be given representation only according to their population. The scheme was also important because the States were to be given representation only according to their population. The scheme was also important because in the states the princes were not to nominate representatives for the Constituent Assembly. This responsibility was to be given to the people of the states. This was a major change in so far as the states were concerned.

The scheme undoubtedly had very salient characteristics and under the circumstances under which it was given, perhaps it provided the best possible solution. But at the same time it had its drawbacks as well, which equally cannot be under-estimated. Under the scheme very few subjects were given to the Centre, even residuary powers were also given to the provinces. In this way a weak Centre was created. For a vast country like India only a strong Centre could effectively work and deliver the goods. Creating a weak Centre was perhaps the greatest drawback of the scheme.

This was bound to create a situation of uncertainty. Then the scheme gave a great blow and set back to India's national unity. The provinces were divided into groups on the basis of religion and group was given full autonomy to frame its own constitution. Not only that, but even each province was also given liberty to leave the group.

Then under the scheme the constiution, which the Assembly was to give, was not going to be a permanent document. It was to be changed after every 10 years. This was bound to create a situation of uncertainty. A Constitution in a federal system is always a permanent document and expected to be a source of confidence both for the Centre as well as the federating States.

Then another drawback of the plan was that its language on very important issues was vague. It was not clear whether it was compulsory for the provinces to join federation or not. In fact language of several articles of the proposed plan *e.g.* 15(5), 19(8) and 19(5) was self-contradictory and subsequently could result in great controversy between two major political parties, namely, the Congress and the Muslim League.

Then another difficulty of the scheme was that the Constituent Assembly, as created by the scheme, was undemocratic the members were to be elected on tbe basis of the strength of each community in the provinces. It was also undemocratic because the states were not as democratic as the provinces.

Then the seeds of mischief were sown in the plan itself when it was said about the states that after paramountcy came to an end, these will have the fullest liberty to either join Indian Union or not. Thus, all that was designed was a disunited rather than a united India.

The Sikhs had a grievance against the plan. According to them their interest were not protected and they were absolutely thrown at the mercy of the Muslims, which they did not like.

The whole plan was very rigid. It was provided that it should be accepted or rejected in to-to. Thus there was no scope for modification of the scheme before its acceptance. Rigidity of scheme undobtedly was unwanted and uncalled for.

The Plan had provided for an interim government. It was, however, not clear for how long will this interim government remain in office. Not only this, but great injustice was done to the Hindus in the scheme of things. In the government the Hindus were given only 6 seats, as against the Muslims who were given 5 seats.

Since the Congress was not given the right to send any Muslim representatives, even out of its own quota. the result was that national character of the Congress, which it was maintaining all along, was thrown into the dust. This was the basic reason why Congress decided not to joint the interim government.

The Hindu Mahasabha objected to the scheme on the plea that it placed the Hindus of certain provinces like Punjab, Assam, Bengal, Sindh and NWFP at the mercy of the Muslims, without taking adequate measures for protecting their rights and interests.

In fact, the whole scheme was a step forward towards creation of a separate state of Pakistan. It had its own advantages but on the whole perhaps no better scheme would have been prepared than what the people got at that time and under those circumstances.

MOUNTBATTEN PLAN

Under the Cabinet Mission Plan both the Congress and the Muslim League were given representation at par and national character of the Congress had been challenged. The result of this mischief was that the Congress declined the offer of the Viceroy to join the interim government. Accordingly on June 16, 1946 Viceroy and the Cabinet Mission issued a statement in which it was stated that he was inviting the leaders of major political parties to join interim government. But the Congresss decided to keep out of it. Muslim League, however, agreed to join that Viceroy, however, felt that a Government which did not include Congress representatives could not be a success and he decided to postpone the formation of an interim government till Congress agreed to join it. On June 26, 1946, Viceroy wrote to Mr. Jinnah that, "Since the Congress and the Muslim League had now accepted the statement of 16th May, it was the intention of the Cabinet Mission and the Viceroy to form a coalition government including both these parties as soon as possible. In view, however, of the long negotiations which has already taken place and since we all had other work to do, we felt that it would be better to have a short interval before proceeding with further negotiations for the formation of an interim government." Meanwhile efforts will be made for the setting up of the Constituent Assembly. Cabinet Mission thereafter left for England on June 29, 1946.

This letter so much annoyed Mr. Jinnah that he demanded that since interim government was not coming into being, therefore, elections to the Constituent Assembly should also not take place. When Viceroy did not agree to this proposal, the Muslim League also decided not to join the interim government. In spite of the fact that the League did not like to go to the polls for electing representatives for the Constituent Assembly, Viceroy decided that the elections should be held so that the process of transfer of responsibility to Indians started. The elections were held in July, 1946. Congress was returned with thumping majority. This very much annoyed the Muslim League which again came out with the usual argument that the Hindu dominated Constituent Assembly was bound to have its own way, sacrificing the interests of the Muslims and other minorities. The League, therefore, decided not to join the Assembly and instead decided to resort to Direct Action on August 16, 1946, to get Pakistan as homeland of the Muslims.

Direct Action Day. In order to press its demand for a homeland the Muslim League decided to bid farewell to Constitutional means and to observe 16th August as Direct Action Day. It was on this day that there was bloodshed in Calcutta and Noakhali. Thousands were killed whereas thousand others were injured. Property worth crores of rupees was destroyed and in the name of religion atrocities were committed on innocent women and children.

On July 22, 1946, negotiations again started for the formation of interim government.Under the revised scheme it was proposed that the Congress will nominate six representatives, including one scheduled castes, Muslim League five and three representatives of minority communities will be nominated by the government and one of them will be a Sikh. The names submitted by one party will not be objected by the other. Distribution of protfolios will be decided by the parties themselves but both the major political parties will share the major portfolios.The interim government will be treated as Dominion Government for all practical purposes. Mr. Jinnah objected to the revised scheme as well on the plea that the Congress should not be given the right of nominating any Muslim and also that distribution of important porfolios on equal basis between the two major communities was an impossibility.

Congress Joins Interim Government. The Congress, however, accepted proposals of the Viceroy and accordingly Pt. Jawahar Lal Nehru was invited to form the government. All subsequent efforts to bring Muslim League in the interim government miserably failed. On September 2, 1946, interim government was installed in power. Finding Congress and other parties in power, Mr. Jinnah also agreed on October, 13, 1946, to join the government "to get a foothold to fight for the cherished goal of Pakistan" and create as many obstructions as possibly could be created. Since, the League was not at all interested in co-operating with the Congress, therefore, the question of joint and collective responsibility did not arise. Muslim League of those days tried its best to ensure that wheels of cabinet coach come as quickly to a standstill as possible. Communal riots and incidences of communal hatred in the country fouled the whole climate.

In the meanwhile Viceroy decided to convene meeting of the Constituent Assembly on December 9, 1946. Mr. Jinnah was afraid of Congress returning with thumping majority in the Constituent Assembly and decided to boycott the Assembly. He also charged the Viceroy of being blind to the situation and in league with the Congress. In order to save the situation from further deterioration Lord Attlee, the British Prime Minister, made last attempt to bring a compromise between the Congress and the Muslim League. He, however, miserably failed and attitude of the Muslim League remained as hard as it was in the past.

British Government was, however, very keen that the power should be transferred to the Indians as early as possible. He, therefore, made a statement in the House of Commons that Britain will leave India by June, 1948. He also said that even if Indian leadership does not come to any compromise by this date, British government will decide then to whom the power of British India may be transferred, *i.e.*, whether to one central authority or to provinces in some of the cases. Since there was a hint that in some cases power might be trasferred to provinces, Muslim League too tried to topple governments it NWFP, Assam and Punjab. Whereas it failed in the case of two first mentioned provinces, in Punjab Sir Sikandar Hyat Khan, the Chief Minister, resigned and Governor took over the adminis-tration of the province. The Congress party, however appreciated the decision of the British government to leave India by a particular date and mentioning nothing about the partition of the country. Gandhiji even said, "So long as I am alive, I will never agree to the partition of India nor will I, if I can help it allow Congress to accept it." But subsequently several other leaders persuaded him and on account of desire to see free India, he was made to agree to the partition of India. In this way Muslim League which followed pressure tactics and policy of communal disharmony seemed near reaching its goal.

MOUNTBATTEN PLAN (JUNE 3, 1947)

Lord Mountbatten came to India on March, 1946 with clear instructions to transfer power to Indians as quickly as possible it could be. He was convinced that partition was no solution to India's constitutional problem. He met Indian leaders and after ascertaining their views he went to England in May 1947. He came back to India and on June 3, 1947 and unfolded his plan of solving problem which was so far evading solution. It was in this plan that proposal was made for the partition of India. Dr. Ishwari Prasad is of the view that role of convincing Congress leadership to accept partition proposal was that of Lady Mountbatten. In his own words, "By remarkable adaptability of character and pleasing manners, she won the hearts of all the great adversaries of the land." Gandhiji even at this late stage wrote in Harijan that the demand for partition of India was both un-Islamic and sinful, because Islam did not preach hatred and partition. He still said that, "They may cut me to pieces but they cannot make me subscribe to something which I consider to be wrong." Dorothy Norman is of the view that partition proposal of Lord Mountbatten matured because during this critical period Gandhiji was kept in pariphery and real negotiation work was done by Nehru and Patel.

Salient features of the scheme are as follows:

(1) There will be two Legislative Assemblies, one of the Hindu and the other of the Muslim dominated areas and each Assembly will decide whether it wishes to be partitioned or not. If either part favoured partition, that will be accepted.

(2) If either of the province opts for partition it will also have to decide whether it will like to join the already established

Constituent Assembly or a new Constituent Assembly which will consist of representatives of those areas which decide not to participate in the existing Constituent Assembly.

(3) Area of Sylhet will decide by referendum whether it will continue to remain part of Assam or join East Bengal, which will form part of Pakistan.

(4) A referendum will be held in NWFP to decide whether the province will like to join India or Pakistan.

(5) The province of Sindh will decide whether as a whole it will like to join existing or new Constituent Assembly.

(6) British Baluchistan will also be given a right to decide whether this Chief Commissioner province will like to stay in India or join newly born State of Pakistan.

(7) In case majority areas of Bengal, Assam and Punjab decide for partition of the provinces then a boundary Commission will be set up to demarcate the boundary.

(8) Both India and Pakistan will be given dominion status.

(9) Boundaries of both India and Pakistan will be decided by a Boundary Commission to be appointed by the Governor-General.

(10) Paramountcy over the states will lapse and the states will be free to decide about the dominion to which they propose to join or to remain independent.

Congress leadership was all along against partition of India and Gandhiji had gone to the extent of saying that India will be partitioned on my dead body but still the partition was accepted. For this one great reason, as already pointed out was, that during those critical days of negotiations leadership went in the hands of Pt. Nehru and Sardar Patel. Then according to the author of "Freedom at Midnight" Congress leadership did not know that Mr. Jinnah was victim of tuberculosis and his end was drawing near. Had they or even Lord Mountbattten come to know of this vital secret, perhaps this tragedy would not have occurred. Then it was also felt by Congress leadership that due to unbending attitude of Muslim League, united India will either be delayed or won at the cost of civil war and for both the situations Congress was not ready. It was hoped that after partition "India and Pakistan will live peacefully with each other, and that all men of goodwill on either side would be free to concentrate on improving the economic conditions of the common people."

THE INDIAN INDEPENDENCE ACT 1947

Once whole partition scheme was agreed by major political parties, stage was set for introducing Independence Bill in the House of Commons, which was introduced on July 4, 1947. This was the culmination of India's struggle against colonialism and imperialism. It was also the victory of communal forces in our national struggle, because the Act provided for the partition of India and formation of an independent and sovereign state of Pakistan. It was also the victory of forces which followed the policy of 'Divide and Rule' on the one hand and 'Divide and Quit' on the other. The Act established that by deliberate manoeuvering a ruling party with the co-operation of minority could veto very effectively the will and wishes of even a strong majority, on one pretext or the other. The Act of 1947 was not a constitution in any manner or even did not provide for any constitution on broad basis. On the other hand, it was an Act which enabled the British government to withdraw from India.

The main provisions of Indian Independence Act, 1947 were as under:

(i) The British government will leave India on 15th August, 1947.

(ii) India will be divided into two sovereign states of India and Pakistan and both these states will become sovereign on this very day.

(iii) The powers previously exercised by the British government in India will be transferred to both these states.

(iv) Office of the Secretary of States for India will be abolished.

(v) Provision was made for the Governor-General for each dominion, who was to be appointed by the Queen of England on the advice of the Dominion government. He was not to act in his individual judgment or dicretion but will act merely as constitutional head of the State.

(vi) Each Dominion was to have a sovereign legislature for rule making purpose. No law made by British Parliament was automatically to apply to India.

(vii) Punjab and Bengal will be divided and its territories will be demarcated by a boundary commission to be headed by Mr. Redcliff.

(viii) A bill passed by the Dominion legislature could not be disallowed by His Majesty.

(ix) Till such time as the Constitution was framed by the Constituent Assembly in any Dominion, it will work as near the Act of 1935 as possible.

(x) Both the Dominions will have their own Constituent Assemblies, which will act as their legislatures as well.

(xi) Governors of the Provinces were to act as constitutional heads of the provinces.

(xii) Reservation of posts for Secretary of State was to discontinue. Those civil service personnel who wanted to resign after transfer of power to both the dominions were to be allowed to do so.

(xiii) Paramontcy of Britain over Indian states and tribal areas was to come to an end on 15th August, 1947. In their case power was not to be transferred to dominions, but it was left to the states to decide whether they would like to join India or Pakistan.

(xiv) The King of England was to drop the title of King Emperor of India.

(xv) Relations of the British government with India henceforth were to be conducted through Commonwealth Relations Office.

(xvi) The territories of Pakistan were to include Eastern Bengal, Western Pakistan, Sindh and British Baluchistan. In case the people of NWFP in a referendum decided to join Pakistan that territory will also join Pakistan.

The Act brought India on the threshold of new era where both the Dominions were to share their own responsiblities without any super power patronage. Lord Attlee said in the House of Commons that, "It is the culminating point in a long course of events." Dawn which respresented Muslim view point in those difficult days called it as "momentus and unique picce of legislation". Lord Samuel called it a "a treaty of peace without war". The Hindustan Times characterised it as the noblest and the greatest law ever enacted by British Paliament. Dr. Rajendra Prasad in his India Divided says, "The period of domination of British over India ends today and our relationship with Britain is henceforth going to rest on a basis of equality of mutual good and mutual profit."

Of course, the Act provided for the freedom of India and the struggle of our freedom fighters bore fruit but it was quite unfortunate that the people of both the Dominions had to undergo untold sufferings and miseries after the partition of the country. It was a period in which inhuman and unhuman acts were committed in the name of religion. Life respect and property of none else but the goondas was safe. All the crimes which religion forbade were committed to glorify that. Not only this, but the scheme was deliberately made mischievous in so far as Indian states were concerned. In fact, Britain left more than 567 independent Indias. It needed a person of will, determination and far sightedness of Sardar Patel who could undo the mischief and knit them in the fabric of one polity and merge them with Indian Union.

On the whole, the Act ended the agonies of freedom fighters and threw upon them the gigantic task of giving a new constitution to India, which could take the nation on the path of peace and prosperity and end the poverty of masses.

SOURCES OF THE INDIAN CONSTITUTION

It was under the provisions of the Cabinet Mission Plan that a Constituent Assembly was established in India. The Constituent Assembly was entrusted with the job of framing a Constitution for India. It was indeed a Herculean task to frame Constitution for a country inhabited by various religions, over 2000 castes and over 1000 dialects spoken by the people. India is a land of diversity; of course with basic unity. The makers of the Constitution were also confronted with challenges which originated from the size of Constituent Assembly, the nature and content of the national struggle and the intellectual, social and political background of the Indian elite. The elite were modern while the society was traditional. Kamal and Mayer have said in their book 'Democratic Politics in India' that "Constitution-making for such a diverse and complex country as India, posed challenging and intricate problems. No doubt, the nationalist movement consolidated many diverse tendencies in India's national life but decisions making on India's institutional strategy was not, however, wholly a product of agreement reached during the movement......the agreements that existed were at a very general level, the deliberations of the Constituent Assembly had to be far more precise." In addition thereto, leaders representing different political parties and socio-religious groups had their own ideas about a Constitution for India. The Hindu Sabha believed in making India a Hindu State while the Socialist Party wanted a socialist orientation. The Congress had also many shades of opinion. It was Gandhi who led the Congress. But even the Congress was not Gandhian. Gandhi said, "Congressmen themselves are not of one mind even on the contents of independence. I do not know how many swear by non-violence of the Charkha or believing in decentralisation, regard the village as the nucleus. I know on the contrary that many would have India become a first class military power and wish for India to have a strong centre and build the whole structure round it" Gandhi regarded the British Parliament as a barren woman but still India followed parliamentary form of democracy.

The founding fathers of the Indian Constitution drew inspiration from many sources. These sources include the imaginative aspirations of the nationalist leaders, the actual working of the Government of India Act, 1935 and the experience gained from the actual working of some of the Constitution of important countries of the world. Our Constitution is not a closed document. It has grown over the years. Its sources thus include not only the sources upon which the founding fathers drew but also the developmental ones such as the judicial decisions, constitutional amendments, constitutional practices and so on.

The sources of the Indian Counstitution can thus be divided into two categories:

I. Seminal Sources. The following are the seminal sources of the constitution:

(1) ***Constituent Assembly Debates.*** A specific Constituent Assembly under the Cabinet Mission plan was constituted to frame the Indian Constitution. Its members included distinguished lawyers, intellectuals and patriots who took two years, eleven months and eighteen days to prepare the Constitution. During the course of this period, debates on all the aspects of the Constitution were held in a free and fair manner. These debates produced an intelligent opinion in the light of which every word of the Constitution was screened carefully and intelligently.

(2) ***Reports of the Committees of the Constituent Assembly.*** The Constituent Assembly had appointed various types of committees to make reprots on different aspects. Some of the most important committees include Union Powers Committee, Union Constitution Committee, Provincial Constitution Committee, Advisory Committee on the rights of citizens, minorities and tribal and excluded areas, Ad hoc Committee regarding the Supreme Court, Committee on financial relations between the Union and States. The reports of these Committees were thoroughly dicussed in the Drafting Committee.

(3) ***The Nehru Report.*** The British Government announced the formation of the Simon Commission for making a report on the working of the Government of India Act, 1919 and suggest constitutional measures required for the efficient administration of India. The Congress decided to boycott this commission because no Indian was taken in it. Instead, it announced the formation of a committee under the leadership of Pt. Moti Lal Nehru to make recommendations about the desired constitutional set-up for India. The Committee made certain recommendations which are known as the Nehru Report.

The main clauses of this Report were:

(a) Grant of Dominion Status to India in the British Empire.

(b) Creation of a federal structure for India.

(c) Parliamentary and responsible Government in Provinces.

(d) Bicameralism at the Centre and unicameralism in Provinces.

(e) Guarantee of Fundamental Rights.

(f) Establishment of Supreme Court as the final court of appeal.

(4) Lahore Session of the Congress. The Congress at its Lahore session held in 1929 resolved to make India a Republic.

(5) Objective Resolution of Jawaharlal Nehru. Jawaharlal Nehru moved in the Constituent Assembly Objective Resolution embodying the aspirations of the nationalist India. The Objective Resolution stated:

(i) This Constituent Assembly declares its firm and solemn resolve to proclaim India as an independent sovereign Republic and draw up for the future Government a Constitution;

(ii) Wherein the territories that now comprise British India, the territories that now form the Indian States, and such other parts of India as are outside British India and the States as well as such other territories as are willing to be constituted into the Independent Sovereign India shall be a union of them all;

(iii) Wherein all power and authority of the sovereign Independent India, its constituent parts and organ of Government are derived from the people;

(iv) Wherein the said territories, whether with their present boundaries or with such others as may be determined by the Constituent Assembly or thereafter according to the law of our Constitution, shall possess and retain the status of autonomous units together with residuary powers, and exercise all powers and functions of Government and administration, save and except such powers and functions as are vested in or assigned to the union, or as inherent or implied in this union resulting therefrom;

(v) Wherein, shall be guaranteed and secured to all the people of India justice–social, economic and political; equality of status of opportunity, and before the law; freedom of thought, expression, belief, faith, worship, vocation association and action, subject to law and public morality;

(vi) Wherein, adequate safeguards be provided for minorities, backward and tribal areas and depressed and other backward classes;

(vii) Whereby, shall be maintained the integrity of the territory of the republic and its sovereign rights on land, sea, air according to justice and the law of the civilised nations; and

(viii) This ancient land attains its rightful and honoured place in this world and makes its willing contribution to the promotion of world-peace and the welfare to mankind."

The Objective Resolution clearly spelled out making India as a sovereign republic where the ultimate supreme power should be vested with the people. The people would get social, economic and political justice, liberties of all types and equality. The uplift of the backward people and areas would be insured and the structure of the country would be federal.

(6) Government of India Act, 1935. At the time the Constitution for free India was being framed, India was governed by the Government of India Act, 1935. The fathers of the Indian Constitution drew heavily on the experience and the provisions of this Act. According to Jennings: The Constitution derives directly from the Government of India Act, 1935 from which, in fact, many of its permisions are copied textually.

The Constitution has been influenced by the 1935 Act in the following points:

(a) Federal Set-up,

(b) Distribution of powers in the three lists,

(c) Provincial autonomy,

(d) Office of Governor,

(e) Bicameral legislature,

(f) Power of issuing ordinances,

(g) Structure of the Surpreme Court.

The present Constitution is described as the glorified version of the 1935 Act. Approximately 250 Articles have been borrowed, either word for word or with minor changes from the Act, with the basic principle remaining unchanged. Dr. Ambedkar, the chairman of the Drafting Committee said, "As to accusation that the Draft Constitution has reproduced a good part of the Government of India Act, 1935, I make no apologies. There is nothing to be ashamed of in borrowing. It involves no plagiarism. Nobody holds any patent rights in the fundamental ideas of a Constitution." However, a lot that did not suit the conditions of free India was discarded.

(7) ***Impact of Various Constitutions.*** The founding fathers of the Indian Constitution were wise enough to borrow from the experience gained in the working of various other Constitutions. It is on this account that the Constitution of India is regarded as the bag of borrowings. However, only those principles were borrowed which could serve well the Indian circumstances and aspirations. There was no blind borrowing.

(a) *British Constitution.* We had drawn inspiration to a great extent from free and democratic institutions at work in Great Britain. Moreover, we had become quite familiar and accustomed to the British constitutional practices. It was but natural that we should have borrowed from the Mother Constitution. The impact of the British Constitution is clear from the following facts.

(i) Constitutional Head of State.

(ii) Lower House of Parliament (Lok Sabha) is more powerful than the Upper House.

(iii) Responsibility of Council to Ministers of Parliament.

(iv) Parliamentary System of Govenment.

(v) Prevalence of Rule of Law

(b) *U.S. Constitution.* The Constitution of the United States had its impact in the following respects:

(i) Preamble of the Constitution.

(ii) Provision of Fundamental Rights.

(iii) Amendment of the Constitution.

(iv) Nature and functions of the Supreme Court.

(v) Functions of the Vice-President.

(vi) Independence of judiciary.

(c) *Irish Constitution.* The Irish Constitution gave us the Directive Principles of State Policy and the method of nomination members to the Rajya Sabha.

(d) *Australian Constitution.* Australian Constitution gave us a long list to concurrent powers and the procedure for solving deadlock over concurrent subjects between the Centre and the States.

(e) *Canadian Constitution.* We borrowed about the provision of strong India, the name 'Union of India' and vesting residuary powers with the Union from Canada.

(f) *Weilmer Constitution of Germany.* The Weilmer Constitution of Germany had its impact upon the powers of the President.

(g) *South African Constitution.* The procedure of amendment with a two-thirds majority in Parliament and the election of the members of the Rajya Sabha on the basis of proportional representation by the State legislatures have been borrowed from the Constitution of South Africa.

II. Developmental Sources. As already stated our Constitution is not a static document. It has grown with the changing needs. Thus amendments, judicial decisions, political practices, parliamentary statute, rules, regulations and ordinances are the developmental sources of the Constitution.

(1) ***Amendments of the Constitution.*** During the course of the 28 years the Constitution has been amended 45 times and a few other amendments have been proposed. In this way, the present shape of the Constitution is quite different from the original document.

The Fundamental Rights have also undergone changes from time to time. The first amendment widened the powers of the State to impose reasonable restrictions on the rights of freedom of speech and expression. The fourth amendment provided that private property can be acquired in the public interest on payment of compensation. The twenty-fourth amendment empowered once again the Parliament of India to introduce changes in any part of the Constitution including the Fundamental Rights. The twenty-fifth amendment replaced the word *'compensation'* by the word *'amount'*. The amount to be paid to the owner of property was to be determined by the law which authorises taking of property itself. By the 42nd amendment, the Directive Principles of State Policy have gained precedence over the Fundamental Rights. A law passed by Parliament or State Legislature for giving effect to any of the Directive

Principles cannot be challenged in any court of law on the ground that it is inconsistent with or takes away or abridges rights conferred by Articles 14, 19 and 31 of the Constitution.

The election disputes of the President, Vice-President, Speaker and the Prime Minister have been withdrawn from the jurisdiction of the courts.

The power of judicial review exercised by the High Courts in matters such as service disputes, election disputes, land reforms disputes etc. under the words *"for any other purpose"* has been curtailed. Such disputes can now be referred to the administrative tribunals. Appeal against the decision of the administrative tribunal can be referred to the Supreme Court. This has been done through the 42nd amendment.

The 42nd amendment has now made it clear once for all that the President shall, in the exercise of his functions, act in accordance with the advice of the Council of Ministers.

Any amendment of the Constitution could be challenged in a court of law. But with the 42nd amendment, the power of the Parliament to amend Constitution is final. Any amendment made by Parliament cannot be challenged in any court of law on any ground whatsoever.

Emergency provisions of the Constitution have undergone significant changes. Emergency declared under Article 352 can now be made applicable to any part of India and not to the whole of India as before. This has been made possible through the 42nd amendment. As amended by the 44th amendment, emergency under this Article will be declared only when the safety and security of the country is endangered either by foreign aggression or armed rebellion from within. Internal disorder in which there is no danger of armed rebellion cannot be made a ground for the declaration of Emergency. Morever, such an Emergency shall be declared by the President only on the advice of the

Council of Ministers on a written request. It will not be declared on the advice of only the Prime Minister as was got done by Indira Gandhi on 25th June, 1976. The Emergency will be approved by both the Houses of Parliament by a majority vote. The approval will have to be obtained within a month of its declaration. Emergency will remain in force for six months and for its extension a resolution will have to be passed by majority. Ten percent or more members of the Lok Sabha can call for a special session in order to get it disapproved. The right *to life, liberty and legal protection* will remain intact even during the course of Emergency. Nobody can be kept under detention for more than two months. This period can be extended only by the advisory board. The chairman of the advisory board must always be a judge of the High Court. Moreover, no censorship will be imposed on the press.

(2) ***Judicial Decisions.*** The judicial decisions given by the Supreme Court on important issues have added new dimensions to the Constitution. It is in the light of such decisions that further constitutional amendments are made in the Constitution. Some of the most important judicial decisions are:

(i) Gopalan v/s State of Madras

(ii) State of Madras v/s Champakam

(iii) Golak Nath v/s State of Punjab

(iv) Keshwanand Bharati v/s Kerala State.

(3) ***Commentaries of the Constitutional Experts.*** While interpreting the Constitution, the views of the distinguished constitutional experts, whether Indian or foreign, enjoy special importance. The most notable constitutional experts are Jennings, Gledhill, Alexandrowitz, D.D. Basu, Palkhiwala, V.N. Shukla etc. Their views are not given legal recognition but due regard is paid to them by the judges. Morever, true significance of any provision of the Constitution can be understood in the light of their views.

(4) ***Parliamentary Statutes.*** Parliament has also made various statutes for furnishing details of the various Articles contained in the Constitution. It is the Constitution which itself empowers the Parliament to enact laws on certain articles for details. These Statutes are considered as constitutional laws.

Without their existence, a detailed study of the Constitution is not possible. Some of the important Statutes are:

(i) Preventive Detention Act, 1950

(ii) Representation of People Act, 1950, 1951.

(iii) Finance Commission Act, 1951.

(iv) President and Vice-President Elections Act, 1952.

(v) Indian Citizenship Act, 1953.

(vi) States Reorganisation Act, 1956.

(vii) Supreme Court (number of Judges) Act, 1956, 1961.

(viii) Vidhan Parishad Act, 1957.

(ix) Pondicherry (Administration) Act, 1957.

(x) Punjab Reorganisation Act, 1966.

(xi) The Unlawful Activities (Prevention) Act, 1967.

(xii) The President (Discharge of Functions) Act, 1967.

(xiii) Official Language Act, 1963, 1968.

(xiv) Maintenance of Internal Security Act, 1971.

(xv) Protection of Foreign Exchange and Anti-smuggling Act, 1974.

(xvi) Protection of Citizens Rights Act, 1976.

(xvii) The President and Vice-Presidential Election (Amendment) Act, 1977.

(5) ***Rules, Regulations, Ordinances etc.*** Each House of Parliament is empowered to make rules for its efficient working. The President has also got the right to make rules for fixing the constitutional subjects. The President is also

empowered to make rules with respect to the conditions of services of the members of the Union Public Service Commission. He can also frame rules to establish peace and efficient administration of the Union Territories. The President has also the power to issue ordinances when the Parliament is not in session. All these rules, regulations and ordinances serve as sources of the Constitution.

(6) ***Constitutional Practices.*** Although the Constitution of India is the most detailed in the world, still certain practices independent of the Constitution have developed in India.

The first example of such a constitutional practice is that the Central Government takes before hand the consent of the State Government in the appointment of its Governor. Moreover, the Governor can be recalled by the Central Government on the advice of the State Government concerned.

Secondly, the Governor should not belong to the State to which he is appointed.

Thirdly, one of the judges of the Supreme Court must belong to the minority community.

Fourthly, the senior-most judge of the Supreme Court should be appointed as the Chief Justice of India. However, this practice was broken by the Indian Government when Justice A.N. Ray was appointed as the Chief Justice of India in supersession of three senior Judges–S. Relat, Grover and Hedge. However, this practice was again revived in the appointment of Chandra Chud as the Chief Justice of India.

Fifthly, the word *'Council of Ministers'* in the Constitution is taken to mean the *'Cabinet'*.

Sixthly, the leader of the majority party in the Lok Sabha is appointed as the Prime Minister.

❐

2

Bases of Indian Constitution

Indian Constitution as a Bag of Borrowings

It was quite natural for the founding fathers of the Indian Constitution to keep all these things in view. Solution of such problems could only be had if they got guidance from the actual working of various constitutions in different countries of the world. They were wise enough to borrow from the experience gained from the working of various other Constitutions. Whatever provision in whatever Constitution could be of any use, was incorporated in the Indian Constitution. It is on this account that the Constitution of India is regarded as the *bag of borrowings.*

The various Constitutions from which the fathers of the Indian Constitution borrowed are the following:

(1) British Constitution. We had drawn inspiration to a great extent from the free and democratic institutions at work in Great Britain. Moreover, we had become quite familiar and accustomed to the British constitutional practices. It was but natural that we should have borrowed from the Mother Constitution. The impact of the British Constitution is clear from the following facts:

(i) The Indian President is a constitutional head like the British King. He is required to act in accordance with the advice tendered to him by the Council of Ministers. Dr. Ambedkar told the Constituent Assembly, "Our president enjoys the same position as enjoyed by the King in the British Constitution. He is the head of the State but not of the executive, he is the representative of the nation but not the administrator of the country."

(ii) The Indian Lok Sabha, like the British House of Commons, is more powerful than the Rajya Sabha.

(iii) India adopted Parliamentary system of Government based on the British model. K.M. Munshi said in the Constituent Assembly, "Our experiment regarding the working of the Parliamentary Administrative system does not permit us to conduct any new experiment."

(iv) The Council of Ministers in India is responsible to Parliament as it is in Great Britain. It can remain in office only so long as it enjoys the confidence of the majority of members of Parliament.

(v) On the British pattern of rule of law, we have introduced equality before law in India.

It should, however, be borne in mind that while the Constitution of Great Britain is largely unwritten, that of India is wholly written.

(2) United States Constitution. The image of the United States before the end of the Second World War was that of a friend of the oppressed and colonial people. It was because the United States had itself freed from colonial rules only in July, 1776. Their Constitution embodies certain fundamental principles enshrining freedom for the people. It was but natural for the founding fathers of our Constitution to have borrowed from them.

The impact of the U.S. Constitution is very clear from the following facts:

(i) We are very much affected by the aims, objectives and principles of the U.S. Constitution. It is clear from the Preamble of the Two Constitutions.

The preamble to the U.S. Constitution reads: "We, the people of the United States do ordain and establish this Constitution for the United States of America."

The preamble to the Indian Constitution reads: "We, the people of Indian... do hereby... enact and give to ourselves this Constitution."

(ii) The Fundamental Rights enshrined in the Indian Constitution resemble those of the U.S. Bill of Rights.

(iii) The functions of both the Vice-President of United States and India are similar to a great extent. The Vice-President of India presides over the meetings of the Rajya Sabha but is not a member of it. Similarly, the Vice-President of the United States presides over the meetings of the Senate but not a member of it.

(iv) The nature and functions of Supreme Court of India are comparable to the U.S. Supreme Court.

(v) The procedure for the amendment of the U.S. Constitution has greatly influenced the Indian Constitution.

(vi) Independence of Judiciary is conspicuous in both the countries.

Prof. Spear holds: "Regarding the Fundamental Rights, Supreme Court and some powers of the President, the Indian Constitution is indebted to the American Constitution."

(3) Irish Constitution. The Directive Principles of State Policy have been borrowed from the Irish Constitution.

Secondly, the provision for nominating members to the Rajya Sabha from amongst the eminent persons in the field of Art, Culture, Science and Social Service have also been taken from the Irish Constitution.

Thirdly, as Prof. Hansen says, "By imitating the system of Roman Catholic religion, articles concerning cow protection have been given a suitable place in the Indian Constitution."

(4) Canadian Constitution. The Canadian Constitution has its impact on the Indian Constitution in the following manner:

(a) The name 'Union of India' for the Indian Republic was borrowed from the Canadian Constitution.

(b) As in Canada, a strong Centre has been provided for in the Indian Constitution.

(c) Like the Canadian Constitution, the Indian Constitution provides that the residuary powers shall be vested in the hands of the Centre.

(5) Australian Constitution. A long list of concurrent powers and the procedure for solving the deadlock over concurrent subjects between the Centre and the States has been borrowed from the Australian Constitution. Dr. Ambedkar clarified in the Constituent Assembly that the concurrent list has been included in the Indian Constitution after getting inspiration from the Australian Constitution.

Secondly, the words *'proved misbehaviour'* and *'inefficiency'* as grounds on the basis of which the judges of the Supreme Court can be removed from office, have also been borrowed from the Australian Constitution.

(6) South African Constitution. The South African Constitution had its impact in the following respects:

(i) The procedure of amendment with a two-third majority in Parliament.

(ii) Election of the Members of Rajya Sabha on the basis of proportional representation by the State legislatures.

(7) Weilmer Constitution of Germany. The President's power to suspend the Fundamental Rights during an Emergency has been borrowed from Section 48 of the Weilmer Constitution of Germany.

Govt of India Act, 1935. In addition to the various Constitutions as enumerated above, the fathers of the Indian Constitution borrowed heavily from the Govt. of India Act, 1935. According to Jennings, "The Constitution derives directly from the Government of India Act, 1935 from which, in fact, many of its provisions are copied textually." Approximately 250 Articles have been borrowed, either word for word with minor changes from the Act, with the basic principles remaining unchanged. It is on this account that the present constitution is described as the glorified versions of the 1935 Act. Dr. Ambedkar, the Chairman of the Drafting Committee said, "As to the accusation that the Draft Constitution has re-produced a good part of the government of India Act, 1935, I make no apologies. There is nothing to be ashamed in borrowing. It involves no plagiarism."

The Indian Constitution has been influenced by the 1935 Act in the following points:

(i) The federal set up has been influenced by the 1935 Act. The federation proposed under the Act was a class by itself. Similar is the position at present. Ours is federation with important unitary features. Rather, it would be more proper to say that it is a unitary constitution with strong federal features.

(ii) The division of subjects into three lists—Union, State and Concurrent—is on the pattern set out on the Act of 1935.

(iii) Provincial autonomy granted in the new Constitution resembles that of 1935 Act.

(iv) The system of bicameral legislature has also been copied from the Act of 1935.

(v) The position of the Governor in the new Constitution is very much similar to that of the Governor under 1935 Act.

(vi) The power of issuing ordinances has also been taken from the Act of 1935.

(vii) Indian Supreme Court set up under the new Constitution bears testimony to the influence it received from the Federal Court set up under the 1935 Act.

No Justification in Calling the Indian Constitution as a Bag of Borrowings. No one can deny that the fathers of the Indian Constitution borrowed from all sources. But, in the words of Dr. Ambedkar, "Nobody holds any patent rights in the fundamental ideas of a Constitution." The Provision inserted in any constitution are not the original discoveries of the fathers of that Constitution. They borrow them from somewhere else. There is nothing wrong in borrowing the experience of another.

It must also be borne in mind that there is no blind borrowing. Only those principles were borrowed which could serve well the Indian circumstances and aspirations. It is in this way not borrowing but shifting. If we have borrowed the parliamentary system from the British experience, we were wise enough to have left the unitary system. We adopted the federal structure as in U.S.A. but not the Presidential form of Government. The procedure for the selection of judges was taken from the British system but the system of judicial review from the United States.

Even in the Constituent Assembly, some of the members remarked that there is nothing original in the Constitution of India. To this, Dr. Ambedkar, the Chairman of the Drafting Committee replied, "One likes to ask whether there can be anything new in a Constitution framed at this hour in the history of the world. More than hundred years have rolled over when the first written Constitution was drafted. It has been followed by many countries reducing their Constitutions to writing. What the scope of a Constitution should be has long been settled. Similarly what are the fundamentals of a Constitution are recognised all over the world. Given these facts, all Constitutions in their main provision must look similar. The only new things, if there can be any, in a Constitution framed so late in the day are variations made to remove the faults and to accommodate it to the need of the country."

In this way, it is not at all justified to call the Indian Constitution as a bag of Borrowings. If we have borrowed mainly from the Government of India Act, 1935 and the British Constitution, it is because of certain reasons. The Government of India Act, 1935 was framed keeping in view the conditions prevalent in India and the aspirations of the people of India. Whatever was not suitable for a free India, we omitted. As regards the British Constitution, we were familiar with the working of its institutions for about hundred years. We could never afford to cut ourselves off from our immediate past. The Constitution of India has been framed in a balanced way. This is what we learn from its practical working.

SALIENT FEATURES OF INDIAN CONSTITUTION

The constitution of India is among the longest in the world. It continued the constitutional development that took place under the British, retaining the basic precepts of the Government of India Act of 1935 and taking from it approximately 250 articles, verbatim or with minor changes.

When India gained independence, the Constituent Assembly, functioning under a modified Government of India Act of 1935, became the Provisional Parliament. Its fundamental task, however, remained that of framing the constitution. Dr. Ambedkar chaired the Drafting Committee and steered the document through nearly a year of debate over its various provisions. Four leaders, Nehru, Patel, Prasad and Maulana Azad, through their commanding grip on the Congress Assembly Party and the assembly's eight committees, constituted a virtual oligarchy within the Assembly. Issues were openly debated, but the influence of the Congress leader was nearly irresistible. Although they themselves were by no means always of one mind, they sought to promote consensus and in the end, the constitution was adopted by acclamation on January 26, 1950, Republic Day, the new constitution went into effect.

The new India was to be a parliamentary democracy, federal, republican and secular. There were some members of the Assembly who pushed for a Gandhian constitution, one that would provide for a decentralised state with the Village Panchayats as its nucleus. The vast majority, however, were, committed from the beginning to a centralised Parliamentary government.

Of this new, native and national constitution of India, the salient features are as follows:

1. ***The Longest and Most Comprehensive Constitution.*** The Constitution of India, according to Ivor Jennings, is "the longest and the most detailed in the world." It is a formidable document having more than 400 Articles spread over nine schedules. The original Constitution, as adopted on 26th January, 1950 had 395 Articles and 8 Schedules. The 9th Schedule was added as a result of the First Constitution Amendment Act (1950) for validating abolition of Zamindari. In respect of its size, it is five times bigger than the U.S. Constitution. The Constitution of Sri Lanka which claims to be sufficiently detailed and comprehensive, is less than half of the size of the Indian Constitution. Its size has been enlarged on account of numerous provisions inserted with a view to covering all the problems peculiar to India. Unlike other constitutions, it does not merely lay down fundamental principles of governance nor does it deal with the federal

Government alone. It makes detailed provision in respect of a number of matters which normally do not form part of other Constitutions.

The extraordinary bulky size of the Constitution is due to the following reasons:

(i) It outlines not only the detailed provisions relating to the governmental system at the Union level but also at the State level.

(ii) Fundamental Rights have been elaborated to the extent as to what limitations and restrictions can be placed on their enjoyment.

(iii) Provisions have been made not only with regard to the distribution of powers and functions but also as to how harmony, co-ordination and adjudication is to be brought about.

(iv) In order to bring about social revolution, Directive Principles have also been enumerated. These Principles are fundamental in the governance of the country.

(v) Even the minutest detail regarding the orgainsation, structure and functions of the Supreme Court and the State High Court has been given.

(vi) Provisions, have been included to ensure independent and impartial functioning of the Union Public Service Commission and the Election Commission.

(vii) Keeping in view the peculiar problems of the Indian people, adequate provisions relating to official language, safeguards for the minorities have been included.

(viii) Emergency provisions have also been made to ensure proper growth of the infant democracy.

2. ***A Sovereign State.*** The Preamble to the Constitution defines new India as a 'Sovereign Secular, Socialist, Democratic Republic'. The word 'Sovereign' denotes that India is no longer a dependency of the British Empire as she was before 15th of August, 1947. Nor is she a dominion as it

was from 15th of August, 1947 to 25th January, 1950. She is now as sovereign as U.S.A, Great Britain or U.S.S.R. No other country has any rights to dictate her terms. She is free from external control and free in internal affairs. She is the master of her destiny and can chalk out an independent state policy of her own without being dictated by any outside power. She is now free to have any type of economic system in the country. No outside power is allowed to interfere in the internal affairs of our country. She is free to establish relations with any foreign country according to her own will. Her membership of the Commonwealth of Nation does not take away from her in any way the status of sovereignty. Nehru emphasized: "The new Commonwealth does not restrict India's independence either in the external or internal sphere. It has no strings attached in it. India is not compelled to stay in the Commonwealth even one minute longer than she may desire to. The agreement is in full accord with the Congress pledge and India's foreign policy of non-alignment with power blocs. It gives to India independence plus security in political and economic spheres." Her membership of the U.N. as that of other countries, does not limit her sovereignty.

3. ***Secular State.*** The Constitution of India lays down features essentially secular in nature. The world 'secular' was not itself mentioned in constitution. It has now been inserted in the Preamble through 42nd Amendment. The Constitution of India has accordingly been described as "the ideal of secular, religiously neutral State". The world 'secular' does not mean irreligious attitudes or opposition to religion. It merely denotes that so far as the State is concerned, it shall not discriminate between one citizen and another on grounds merely of differences in the religious beliefs of the people. Nor for that reason will the persons belonging to any particular religious faith be entitled to any special rights or privileges. Article 25 of our Constitution, therefore,

says: 'Subject to public order, morality and health, all persons are equally entitled to freedom of conscience and the right fully to profess, practice and propagate religions."

The Indian State, according to Venkataraman is "neither religious nor anti-religious, but is wholly detached from religious dogmas and activities and thus neutral in religious matters." This is exactly what we mean by the secularism of the Indian State. Every citizen, irrespective of his religion, race or creed is guaranteed by the Constitution of India, equal rights. The concept of secularism is not negative but a dynamic ideal. It seeks to create opportunities for all members of the great family of the people of India, whatever their race, religious or social background may be, to find full self-expression in their own way, through their own religion, distinctive culture and traditions.

4. ***Socialist State.*** It was through the 42nd Amendment that word *'Socialist'* was inserted in the Preamble. This was done to emphasize the socialist nature of the Indian Constitution. Even though the word 'socialist' was not used, the Indian Constitution laid emphasis on socialism through various Directive Principles of State Policy. Art. 39 lays down that the State shall ensure that the property does not get concentrated in few hands. The Directive Principles aim at the elimination of the exploitation of children, inequality among men and women, and unemployment. The State must take steps to raise the standard of living of the poor and the downtrodden.

5. ***Democratic State.*** The term 'Democratic' signifies that the Indian Constitution seeks to establish a form of Government which derives its authority from the will of the people. It is the people themselves who elect the rulers of the country, who are accountable to them for their omissions and commissions. Besides, the State does not discriminate against any citizen on grounds of religion, birth, sex, caste, colour etc. Constitution guarantees in

every manner possible a sense of justice, equality, freedom and security to all minorities in India. According to Panikkar, "Every section of the Constitution provides evidence... that the religion, culture and interests or all alike are safeguarded in the Constitution, and the sense of distrust and fear, which had far so long made India a cockpit of communal strife, may now be laid at rest." The word democracy indeed represents much more. It ensures not only political democracy as enshrined in the fundamental rights but also social and economic democracy as enshrined in the Directive Principles. This makes India a unique democracy in contradiction from the U.S.A. which ensures only political democracy and the U.S.S.R. which ensures only economic democracy.

6. ***A Republic.*** The term 'Republic' indicates that India has chosen to have an elected head. The President of India–her chief executive–is not a hereditary monarch as the British King but an elected head for a limited period. According to T.K. Tope "The Indian Republic is to be distinguished from the ancient Greek and the ancient Indian republics which were essentially, aristocratic, and also from the modern republic like that of U.S.S.R. which is of dictatorial nature. The Indian republic is a democratic republic."

7. ***Parliamentary Form of Government.*** The Indian Constitution provides for a parliamentary form of Government, both at the Centre and the States. The President of India and the Governors in their respective States are only constitutional heads. The executive is drawn from and is responsible to the legislature, both at the Centre and the State level. The essence of Parliamentary democracy is the responsibility of the Cabinet to parliament for what it omits and commits. It can remain in office only so long as it enjoys confidence of the majority of members of Parliament. In all its functions of law making, financial and constitutional, the Parliament has followed to be led by the Cabinet.

The members of the Council of Ministers are collectively responsible to the Parliament "for whatever they did jointly or severally". They "are able to accept this joint responsibility because they consider all matters of importance sitting together as a Committee. All the policy decisions are arrived at through joint deliberations and by unanimous agreement". Actually, the principle of collective responsibility has not worked well. Dr. Ambedkar while tendering resignation in 1951 said that he was obliged, "to take joint responsibility without any opportunity to take part in the shaping of policy. This is an impossible position." In the Nehru administration, decisions on foreign policy were taken by Nehru himself without making any reference to the Cabinet Sub-committee on Foreign Affairs. Then after the Chinese aggression, V.K. Krishna Menon was made a scape-goat in 1963 when the whole Cabinet ought to have resigned for its failure with respect to foreign policy. Similarly was A.P. Jain made scape-goat on the issue of failure on food and agriculture production. The matters appear to be worse in the Indian administration.

The Parliament has maintained by and large due control over administration. The Mundra Affair was brought to the notice of Parliament by Feroze Gandhi as a result of which T.T. Krishnamachari had to resign as the Finance Minister. Krishna Menon had to resign on the issue of the unpreparedness of the defence forces at the time of the Chinese invasion in 1962. Kairon had to resign in 1964 on the findings of the Das Commission which was appointed to investigate charges of nepotism against him. Only recently the Opposition succeeded in going through the Report prepared by the C.B.I. on the Import Licence Scandal. The Parliament also succeeded in getting released the correspondence between Morarji Desai and Charan Singh in which they levelled charges against each other.

8. ***Sovereignty of the People.*** The Preamble to the Constitution clearly proclaims the sovereignty of the people of India. It

lays down: "We the people of India having solemnly resolved to constitute India into a sovereign democratic republic." This idea is further re-affirmed in several other places in the Constitution, particularly in the chapter dealing with elections. In terms of Article 326 "the election to the House of People and to the Legislative Assembly of every State shall be on the basis of adult sufferage." Further, the people have themselves adopted and enacted their Constitution. the Preamble to the Constitution reads: "We the people of India... In our Constituent Assembly this 26th day of November 1949 do hereby Adopt, Enact and Give to Ourselves, this Constitution." The people are also the ultimate masters under the Constitution. If the Constitution is to be amended, the Parliament under Article 368, has the power to do so. In Gopalan V/s State of Madras, Mr. Justice Shastri observed: "There can be no doubt that the people of India in exercise of their sovereign will as expressed in the Preamble, adopt the democratic ideal which assures to the citizens the dignity of the individual and other cherished human values as a means to the full evolution and expression of his personality, and in delegating to the Legislature, the Executive and the Judiciary, their respective powers in the Constitution, reserved to themselves certain Fundamental Rights."

9. ***Qualified Rigidity and Flexibility.*** The Constitution of India is neither so flexible as the Constitution of England, nor so rigid as the Constitution of U.S.A. It is rather a strange mixture, with appropriate modifications, to suit Indian condition. In so far as the constitutional amendment is concerned, the provision of our Constitution can be grouped into three categories:

   (a) *Amendment by Parliament by Simple Majority.* It applies to provision relating to the creation of new States by means of transferring some parts of the existing State or uniting the territories of the units of the

Indian Union, parliamentary quorum. Parliamentary privileges, rules of procedure, abolition or creation of Second Chambers in the State legislature, citizenship of India, etc.

(b) *Amendment by Parliament by Special Majority and by State Legislature by Simple Majority.* It applies to provisions relating to federal framework, as the election of the President, executive authority of the Union and States, Supreme Court of India, High Courts in States, distribution of legislative powers between the Union and States, etc.

(c) *Amendment by Parliament by Special Majority.* It applies to Part III of the Constitution dealing with Fundamental Rights and Part IV of the Constitution dealing with Directive Principles of State Policy.

Viewed as a whole, the Indian Constitution is to a great extent flexible with some things of rigidity. Wehare was obliged to say that the Indian Constitution has succeeded in "striking a good balance." Speaking about the adoptability of the Constitution to the changing circumstances, Ambedkar said, "This Assembly has only refrained from putting seal on finality and infallibility upon the Constitution by denying the people the right to amend the Constitution as in Canada, or making the amendment of the Constitution subject to the fulfilment of extraordinary terms and conditions as in America or Australia, but has provided a most facile procedure." It is thus fairly established that the Constitution of India is more flexible than rigid.

10. *Universal Adult Suffrage.* The Indian Constitution has incorporated the principle of adult suffrage and has abolished the old system of communal electorates. Now every person of 18 years of age or above, except those debarred on few grounds of criminality or mental health, have the right to vote. This is indeed a great achievement of nascent Indian democracy where the number of voters at the time of the seventh Election to the Lok Sabha held in 1980 exceeded 35 crores. Moreover the evil of communal electorate that ate the vitals of national integration, has also been done away with.

11. ***Fundamental Rights.*** The Constitution in its Part III embodies a set of Fundamental Rights which are guaranteed to all citizens and, in some cases, even to those who are not citizens. They are termed as the Magna Carta of the essential freedoms of the Indian people. These rights have a justifiable character in spite of the fact that the State may impose reasonable restrictions on their use and enjoyment. Nehru called these Fundamental Rights as the "Conscience of the Constitution."

The Fundamental Rights guaranteed under the Indian Constitution deal with equality before law, prohibition against discrimination on grounds of opportunity in matters of public employment, right of freedom of speech and expression, right to form associations or Unions, right to acquire, hold or dispose of property, right to practise any profession or carry on any occupation, trade or business, right not to be deprived of life or personal liberty except according to procedure established by law, right to freedom of conscience and to freely profess and practise religion, right to one's own culture and to study in any institution.

Some of the Rights fall in the category of negative injunctions prohibiting the State to commit certain acts, while others fall in the category of positive commandments conferring certain benefits upon the individual. Quoting as example, we can say that the State is restricted to take any action deny to any person equality before law while an individual has the right to the enjoyment of certain freedoms. These rights are not absolute but at the same time they are fully enforceable by the Court. It is open to the Court to determine whether the restriction imposed on the exercise of Fundamental Rights are reasonable or not.

However, the President of India can suspend any of the Fundamental Rights except the right to life, liberty and legal protection during the period of Emergency declared under Art. 356. Before the 44th Amendment, the President could suspend any of the Fundamental Rights. It is by virtue of the 44th Amendment that the President has been debarred from suspending the right to life, liberty and legal protection.

12. ***Fundamental Rights can be Amended.*** It has now been established that the Fundamental Rights are not immutable. They are subject to amendment by Parliament by ordinary legislative process. Such a bill should, however, be passed by both the Houses by special majority i.e. absolute majority of the whole House and two-thirds majority of the members present and voting. The Parliament can as such introduce as many amendments as it likes by following the special procedure. The right had to be ascertained after the Supreme Court gave its verdict in the Golak Nath *Vs.* the State of Punjab (1967) case that Fundamental Rights cannot be amended by Parliament. The Parliament accordingly passed 24th Constitution Amendment Act of 1971. On this amendment being challenged, Chief Justice S.M. Sikri, in the Fundamental Rights case of 1973, said, "Applied to Fundamental Rights it would mean that while Fundamental Rights cannot be abrogated reasonable abridgements of Fundamental Rights can be effected in the public interest." In general terms it may be said that the Fundamental Rights Case of 1973 allowed Parliament to amend Fundamental Rights to the extent that the basic feature of the Constitution are not changed.

Now, through the 42nd Amendment any amendment introduced in any part of the Constitution cannot be challenged in any court of law. It means Parliament has assumed supremacy even over Fundamental Rights. The Janta Government through the 44th Amendment sought to change this provision but it was rejected by the Congress dominated Rajya Sabha.

13. ***Directive Principles of State Policy.*** The Directive Principles of State Policy form yet another important feature of Indian Constitution. They are, according to Ambedkar, a "Novel feature." While the Fundamental Rights stipulate political democracy, the Directive Principles stipulate social and economic democracy. As such, both Part III and IV of our Constitution, taken together, are what may be said to constitute real democracy in India. "If a Chapter on Fundamental Rights is a must for a State of the modern democratic type with a written Constitution, a Chapter on the Directive Principles of State Policy is a must for a Welfare State with a written Constitution." In the words of M.C. Setalvad; "Although the Directive Principles of State Policy confer no legal rights and create no legal remedies they appear to be like an Instrument of Instructions, or general recommendations addressed to all authorities in the Union reminding them of the basic principles of new social and economic order which the Constitution aims at building. These fundamental axioms of State policy, though of no legal effect, have served as useful beacon-lights to courts."

    The Directive Principles lay down emphatically that the State shall strive to ensure for its people adequate means of livelihood, fair distribution of wealth, equal pay for equal work, protection of child and adult labour, employment, and free and compulsory education for children up to the age of 14. They also lay down that the States shall make effective provisions for public assistance in the event of unemployment, old age, sickness, disability and raising the level of nutrition as also of health.

    Though not justifiable, they are to be regarded as "fundamental in the governance of the country." The Directive Principles have as such offered a debatable issue. An English writer describes them as "a little more than a manifesto of aims and aspirations." But Ambedker said, "We have deliberately introduced in the language that we have used in the Directive Principles something which is not fixed or rigid. We have left enough room for the people of different ways of thinkings, with regard to the reaching of the ideal of economic democracy, to strive in their own way, to persuade the electorate that it is the best way for reaching economic democracy the fullest opportunity to act in the way in which they want to act."

14. *Fundamental Duties.* It is well known that rights without duties have no meaning. It is because no one can enjoy rights in the absence of duties and obligations. Still, our Constitution had made no mention of the duties of the people. It was through the introduction of the 42nd Amendment that a comprehensive list of the fundamental duties has been inserted in our Constitution.

Art. 51-A lays down that it shall be the duty of every citizen of India:

(a) To abide by the Constitution and respect its ideals and institutions, the National Flag and the National Anthem;

(b) To cherish and follow the nobel ideals which inspired our national struggle for freedom;

(c) To uphold and protect sovereignty, unity and integrity of India;

(d) To defend the country and render national service when called upon to do so;

(e) To promote harmony and the spirit of common brotherhood amongst all the people of India transcending religious, linguistic and regional or sectional diversities; to renounce practices derogatory to the dignity of women:

(f) To protect and improve the cultural environment including forests, rivers and wild life and to have compassion for living creatures:

(g) To value and preserve the rich heritage of our composite culture;

(h) To develop the scientific temper, humanism and the spirit of enquiry and reform;

(i) To safeguards public property and to avoid violence:

(j) To strive towards excellence in all spheres of individual and collective activity so that the nation constantly rises to higher levels of endeavours and achievements.

15. ***Supremacy of Directive Principles over Fundamental Rights.*** Before the introduction of the 42nd Amendment, the Fundamental Rights enjoyed supremacy over the Directive Principles. It was because of the fact that Fundamental rights were justifiable while the Directive Principles were not.

However, with the introduction of the 42nd Amendment, the position has completely changed. It has been provided that any law passed by any legislature, whether central or State, with a view to implementing Directive Principles cannot be challenged on the ground that it goes against any of the Fundamental Rights guaranteed.

16. ***Single Citizenship.*** Although India has a federal government yet double citizenship, as provided for in the U.S. constitution, has not been provided for. All the Indians irrespective of their domicile, enjoy a single citizenship of India whereas in United States all the citizens enjoy the right of double citizenship. Since American are considered to be the citizens of the State where they are domiciled and then they are the citizens of the U.S.A. as a whole. In both these capacities, they enjoy different rights and owe different obligations. The principle of single citizenship was provided for in the Indian constitution in order to foster strong bond of social and political unity among the people of India, who are hitherto divided on account óf racial discrimination, variety of languages and multiplicity of religious and cultural background.

17. ***Independence of Judiciary.*** The framers of the constitution were aware that democratic freedoms were meaningless in

the absence of an independent machinery to safeguard them. No subordinate or agent of the Government could be trusted to be just and impartial in judging the merits of a conflict in which the Government itself was a party. Similarly, a judiciary subordinate either to the centre or the states could not be trusted as an impartial arbiter of conflicts and controversies between the centre and the states. These were the compelling reasons for the creation of an independent judiciary as an integral part of the constitution and for the adoption of judicial independence as a basic principle of the constitution.

In its bid to establish complete independence of the judiciary, the constitution has first erected a wall of separation between the executive and the judiciary. After effecting such separation, it has created conditions that are conducive to making the judiciary independent. Thus, rigid qualifications are laid down for the appointment of judges and provision has been made for compulsory consultation of the Chief Justice of India in the appointment of every judge of the Supreme Court and the High Courts. They are given high salaries, their conditions of service cannot be altered to their disadvantage and their conduct is made a subject beyond the scope of discussion in the legislature. They can be removed from office only for proved mis-behaviour. For this purpose, both the Houses of Parliament will have to pass resolutions against a judge supported by a two-third majority of those who sit and vote and at least an absolute majority of the total membership of the House.

18. ***Bicameral Legislature.*** Our Parliament has two Houses– the Lok Sabha and the Rajya Sabha. The Lok Sabha is the lower House. It represents the whole nation. The Rajya Sabha is the upper House. It represents the States. The maximum strength of the Lok Sabha has been fixed at 545 by the 31st Amendment. However, at present it consists of 543 members. The maximum strength of Rajya Sabha has been fixed at 250. Out of this total members, 12 members

are nominated by the President. The remaining 238 members represent the state and union territories in proportion to their population. There are at present 240 members of the Rajya Sabha. The Lok Sabha is more powerful than the Rajya Sabha.

19. ***Administrative Tribunals.*** With the introduction of the 42nd Amendment, a new part, XIV-A, has been inserted in the Constitution. It deals with the creation of Tribunals to settle matters. Article 323-A lays down that Parliament may by law provide for the adjudication by administrative tribunals of disputes and complaints with respect to recruitment and conditions of service of persons appointed to public services and posts in connection with the affairs of the Union of any State or of any local or other authority within the territory of India or under the control of the Government of India or of any corporation owned or controlled by the government. Parliament is the competent authority to provide for the establishment of an administrative tribunal for the Union and a separate administrative tribunal for each State or two or more States. The procedure, jurisdiction, powers and authority of these tribunals is to be determined by the Parliament.

    If terms of Art. 323-B, appropriate legislature may, by law, provide for the adjudication by tribunals of any disputes, complaints or offences with respect to all or any of the matters specified in clause 2 of the said article. These matters include foreign exchange, import and export, levy, assessment, collection and enforcements of any tax; industrial and labour disputes, land reforms; ceiling on urban property; production, procurement supply and distribution of foodstuffs, etc.

20. ***Emergency Powers of the President.*** With a view to guarding against disintegration, the Constitution has placed enormous powers in hands of the President to declare Emergency. He can declare three types of emergency.

(a) *National Emergency.* When there is the danger of war, foreign aggression or armed rebellion.

(b) *State Emergency.* When there is break-down of Constitution machinery in a State.

(c) *Financial Emergency.* When the financial stability or the credit of India has fallen in danger.

21. ***Rights of Minorities.*** The Constitution does not merely safeguard the interests of the majority community. The minorities have been equally protected so far as their religious, cultural, economic and political privileges are concerned. The Constitution states:–

Section 15 (1): All citizens of India, irrespective of differences in religion, caste, colour, creed or sex, shall enjoy equal rights.

Section 25 (1): The wearing and carrying of Kirpans shall be deemed to be included in the profession of Sikh Religion.

Section 29 (1): Any section of citizens residing in the territory of India or any part thereof, having distinct language, script or culture of its own shall have the right to conserve the same.

Section 46: The state shall promote with special care the educational and economic interests of the weaker sections of the people, and in particular of the scheduled castes and scheduled tribes, and shall protect them from social injustice and all forms of exploitation.

22. ***Compromise Between Judicial Review and Parliamentary Supremacy.*** "Parliament in India is not as supreme as the British Parliament. At the same time judiciary in India is not as supreme as in the United States of America which recognises no limit on the scope of judicial review."

The Indian constitution wonderfully adopts the via media between the American system of judicial supremacy and the English principle of Parliamentary supremacy, by endowing the judiciary with the power of declaring a law as unconstitutional if it is beyond the competence of the legislature according to the distribution of powers provided by the constitution, or if it is in contravention of the fundamental rights guaranteed by the constitution; but at the same time, depriving the judiciary of any power of 'Judicial review' of the wisdom of legislative policy. Thus, it has avoided expressions like 'due process', and made fundamental rights such as that of liberty and property subject to regulation by the legislature. Further, the major portion of the constitution is liable to be amended by the Union Parliament by a special majority, if in any case the judiciary proves too obstruive. The theory underlying the Indian Constitution in this respect can hardly be better expressed than in the words of Jawaharlal Nehru: "No supreme court, no judiciary, can stand in judgment over the sovereign will of Parliament, representing the will of the entire community. It can pull up that sovereign will if it goes wrong, but, in the ultimate analysis, where the future of the community is concerned, no judiciary can come in the way... Ultimately, the fact remains that the Legislature must be supreme and must not be interfered with by the Courts of Law in such measures as social reform."

Criticism of the Indian Constitution

The constitution of India is remarkable for many outstanding features which will distinguish it from other constitutions, even though there were members in the Constituent Assembly who criticised the constitution which was going to be adopted as a 'slavish imitat on of the west' or 'not suited to the genius' of the people. Another Assembly member charged that this constitution will not prove suitable and will break down soon after being brought into operation. The main criticism levelled against the constitution are as follows;

1. **The Elephantine Size of the Constitution.** The constitution of India is being criticised on the ground that it is the most lengthy and detailed constitutional document the world has so far produced. In the words of Ivor Jeanings–"The provisions borrowed were not always well selected and that the constitution, generally speaking, was too long and complicated."

2. **Carbon Copy of the Act of 1935.** The constitution of India is called as the carbon copy of the Act of 1935. The fathers of the constitution have borrowed a large number of provisions from the Act of 1935 and made them part of the new constitution. Making a specific reference to this aspect of the constitution, Ambedkar, the Chairman of the Drafting Committee, said in the Constituent Assembly; "As to the accusation that the Draft constitution has reproduced a good part of the provisions of the Government of India Act, 1935, I make no apologies. There is nothing to be ashamed in borrowing. It involves no plagiarism. Nobody holds any patent rights in the fundamental ideas of a constitution. What I am sorry about is that the provisions taken from the Government of India Act, 1935, relate mostly to the details of administration."

3. **Paradise of the Lawyers.** One of the frequent criticism of the constitution was that it was a lawyer's paradise. Making a general comment on the constitution, a member said that "the Draft tends to make people more litigious, more inclined to go to law court... If I may say so, the Draft is really a lawyer's paradise. It opens up vast avenues of litigation and will give our able and ingenious lawyers plenty of work to do."

   It is true that the constitution is a compex document. The language in which it was drafted is that which is familiar only in Courts of Law. A striking feature of the constitution in this context is the numerous exception, qualifications and explanations that one finds along with almost every provision. Only an experienced lawyer, well versed in constitutional law, can understand the implications of the legal language in which most of these provisions are couched.

4. **A Borrowed Constitution.** It is said that the Indian constitution is a bag of borrowings or is a more paper and scissors work. Parliamentary form of government is borrowed from the British constitution while federalism

and judicial review is borrowed from the U.S. Constitution. However, the credit of its framers lies in gathering the best features of each of the existing constitutions and in modifying them with a view to avoiding the faults that have been disclosed in their working and to adopting them to the existing conditions and needs of this country. So, if it is a 'patchwork' it is a 'beautiful patchwork'.

5. **Un-Gandhian Constitution.** The constitution has been criticised by a small but vocal section on the ground that it is un-Gandhian. The constitution did not embody the principles for which Mahatma Gandhi stood or the ideology of the Indian National Congress. Others thought that it should have been raised and built upon village Panchayats and district Panchayats.
6. **Centre has been Made Too strong.** According to some critics, the centre has been made too strong. There is too much centralisation and that the states have been reduced to municipalities.
7. **Un-Indian.** The new constitution is called as un-Indian or anti-Indian that no part of the constitution represents the ancient polity of India, its genious and the spirit of its hallowed and glorious traditions. "We wanted the music of Veena or Sitar," lamented an Assembly member, "but here we have the music of an English band." The ideals on which this constitution is framed have no manifest relation to the fundamental spirit of India; charged another member of the Constituent Assembly.

HISTORY OF THE PREAMBLE

In order to appreciate the nature of the Preamble of the Indian constitution, we must first of all look into the historic objectives resolution moved by Jawahar Lal Nehru on December 13, 1946 and that was adopted by the Constituent Assembly on January 22, 1947. In fact, the Constituent Assembly held its first meeting on December 9, 1946 and the first task of the assembly was the formulation of the objectives and the guiding principles which were to form the basis of the constitution. It was this great Charter that influenced the eventual shaping of the fundamental law of our land through all subsequent stages. The objectives resolution reads as follows:

(i) The Constituent Assembly declares its firm and solemn resolve to proclaim India as an Independent Sovereign Republic and to draw up for her future governance a constitution;

(ii) Wherein the territories that now comprise British India, the territories now form the Indian states and such other parts of India as are outside British India and the states as well as such other territories as are willing to be constituted into the Independent Sovereign India, shall be a Union of them of all;

(iii) Wherein the said territories, whether with their present boundaries or with such others as may be determined by the Constituent Assembly and thereafter according to the law of the constitution, shall possess and retain the status of autonomous units, together with residuary powers and exercise all powers and functions of government and administration, save and except such powers and functions as are vested or assigned to the Union, or as are inherent or implied in the Union or resulting therefrom;

(iv) Wherein all powers and authority of the Sovereign Independent India, as its constituent parts and organs of government, are derived from the people;

(v) Wherein shall be guaranteed and secured to all the people of India justice, social, economic and political; equality of status, of opportunity, and before the law; freedom of thought, expression, belief, faith, worship, vocation, association and action, subject to law and public morality;

(vi) Wherein adequate safeguards shall be provided for minorities, backward and tribal areas and depressed and other backward classes;

(vii) Whereby shall be maintained the integrity of the territories of the Republic and its sovereign rights on land, sea and air according to justice and the law of civilised nations; and

(viii) This ancient land attains its rightful and honoured place in the world and makes its full and willing contribution to the promotion of world peace and the welfare of mankind.

The Drafting Committee of the Assembly in formulating the Preamble in the light of the 'Objective Resolution' felt that the Preamble, should be restricted to defining the essential features of the new state and its basic socio-political objectives and that the other matters dealt within the Resolution could be more appropriately provided for in the substantive parts of the constitution. The committee adopted the expression 'Sovereign Democratic Republic' in place of 'Sovereign Independent Republic' as used in the Objectives Resolution, for it thought that independence was implied in the word 'Sovereign.' The committee also added a clause about fraternity which did not occur in the Objective Resolution. "The committee felt that the need for fraternal concord and goodwill in India was never greater than now and that this particular aim of the new constitution should be emphasised by special mention in the Preamble." In other respects the committee tried to embody in the Preamble "the spirit and, as far as possible, the language of the Objective Resolution."

THE PREAMBLE OF THE CONSTITUTION

The Preamble of the constitution of India reads:

"We the people of India, having solemnly resolved to constitute India into a Sovereign, Socialist, Secular, Democratic Republic and to secure to all its citizens:

Justice, social, economic and political;

Liberty of thought, expression, belief, faith and worship;

Equality of status and opportunity; and to promote among them all

Fraternity assuring the dignity of the individual and the unity and integrity of the Nation;

In our constituent assembly this twenty-sixth day of November, 1949, do hereby

Adopt, Enact and Give to Ourselves this Constitution."

The draft of the Preamble was considered by the Assembly last after considering other provisions of the Draft constitution "to see that it was in conformity with the constitution." A number of amendments were moved and rejected. A motion was, therefore, adopted by the Assembly that "the Preamble stands parts of the constitution." The words and figure "this twenty-sixth day of November 1949" introduced in the last paragraph indicate the date on which the constitution was finally adopted by the Assembly.

AMENDMENT OF THE PREAMBLE

By section 2 of the constitution (42nd amendment) Act, 1976, two amendments were made in Preamble. First, for the words 'Sovereign Democratic Republic' the words 'Sovereign Socialist Secular Democratic Republic' were substituted and secondly, for the words 'Unity of the Nation' the words 'Unity and Integrity of the Nation' were substituted.

The Preamble being a part of the constitution, is open to amendment in the exercise of Parliament's constituent power under Article 368 subject to the limitation that to the extent it reflects the basic structure or framework of the constitution it cannot be amended. The amendments made by the 42nd Amendment in the Preamble have been held to be valid. Those amendments are not only within the framework of the constitution but they give vitality to its philosophy, they afford strength and succor to its foundations.

IMPORTANCE OF THE PREAMBLE TO THE INDIAN CONSTITUTION

Our constitution, like many other Constitutions of Democratic States of the world, begins with a foreword, a preface, or what is technically known as the preamble. The Preamble is not a legal part of the Constitution yet it is binding upon the present and future governments of the Country. It is the soul and spirit of the Constitution. It reflects the aspirations of the makers of the Constitution about the objectives of the State. While giving the importance of the Preamble to the Indian Constitution, Pt. Thakur Dass Bhargava said, "The Preamble is the most precious part of the Constitution. It is key to the constitution... It is a jewel in the constitution. It is superb Prose-Poem, nay, it is perfection in itself."

The Preamble of the Indian Constitution throws light on three aspects:

1. Source of Constitutional Authority.
2. Nature of the State.
3. Objectives of the Constitution.

1. Source of Constitutional Authority. The Preamble tells in very clear terms that the people of India are the final authority to have made this Constitution. In this way, it proclaims that sovereign power resides with the people of India. It lays down: "We the people of India having solemnly resolved to constitute India into a sovereign democratic republic..." These words remind us about the fulfilment of the ideal that the nationalist people of India set before themselves on 26th January, 1929 at the bank of the Ravi at the Lahore Session of the Congress. The people have themselves adopted and enacted them. The Preamble to the Constitution further reads: "We the people of India... In our Constituent Assembly this 29th day of November 1949 do hereby Adopt, Enact and Give to Ourselves, this Constitution."

The contention that sovereignty resides with the people is reaffirmed at several other places of the Constitution also. This is particularly evident in the chapter dealing with elections. In terms of Article 326, "The elections to the House of People and to the Legislative Assembly of every State shall be on the basis of adult suffrage."

The people are the ultimate masters under the Constitution. If the Constitution is to be amended, the Parliament under Article 368 has the power to do so. In Gopalan Vs. State of Madras, Mr. Justice Shastri observed: "There can be no doubt that the people of India in exercise of their sovereign will as expressed in the Preamble, adopted the democratic ideal which assures to the citizens the dignity of the individual and other cherished human values as a means to the full evolution and expression of his personality, and in delegating to the Legislature, the Executive and the Judiciary, their respective powers in the Constitution, reserved to themselves certain fundamental rights..."

2. Nature of the State. The Preamble throws light on the nature of the State that we shall have in India. The nature of the State can be studied under the following heads:

(i) ***A Sovereign State.*** The Preamble to the Constitution defines new India as a 'Sovereign Socialist, Secular, Democratic Republic.' The word 'Sovereign' denotes that India is no longer a dependency of the British Empire as she was before 15th of August, 1947. Nor is she a dominion as it was from 15th of August, 1947 to 25th January, 1950. She is now as sovereign as U.S. Great Britain or U.S.S.R. No other country has any right to dictate her terms. She is free from external control and free in internal affairs. She is the master of her own destiny and can chalk out an independent state policy of her own without being dictated by any outside power. She is now free to have any type of economic system, in the country. No outside power is allowed to interfere in the internal affairs of our country. She is free to establish relations with any foreign country according to her own will. Her membership of the Commonwealth of Nations does not in any way take away the status of sovereignty. Nehru emphasized: "The new Commonwealth does not restrict India's independence either in the external or internal sphere. It has no strings attached in it. India is not compelled to stay in the Commonwealth even one minute longer than she may desire to. The agreement is in full accord with the Congress pledge and India's foreign policy of non-alignment with power blocs. It gives of India, independence plus security in political and economic sphere." Her membership of the U.N.as that of other countries, does not limit her sovereignty.

(ii) ***Democratic State.*** The term 'Democratic' signifies that the Indian Constitution seeks to establish a form of Government which derives its authority from the will of the people. It is the people themselves who elect the rulers of the country. They are accountable to the people for their omissions and commissions. Besides, the State does not discriminate against any citizen on the grounds of religion, birth, sex, caste, colour etc. The Constitution guarantees in every manner possible a sense of justice, equality freedom and security to all minorities in India. According to Panikkar, "Every section of the Constitution provides evidence... that the religion, culture and interests of all alike are safeguarded in the Constitution, and the sense of distrust and fear, which had for so long made India a cockpit of communal strife, may now be laid at rest." The word democracy indeed represents much more. It ensures not only political democracy as enshrined in the Fundamental Right but also social and economic democracy as enshrined in the Directive Principles. This makes India a unique democracy in contradiction from the U.S.A. which ensures only political democracy and the U.S.S.R. which ensures only economic democracy.

(iii) ***Socialist State.*** The word 'socialist' has been added in the Preamble by virtue of the 42nd Amendment to the constitution. Various provisions in the constitution including the Directive Principles of state policy sought to establish a socialist state in India. However, the word socialism was nowhere used. It was with this end in view of laying emphasis on this aspect that the word socialist has now been added in the Preamble.

The word socialism is difficult to define. However, a socialist state is one in which the means of production such as land, mineral-resources, mills and factories and the means of distribution are in the hands of government. In this system, the distribution of national income is done in such a manner that there are not very wide inequalities in the incomes that the people receive for their work. But in the context in which it has been inserted in the Preamble, it refers to democratic socialism of the Indian type. It is through democratic means that socialism suitable to the Indian conditions and circumstances is to be brought. Socialism has been sought to be brought about by the Directive Principles of State Policy aimed at equal distribution of wealth; end of exploitation, inequality among men and women, unemployment: and improving the standard of living of the poor and downtrodden people.

The 42nd Amendment has established the supremacy of the Directive Principles of State Policy over the Fundamental Rights. Any law passed by the State or Union legislature with a view to implementing the Directive Principles shall not be held illegal on the grounds that it takes away certain fundamental rights of the citizens as guaranteed under Articles 14, 19 and 34 of the constitution.

(iv) Secular State. The word 'Secular' has been added in the Preamble by virtue of the 42nd Amendment to the Constitution. Various provisions in the Constitution sought to establish a Secular State in India. However, the word 'secular' was nowhere used. It was with this end in view of laying emphasis on this aspect that the word 'secular' has now been added in the Preamble.

Secularism implies four things:

First, India would not be a religious or theocratic State.

Secondly, it would not extend special favours to a particular religion.

Thirdly, the State would have no official religion of its own.

Fourthly, the people of India would be free to profess, practise or propagate any religion they like.

Unlike Pakistan or Great Britain, India has no State religion. All the religions are duly honoured. All the religions in India are free to propagate their ideals. No religion can interfere in the religious activities of another religion. In the institutions that are maintained and run out of the State funds, religious instructions of any kind are not permitted. However, private institutions run out of the funds of a trust can impart religious instruction of their faith. However, no person can be forced to follow those religious instructions.

Not only that, our Constitution guarantees equal opportunities for appointment to public posts irrespective of considerations of religion, caste, colour, sex or place of birth. This does not, however, mean that special safeguards and reservations can not be made to promote the interest of backward classes. There shall be equality before law. Article 14 declares that the State shall not deny to any person equality before law or equal protection of laws within the territory of India. There shall be no discrimination against any citizen on the grounds only of religion, race, sex, cast, place of birth or any of them.

In terms of Art. 30, "The State shall not discriminate in granting aid to educational institutions on the ground that it is under the management of a minority, whether based on religion or language."

(v) ***Republican State.*** Republican State means State whose head is elected by the people for a fixed period of time. A nominated official like a Governor General or a hereditary King or Queen shall not be the head of the State. Accordingly, the President of India–the chief executive–is elected by the people. He is not hereditary-like the British King. He is elected for a fixed period. According to T.K. Tope, "The Indian republic is to be distinguished from the ancient Greek and the ancient Indian republics which were essentially aristocratic, and also from the modern republic like that of the USSR which is of dictatorial nature. The Indian republic is a democratic republic."

3. Objectives of the Constitution. The Preamble includes certain objectives also. French Revolution proclaimed "Liberty, Equality and Fraternity" but the Indian Constitution adds justice also to the objectives to be achieved.

Accordingly, the Constitution as also the ordinary laws of the land must be based on justice and should guarantee individual liberty, promote equality and foster a spirit of brotherhood among the citizens of India irrespective of caste, creed, religion, law, age and sex.

The following are the objectives of the Constitution:

(i) Justice. The Preamble makes it amply clear that all the people of India will get social, economic and political justice.

(a) Social Justice. Social justice means that no discrimination shall be made on basis of religion, caste, creed, sex, colour place of birth or any such ground. All will enjoy equality.

(b) Political Justice. Political justice means that everyone irrespective of considerations of caste, colour, creed, religion, sex, birth or the like shall get equal opportunities in the exercise of the right to vote, to seek election etc.

(c) Economic Justice. Economic justice means that all people shall get equal opportunity to earn their livelihood. They should get reasonable remuneration for their work. No discrimination should be made between man and woman for equal work done by them. The Directive Principles of State Policy deal with economic and social justice. It has been laid down that the State shall endeavour not to allow concentration of wealth in fewer hands. The State shall make arrangements to ensure against illness, unemployment, old age, etc.

(ii) Liberty. Liberty is the essential pre-requisite for the existence of democracy. Our democracy would have been meaningless if there were no liberty. Our Preamble lists liberty of thought, expression, belief, faith and worship. These liberties have been duly guaranteed to the people of India through Fundamental Rights.

(iii) ***Equality.*** Liberty has meaning only if there is equality. Inequality has been the bane of Indian society. Unless inequality is removed from the socio-economic structure of India, even the Fundamental Rights lose their importance. Equality of opportunities has been ensured "by making illegal all discrimination by the State between citizen and citizen on the grounds of religion, race, caste, sex, or place of birth." It is also ensured by Art. 14 which guarantees equality before law and equal protection of law. Equality of status is assured by Art. 17 and 18 which prohibits untouchability and abolishes titles.

(iv) ***Fraternity.*** Fraternity means feeling of brotherhood and national integration. This feeling deserves to be given top-most consideration in view of the fact that the people of India profess different religions, speak different languages and have affinity with different castes. None can close its eyes in India to the danger posed by these divisive forces. These very forces caused the division of our country. According to M.V. Pylee, "Through the establishment of a new Nation based upon justice, liberty and equality, must feel that they are children of the same soil, of the same motherland, members of the same fraternity."

(v) ***Unity and Integrity of the Nation.*** The word 'integrity' has been added by virtue of the 42nd Amendment. So long as unity and integrity of the nation is not assured, liberty cannot continue. The British Government could continue to rule over India by following the policy of 'divide and rule'. It is to ensure the unity and integrity of India that 18 languages have been recognised in our Constitution, India has been made a secular State, equality has been assured to all, one Constitution has been promulgated for the whole of India, only one citizenship has been conferred on the Indians and so on.

(vi) ***Dignity of the Individual.*** The Preamble also lays down that the dignity of the individual shall be maintained, assured and upheld. Maintenance of the dignity of an

individual is a necessary condition for the maintenance of freedom. It is for the maintenance of individual dignity that all the citizens of India have been given Fundamental Rights without any distinction.

FUNDAMENTAL RIGHTS

A part of the Constitution is devoted to Fundamental Rights, which Indians can enjoy during normal times. These Rights can, however, be snatched away from citizens during emergencies. The Rights, among other things, include right to freedom of assembly, association, faith, expression, etc. These are justifiable and courts of law are competent to declare any law, which is violative of these rights as unconstitutional or *ultra-vires* of the constitution, if need be. Such an action can be taken only if an appeal is made by a citizen to review a law or an executive order, which in his opinion is *ultra-vires* of the constitution.

Inclusion of fundamental rights as a constitutional guarantee as said above is comparatively of recent origin. It was felt after French Revolution and the U.S. struggle for freedom that nations of the world should seriously think of giving some basic rights to their people. It was in 1789 that French National Assembly adopted the Declaration of Rights of Man. The Constitution of the USA also incorporated a chapter on Fundamental Rights. In 1945, Universal Declaration of Human Rights was made, which was adopted by the General Assembly of UNO on December 10,1948, which included social, economic, political and cultural rights of the people. In India, it was in Nehru Committee Report of 1928, that suggestion was made for the inclusion of religious and cultural rights as basic rights of the citizens. Simon Commission which visited India to review India's constitutional progress did not favour the idea of inclusion of Fundamental Rights in the constitution. So was the view point of Joint Parliamentary Committee on Indian Constitution Reforms (1933-34). Sapru Committee Report on Constitutional Proposals (1945), however, supported the idea of inclusion of Rights in our Constitution. Constitution makers in India were guided by public sentiments and national demand in this regard and accordingly a chapter on Fundamental Rights was added to the constitution.

PECULIAR FEATURES OF FUNDAMENTAL RIGHTS

In India Fundamental Rights have some peculiar features. Whereas in some respects these are in accordance with the Rights extended to the people of other countries, in other respects these differ from them as well. The Rights guaranteed to the people are not absolute. Each right is conditioned by certain duties. There is no Right which has no corresponding obligations. It is, however, worth remembering that the constitution has very extensively elaborated rights and the courts of law have very little to twist these to suit to their convenience or take shelter of duties.

Another feature of these rights is that these are justifiable. It implies that the Rights are above everything in the land. All the executive actions or laws passed by our legislatures must be in conformity with fundamental Rights. If any law passed by the executive government is considered against any of the Fundamental Rights the citizens have every right to approach the court of law which have the power of judicial review.If the courts, after examination, are satisfied that a particular law passed by the legislature, is not in conformity with the constitution and violates a Fundamental Right that can be declared unconstitutional or *ultra vires* of the Constitution.

Then another feature is that Fundamental Rights have been very much elaborated. It is said that these have been so much elaborated that no other constitution has discussed these in such a great length and with such minute details, as Constitution of India. It is said that "it is unique feature of the Indian Constitution that it sets out in the Constitution itself the most elaborate declaration of human rights yet framed by any state."

Fundamental Rights as embodied in our constitution can be divided into two broad categories. namely those which impose certain restrictions of negative character on the state without confering special privileges on the citizens. Then there are positive rights which confer privileges on the people, *e.g.* Article 18 desires that the state will not to confer any special titles on the citizens. Art. 17, similarly abolishes untouchability. These can easily be covered in the former category. Right liberty, equality or freedom to express or worship come under the second category.

Then another feature of these rights is that these make a distinction between the citizens and the aliens. Whereas rights to freedom to worship and equality before law are available even to, aliens right to freedom and speech and assembly is available only to the citizens. Thus all rights are not available to all living in India. Similarly there are certain rights which are denied to a particular section (s) of society *e.g.* armed forces personnel do not enjoy political rights.

Then another feature of our rights is that these are available only against the state and not against any private party. If state violates any right the aggrieved party can seek redress through courts of law but if some violation is by an individual, he or she will have to take recourse to ordinary law of the land.

One of the most important and significant feature of our Rights is that these can be suspended. It is peculiar in the sense that no constitution of the world has made any such provision. According to our constitution as soon as state of emergency is declared in the country Fundamental Rights stand suspended and the courts of law are debarred to enforce these. It is this provision which was very vehemently and bitterly opposed in the Constituent Assembly. The opposition felt that it was the darkest day of our history when a provision was made for denying Fundamental Rights to our people. In the words of H.V. Kamath, "If we get peace in that state it will be the peace of the grave and the void of the desert. When the tempests blow, the weight of this great negation will be so very heavy that the whole edifice will collapse." Dr. Ambedkar, however, felt that the inclusion of such a provision was essential to save the country from disruptive elements and also a guarantee to the people to have maximum freedom. In his own words, "This provision is absolutely necessary. It will save democracy from danger and extinction."

Not only in emergencies, but even in normal times Articles 33 and 34 of the Constitution empower the Parliament to decide about applicability and extension of fundamental rights to the people working in the armed forces or engaged in services responsible for the maintenance of peace and order. To that extent the application of fundamental rights can be suspended by an Act of Parliament. Under emergencies, the people are denied to take shelter under the roof of judiciary in so far as Fundamental Rights are concerned. These also stand suspended when the people are arrested under Preventive Detention Act, which empowers the state to arrest a person for his being a danger to the security of the state.

RESTRICTIONS ON FUNDAMENTAL RIGHTS

Under the constitution, the state can put some restrictions on the operation of Fundamental Rights but it is for the courts of law to see whether the restrictions imposed are justified or not. But in India these rights have been divided into two categories. Some rights are available to the citizens alone, while others are available to all those living in this country, whether they are citizens or not. Thus, whereas freedom of speech, assembly and expression come under the first category, in the second category fall right against exploitation and freedom of religion, etc.

Fundamental Rights in India are a guarantee against the state action but in some cases, these restrictions are also against specific class of persons or against all persons within the territory of India. Article 15(2) prohibits discrimination on grounds of religion, race, caste and sex, etc., whereas Article 17 forbids practice of untouchability in any form. Under Article 23 beggary is forbidden, whereas Article 24 prohibits employment of children below the age of 14 in any factory or mine. These are such restrictions which are against private individuals. On the other hand, there are provisions which deal with the state e.g. under Article 14 it is provided that the state shall not deny to any person equality before law whereas Article 15 says that state shall not discriminate against any citizen on grounds of religion, race, caste and sex. Whereas Article 16 ensures equality of opportunity, Article 18 prohibits the state on conferring any titles. The state in India has been conferring titles like Bharat Ratna, Padam Vibhushan, Padam Bhushan and Padam Shri on the citizens of India for their meritorious services on the plea that these did not infringe Art. 18 of the Constitution. But in 1977, when Janata

Government came to power it dispensed with such titles on the ground that these were not in keeping with spirit of Article 18 of the Constitution. In 1980, when Janata Government was ousted from power these honours were again bestowed on the citizens and Mother Terasa was awarded Bharat Ratna in that year. Since then every year these honours/titles are being conferred on the citizens of India.

The 'state' can amend, modify or abridge Fundamental Rights. Under Article 12 of the Constitution an effort was made to define the term 'state'. It was then said that the state in India shall mean government and Parliament of India, government and legislatures of the states and all local and other authorities within the Union of India, any departmental organ of the Government of India, any public authority exercising statutory powers, but state excludes judiciary and hence the judgments of the courts cannot be challenged on the ground that these contravene Fundamental Rights." D.D. Basu is of the view that "The Courts, like any other organ of the state, are limited by the mandatory provision of the constitution and they can hardly be allowed to over-ride the fundamental rights under the sheild that they have, within their jurisdiction, the right to make an erroneous decision."

Fundamental Rights, as provided in Part III of the Constitution, do not provide constitutional remedy, in case of their infringement by private individuals, except as otherwise provided.

In the case of Behram Khursid Pesikada Vs. State of Bombay, it has been held that the 'Doctrine of Waiver' enunciated in America cannot be applied in India. The court held the view that the Fundamental Rights as incorporated in the constitution are not primarily for individual benefit but have been put in the constitution as a matter of public policy. The courts have maintained that it is not open to an individual to relieve the state of an obligation imposed upon the state by Article 14 of the constitution.

Under the Constitution fundamental rights can be suspended and it is left to the courts to put reasonable restrictions on them. The Parliament can restrict or even abrogate by law to the members of the armed forces, with a view to ensuring proper discharge of their duties and enforcing discipline among them.

After the passing of Forty-Fourth Constitution Amendment Act (Articles 35 and 359) it is provided that Article 19 of the constitution will only be suspended when there is emergency in the country due to actual outbreak of war or threat of external aggression and not on the ground of apprehended armed rebellion.

Then comes the power of the Parliament to take away Fundamental Rights guaranteed by the Constitution to the citizens of India. The Constitution has devoted a part to Fundamental Rights, which are available to the citizens and other living in India. Parliament has a right to amend the Constitution. A question, therefore, arises whether by a constitutional amendment can Parliament amend fundamental rights or even take away these rights? In other words, are Rights above the amending powers of Parliament or not. In the famous Golak Nath case it has been held by the Supreme Court that under Article 368 of the Constitution, Parliament cannot modify, restrict or impair Fundamental Rights. But the position was again reviewed in the case of His Holiness Kesvananda Bharti Vs. State of Kerala and Others. In this case a Bench of 13 judges of Supreme Court held that the Constitution invested the Parliament the right to alter, abridge or abrogate Fundamental Rights guaranteed by the Constitution. In this way the Parliament, by a constitutional amendment can curtail, suspend or modify these Rights. In this very case the court held the view that the Parliament could not change basic structure of the Constitution. But in the view of the court fundamental rights do not come under the orbit of basic structure. The court, however, did not specify as to what was covered under basic structure. It was left undefined or unspecific. Articles 31 and 32 and 358 and 359 of the Constitution which deal with Fundamental Rights were touched by Forty-Second Constitution Amendment Act, whereas Forty-Fourth Constitution Amendment Act again touched these Articles of the Constitution. In this way, the Parliament has amended these Rights and can even put restrictions on these as well in the way it likes.

But again in May, 1980 the Supreme Court held that the Parliament has not got unlimited rights to amend the Constitution. In the view of the Court the Parliament by a constitutional amendment cannot provide that the courts have no right to interfere in certain matters.

The Constitution provides that no law of the land shall be against Fundamental Rights. In this regard the term law is very wide. It includes not only the laws in force but also the ordinances, orders, bye laws, rules, regulations, notifications, customs and usages having the force of law.

SOCIAL FACTORS

The social factors that had their impact on the framing of the Indian Constitution are discussed as under:

1. Communalism. The basic fact to be kept in view was the existence of communalism in India. Communalism means giving loyalty to one's own community against the whole nation or country. Communalism is a legacy of the British Raj in India. There was no communalism as such before the coming of the British Raj to India. The Muslim rulers no doubt indulged in conversion of the Hindus to their religion but the people did not fight among themselves on the basis of their religion. Communalism grew as a result of the policy of 'Divide and Rule' followed by the British Government under which the Muslim Community was shown undue favour and nepotism. In an effort to get favoured treatment, the Muslims opposed forcefully the nationalist movement launched by the Hindus. The Indian National Congress worked for the attainment of freedom. But the Muslim League opposed the very idea of independence for India. It demanded certain safeguards before the British left them to the mercy of the Hindus. The British Government had granted them the concession of communal electorates as early as through the Act of 1909. A strong feeling of two communities in India was created. The Muslim League propagated 'Two Nation Theory'. It was thus the primary duty of the fathers of the constitution to create a feeling of oneness and one nation.

2. Linguism. Even more serious than the problems of communalism, there is the problem of linguism in India. The Linguistic

Survey of India published in 1927 stated that there are in India 179 languages and 544 dialects (and in all 1652 mother tongues). The 1971 Census of India shows that there are 1108 different languages. There was the urge to discourage the learning of other languages. The Southern India even now hates the idea of Hindi on the pretext of Hindi imperialism. The supporters of Hindi, on the other hand, want to force it on non-Hindi areas. The fathers of the Constitution had to solve this problem by keeping English as the official language of India to be replaced by Hindi after fifteen years. It is by subsequent legislation that English has been allowed to continue as link language indefinitely.

3. Racial Diversity. Still more dangerous was the impact of racial diversity. The southern people claim themselves to be the Dravidians who were the original inhabitants of India. They claim that the Northern States are inhabited by the Aryans who invaded and settled in India. The Eastern States show Mangol influence. We are well aware of the fact that the D.M.K. advocated secession. It was on this account that the 16th Amendment was introduced in 1963. The fathers of the Constitution had to make a constitution that could maintain the integrity of India.

4. Casteism. The caste system is a unique and unparalleled institution that exists only in India. To begin with, it denoted a system of division of labour. But it has undergone many changes since then. This system has promoted feelings of inequality. Several social and religious reformers tried to put an end to this discrimination, but the situation went from bad to worse. The British Government made an attempt to exploit caste feelings by reserving separate seats for the Harijans also on the lines of communal electorate. This was resisted by Mahatma Gandhi with all the force at his command. Certain castes in India were backward. They could came up to level with others only if certain special safeguards were provided for them. The Constitution provides special facilities for the backward people. It will be relevant to mention here that Dr. Ambedkar, the Chairman of the Drafting Committee, belonged to the scheduled caste.

5. Special Needs of the Tribal and Backward Areas. There were certain areas which were backward in every respect. They had no educational facilities, no means of transport and communication, no medical facilities and the like. Naturally, those areas needed special attention if any progress was to be made in those areas. It is with this spirit in mind on the part of the Constituent Assembly that special facilities and concessions have been given to the tribal and backward areas.

6. Discrimination Based on Sex. We have had in India discrimination against the female sex. They have since been regarded as inferior and subordinate to men. Even in case of payment of wages, discrimination is made against them. It was this realisation on the part of the fathers of our Constitution that it has now been made obligatory to pay equal wages to women for equal hours of labour. Moreover, special securities have been provided for them.

ECONOMIC FACTORS

No one can deny that India is poor in spite of rich resources. This was all due to the ignorance of the people and the apathy of the British Government. India could make no development for want of scientific outlook. India remained tied to old bullock-driven economy. This resulted in unemployment and half-employment. Consequently, the standard of living of the people in India was very poor. Even the Government lacked resources. It was on this consideration that our Constitution has put provisions relating to economic democracy under the Directive Principles of State Policy. They are as a sort of reminder to the legislatures to always bear in mind that their law should reflect the ideals enshrined in them. But unlike the Fundamental Rights, they are not justifiable because the Constituent Assembly was well aware of the fact that the Government had no resources to put them immediately into practice.

POLITICAL FACTORS

From the political aspect also, India had many problems to tackle.

(1) Integration of Indian States. At the time India got freedom, there were 562 Indian States. It should be remembered that India at that time was divided into two broad parts–British India and the Indian India. The British India comprised of Provinces which were under the administration of the British Government. The Indian India comprised of States ruled by Indian Rajas and Nawabs. The Indian Independence Act, 1947 laid down that the Indian States were free either to join India or Pakistan or even remain independent. This created a very big problem. Their independence would have meant troubles of great dimensions. We can see Pakistan alone is creating many troubles. If these States remained independent, there would have been many more Pakistans for India to face. The Constituent Assembly provided provisions under which these States could be integrated with India.

Moreover, these States had different standards of living and different degrees of development. It was with this consideration in view that the States were divided into different categories.

(2) Provision of Federation. The founding fathers preferred federal constitutional structure for India because of certain factors:

(a) India as a whole is a vast land having areas in various stages of development. While Kerala had the highest percentage of literacy, other States are very much backward in this respect. There is a wide difference in agricultural sphere also. Neither is the weather uniform nor is the productive capacity of the land. Minerals are abundant in Bihar. In Punjab, there is a network of canals. In this way, a uniform agricultural and industrial policy was not possible for the whole country. The vastness of the country and difference in local needs had so great an impact that could not be overlooked by the fathers of the Constitution. The only reasonable solution of these differences was federation.

(b) The foundation of federalism had already been laid by the 1935 Act. The Indian Constitution in its federal aspect is very much influenced by that Act.

(c) It would have been very difficult to rule such a big country from one centre. As justice P.N. Sapru said: "Our founding fathers wisely did not establish for this country a completely unitary sovereignty among various units composing it. Any such attempt would have completely broken down as India is too vast a country to be governed as a completely unitary State."

(d) Federalism seemed to offer a natural, and perhaps the only satisfactory solution to the Hindu-Muslim question. The Muslims in India looked upon themselves as perfectly safeguarded in the Indian Polity while enjoying autonomy in areas where they were in majority. According to Sir Mohd. Iqbal, "The Muslims demand federation because it is pre-eminently a solution of India's most difficult problem, the communal problem... The unity of India must be sought not in the negation but in the harmony and co-operation of the many."

But it is surprising that the Constitution has been termed a Union of India and the term federation is missing. This was done intentionally to avoid rigidity and legalism of the American federalism. Our Constitution was intended to serve as unitary in times of emergency. It must be remembered that the Constitution was framed under the dark shadow of events like the attack of Pakistan on Kashmir, the Communist rebellion in Telangana and the Razakar trouble in Hyderabad. All these problems posed a serious threat to the very existence of the country. In addition thereto, the international situation had also a great impact. The rising India wanted to play a role in accordance with her size and geographical importance. The formation of the United Nations, the commencement of cold war between the two blocs, the emergence of a large number of free independent countries in Asia and Africa and the question of economic reconstruction warranted a strong and powerful India.

(3) Aspiration of the People. All through the struggle for freedom, the people of India aspired for a parliamentary and republican form of Government. The concessions granted by the Acts of 1919 and 1935 did not satisfy them. Naturally, the framers of the Constitution adopted these ideals and aspirations of the people.

(4) Influence of Mahatma Gandhi. The Directive Principles of State Policy reflect clearly the influence of Mahatma Gandhi. Provisions such as prohibition, cottage industries, ban on cow slaughter etc. reflect Gandhian ideals. Mahatma Gandhi said in 1931: "I shall work for an Indian which the poorest shall feel that it is their country, in whose making, they have an effective voice, an India in which there shall be no high class and low class people; an India in which all communities shall live in perfect harmony. There can be no room in such an India for the curse of untouchability or the curse of intoxicating drinks and drugs. The women shall enjoy the same rights as men. Since we shall be at peace with all the rest of the world, neither exploiting not being exploited..."

NATURE OF THE FUNDAMENTAL RIGHTS

The Fundamental Rights provided by the Indian Constitution are most elaborate. It provides for seven Fundamental Rights in the minutest details alongwith an elaborate list of limitations imposed upon them. The chapter on Fundamental Rights contains as many as twenty-four Articles.

The Fundamental Rights guaranteed by the Indian Constitution can be divided into two categories—negative and positive. Negative rights impose constitutional restrictions upon the state. They do not bestow any positive right upon the individual. Article 17 does not provide any special privilege for untouchables. It only removes a social evil. Article 18 forbids the state to confer any title, other than a military or academic distinction, on any individual. This is also a negative right because it does not provide for any positive privilege. On the other hand, right to freedom, right to property, right, to religion and cultural and educational right are considered as positive rights. It is very difficult to draw a line of distinction between the positive and the negative rights. But' some constitutional experts are of the opinion that there is one distinction, namely, that the negative rights are absolute and the positive rights are hedged with restrictions.

The Fundamental Rights provided by the Indian Constitution are not more pious declarations. The insertion of fundamental rights in the Constitution would not serve any fruitful purpose if they are not easily and effectively enforced. Fundamental Rights are also inserted in the Fascist Constitutions but in reality they remain only on paper. "Mere insertion of fundamental rights on the Constitution is of no use unless there is an effective and easy remedy provided for enforcing them, or unless their enjoyment is effectively guaranteed by a provision for judicial process and judicial review".

The Indian Constitution provides for a special fundamental right—the Rights to Constitutional Remedies. The Supreme Court is the guardian of the Fundamental Rights. According to Articles 226, the High Courts are also empowered to issue writs for the enforcement of the Fundamental Rights provided by the Constitution. Thus, these rights are justiciable and sufficient provisions have been made for their protection and enforcement if they are interfered with or encroached upon or violated.

The Fundamental Rights guaranteed by the Constitution are not absolute in character. These rights are relative and they are subject to the public good and the safety of the State. There can be no gain say that the rights of the individual are important and that the State exists for the individuals. But at the same time when the safety of the state is in danger the State must have the power to abridge, suspend or, if necessary, abrogate the rights of the individual which are detrimental to its safety and territorial integrity. In the words of Dr. Ambedkar, "what the Draft Constitution has done is that instead of formulating Fundamental Rights in absolute terms and depending upon the Supreme Court to come to the rescue of Parliament by inventing the doctrine of police power, it permits the state directly to impose restrictions on the Fundamental Rights. There is thus, no difference in the result". By the enumeration of the Fundamental Rights in the Constitution they have been made an integral part of the Supreme law of the country. But the constitutional authority of the sovereign Parliament to amend the Constitution and also the Fundamental Rights contained therein cannot be questioned. T.T. Krishnamachari has observed that there could be no absolute right and that every right had to be abridged in some manner or other under certain circumstances. He was of the view that the Drafting Committee had chosen the "golden mean" of providing the essential rights of the individual and at the same time putting hedges on them so as to ensure that the "State...which we are trying to bring into being... will continue unhampered and flourish".

The Fundamental Rights are restricted by the Constitution. They are also restricted and if necessary can be abrogated by an amendment of the Constitution. The Indian Constitution provides the procedure for its own amendment. Fundamental Rights may be restricted or abrogated in their application to the members of the Armed Forces or the forces charged with the maintenance of public order (Act. 33). These provisions are also applicable to the ordinary police force. According to Article 34, Parliament is empowered to pass an indemnity law legalising acts done during the enforcement to martial law. When emergency is proclaimed by the President certain Fundamental Rights may be suspended. The right to constitutional remedies for the enforcement of the Fundamental Rights may be suspended during the emergency.

Though the rights guaranteed by the Indian Constitution can be suspended or abrogated, yet they are called fundamental because the denial of these basic rights would make the personality of the individual stunted in its growth. The Fundamental Rights are essential for the protection of the interests of the minorities from the arbitrary interference of the transient majorities. It is not possible to have a democratic society in the absence of these rights. In a democratic society the individual needs certain rights for the full moral spiritual development of his personality. These rights are called fundamental because by their enumeration in the Constitution they have been made a part and parcel of the fundamental law of the land. These rights cannot be normality infringed, interfered or abrogated, except by the procedure laid down in the Constitution itself. Further, these rights are considered fundamental because they are justiciable and are guaranteed to all the citizens of India. They are also binding on all public authorities in India.

SPECIFIC FUNDAMENTAL RIGHTS

The Fundamental Rights which are enumerated in the Indian Constitution are as follows: *(i)* Right to equality, *(ii)* Right to freedom, *(iii)* Right against exploitation, *(iv)* Right to freedom of religion, *(v)* Cultural and educational rights, *(vi)* Right to property *(vii)* Right to constitutional remedies.

Right to Equality (Arts. 14 to 18). This right provides for equality before the law, social equality and equality of opportunity in public employment. The right to equality guaranteed by the Indian Constitution is essentially negative in character and has no socialist implications. This right prohibits any discrimination against any citizen or grounds of religion, race, caste, sex or place of birth. It aims at mitigating the cruder forms of social inequality.

According to Article 14, "the State shall not deny to any person equality before the law or the equal protection of the laws within the territory of India". This means equality of rights and duties because perfect equality of all the individuals is impossible. Broadly speaking, this means that all are equal before the eyes of law. All persons are equally subject to the ordinary law of the land administered by the ordinary law courts. Like the British Rule of Law it also declares that all citizens including the officials are subject to the same laws and the same courts. According to this Article, no person is to be denied the equal protection of the laws within the territory of India.

The two phrases "equality before the law" and the equal protection of the laws" have been taken from the British and the American Constitutions respectively. Equality before the law is one of the three interpretations of the Rule of Law of Dicey who defines it as, "the equal subjection of all classes to be ordinary law of the land administered by ordinary law courts". According to the interpretation of Sir Ivor Jennings, equality before the law means that, "among equals the laws should be equal and should be equally administered, that like be treated alike".

Equality does not mean absolute identity. In the general interest of the society people and their property need to be differently classified. This distinction and the classification, however, should not be arbitrary. It must be based upon just and proper differences which should form the basis of such classification, Justice Mukherjee of the Indian Supreme Court in a judgement has explained the true meaning and scope of the right to equal protection of laws in these words: "It must be admitted that the guarantee against the denial of equal protection of the laws dos not mean that identically the same rules of the law should be made applicable to all persons within the territory of India in spite of differences of circumstances and conditions. As has been said by the Supreme Court of America, 'equal protection of laws is a pledge of the protection of equal laws', and this means 'subjection to equal laws applying alike to all in the same situation'. In other words, there should be no discrimination between the one person and another if an regards the subject matter of the legislation their position is the same. There can be certainly a law applying to one person or to one group of persons and it cannot be held to be unconstitutional if it is not discriminatory in its character. It would be bad law if it arbitrarily selects one individual or a class of individuals, one corporation or a class of corporations and visits a penalty upon them, which is not imposed upon others, guilty of like delinquency. The legislature undoubtedly has a wide field of choice in determining and classifying the subject of its laws, and if the law deals alike with all of a certain class, it is normally not obnoxious to the charge of denial of equal protection but the classification should never be arbitrary. It must always rest upon some real and substantial distinction bearing a reasonable and just relation to the things in respect to which the classification is made, and classification made without any substantial basis should be regarded as invalid". Right to equality also provides that no citizen can be subjected to any disability on the ground of race, religion, caste, sex or place of birth in such matters as access to place of public entertainment, use of public wells, tanks, roads, etc. This right provides for equal opportunity. All citizens of India shall enjoy equal opportunity in matters of employment or appointment to any office under the State.

According to Article 17, "untouchability is abolished and its practice in any form is forbidden. The enforcement of any disability arising out of untouchability shall be an offence punishable in accordance with law".

Lastly, according to Article 18(1), "No title, not being a military or academic distinction, shall be conferred by the state". Thus the state is prohibited to confer titles other than military and academic distinction. Citizens of India are prohibited to accept any titles from foreign states without the permission of the President of India.

However, it may be noted that the Parliament has got the power to prescribe residential qualification in regard to employments within particular states or local areas. It also has the power to reserve posts for the backward classes, Equality of access to public places shall not prohibit the state from making special provision for women and children.

In the year 1951, the first amendment of the Constitution provided that right to equality will not prevent the state from making special provisions for the advancement of any socially and educationally backward classes of citizens or for the Scheduled Castes or the Tribes. This amendment became necessary because the Madras High Court declared a circular of the Madras Government, reserving seats in certain technical educational institutions for the students belonging to certain castes and communities, *ultra vires*.

By way of criticism it may be pointed out that the grant of special privileges to some backward communities for almost an indefinite period would create psychological barriers in the society. This would aggravate the class consciousness of different communities and hamper the efforts for social cohesion. As a result of this the integration of the different social classes and communities would become increasingly difficult. Further, the indefinite dependence on special privilege, financial grants and reservation of posts would adversely affect individual initiative and efficiency. Employment of special privileges has a tendency for perpetuation.

Right to Freedom (Arts. 19 to 22). The usual liberties of the individual are embodied in Article 19, which lays down: "All citizens shall have the right:

(a) to freedom of speech and expression;

(b) to assemble peaceably and without arms;

(c) to form associations or unions;

(d) to move freely throughout the territory of India;

(e) to reside and settle in any part of the territory of India;

(f) to acquire, hold and dispose of property; and

(g) to practice any profession or to carry on any occupation, trade or business" (Article 19(1).

A number of restrictions have been imposed on the rights enumerated above. In the interest of morality, decency, public order and security of the state, these rights can be restricted. These limitations are enumerated in Clauses (2) to (6) of Article 19. The state has the right to make laws relating to slander, defamation, libel and contempt of court. The first Amendment Act of 1951, has empowered the state to impose certain restrictions on the freedom of speech and expression in the interest of public order and the maintenance of friendly relations with foreign countries. It also empowers the state to carry on trade, business or industry whether to the total or the partial exclusion of citizens. Freedom of association and assembly is subjected to the right of the state to impose reasonable restrictions. These restrictions are considered essential for checking the abuse of freedom.

The original provision of the Constitution regarding the freedom of speech was exceptionally wide. This may be attributed to the American influence on the framers of the Constitution. The circumstances in which freedom of speech could be curtailed has been explained by Justice Brandeis. According to him, "to justify suppression of freedom of speech there must be reasonable ground to fear that serious evil will result if freedom of speech is practised. There must be reasonable ground to believe that the danger apprehended is imminent. There must be reasonable ground that the evil to be prevented is a serious one". An equally broad interpretation of the right of free speech under the original provision has been given by the Indian Supreme Court in the case of Romesh Thappar *V.* The State of Madras. It was observed that the Constitution has "placed in a distinct category these offences against public order which aim at undermining the security of the state or overthrowing it and made the prevention of the sole justification of legislative abridgement of the freedom of speech and expression, that is to say, nothing less than endangering the foundations of the state or threatening its overthrow could justify the curtailment of the freedom of speech and expression".

The first Amendment Act of 1951, has considerably reduced the scope of the right to freedom of speech. It provides that "reasonable restriction" may be imposed by the state on the right to freedom of speech in the interests of the security of the state, the maintenance of friendly relations with foreign states, public order, decency, morality or contempt of court, defamation or incitement to an offence. Thus, the scope of state interference in the right to freedom of speech has been widened. If the courts are satisfied about the reasonableness, the legislature and the executive are free to impose any number of restrictions on the individual's right to freedom of speech.

In several cases the Supreme Court has interpreted the phrase reasonable restriction. It has been held that, "the phrase 'reasonable restriction' connotes that the limitation imposed on a person should not be arbitrary or of an excessive nature, beyond what is required in the interests of the public...Legislation which arbitrarily or excessively invades the rights cannot be said to contain the quality of reasonableness and unless it strikes a proper balance between the freedom guaranteed in Art. 19(1) (g) and the social control permitted by Cl. (6) of Art, 19 it must be held to be wanting in quality." It was observed that, "the determination by the Legislature of what constitutes a reasonable restriction is not final or conclusive, it is subject to supervision by the court". In the matter of fundamental rights the Supreme Court watches and guards the rights guaranteed by the Constitution and in exercising its functions, it has the power to set aside an Act of the Legislature if it is in violation of the freedoms guaranteed by the Constitution. The Indian Constitution gives due emphasis to personal liberty and the principle Rule of Law. In its narrower sense personal liberty means freedom from arbitrary arrest and imprisonment or deprivation of life or detention of conviction. Right to freedom provides that no person shall be convicted of an offence except for a definite breach' of the law in force at the time of its commission. The operation of the criminal law in an expost facto manner is forbidden by the Constitution. It also provides that no punishment grater than that provided by the law at the time of commission of the offence can be inflicted. No person accused of any offence will be compelled to be a witness against himself and no person will be prosecuted and punished twice for the same offence. It is laid down that no person shall be deprived of his life or personal liberty except "according to the procedure established by law".

The use of the phrase procedure established by law requires elaborate discussion. The framers of the Indian Constitution preferred the phrase procedure established by law as against the due process of law of the fifth and the fourteenth amendments of the American Constitution because the former is more defined in its scope than the latter. The entire edifice of judicial supremacy in the U.S.A is built upon the concept of the due process of law. This phrase has never been defined by the American Supreme Court. This means nothing but an ideal standard which is there in the minds of the judges according to which they determine the constitutionality of a particular legislation. "Whatever it means to the present time, it is what the Supreme Court says it means". The purpose of the due process clause has been to give the power to the Supreme Court to determine the constitution did not like that the legislature should be thwarted by the judiciary. It was apprehended that, as in the U.S.A. the phrase due process would prove a serious handicap to progressive social legislation.

It is precisely for this reason that the framers of our constitution have discarded the term due process of law and have used its substitute, procedure established by law, which was borrowed from the new Japanese Constitution. This has considerably weakened the safeguards of personal liberty because the powers of the legislature in prescribing any procedure cannot be challenged. The phrase 'procedure established by law is also subject to multifarious interpretations. In the case of A.K. Gopalan *V.* State of Madras the Chief Justice of India held a that 'law' in Article 21 means, 'Law enacted by the State' or law in force at the time". The majority view in this case asserted that the procedure established by law cannot be interpreted to lay down a vague standard such as the principles of natural law. Mr. Justice Fazl Ali, however, gave his dissenting opinion that this includes, "certain fundamental principles of justice which inhere in every system of law".

Article 22(1) lays: "No person who is arrested shall be detained in custody without being informed as soon as may be, of the ground of such arrest nor shall be denied the right to consult, and to be defended by a legal practitioner of his choice". Every person who is arrested and detained must be produced before the nearest magistrate within twenty four hours of his arrest (excluding the time necessary for the journey) and cannot be detained in custody longer than that without the authority of a Magistrate.

The state, however, has the power of preventive detention in case of enemy aliens and even citizens. Such detainees do not enjoy the safeguards against arbitrary arrest mentioned in Article 22(1). Certain other safeguards are laid down for such cases. No person can be kept under detention for more than three months if it is not approved by an advisory committee consisting of persons of the status of High Court Judges. Parliament is empowered to fix the maximum period of detention in any class or classes of cases. The procedure to be followed by the advisory committee may also be prescribed by the Parliament. Parliament may also fix the maximum period beyond which detention cannot be continued. The person under detention has a constitutional right to be informed, as soon as may be of the grounds of his detention and he must be given the earliest opportunity to represent against the order of detention. The authority issuing the order, however, may refuse to disclose any acts which it does not consider to be in the public interest.

The provision of preventive detention has been subjected to severe criticism. In the Constitution Assembly it was denounced in unreserved terms Pandit Thakur Das Bhargava described these articles as, "the crown of our failures". It was described as a chart of oppression and denial of liberty" by Dr. Bakshi Tekchand. The initial period of three months was considered to be too large and it was argued that the period of detention should be reduced to one month or 15 days. A.K. Gopalan criticised it on the ground that, 'it is designed to crush political rivals of the Congresis'. In the Constituent Assembly it was pointed out that the rights guaranteed by the Constitution are worthless and that "the provison abrogate the freedoms" granted.

The framers of the Constitution probably realised that personal liberty is not only menaced by the state authority but also by the individuals and groups who seek to impose their will upon others by secretive and violent methods. The security of the state and the freedom of the individual will be jeopardised if the hands of the government are not strengthened against the anti-social elements and their obnoxious activities. There is no government in the world which does not enjoy such powers and hence it would have been unfair not to grant such powers to the Indian Government. The provision of the rights in the Constitution and the limitations strike a balance. The Constitution has achieved "a fairly reasonable enumeration of our rights and a reasonably conservative abridgement of the same" which was essential under the existing conditions.

At the same time, it is to be noted that the power of preventive detention is a dangerous weapon which can be used for political victimisation. The people, therefore, have to be alert and they must check the arbitrary use of this power. Public opinion has to be roused against the loop-holes in the provisions regarding detention without trial.

Right Against Exploitation (Arts. 23-24). According, to Article 23, traffic in human beings and bagar and other similar forms of .forced labour are prohibited and any violation of this provision shall be an offence punishable in accordance with law. But nothing in this Article shall prevent the state from imposing compulsory service for public purposes without making any discrimination on grounds only of race, religion caste or class or any of them. The state can impose compulsory service for public purposes.

This provision became necessary because in 1984, the practice of forced labour and some sort of traffic in human beings was prevalent in some parts of the country. The framers of the constitution wanted to end these shameful practices. But the Rights against Exploitation are almost useless platitudes, According to Dr. K.V. Rao these Articles in the group of rights entitled, "Right against Exploitation" confer no right on anyone nor an enforceable punishment. It is criticised that phrases like 'traffic in human beings', begar and hazardous have not been defined. Whether 'these are to be defined by the courts or the Parliament and who shall enforce them and against whom are some of the important points which have been left undecided. In order to be enforced the violation of these rights must be made cognizable offences in which case Article 32 becomes meaningless. Another thing which is to be noted is that prostitution is not prohibited. Only living on the prostitution of other is prohibited.

Similarly, employment of children is not prohibited, only their employment in hazardous work is prohibited. According to Dr. Jennings, right against exploitation is more in the nature of imposing duties on private persons than laying down a right.

Article 24, provided that no child below the age of 14 years shall be employed to work in any factory or mine or engaged in any other hazardous employment. Labour laws prohibiting the employment of children in factories or mines have been passed. But the state must make provision for poor houses or work houses for providing suitable work of children coming from very poor families to enable them to earn their livelihood.

Right to Freedom of Religion (Act 25–28). India is a milti-religious state inhabited by people of almost all the religious' faiths. The framers of the Constitution could not forget the historic role of religion in the politics of the country and therefore, it was necessary for them to face squarely the question of the role of religion in the new republic. The leaders of India were wedded to the concept of a secular state. Jawaharlal Nehru was opposed to a caste ridden society and wanted "a national state which includes people of all religions and shades of opinion and is essentially secular as a state." Religious freedom was considered essential in India for divesting from the minds of the citizens any fear of state interference. Gandhiji, the apostle of truth and non-violence, was deeply convinced about the merit and truth in all religions and strongly felt that "any form of political association based exclusively on adherence to a particular religion was worse than undemocratic".

Article 25, aims at the establishment of the secular character of the Indian polity. According to this Article all persons are equally entitled to freedom of conscience and the right freely to profess, practice and propagate religion subject to public order, morality and health. Positively, this right safeguards the free exercise of religion by everybody subject to public order morality and health; and negatively, it prohibits the state from compelling by law any person to practice any particular creed or religion. Again, it may be noted that the recognition of the right to freedom of conscience and the free profession, practice and propagation of religion shall not affect the operation of any existing law or prevent the state from making any law regulating or restricting any economic financial, political or other secular activity which may be associated with religious practice. Nothing in this Article shall affect any provision of social welfare and reform or the throwing open of Hindu religious institutions of a public character to all classes and sections of Hindus.

Article 26, is a necessary concomitant of Article 25. Without the freedom to maintain and establish religious institutions, the mere freedom to religion and religious propaganda would have become absolutely meaningless. Article 26, provides that, subject to public order, morality and health, every religious denomination or any section thereof shall have the right *(i)* to establish and maintain institutions for religious and charitable purposes, *(ii)* to manage its own affairs in matters of religion, *(iii)* to own and acquire movable and immovable property, *(iv)* to administer such property in accordance with law.

Article 27, provides that no person shall be compelled to pay any taxes which would be spent for the promotion or maintenance of any particular religion or religious denomination. This Article is a further step ahead in the emphasis of the secular character of the Indian polity. The state cannot make any special financial provision for the development of any particular religion.

Article 28: "*(1)* No religious instruction shall be provided in any educational institution wholly maintained out of state funds. *(2)* Nothing in clause *(1)* shall apply to an educational institution which is administered by the state but has been established under any endowment or trust which requires that religious instruction shall be imparted in such institution. *(3)* No person attending any educational institution recognised by the state or receiving aid out of the state funds shall be required to take part in any religious instruction that may be imparted in such institution or to attend any religious worship that may be conducted in such institution or in any premises attached thereto, unless such person, or if such person is a minor, his guardian has given consent there to."

Cultural and Educational Rights, (Article 29-30). India is a multi-lingual state. It comprise a very wide tract of territory consisting of people with different cultures and traditions. In ethnic origin and culture a Punjabi has greater affinity with a Pathan from Afghanistan than with an Indian from Tamilnadu. Besides the fourteen recognised languages, apart from English, there are more than two hundred spoken dialects in India. Unless we remember this it will be difficult to realise the significance of culture and educational rights guaranteed by the Indian Constitution.

Article 29(1) : "*(i)* Any section of the citizen residing in the territory of India or any part thereof having a distinct language, script or culture of its own shall have the right to conserve the same. *(ii)* No citizen shall be denied admission into any educational institution maintained by the state or receiving aid out of state funds or grounds only of religion, race, caste, language or any of them".

Article 30(1) : "*(i)* All minorities whether based on religion or language shall have the right to establish and administer educational institution of their choice. *(ii)* The State shall not, in granting aid to educational institutions discriminate against any educational institution on the ground that it is under the management of a minority whether based on religion or language".

Thus, the minorities have the constitutional right to establish educational institutions of their choice which they think suitable to conserve their own language and culture. The State has to adopt an impartial attitude at the time of granting aid to the institutions run by the minorities.

By way of criticism it may be pointed out that the words 'culture' and 'conserve' in the Article mentioned above have not been defined. In the words of Dr. K.V. Rao, they are not only delightfully vague but dangerously so". Culture may be interpreted as a moral and social order based upon religion. Article 29, (ii) confers the right on the monorities to seek admission in any educational institution. But how far the right is effective? When teaching in mother tongue becomes vogue the minorities will be barred automatically from seeking admission into the educational institutions.

Moreover, on grounds of minimum educational qualifications, age, health, character and previous conduct admission into educational institutions can be refused. The degree of one university may not be recognised by another university. In the words of Dr. K.V. Rao, if the Makers thought they had conferred any right by Article 29, they were mistaken".

Right to Property (Article 31.31-A, 31-B). Article 31, "*(1)* No person shall be deprived of his property save by authority of law. *(2)* No property movable or immovable including any interest in or in any company owning any commercial of industrial undertaking shall be taken possession of or acquired for public purposes under any law authorising the taking of such possession or such acquisition unless the law provides for compensation for the property taken possession of or acquired and either fixes the amount of compensation or specifies the principles on which and the manner in which, compensation is to be determined and given".

Clauses (3) to (6) Art. 31 and Art. 31-A and 31-B, provide exception to the general provisions of acquisition and requisition of property by the state for public purposes and compensation to be paid therefor.

Such exceptions to the right to property are also noticed in other constitutions of the word. In states like U.S.A. and Australia, private property can be acquired for public purposes under the authority of the principle of "eminent domain" subject to payment of fair or just compensation. In the U.S.A the courts are competent to decided whether the compensation is fair or not. Compensation has been made a necessary condition of compulsory acquisition for public purposes. In India the Constitution does not mention about its being fair or just. According to Dr. M.P. Sharma, the omission is deliberate and its intention is to bar out the interference of the courts from the matter and prevent litigation. It was observed by Pandit Pant, the then Chief Minister of U.P., "We wish to pay equitable compensation to everybody but we do not want to be involved in litigation in any case whatsoever". Many members of the Constituent Assembly also asserted that the amount of compensation should be determined by the legislature and the judiciary should not be allowed to challenge the Parliament which embodies the sovereign will of the nation. Pandit Nehru emphasised that, "within limits, no judge and no Supreme Court can make itself a third chamber". But K.M. Munshi was right when he pointed out in the Constituent Assembly that it was not possible to by-pass the courts. If it is said that, "this shall not be questioned in a court of law", then the courts will try to adjudicate on the meaning of "questioned in a court of law." The apprehensions of K.M. Munshi came true.

Two divergent views were expressed in the Constituent Assembly. One group led by Pandit Nehru insisted that the Parliament's sovereignty should not be challenged by the judiciary and the courts could not become" "a third chamber" Nehru was of the view that the Parliament should fix the compensation. The nature and the Principles of compensation should not be questioned by the judiciary. On the other hand, there was another group which insisted that the judiciary should enjoy the power to determine the reasonableness of compensation. However, there was a compromise. It was thought that the Legislature would fix the principles and the courts could go only into the question of fact whether compensation or principles of compensation were mentioned at all in Act but not into reasonableness of compensation".

The definition of the two words 'public purpose' and compensation has posed the greatest problem and, as a consequence, whether the nationalisation of industry and land reforms are possible within the framework of the Constitution has become a debatable point. Despite the incorporation of clauses (4) and (6) in Article 31, to shield Zamindari Abolition Acts of Bihar, U.P. and Madras judicial interference could not be eliminated. The courts declared these Acts as unconstitutional on the ground that they violated the other Fundamental Rights guaranteed by the Constitution. The Patna High Court declared the Bihar Zamindari Abolition Act unconstitutional. In the initial stage when the Zamindari Abolition Acts were brought before the courts, they began to question the principles of compensation as well as the question whether 'Public purpose' was involved or not. Latter on the courts, however, took a liberal view. The makers of the

Constitution deliberately avoided the use of words like 'fair', 'just' or 'reasonable' compensation in order to give the power in the hands of the Parliament to have the final say in the matter. But the courts held that compensation meant the 'equivalent' of the property deprived of and it should be adequate and not discriminatory. Compensation, however, need not be paid in terms of money. Thus, it was decided that the compensation implies that it should be just and equivalent and was a justiciable issue. This was contrary to the expectations of the framers of the Constitution. They did not want either the compensation to be "just and equivalent" or that the courts should have the final say in the matter.

But it was not possible to keep the land reforms legislation outside the purview of the courts. The legislators wanted to overcome this difficulty, because it was thought to be a great hindrance to the attainment of socialistic pattern of society. Hence, the Constitution was amended twice to put these issues beyond the jurisdiction of the courts and again a third time in 1964, to define estates. The Supreme Court decision in 1961, that 'estate' as used in the Constitution referred only to Zamindari tenures but not to roytwari property and full compensation should be given if surplus land was taken away from the Zamindari, necessitated the amendment of 1964. This amendment defined estate in a more comprehensive way as to include any proprietary right in land.

Article 31A, stated that no law providing for the acquisition by the state of an estate or of any rights therein or for the extinguishment or modification of any such rights or the taking over of the management of any property by the State for limited period either in public interest or in order to secure the proper management of the property shall be held void on the ground that it was in conflict with Fundamental Rights as provided by Articles 14, 19 or 31.

Article 31B, added a new schedule (ninth) to the Constitution, giving a list of 13 Zamindari Abolition laws whose validity could not be questioned by the courts, under the provisions of the previous Article and which would remain valid not withstanding and judgement, decree or order of any court or tribunal to the country. The purpose of this Article was to keep certain land-reform measures beyond the purview of the judiciary.

But the insertion of the new Article 31-A and 31-B, in the Constitution did not solve the real problem. In Sholapur case it was decided, *inter alia*, that since the ordinance taking over the management of the Sholapur Mills did not make any provision for compensation, it amounted to infringement of Article 31. The Supreme Court of India also declared the Bank Nationalisation Ordinance of 1969, unconstitutional because it was discriminatory. While other banks were not touched, the fourteen nationalised banks were not allowed to carry on banking business without the approval of the government.

On 12th April, 1955 the Constitution (Fourth Amendment), Act was passed to surmount some of the difficulties created by the decisions of the Supreme Court. Pandit Nehru said in the Parliament that while interpreting the laws the Supreme Court and the Country. While explaining the objects of the bill he said, "we are not suggesting any arbitrary confiscatory or expropriatary action. In fact the law provides that acquisition of property be by law and compensation should be paid. But the quantum of compensation will be determined by the legislature".

The amendment of 1955, provided that the adequacy of compensation cannot be questioned in a court. By this amendment the original principle of the Constitution that in matters of social, political and economic policy it is the legislature and the judiciary which is supreme was emphasised. The amendment makes it amply clear that no law which provides for the transfer of the ownership or right to possession of any property to the State or to a corporation owned or controlled by the state can be declared invalid by the court on the grounds of the inadequacy of compensation.

This amendment was vehemently condemned by protagonists of the right to property. They argued that this amendment is a negation of the right to property guaranteed by the Constitution because it has made the right to property non-justiciable. On the other hand, the communists, socialists and the extremists in the Congress ardently supported it.

The right to property requires dispassionate consideration and the extremes are to be avoided. The right to property is brought under fire no less vigorously at present than it was in the past. After the invalidation of the Bank Nationalisation Ordinance many statesmen, politicians and intellectuals suggested that right to property should no longer be a fundamental right. It should only be a legal right like the other rights, say the right to vote. The most unfortunate thing is the criticism of the Supreme Court as the citadel of the reactionary forces and the obstacle to the attainment of the socialistic pattern of society. The Supreme Court is one of the main pillars of support for a democratic government and it cannot be expected to sail favourably with the fluctuating and transient political opinions of the country. Socialism must function within the framework of the Constitution and there is ample scope for that. What is really lacking is the sincerity of the leaders, if they take recourse to undemocratic and extra constitutional measures of the Supreme Court as the guardian of the Constitution must invalidate such measures. However, one thing has to be noted in this context that large properties in land or means of production are determental to the general interest of the society. Concentration of wealth in the hands of a few people has to be scaled down and there must be equitable distribution of wealth. Hence, the amendment was justified in the context of the dynamics and tempo of the new social forces that had been set in operation to shape India's destiny.

Further, in accordance with the Constitution's Twenty-fifth Amendment Act, 1971, after Article 318, 31C was inserted saying: "Notwithstanding anything contained in Article 13, no law giving effect to the policy of the State towards. Securing the principles specified in clause (b) or clause (c) of Article 39 span be deemed to be void on the ground that it is inconsistent with, or takes away or abridges any of the rights conferred by Article 14, Article 19 or Article 31 and no law containing a declaration that it is for giving effect to such policy shall be called in question in any court on the ground that it does not give effect to such policy.

Provided that where such law is made by the legislature of a State, the provisions of this Article shall not apply thereto unless such law, having been referred for the consideration of the President has received his assent.

According to the Forty-second Amendment of the Constitution Article 31D, has been inserted saying: "Not-withstanding anything contained in Article 13, no law providing for, *(A)* the prohibition or prevention of anti-national activities, *(B)* the prevention of formation of or the prohibition of anti-national associations, shall be deemed to be void on the ground that it is inconsistent with or takes away or abridges any of the rights conferred by Articles 14, 19 or 31. Further, it is providing that Parliament alone shall have the power to make laws with respect to any of the matters in this, regard".

Right to Property which was amended several times in the past and was severely mutilated was deleted from the category of Fundamental Right, finally, during the Janata Government regime. The Right was responsible for most of the conflicts between the Legislature and the Judiciary. Right to property however, would be given express recognition as a legal right and no person shall be deprived of his property save in accordance with law.

Ever since the inception of the Constitution, the Fundamental Right to Property has been progressively restricted by several Amendment, Acts, namely, the First Amendment Act, 1951, the Fourth Amendment Act, 1955, the Seventeenth Amendment Act, 1964, the Twenty-fifth Amendment Act, 1971 and the Forty-second Amendment Act, 1976. All these successive Amendment Acts have severely eroded the Right to Property to such an extent that there was a genuine doubt, whether this Right was protected in any way from legislative encroachment. This doubt was cleared for all times to come by its total deletion from the category of Fundamental Rights during the regime of the Janata Government.

Right to Constitutional Remedies (Arts. 32—35). This provision is extraordinarily important because it gives meaning and fulfilment to the other fundamental rights guaranteed by the Constitution. A mere declaration and insertion of fundamental rights in the Constitution is useless, unless there is an effective and easy remedy or machinery provided in the Constitution itself for enforcing these rights, or unless their enjoyment is effectively guaranteed by provision for judicial review". Referring to this provision Dr. Ambedkar said, "If I was asked to name any particular Article in this Constitution as the most important Article without which this Constitution could be a mullity, I could not refer to any other Article except this one. It is the very soul of the Constitution and the very heart of it."

Article 32 : *(1)* The right to move the Supreme Court by appropriate proceedings for the enforcement of the rights conferred by this part is guaranteed. *(2)* The Supreme Court shall have power to issue directions or orders or writs in the nature of habeas corpus, mandamus, prohibition, *quo warranto* and *certiorari*, whichever may be appropriate for the enforcement of any of the rights conferred by this part. *(3)* Without prejudice to the powers conferred on the Supreme Court by clauses (1) and (2), Parliament may by law empower any other court to exercise with in local limits of its jurisdiction all or any of the power exercisable by the Supreme Court under clause (2). (4) The right guaranteed by this Article shall not be suspended except or otherwise provided for by the Constitution."

In case of violation of the fundamental rights the individual has the right to move the Supreme Court by appropriate proceeding and the Supreme Court has the power to issue direction, orders or writs as mentioned above whichever may be appropriate for the enforcement of any of the fundamental rights. Justice Mukherjee of the Supreme Court has defined the scope of the power to issue directions, orders or writs in the following words: "Article 32, as its provisions show, is not directly concerned with the determination of constitutional validity of particular legislative enactments. What it aims at is the enforcing of fundamental rights guaranteed by the Constitution no matter whether the necessity for the enforcement arises out of an action of the executive or of legislature. To make out a case under this Article, it is incumbent upon the petitioner to establish not merely that the law complained of is beyond the competence of the particular legislature as not being covered by any items of the legislative list, but that it affects or invades his fundamental rights guaranteed by the Constitution of which he could seek enforcement by an appropriate writ or order. The rights that could be enforced under Article 32, must ordinarily be the rights of the petitioner himself who complains of infraction of such rights and approaches the court for relief."

Article 32, is a remedial right for the enforcement of the fundamental rights guaranteed by the Constitution and this right has also been made fundamental by its incorporation in Part III of the Constitution. Thus, the Supreme Court is made the protector and the guarantor of the fundamental rights. The Supreme Court, therefore, is duty bound to entertain all applications seeking protection against infringements of fundamental rights. The Constitution has empowered the Supreme Court and the High Courts to issue orders, directions and writs. Parliament also has the power to authorise any other courts in India to issue order or directions in the nature of the above-mentioned writs within the local limits, without prejudice to the powers of the Supreme Court to issue these orders. The jurisdiction of the Supreme Court, the High Courts and other courts will be concurrent. However, apart from these remedies any law can be questioned in a court by any person on the ground that it violates the Constitution.

The right to move the Supreme Court and the power of the Supreme Court to issue writs cannot be suspended except as otherwise provided for by the Constitution. But it is criticised that this right can be suspended under Article 359, which has robbed the vital essence of the fundamental rights. The fundamental rights can be suspended, abrogated when emergency is proclaimed by the President under Article 352. It may be pointed out in this connection that our fundamental rights are not absolute and they strike a balance between the demands of the individual and the needs of the States. It must be realised that the safety of the State is more important than the rights of the individual. When the life of the State is itself in jeopardy, it must take drastic steps to protect itself and under such circumstances the rights of the individual must be subordinated to the supreme need of the safety of the State. Hence, during emergency the rights remain suspended. Such an order may extend to the whole or any part of the territory of India. The constitutional remedies for the enforcement of the fundamental rights cannot be suspended during normal times without the amendment of the Constitution by the Parliament. But during the emergency the right to constitutional remedies can be suspended by the President by an executive decree. It is true that the nature and the scope of this power is absolute and unlimited and may be open to abuse but in the larger interests of the State such power is deemed necessary."

According to Article 33, Parliament has the power to modify the rights guaranteed to the citizens, which may in their application to the members of the Armed Forces or the Forces charged with the maintenance of public order be restricted or abrogated so as to ensure the proper discharge I of their duties and the maintenance of discipline among them.

Article 34: Notwithstanding the provisions regarding fundamental rights in Part III, "Parliament may be law indemnify any person in the service of the Union or of a State or any other person in respect of any act done by him in connection with the maintenance or restoration of order in any area within the territory of India where martial law was in force or validate any sentence passed, punishments inflicted, forfeiture ordered or other act done under martial law in such area."

Article 35, makes it clear that laws regarding matters relating to fundamental rights are to be enacted by the Parliament alone and the State legislatures have no power to deal with these matters.

Provisions for the Issue of Writs. The power of the Supreme Court to issue the different writs has been discussed earlier. They are like the original prerogative writs and under the Constitution they are made statutory remedies. A brief analysis of the writs is given below:

Habeas Corpus (You may have the body). It is the most important prerogative writ. This writ protects the personal liberty of the individual and is considered as a landmark of liberty. It provides a remedy for a person who has been wrongfully detained or restrained. The courts can order the authorities to produce before them any person who has been arrested and detained by them for the purpose of determing the legality of his detention. This writ is issued to whoever holds an individual in captivity. If the court is not satisfied with the cause of such detention and finds anything wrong with the confinement, it can order for the immediate release of the detenue. Any person can set the machinery in motion for purpose of the issue of such a writ by notice of motion, or application supported by an affidavit of facts.

Mandamus (We command). This is a high prerogative writ of a most extensive remedial nature. It is an order to public body or person to do what is its or his duty, provided it is a public duty affecting the right of an individual. It is mainly used for public purposes and for the enforcement of public duties. It also enforces some private rights when they are withheld by public officers. This writ is aimed at correcting the acts of omission on the part of authorities which ciolate the fundamental rights of the citizens.

Prohibition. This is a judicial writ issued by a court of superior jurisdiction and directed to the inferior court or tribunal, preventing it from acting without proper jurisdiction. By this writ the court of higher jurisdiction can compel courts entrusted with judicial duties to keep within the limits of their jurisdiction. The writ of prohibition is used at an earlier stage to prevent the wrong action by the authorities and in this sense it is a preventive step, whereas the writ of mandamus is sought to be used after the wrong has been committed and as such it is the cure. This writ can be issued to non-judicial bodies in cases where such bodies take quasi-judicial decisions. The writ is issued on a notice of motion or on application supported by affidavit and the inferior court may be asked to show cause as to how it is concerned with the matter not within its jurisdiction. This writ orders for the immediate cessation of the trial of the case in the court of a lower jurisdiction. If the judge or any party proceeds with the case after the writ of prohibition has been issued the court issuing the writ may proceed against them for contempt.

Certiorari. This writ is an order commonly issued by a superior court to withdraw a case or trial from an inferior court or tribunal when the subordinate court or tribunal is acting without jurisdiction or in excess of it or in violation of the principals of natural justice or refuses to exercise a jurisdiction vested in it. By this writ the superior court prevents the courts of special jurisdiction (including authorities exercising quasi-judicial function) and the inferior courts from exceeding the proper functions.

Quo Warranto. This writ prevents the illegal assumption of any public office or usurpation of any public office by a person till the matter is finally decided by the court. Where a person acts in an office in which he is not entitled to act, an injunction may be granted in the nature of the writ of quo-warranto restraining from so acting.

FUNDAMENTAL DUTIES

In June, 1975, Mrs. Gandhi proclaimed Internal Emergency because of apprehended internal disturbances following the adverse judgement of the Allahabad High Court against her. Certain drastic amendments were made to the Constitution during this period. The main purpose of these amendments was to contain the apprehended disturbance and large scale violation of constitutional provisions and law and order. The government wanted to strengthen its hands and the 42nd Amendment was passed. As per the provisions of the 42nd Amendment of the Indian Constitution.

Part IV A is inserted titled, "Fundamental Duties" saying: It shall be the duty of every citizen of India:

(a) to abide by the Constitution and respect its ideals and institutions, the national flag and the national anthem;

(b) to cherish and follow the noble ideas which inspired our national struggle for freedom;

(c) to uphold and protect the sovereignty, unity and integrity of India;

(d) to defend the country and render national service when called upon to do so;

(e) to promote harmony and the spirit of common brotherhood amongst all people of India transcending religious, linguistic and regional or sectional diversities, to renounce practice derogatory to the dignity of women;

(f) to value and preserve the rich heritage of our composite culture;

(g) to protect and improve the natural environment including forest, lakes, rivers and wild life and to have compassion for living creatures;

(h) to develop the scientific temper, harmonism and spirit of enquiry and reform;

(i) to safeguard public property and to abjure violence; and

(j) to strive towards excellence in all spheres of individual and collective activity so that the nation constantly rises to higher levels of endeavour and achievement.

The 42nd Amendment of the Indian Constitution was effected during the time of Emergency. There was the feeling that in India people were demanding too much of rights without being prepared to fulfil their constitutional obligations or duties. Rights and duties are complementary to each other. Mere insistence on rights is likely to vitiate the constitutional process. The Constitution of U.S.S.R. also provided the inspiration for inclusion of the provision of Fundamental Duties in our Constitution.

DIRECTIVE PRINCIPLES OF STATE POLICY

The framers of the Indian Constitution followed the Irish precedent in making a declaration of social and economic policy in the framework of the Constitution. The Weimar Constitution of Germany for the first time made a constitutional declaration of the social and economic policies in 1919. Since that time many countries have followed the practice of incorporating a number of directives in the constitutions of their country, e.g. the Constitution of Austria (1929), Spain (1931), Eire (1937), New York State (1941), Brazil (1942), France (1946), Italy (1947) and East Germany (1949). They are also incorporated in the Constitutions of Czechoslovakia, China and Yugoslavia. These principle are included in the chapter on Fundamental Rights in the Constitution of USSR in most of the Constitutions no distinction is made between justiciable and other rights. But India has followed the Irish example where the justiciable rights of the individual are separated from non-justiciable social policy.

The founding fathers of the Indian Constitution were convinced that Indian should be made a welfare state. They were also greatly influenced by the trading surge of socialism. But they did not like to prescribe any cut and dried scheme to be followed by everybody. They only desired to prescribe that every government shall try to bring about economic democracy. Mere political democracy in the absence of economic democracy would be devoid of its vital substance. Hence, for the attainment of economic democracy certain provisions have been made in the form of directives to the legislature and the executive. The legislatures of the Union and the States while making the law and the governments while executing the law should keep these directives in mind. Whether the judiciary shall keep them in mind while interpreting the laws is not clear in the Constitution. But as the directives are fundamental in the Governance of the country, they may be used in case of doubt in the interpretation of legislation.

The purpose of incorporating the Directives of State Policy in a separate chapter of the Constitution has been explained by Dr. B.R. Ambedkar in the following words: "It was not the intention of the framers to prescribe any rigid programme for the attainment of the ideal of economic democracy. Parties were to be completely free to advocate their own programmes and appeal to the electorate for a mandate for them. But the framers desired to prescribe that every government shall try to bring about economic democracy."

Most of the Directive Principles aim at the establishment of a welfare state based on socialistic principles. They constitute a very comprehensive political, social and economic programme for a modern "democratic state," The framers of the Constitution considered that these are the basic principles of a new economic and social order. But as no legal effect could be given to these principles they were incorporated in the Constitution in the form of directives to the legislature and the executive. They are mostly in the nature of moral precepts and economic maxims unexceptionable in content having to legal force. They may be used for political criticism, They confer no legal rights and create no legal remedies."

Distinction between Fundamental Rights and Directive Principles. There is a difference between the Fundamental Rights mentioned in Chapter III and the Directive Principles mentioned in Chapter IV Of the Indian Constitution. The Fundamental Rights are justiciable. If a Fundamental Right is violated a legal remedy is provided for that. But the Directive Principles are non-justiciable and if they are violated there is no provision of legal remedy Article 38, says that the state shall strive. It does not mean that the state must fulfil these principles. If for example, the state does not make provisions for compulsory free 'education for children under the age of 14 or if the judiciary is not separated from the executive nobody can challenge it in the court of law. However, on thing should be kept in mind that the Directive Principles have been declared as fundamental in the governance of the country. This mean that these principles are not to be lightly taken and the legislatures and the governments must maen sincere efforts to fulfil these principles. In the words of Dr. Ambedkar, "the word strive" was purposely used because their intention was that however adverse the circumstances that stand in the way for a government in giving effect to these principles and however unpropitious the time may be, they should always strive for the fulfilment of the principles. Otherwise, it would be open to the government to say, that the circumstances were not good and the finances were so bad that they could not implement them.

The Directive Principles are subsidiary to the Fundamental Rights and in case of conflict with Fundamental—Rights they shall be declared unconstitutional. In the case of State of Madras V. Champakan Dorairajan, the Supreme Court observed: "The Directive Principles of State Policy which are expressly made unenforceable by a Court cannot over-ride the provisions in Part III which are made enforceable by appropriate writs, orders of directions under Article 32." Thus the Directive Principles must have to conform to and run subsidiary to the chapter on Fundamental Rights. The State can act in accordance with the Directive Principles if that does not amount to the infringement of the Fundamental Rights conferred by the Constitution. The legal superiority of the Fundamental Rights over the Directive Principles has been established by the decisions of the Supreme Court of India.

Another difference between the Fundamental Rights and the Directive Principles is that the former are negative in character whereas the latter are positive. The Fundamental Rights are in the nature of injunctions requiring the state not to do certain acts and are prohibitive in character. The Directive Principles, on the other hand, are positive directions to the state to perform certain things for the good of the citizens. They urge that it is the duty of the state to implement the social and economic policy as embodied in the directives for the attainment of economic democracy and social justice. In the words of Gledhill, "Fundamental Rights are injuctions to prohibit the government from doing certain things; the Directive Principles are affirmative instructions to the government to do certain things."

CLASSIFICATION OF DIRECTIVE PRINCIPLES

The Directive Principles are embodied in as many as 16 Articles. It is difficult to classify these principles because they are not arranged in accordance with any logical plan. They cover a wide range of state activities. They are concerned with the social, economic, legal, educational and international principles. For the purpose of a systematic study these principles have been classified into three categories, namely, the socialistic, Gandhian and liberal. However, there are certain principles which cannot be included in either of these categories. These may be included in a fourth category called as the general category.

(a) Socialistic Principles. Most of these Directive Principles aim at the attainment of a socialist society. The socialistic principles were considered essential for the purpose of establishing a welfare state.

Article 38, provides that the State shall strive to promote the welfare of the people by securing and protecting a social order in which justice, social, economic and political, shall inform all the institutions of national life.

Article 39, provides that the State shall direct its policy towards securing, *(i)* the citizens, men and women equally, have the right to an adequate means of livelihood; *(ii)* that the ownership and control of the material resources of the community are so distributed as to subserve the common good; *(iii)* that the operation of the economic system does not result in concentration of wealth and means of production to the common detriment; *(iv)* that there is equal pay for equal work for both men and women; *(v)* that the health and strength of workers, men and women, and the tender age of children are not abused and that citizens are not forced to enter vocations unsuitable to their age; *(vi)* that childhood and youth are protected against exploitation and moral and material abandonment.

Article 41, seeks to ensure the right to work, to education and to public assistance in case of unemployment, old age, sickness and disablement and other cases of underserved want. Article 42, provides that provisions shall be made by the State for securing just and human conditions of work and for maternity relief. Article 43, exhorts the State to secure to all worker-industrial, agricultural or otherwise—work, a living wages, conditions of work ensuring a decent standard of life and full enjoyment of leisure and social and cultural opportunities. Article 46, provides that the State shall take special care of the economic and the educational interests of the weaker section of the society and in particular of the Scheduled Castes and Scheduled Tribes and to protect them from social injustice and all forms of exploitation. According to Article 47, the State is made duty bound to raise the level of nutrition and the standard of living of its people and the improvement of the public health.

(b) Gandhian Principles. The framers of the Constitution were greatly influenced by Gandhian ideology. During his life Gandhiji become the undisputed leader of Congress party and the nation as well. The Gandhian philosophy finds its expression in many Articles of this chapter. It can be noticed in the following principles:

(i) The state shall organise village panchayats and endow them with such powers as may enable them to function as units of self-government.

(ii) The State shall promote, with special care, the educational and economic interests of Harijans, Scheduled Tribes and weaker sections of the community.

(iii) The State shall endeavour to promote cottage industries on individual or co-operative basic in rural areas.

(iv) The State shall take steps for preserving and improving the breeds of milch and draught cattle, including cows and calves and for prohibiting their slaughter.

(v) The State shall endeavour to effect prohibition of the consumption, except for medicinal purposes, of intoxicating drug and drinks which are injurious to health.

(c) Liberal Principles. This category of the Directive Principles contains what may be called the liberal principles. These principles were advocated by the liberal intellecturals for the betterment of the citizens of India. The liberal principles are embodied in the following provision of the Constitution:

(i) The State shall endeavour to secure for the citizens a uniform civil code throughout the territory of India.

(ii) The State shall endeavour to provide within a period of ten years from commencement of the Constitution for free and compulsory education for children below and up to 14 years of age.

(iii) The State shall endeavour to organise agriculture and animal husbandry on modern and scientific lines.

(iv) The State shall take steps to separate the judiciary from the executive in the public service of the State.

(v) The State shall endeavour to promote international peace and security; maintain just and honourable relations between nations; foster respect for international law and treaty obligations; encourage settlement of international disputes by arbitration.

(d) General Principles. As it has been said earlier, there are certain Articles in this chapter which cannot be included in anyone of the three categories into which the Directive Principles have been classified by Dr. M.P. Sharma. These principles may be included in the category of general principles. Articles 36 and 37 deal with the definitions and application of the Directive Principles. According to Article 36, unless the context otherwise requires, the State shall have the same meaning as in Part III of the Constitution. Article 37, provides that these principles shall not be enforceable by any court of law and at the same time declares that they are nevertheless fundamental in the governance of the country and it shall be the duty of the State to apply these principles in making laws. Article 49, which provides that it is the obligation of the State to protect every monument of place or object of artistic or historic interest which Parliament of India has declared of national importance, may be included in this category.

Criticism of the Directive Principles. The Directive Principles have been subjected to serious and searching criticisms. They are considered as mere platitudes without having any practical use for the people. There is no immediate practical social and economic programme and as such they fall flat upon the people. These principles do not have any attraction for the masses because. They are silent about the means of implementation. The formulation of the directives of State policy can hardly be considered inspiring. It is both vague and repetitive. The directives are neither properly classified nor logically arranged". The Directive Principles are evasive and ambiguous and by mixing up important matters like prohibition, compulsory education for the children below and up to the age of 14 etc. With relatively less important matters such as that the State shall protect places of artistic or historic interest, they have reduced their urgency and importance. The Directive Principles like the formulation of rights in some of the European Constitutions do not have clear objectives and are evasive on the decisive social issues of labour management relations and the property complex as the key to the alternatives of private capitalism or socialisation, laissez faire of planning.

As there is no legal force behind them, the Directive Principles are dubbed as mere pious ambitions, or superfluous platitudes or political manifesto devoid of any constitutional importance. A member of the Constituent Assembly (Nassiruddin) described these principles as a set of New Year resolutions. In the words of Professor K.T. Shah these principles are like a cheque on a bank, payable only when the resources of the bank permit". It is pointed out that mere platitudes have no place in the Constitution. Principles which are legally enforceable should not have been mentioned in the Constitution. They unnecessarily increase the bulk of the Constitution. Sir B.N. Rau is of the opinion that the Directive Principles of State Policy are in the nature of moral precepts for the State authorities and are open to the facile criticism that the Constitution is not the place for moral precepts. The Directive Principles have been characterised by K.C. Whear as a manifesto of aims and aspirations. The illogical arrangement and the curious combination of the different principles have also been criticised by many critics of the Indian Constitution. It combines rather incongrously the modern with the old and provisions suggested by reason and science with provisions based purely on sentiment and prejudice.

Some critics are of the opinion that the Directive Principles are redundant and are incompatible with the sovereign status of the country. There is hardly any necessity of such instructions for a sovereign country. Moreover, the Directive Principles cannot be followed and implemented at all times and under all circumstances. A sovereign State must have the freedom to change its policy in accordance with the requirements of the time. It would be unwise to restrict its activities through certain rigid principles formulated at a particular time. In a parliamentary democracy different political parties have the freedom to have their independent social, economic and political programmes with which they would try to seek the mandate from the people. Thus, with every change in the government there is the likelihood of a change in the political philosophy which differs from party to party. Hence, the Directive Principles of State Policy which constitute a political philosophy can never be expected to be followed by all the governments for all times to come. They are rightly described as parade of high sounding sentiments couched in vain glorious verbiage."

In an age of reality the practicability, the soundness of the Directive Principles have also been challenged. The principle concerning prohibition is severely criticised as it causes great loss to the national exchequer. It does not serve any useful purpose. Morality cannot be enforced with the help of laws. It is pointed out that prohibition can hardly change drunkards into moralists. On the contrary, it will provide incentive to crimes of illicit distillation and illegal gratification of officers who become instruments in the hands of those who carry on this illegal trade. Thus, the Directive Principle contain an overdose of idealism without looking for their practicability. Dr. Jennings has rightly remarked that, "the ghosts of Sidney and Beatrice Webb stalk through the text of Part IV of the Constitution".

In the Constituent Assembly some members expressed the apprehension that the Directive Principles may become the cause of conflict between the President of India and the Prime Minister and between the Governors and their provincial Ministers. If the Prime Minister gets a law passed by the Parliament, which violates the Directive Principles, the President may withhold his assent from such a bill on the ground that since these principles are "fundamental in the governance of the country" the Ministry has no right to ignore them. Such cases, however, have not occurred but this does not rule out possibility of their occurrence in future. The same thing may also be followed in the provincial spheres. This may endanger the smooth functioning of parliamentary democracy in the country.

It is rightly pointed out that this chapter does talk of the end but ignores the means. Dr. Jennings is sincere in expressing his apprehensions that these principles may not simply become outmoded and antiquated in the next century. They might act as citadels of reaction as well as thus clog national progress.

The vehement criticism of the Directive Principles may lead us to believe that they are useless and meaningless maxims or moral precepts. But there is great justification for their enumeration in the Constitution. In the words of G.N. Joshi, "All these provisions constitute a very comprehensive political, social and economic programme of a modern democratic state and indeed, read like a political manifesto. It would appear that they are meant to generate an atmosphere favourable to the growth of the democratic Republic". The main criticism against the Directives is that there is no legal force behind then. But in a democracy the force of public opinion is more effective and powerful than the legal force. The Directives which aim at the attainment and the establishment of the welfare state and a socialistic pattern of society are vigorously backed by public opinion. No government can dare to violate these principles because such violation will not be tolerated by them. The Directives work as constant reminders to the executive and the legislature to make and implement progressive legislation. If the Directives are not implemented by the government this would form a very good ground for its political criticism.

The Directive Principles have great educative value. They make the people conscious about the social, economic and political programmes envisaged by the Constitution. The government also becomes aware of its constitutional obligations. In the light of the constitutional declarations the people scrutinise the policies and the programmes of the government. If there is any deviation from the principles of the Constitution, then the activities of the government are brought under fire. The chapter on Fundamental Rights has provided political democracy. But it need not be stated that political democracy is meaningless without economic democracy. The Directive Principles aim at the establishment of economic democracy. By the enumeration of the Directive Principles, as has been stated by Dr. Ambedkar, the framers desired to prescribe that every government shall try to bring about economic democracy. Further Dr. Ambedkar is of the view that whichever political party may come to power irrespective of the fact whether it is conservative or redical, the Directive Principles have left enough room for people of different ways of thinking with regard to the reaching of the ideal of economic democracy. In the words of Raghava Chariar, "Whoever may capture the government power they will have to respect these instruments of instruction. He may certainly have to answer for them before the electoral when the next election comes."

The Directive Principles, though not legally enforceable, are nevertheless fundamental 'in the government of the country. A philosophy of new social and economic order is embodied in the Principles. The framers of the Constitution could not have ignored the impact of socialism in the middle of the twentieth century. Article 38, prescribes: "The state shall strive to promote the welfare of the people by securing and protecting as effectively as it may a social order, in which justice, social economic and political shall inform all the institutions of national life." The socialistic principles are further enumerated by Article 39.

The constitutional sanctity of the Directive Principles has been recognised by the judiciary. The violation of the Directives is as contrary to the Constitution as the violation of a principle legally enforceable. According to Gledhill, "If the Indian Constitution becomes vested with the hope of sanctity essential to its durability, it will be difficult for any public figure to propose any legislative measures without making an appeal to Fundamental Rights or Directive Principles. Measures will be attacked by the opposition as unconstitutional 'insofar as they conflict with the Directive Principles". In Gopalan V. State of Madras, Kania C.J. opined that the Directive Principles form a part of the Constitution and as such do not represent a temporary will of the majority, but the deliberate wisdom of the nation expressed through the Constituent Assembly. By declaring them to be fundamental in the governance of the country, the Constitution has invested them with a certain sanctity.

The Directive Principles have greatly helped in avoiding the ambiguities of the Constitution. As these Principles form a part of the Constitution, a reference can be made to them whenever and difficulty arises regarding the interpretation of some of the vague provisions of the Constitution. The Directive Principles have been of immense help in the interpretation of the Fundamental Rights. The imposition of reasonable restrictions on Fundamental Rights in the public interest is permitted by Article 19. If a question as to whether a certain matter is in the interest of the public or not arises a reference to the Directive Principles can be made to come out of the thickest of constitutional ambiguities. In Goplan V. State of Madras Kania C.J. observed: "It has no doubt been repeatedly made clear that the courts cannot uphold a Directive Principle when it comes in consist with a specific provision of the Constitution relating to Fundamental Rights. However, in the interpretation of these provisions, the Directive Principles can serve a very useful purpose. Most of the Fundamental Rights are subject to reasonable restrictions which may be imposed for public purpose, or in public interest. The courts can be and have been guided by the Directive Principles in determining whether the actual restrictions placed by law on the exercise of Fundamental Rights are reasonable or in public interest or whether they subserve a public purpose."

In several cases the Supreme Court has made references to the Directive Principles while determining the controversial issues. In the case of Bijoy Cotton Mills V. State of Ajmer, the constitutional validity of the Minimum Wage Act, (1948) was upheld by the Supreme Court. It was decided that the fixation of wages for labourers did not violate freedom of trade and in support of this court cited Article 43, dealing with the Directive Principles. In the case, The State of Bombay V. F. M. Balsara, the Supreme Court decided that the restriction imposed by the Bombay Prohibition Act was reasonable restriction on the right to acquire any profession or carry on any trade. In support of its decision the Supreme Court cited Article 47, dealing with the Directive Principles which aim at prohibition. Professor Alexandrowicz observes that the courts should give the greatest possible weight to the Directive Principles for the purpose of their interpretations of the provisions relating to Fundamental Rights. The utility of the Directive Principles has been correctly assessed by M.C. Setalwad in the following words: "These fundamental axioms of state policy though of no legal effect have served as a useful beacon light to courts. Restrictions imposed by law on the freedom of citizens may well be responsible if they are imposed in furtherance of the Directive Principles."

An Assessment. From the foregoing analysis it is evident that although, the Fundamental Rights were amended several times by various amendments the Directive Principles were not amended until the passage of the Forty-second Amendment of 1976.

The Forty-second Amendment Act, 1976 inserted the provision in Article 39, saying, "that children are given opportunities and facilities to develop in a healthy manner and in conditions of freedom and dignity and that children and youth are protected against exploitation and against moral and material abandonment."

A new article, Article 39-A, was inserted which provided that the State shall strive to secure that the operation of the legal system promotes justice, on a basis of equal opportunity and shall in particular, provide free legal aid by suitable legislation or schemes or any other way, to ensure that opportunities for securing justice are not denied to any citizen by reason of economic or other disabilities.

After Article 43, Article 43-A, was inserted, which provided that the State shall take steps, by suitable legislation or in any other way, to secure the participation of workers in the management of undertakings, establishments or other organisations engaged in any industry.

In addition to the above amendments to the Directive Principles, the Forty-second Amendment, inserted Article 48-A, which provided that the State shall endeavour to protect and improve the environment and to safeguard the forests and wild life of the country.

A comperative analysis of the various amendments effected to Fundamental Rights and Directive Principles would show that while the scope of Fundamental Rights has been either curtailed, limited or abridged by these amendments the scope of Directive Principles has been enlarged.

The difference between Fundamental Rights and Directive Principles is that while the Fundamental Rights are justiciable the Directive Principles are not justiciable. In case of conflict between these two categories, the Judiciary upheld the primary of Fundamental Rights over the Directive Principles. In the case of Gopalan Vs. State of Madras it was observed that : "It has no doubt been repeatedly made clear that the Courts cannot uphold a Directive Principle when it comes in conflict with a specific provision of the constitution relating to Fundamental Rights. However, in the interpretation of these provisions, the Directive Principles can serve a very useful purpose. Most of the Fundamental Rights are subject to reasonable restrictions which may be imposed for public purpose, or in public interest. The courts can be and have been guided by the Directive Principles in determining whether the actual restrictions placed by law on the exercise of Fundamental Rights are reasonable or in public interest or whether they subserve a public purpose". The relationship between—Fundamental Rights and Directive Principles was more explicitly analysed in the State of Madras Vs. Champakan Dorarirajan case. In the case it was observed that: "The Directive Principles of state policy which are made expressly unenforceable by a court cannot over-ride the provisions in Part III which are made enforceable by appropriate writs, orders or directions under Article 32". This primacy of Fundamental Rights over the Directive Principles was specifically accepted by Article 37, of the Constitution. Referring to the Directive it is said that, "The provisions contained in this part shall not be enforceable by any court, but the principles therein laid down are nonetheless fundamental in the governance of the country and it shall be the duty of the State to apply these Principles in making laws".

In the Champakan Dorairajan case the Supreme Court was of the view: "That the chapter on Fundamental Rights is sacrosanct and not liable to the abridged by any legislative or executive act or order, except to the extent provided in the appropriate Article in Part Ill. The Directive Principles of State Policy have to conform to and run subsidiary to the chapter the Fundamental Rights. That is the correct way in which the provisions found in Parts III and IV have to be understood". The Courts cannot declare a law to be invalid merely on the ground that it violates the provisions mentioned in Chapter IV of the Constitution. But the numerous developments in the Indian socio-political system have been responsible for a basic change in the philosophy of the Indian Constitution in many respects despite the rulings of the Supreme Court in the Kesavananda Bharati Case, 1973. In this case the Supreme Court was of the opinion that although the Parliament has the power to amend any part of the Constitution including provisions enumerated in Part Ill, it cannot amend the basic structure of the Indian Constitution. But many provisions of the Forty-second Amendment have resulted in changing the basic structure of the Indian Constitution. It has also transformed the basic philosophy of our political system.

The Constitution itself has been amended several times to modify those Fundamental Rights which were obstacles to the State in its task of effecting socio-economic reforms as required by certain Directives. The Twenty-fifth Amendment Act, 1971 gave precedence to the Directive Principles embodied in Article 39(b) and (c) over the Fundamental Rights embodied in Articles 14, 19 and 31. The Forty-second Amendment Act, 1976, has gone further by expressly giving precedence to all the Directive Principles of State Policy over Articles 14, 19 and 31. The implication is crystal clear. At present no law seeking to implement any Directive Principle shall be deemed to be void on the ground that it is inconsistent with takes away or abridges any of the stated Fundamental Rights. Thus, the basic philosophy of the Indian Constitution has been radically changed and the Directive Principles have assumed primacy over the Fundamental Rights. The Fundamental Rights of the individual have been made subservient to the rights of society as enumerated in the Chapter on the Directive Principles of State Policy. Most important democratic rights like Right to Equality and Right to Freedom are also surrendered at the altar of this changed philosophy. This is likely to result in legislative in roads into the most important Fundamental Rights and may consequently lead to the destruction of the basic structure of the Constitution. This is definitely antagonistic to the philosophy of the original framers of the Constitution who conceived these two categories of rights as complimentary to each other and in reality both were visualised to serve the interest of the people. There is no basic incompatibility between the two. The Supreme Court has rightly observed. A harmonious interpretation has to be placed upon the Constitution, and so interpreted, it means that the State should certainly implement the Directive Principles, but it must do so in such a way that its laws do not take away or abridge the Fundamental Rights, for otherwise the protecting provisions of chapter III will be a mere heap of sand".

❐

3

Constitution and Amendments

It is impossible to think of a country without a constitution of some kind. The constitution of a country may be enacted or it may be largely based upon conventions. The Constitution of the U.S.A. is an example of an enacted constitution, whereas the British Constitution is mostly grounded in conventions. A constitution indicates the pattern of the state. It binds the ruler and the ruled and makes possible the proper adjustment of the power-relationship. The Americans for the first time realised the importance of the constitution. But in the 19th century when constitutionalism became the main basis of democracy, the framing of a constitution for the sound governance of a country was felt obligatory. The importance of a constitution may be explained in the words of Jellink: "A state without a constitution would not be a state but a regime of anarchy".

It was precisely this consideration which was uppermost in the minds of the national leaders of India. They wanted to give India the best possible constitution. They did not start with a clean state. The constitutions of the different States were there as guidelines. It was a question of selection and assimilation. The Constituent Assembly took inordinate time in drafting and adopting the Constitution. The salient features of the Constitution are discussed below:

Impact of the Government of India, Act 1935. The new Constitution of India, which came into force on 26 January, 1950, does not make a complete or an abrupt break with the past. It has derived many features from the Government of India Act of 1935. Important features of the new Constitution like the Constitution of the executive, the legislature and the judiciary and their mutual relations have been derived from the Act of 1935. Its federal characteristic has been taken from the Government of India Act, 1935. According to some writers on the Indian Constitution the whole of the existing administrative set-up of the country has been accepted by the new Constitution from the Act of 1935, either expressly or by implication.

Influence of other Constitutions. Besides the influence of the Act of 1935, the Constitutions of other foreign countries have also influenced the Indian Constitution. The framers of our Constitution have borrowed many importance features, like parliamentary democracy, rule of law, bicameralism and privileges of the legislature from the British Constitutional system.

The Indian Constitution has also been influenced by the American Constitution. The federal scheme, the fundamental rights and the concept of Judicial review have been borrowed from the Constitution of the U.S.A. But as far as the federal scheme is concerned, the influence of the Canadian Constitution is greater than the American Constitution. Like the Canadian federation, we have a strong centre in India, and the distribution of powers and the advisory jurisdiction of the Supreme Court are mainly due to Canadian influence. Like the Canadian Constitution, in India the residuary powers are also vested in the Central Government. The provision for the joint sitting of the two Houses and the provision of Concurrent List are taken from the Australian Constitution. The makers of our Constitution have borrowed the provision of Directive Principles of State Policy from the Irish Constitution. We have accepted the Emergency Provisions of our Constitution from the Weimar Constitution of Germany. The method followed for the amendment of the Indian Constitution resembles that of South Africa. It is also note-worthy that the important principles of the French Revolution have been incorporated in the preamble to our Constitution.

The Preamble of the Constitution. Strictly speaking, the preamble does not form a part of the constitution. But every constitution begins with a preamble. It embodies the spirit of the constitution and speaks about the goals that are to be followed by the state in the course of its governance. A constitution of a country is not an end in itself, but a means for the attainment of higher ideals. The constitution of India reflects the ideals and aspirations of the people towards freedom and a better life for the common man.

Significantly enough, the preamble to the Indian Constitution embodies all the main principles of the Resolution on Aims and objectives adopted by the Constituent Assembly on the motion of Pandit Jawharlal Nehru on January. 25 1947. It reads:

WE THE PEOPLE OF INDIA, having solemnly resolved the constitute India into a Sovereign, Socialist, Secular, Democratic Republic and to secure to all its citizens;

JUSTICE, social, economic and political;

LIBERTY of thought, expression, belief, faith and worship;

EQUALITY of status and of opportunity; and to promote among them all;

FRATERNITY assuring the dignity of the individual and the unity and integrity of the Nations;

IN OUR CONSTITUENT ASSEMBLY this twenty-sixth day of November 1949, do hereby Adopt, Enact And Give Ourselves This Constitution".

The preamble proclaims India as a sovereign democratic republic. It proclaims the supremacy of Indian people by attributing ultimate power to them. The constitution has been proclaimed in the name of the people which indicates that it is not an alien or imposed constitution and it has been derived from the authority of the people. The preamble specially mentions that the people of India shall be provided social, economic and political justice; equality of status and opportunity; equality before law and freedom of thought, expression, belief fatih, worship, vocation, association and action. Now emphasis has been placed on the secular and socialistic basis of our constitution.

India is proclaimed in the preamble as a sovereign democratic republic, India is free from the control of any other power in her internal and external affairs. She is free to follow an independent foreign policy and any internal policy that she thinks desirable for promoting the general interest of the people. India is a full member of the U.N. and enjoys full international personality, like the other sovereign states, in the comity of Nations. The Government of India enjoys supreme powers over all individuals and associations within the territory of the country. The preamble emphasises the democratic character of our constitution.

India has followed parliamentary democracy as its form of government. There is the provision of election at regular and fixed intervals, to ascertain the opinion of the people and to elect the representatives to the Parliament and the different state legislatures. The government derives its authority from the people. The executive is responsible to the legislature and through it to the people of India. The constitution also guarantees several fundamental rights to the citizens. It is proclaimed as a secular and socialistic state.

The preamble refers to the republican form of government it means that no monarch or king can be the head of India. The head of the state must be either indirectly or directly elected. He cannot come to office through hereditary or selective method. The Indian Constitution provides for indirect election of the President.

It is pointed out by some critics that India's membership of the Commonwealth of Nations is incompatible with her sovereign status. But this criticism appears to be incorrect. The Commonwealth of Nations is a voluntary organisation of sovereign states based upon perfect equality and friendship. The decisions of the Commonwealth Conferences are not binding upon any country. Any country can withdraw its membership from the Commonwealth of Nations at any time. No country can be compelled to join a war or to sign a treaty or alliance against her will. Thus India's membership of the Commonwealth does not in any way take away its sovereign status. The British Government or the British Parliament have absolutely no control whatsoever on the internal and external affairs of India. On more than one occasion India has made bitter criticism of the British colonial policy.

The Preamble of the Indian Constitution guarantees democracy both as a form of government and as a way of life. The people of India exercise their sovereignty through the elected Parliament. In our Constitution we do not have the provisions like referendum, the initiative and the recall which are the means of direct control by the people over the government. But there is the provision of election at fixed interval and the supreme power vests with the people to choose their own government.

The Preamble refers to political justice, which is closely connected with the system of a democratic republic. In India there is complete equality between the sexes before the law and in the political sphere. Moreover, India has adopted the system of universal adult franchise. By this every citizen of India is enabled to effectively participate in the democratic process of the country. The principle of one man, one vote stands for the equality of all irrespective of the considerations of Caste, Creed, Colour or Sex.

Social justice as guaranteed by the Preamble implies that in the matter of appointment or employment under the state, no discrimination shall be made between one citizen and another merely on the ground of religion, race, caste, sex or place of birth. No citizen shall be deprived of access to any public place or of the enjoyment of any public amenity or privilege. In the context of the tyranny of caste system and the scourge of untouchability, the concept of social justice as enshrined in the Preamble is highly laudable.

But political and social democracy are meaningless if they do not aim at achieving economic democracy or distributive justice. Pandit Jawharlal Nehru rightly observed, "Democracy has been spoken of chiefly in the past as political democracy, roughly represented by every person having a vote. But a vote by itself does not represent very much to a person who is down and out, to a person, let us say, who is starving or hungry. Political democracy, by itself is not enough except that it may be used to obtain a gradually increasing measure of economic democracy, equality, the spread of the good things of life to others and removal of gross inequalities".

The citizens of India have been guaranteed by the Preamble, "liberty of thought, expression, belief, faith and worship". These liberties are essential in a democratic system for the fullest development of the personality of the individual. These human rights are elaborately mentioned in Chapter III of the Constitution in the form of Fundamental Rights.

In the Preamble there is also reference to fraternal concord or mutual fellowship among all section of people, which is very vital for a democratic society. The ideas of liberty, equality and farternity are the three cardinal principles incorporated in the Preamble.

The dignity of the individual is also very important in a democracy. There must be respect for the personality of the individual which is the perennial fountain of inspiration for a democratic society.

In addition to these cardinal principles of the Preamble unity of the nation is a goal of the utmost importance. Unity and integrity of the nation must be kept above all other considerations. A strong sense of nationalism has to be promoted among the people.

Terms like "Secular" and "Socialist" which were introduced by the 42nd Amendment of the Constitution have tried to make these values enshrined in the Constitution more explicitly.

A Detailed Constitution. India has the lengthiest and most comprehensive written constitution in the whole world. It consists of 395 Articles and 9 Schedules and is about seven times the size of the Constitution of the U.S.A. So many factors have contributed to the bulky size of the Indian Constitution. The framers of the Indian Constitution have followed in to most of the provisions of the government of India Act, 1935, which was the lengthiest statute ever passed by the British Parliament. In addition to this factor the founding fathers of the Indian Constitution were trying to provide for a democratic Constitution for a country, which did not have specific democratic traditions. They, therefore did not like to leave anything to chance and speculation and put everything in writing. The Indian Constitution contains detailed provisions not only relating to the Union Government but also to the Government of the States, Fundamental Rights. Directive Principles of State Policy, the different Services, the Supreme Court and the High Courts, Emergency Provisions, official language and provisions relating to the Scheduled Castes and Scheduled Tribes etc. It defines the organisation and functions of the three principal organs of the State, namely, the Executive, the Legislature and the Judiciary. It provides for the division of powers into three detailed lists, such as, the Union List, the State List and the Concurrent List. It contains provisions concerning relations between the Union and the States, finance, property, contracts and suits, trade and intercourse within the territory of India. All these factors have been responsible to make the Indian Constitution very lengthy.

Balance between Rigidity and Flexibility. The Indian Constitution maintains a balance between rigidity and flexibility. Technically speaking a constitution is called flexible when there is no difference between the constitutional and the ordinary laws of the land and the laws of the Constitution can be amended by the Legislature through the ordinary legislative procedure. The British Constitution is the most glaring example of a flexible constitution. On the other hand, under a rigid constitution, the constitutional laws are declared superior to the ordinary laws of the land and for amending the provisions of the constitution a difficult and a cumbersome procedure is followed. A rigid constitution is amendable only either by the joint action of the federal and state legislatures or by an independent third authority. In a federal system of government there must be a rigid constitution.

The Constitution of India is both rigid and flexible because it contains both rigid and flexible features. It is flexible in comparison to the American Constitution which is extremely rigid. But it is rigid when compared with the British Constitution, as the process of amendment as regards certain features in the Indian Constitution is difficult.

There are three procedures for the amendment of the Indian Constitution: *(1)* A large number of provisions can be amended by the Union Parliament by a simple majority of the members present and voting in each House. This method of amendment is used for the reorganisation of the existing states, the creation of new state, the creation or abolition of upper chambers in the states, citizenship etc. *(2)* A Bill containing the provisions of amendment may be passed by the Union Parliament by a two-thirds majority of the members present and voting as well as by the absolute majority of the total membership of each House and also ratified by at least the legislatures of half of the states. This process of amendment relates to the election of the President, the Supreme Court, division of powers between the Union and States etc. *(3)* Several other provision can be amended by two-thirds majority of the members present and voting as an absolute majority of the total membership of each House.

A Federal Polity with a Strong Centre. To counteract the fissiparous tendencies in India the framers of the Constitution provided for a strong central government. The unitary bias is evident from the fact that framers of the Constitution have used the term "union" and not the term "federal". In the words of Prof. D.N. Banerjee, "India's Constitution is federal in form with a pronounced unitrary bias". The Indian Constitution provides for a unitary state with subsidiary federal features rather than a federal state with subsidiary unitary features. The framers of the Indian Constitution have followed the Canadian model rather than the American model of federation. India may be said to be federation with a very powerful Centre. The process of formation being from unitary to federal—from centralisation to decentralisation. A strong centre has been deliberately created to give more stress on the unity of the country and also to avoid the disintegrating tendencies which were responsible for the long subjugation of India to foreign rule. Though the normal federal features, *viz. (a)* supremacy of the Constitution, *(b)* division of powers between the federal government and the component units, and *(c)* an independent and impartial judiciary are present in India, yet the supremacy of the Centre over the States has made it more unitary than federal.

There has been a great controversy among political scientists as to whether India has a truly federal polity or not. Professor K.C. Wheare describes the Indian Constitution in the following words: "It establishes, indeed, a system of government which is at most quasi-federal, almost devolutionary in character; a unitary state with subsidiary federal features rather than a federal state with subsidiary unitary features". Some Indian writers object to the use of the phrase "quasi-federal" in the context of the Indian Constitution. It may be remarked that the observations of K.C. Wheare contain partial truth. It is also futile to quarrel over the nomenclature. At the same time we have to keep in mind that federalism is a relative and dynamic concept and it is futile to search for a universal pattern of federalism applicable to all countries or circumstances.

Parliamentary Democracy with an Elected President. India has followed parliamentary democracy and as such the Constitution provides for a parliamentary executive. There is dual executive in India, *viz.* the *de jure* and the *de facto*. The President of India is the nominal or the *de jure* executive and the Council of Ministers is the *de facto* or real executive. All the powers are exercised by the Council of Ministers in the name of the President. The President is the head of the state but not the head of the executive. The executive is headed by the Prime Minister. The President is the Constitutional head of the state like the British Monarch. The Indian Constitution provides for the indirect election of the President by an electoral college consisting of the elected members of the Parliament and the State Legislative Assemblies. The President acts upon the aid and advise of the Council of Ministers. After every general elections the leader of the majority party in the Parliament is called by the President to form the government. The President has no discretion in this matter. However, if no single political party comes with majority, the President might have to play an effective role in the formation of the government. The Parliamentary system of government is also followed in the provincial sphere. The Governor, who is the constitutional head of the State, is appointed by the President and is accountable to him He holds his office during the pleasure of the President. Just as at the centre the real powers are vested in the Prime Minister and the Council of Ministers, so also in the provincial sphere the real powers are vested in the Chief Minister and the Council of Ministers. As long as the Governor acts as the constitutional head of the state he is expected to act upon the advice of the Council of Ministers.

A Secular State. The Preamble of the Constitution makes a specific mention about the establishment of a secular state, and the spirit of the constitution is very clear. It seeks to establish a secular state. In the provision of fundamental rights it is made amply clear that all the citizen of India shall enjoy equal rights irrespective of caste, creed, colour or religion. The state maintains perfect neutrality in the matters of faith and religion. It does not take any interest in the propagation of a particular religion. In India, educational institutions, are prohibited from imparting religious instructions if they are wholly or partly subsidised from state funds. According to Article 15, discrimination against any citizen on ground of his religion in matters of public employments and offices, or access to places of public resort, is forbidden India has no official religion, nor can it endow or establish any official religion. Secularism of the state, however, cannot desist the state from regulating any economic, political or other secular activity connected with religion. It cannot prevent the state from taking steps for social welfare or religious reforms.

An Integrated Judiciary. The Indian Constitution provides for an independent and integrated judicial organisation. An independent judiciary is the sine-qua-non of a democratic state. Moreover, the federal structure of Indian has vested the judiciary with extra powers, as it has to interpret the constitution and decided the disputes arising under the constitution. The salary, method of appointment, removal, leave and allowances of the judges have been provided by the constitution to guarantee them the required independence and impartiality.

The Indian Constitution provides for a single integrated judicial system beginning from the top to the bottom. The Supreme Court of India is at the top and at the lowest level there are courts of the Munsif and the other judicial Magistrates. In every state there is a High Court and under the High Court there is the Court of the District and Sessions Judge.

The Supreme Court of India is free from the control of either the executive or legislature. It is empowered to decide the disputes between the Union and the States. The Supreme Court and the High Courts enjoy the powers of judicial review. If the laws passed by the union legislature or the state legislatures contravene the provisions of the Constitution, the Supreme Court can declare such laws as unconstitutional or ultravires.

Single Citizenship. The Indian Constitution provides for single citizenship. In India, wherever an individual might have been born, he is an Indian citizen. An Indian citizen can settle in any part of the country except Kashmir, and be engaged in any vocation according to his choice. The framers of the Constitution have provided for single citizenship to counteract against the fissiparous tendencies existing in the country. This emphasises the unity and integrity of the country and excludes the possibility of any discrimination by any particular state in favour of its own citizens. But in spite of this provision there are tendencies of regionalism and parochialism resulting in the dangerous concept of the "son of the soil". Steps should be taken to successfully check this development in India. In our country the Union Parliament has the exclusive powers to make laws relating to the acquisition and termination of citizenship. It can regulate citizenship by the ordinary process of legislation. No State has got the power to confer citizenship or to pass laws pertaining to conferment of citizenship on any individual.

AMENDMENT PROCEDURE OF THE INDIAN CONSTITUTION

A Constitution is the basic document which determines the fundamental relationship between the different organs of the Government, the nature of the executive, legislature and the judiciary and the relationship between the government and the judiciary and the relationship between the government and the governed. It may be wholly enacted or partly enacted and partly in the form of conventions. It may be one document or a number of documents consisting of the fundamental laws of the land. It is framed and adopted at a particular point of time and is bound to contain its own limitations. If it does not grow with the time and adapt itself to the changing circumstances and the needs of the people, it might be destroyed. A constitution, therefore, should have sufficient elbow-room for its growth. From this point of view, the procedure of amendment of the Constitution should not be unduly complicated and rigid. The framers of the Indian Constitution were conscious of this fact. At the same time, they were equally aware of the fact that too much flexibility of the Constitution, would make it a plaything of the whims and caprices of the ruling party. The framers of the Indian Constitution have tried to avoid extreme rigidity and extreme flexibility and have steered a middle course. In the words of Pandit Jawaharlal Nehru: "While we want this Constitution to be as solid and permanent as we can make it, there is no permanence in Constitution. There should be a certain flexibility. If you make anything rigid and permanent, you stop the nation's growth, of a living, vital organic people in any event, we could not make this Constitution so rigid that it cannot be adapted to changing conditions. When the world is in a period of transition, what we may do today may not be wholly applicable tomorrow".

Procedure for Amendment. There are three different methods for the amendment of the Indian Constitution. This has been done in accordance with the requirements of a federal Constitution, Each method has to be applied in connection with certain specific provisions. While some provisions of the Constitution can be easily amended, the others require a comparatively difficult procedure for their amendment. These methods of constitutional amendment may be analysed as follows:

(1) Article 368, of the Constitution provides for the amendment of the Constitution of India. According to the First provision of this Article the federal provisions of the Constitution can be amended when the bill for the constitutional amendment is passed in both the houses voting separately with *(a)* majority of the total membership of the house and *(b)* two-third of the members present and voting therein. This bill is then sent to the States and it should be approved by at least half of the State Legislatures, before be approved by at least half of the State Legislatures, before it is presented to the President for his assent. After getting the Presidential assent the constitutional amendments become a part and parcle of the Constitution. The proposal for constitutional amendment may be introduced in any house of the Indian Parliament and no specific majority has been prescribed for the introduction of the Bill for constitutional amendment. It may be mentioned that in respect of the federal provisions the States in India do not enjoy and initiative for introducing Constitutional amendments as is the practice in the

United States of America. However, for the amendment of the federal provision, consent of at least half of the State Legislatures is required.

This method of amendment is applied for the amendment of the following provisions of the Constitution:

(i) Election of the President (Articles 54 and 55).

(ii) The extent of the executive authority of the Union and States (Article 73 and 162 respectively).

(iii) Union Judiciary (Chapter V of Part-VI).

(iv) The High Courts in the States (Article-241).

(v) The Legislative Lists.

(vi) Representation of States in the Parliament.

(vii) Procedure of Amendment (Article-368).

(2) The second method of amendment is comparatively easier. A Bill for constitutional amendment has to be passed by two-third majority of the members present and voting as well as by the total membership of the house. Then it is sent to the other house where it is to be passed by a similar method. After the consent of the President this amendment Bill is considered to have been passed. Most of the provisions of the Constitution including Part-Ill and Part-IV dealing with Fundamental Rights and Directive Priniciple of State Policy, fall in this category.

(3) Besides, these two there is also a third method of amending the Constitution which makes it highly flexible. A large number of provision of the Constitution can be amended by both the houses of the Parliament by a simple majority of the members present and voting. As regards the amendment provisions of the Constitution falling in this category, Parliament may act at its own initiative or on the recommendation of some other agency. Forming of new States, increasing or decreasing the boundary or the area of any State, changing the name of any State, creating or abolishing the Legislative Council of any State fall in this category. Several Articles like 73(2), 75, 97, 100(3), 105(3), 106, 118(2), 120(2), 164(5), 221(2), 242(1) and 348(1) provide for their own alteration through the standard pattern of adding the proviso until Parliament otherwise provides".

Appraisal. The process of Amendment of Indian Constitution contains certain distinct features when compared to the other constitutions of the World. The Indian Constitution does not provide for any different body for amending the Constitution. The constituent-power is vested in the Parliament. The State Legislature do not enjoy any power for introducing Bills for constitutional amendment. There is no provision for initiative and referendum and the prior permission of the President is not required for the introduction of the constitutional amendment Bills. All provisions of the Indian Constitution are subject to amendment and the process of amendment as incorporated in Article 368, may itself be changed by amendment. Another distinguished feature of the Indian Constitution is that the ratification by the States in respect of the amendment of certain provisions is more liberal than the American Constitution. While the American Constitution requires ratification by not less than 3/4 of the States, the Indian Constitution provides for ratification by not less than half of the States.

The Indian Constitution is silent as to what is to be done when the two houses of the Parliament disagree over an amendment to the Constitution.

In the U.S.A the constitutional amendments passed by the requisite majority of the Congress and the State Legislatures or conventions are not even presented to the President for his assent. But in India, originally Article 368, laid down that after an Amendment Bill had been passed by Parliament, "it shall be presented to the President for his assent and upon such assent being given to the Bill, the Constitution shall stand amended in accordance with the terms of the Bill". Thus, it was not specifically mentioned whether it was obligatory on the part of the President to give his assent to the Amendment Bills duly passed by the Parliament. But the Constitution (Twenty-fourth Amendment) Act, 1971, categorically provided that, "It shall be presented to the President, who shall give his assent to the Bill, thereupon".

No time limit has been prescribed within which the State Legislatures, should either ratify or reject the Bill for constitutional amendment. The Bills may be killed by following a delaying tactics for an indefinite period, if different political parties, other than the party having majority at the Centre, have majority in the States. The sanctity of Fundamental Rights is lost as they are left entirely to the mercy of the Union or Parliament.

There is grave violation of the federal principles as vital provisions like creation of new states and the alteration of the boundaries of the existing States can be done by the ordinary process of law making and do not require the consent of the States.

The Parliament's right to amend any part of the Constitution was accepted by the Supreme Court until is decision in the Golaknath case. In this case the Supreme Court challenged the right of the Parliament to amend the Fundamental Rights in any manner it likes. However, this decision was reversed by the Court in the Kesavanand Bharati case. In this case it was held that the Parliament could amend any provision of the Constitution excepting the 'Basic features' of the Constitution. The Parliament passed the Twenty-Fourth Amendment Act, 1971 in order to assert that there was no limitations on the constituent powers of the Parliament, which had the power to amend, change or alter any part of the Constitution including the provisions mentioned in Part-Ill of the Constitution, namely Fundamental Rights. This was done by amending Article-13 and 368 to make it clear that the provision in Article-13(2), abridging or taking away any Fundamental Right was not applicable to constitutional amendments made in accordance with Article-368. Referring to Article-13, it was stated in this Amendment that, "Nothing in this Article shall apply to any amendment of this Constitution made under Article-368" originally the marginal heading of Article-368, was "Procedure for Amendment of the Constitution". This was substituted by the heading : "Power of Parliament to amend the Constitution" and the procedure therefor: "Notwithstanding anything in this Constitution, Parliament may in exercise of its constituent power, amend by way of addition, variation or repeal, any provision of this Constitution in accordance with the procedure laid down in this Article".

Article 368, was further amended by the Forty-Second Amendment Act, which declared that Parliament's power to amend the Constitution under Article 368, is without limits and this is not subject to the Court's power of judicial review.

Judging from the fact that the Indian Constitution, has so far been amended for fifty-six times, it can be said that, the fear of the critics like Dr. Ivor Jennings who thought that the Indian Constitution would prove to be too rigid for change has been belied. Rather the frequent amendments and the case with which have been made have subjected the Indian Constitution to the criticism of too much flexibility. Even the so called 'Basic features' have not been spared. Thus, it can be observed that the Constitution of India instead of being rigid is flexible enough to admit necessary amendments to the Constitution.

CONSTITUTIONAL AMENDMENTS

A brief analysis of the Constitutional Amendments is given below as evidence of the Adaptability of the Indian Constitution:

First Amendment, 1951. This Act Amended Article-19, of the original Constitution dealing with the provision of freedom of speech and expression. It provided that nothing shall prevent the State from imposing reasonable restrictions on speech, in the interest of the security of the State, friendly relations with foreign states, public order, decency or morality, or in relation to contempt of court or defamation or incitement to violence. The state is also empowered to make any special provision for the socially and educationally backward classes of citizens. By this amendment the State was also empowered to acquire private property, including industrial and business firms, for public purposes after payment of due compensation. This amendment was necessitated by the decisions of the Supreme Court in two cases, namely, Ramesh Thapar V. State of Madras, 1950 and Brij Bhushan V. State of Delhi, 1950.

Second Amendment, 1952. This amendment was required for readjusting the scale of representation in the House of People. Due to an increase in the population, the upper limit of representation was abolished. At present it is provided that there shall be not more than one member for every 5,00,000 people.

Third Amendment, 1954. This amendment placed food-stuffs, cattle fodder, raw cotton, raw jute, oil seeds and oil etc. in the concurrent list to enable the Central Government to have full control over industries producing or dealing with such commodities.

Fourth Amendment, 1955. This amendment was required for eradicating the defects of the first amendment with regard to the acquisition of private property by the State. It provided that in case of acquisition of private property by the State for public purpose, the quantum of compensation shall be decided by the State Legislatures or the Union Parliament. The amount of compensation in all such cases could not be subject of litigation in any court of law.

Fifth Amendment, 1955. The President was empowered by this amendment to fix a time limit for State Legislatures to express their views on proposed central legislations affecting the area and boundaries of the respective states.

Sixth Amendment, 1956. The Central Government was empowered by this amendment to levy taxes on all articles of inter-state trade with the exception of purchase and sale of newspapers. The income from these sources may be distributed among the states by the Union Government.

Seventh Amendment, 1956. 1. This amendment abolished the distinction between Parts A, B, C and D States and India was divided into fourteen (now twenty-two) states and six (now nine) Union Territories.

2. One Governor could be appointed for two or more states.

3. The maximum strength of Lok Sabha was raised to 520. Out of this number 500 were to represent States and not more than 20 were to represent Union Territories.

4. A common High Court could be set-up for two or more States.

5. The membership of the Legislative Assemblies should not exceed 500 and should not be less than 60.

6. Retired High Court Judges were allowed to practice in High Courts other than their own and also in the Supreme Court.

7. It was provided that children belonging to linguistic minorities should get adequate facilities to learn through their mother-tongue in the preliminary stage of education.

Eight Amendment, 1959. Article 334, was amended so as to extend the special provision in respect of the reservation of states for the Scheduled Castes and Scheduled Tribes and the representation of the Anglo-Indian community by nomination in the Lok Sabha and the State Legislative Assembly for a further period of ten years from January 26,1960.

Ninth Amendment, 1960. The first schedule to the Constitution was amended in order to give effect to the transfer of certain territories to Pakistan, in pursuance of the agreement between India and Pakistan in 1958.

Tenth Amendment, 1961. It integrated the areas of Dadra and Nagar Haveli (which were former Portuguese possessions) with India and provided for their administration under the regulation making powers of the President.

Eleventh Amendment, 1961. This amendment provided that the Election of the President and the Vice-President cannot be challenged on the ground of any vacancy in the appropriate electoral college. The provision of the joint sitting of both the Houses of Parliament for the election of the Vice-President was amended. It provided that the Vice-President would be elected by an electoral college consisting of the members of both the Houses of Parliament.

Twelfth Amendment, 1962. The Constitution was amended to include Goa, Daman and Diu, formerly Portuguese enclaves, among the Union Territories.

Thirteenth Amendment, 1962. It created a separate State of Nagaland within the Union in pursuance of an agreement between the Government of India and the Naga People's Convention.

Fourteenth Amendment, 1962. It provided for *(i)* the creation of Legislatures and Council of Ministers for Union Territories; *(ii)* The Conversion of Pondicherry, Karikal, Mahe and Taman (the former French possessions) into Union Territories; *(iii)* Constitution of another Union Territory for Goa, Daman and Diu with a separate legislature.

Fifteenth Amendment, 1963. By this amendment the age of retirement of High Court Judges was raised from 60 to 62 years. The President was empowered to determine the correct age of Supreme Court and High Court Judges in consultation with the Chief Justice of India in case of doubt. It also restricted the right of the civil servants to only one enquiry in case of departmental action.

Sixteenth Amendment, 1963. Article 19, of the Constitution was amended to enable the States to make Laws against secessionist activities. Politic parties were prohibited to make secession from India an election issue. It also provided that every candidate for membership of Parliament or of a State Legislature, Union and State Minister, M.Ps. and M.L.As., Judges of Supreme Court and High Courts and Comptroller and Auditor-General of India should take an oath to uphold the sovereignty and the territorial integrity of India.

Seventeenth Amendment, 1963. This controversial amendment was necessary to revalidate agrarian laws of various states. The Government was authorised to acquire the self-cultivated lands from the royats above the ceiling after payment of compensation.

Eighteenth Amendment, 1966. It enabled the bifurcation of the State of Punjab into Punjab and Hariyana and some parts of the erstwhile Punjab were merged into Himachal Pradesh.

Nineteenth Amendment, 1966. The power of Election Tribunal to hear cases of election malpratices was abolished and the High Courts were empowered to deal with such cases.

Twentieth Amendment, 1966. It validated the judgments decrees, orders and sentences passed by all District Judges in the State and also validated their appointments, postings and transfers.

Twenty-First Amendment, 1967. Sindhi has been included in the VIII Schedule as the 15th Indian Language.

Twenty-second Amendment, 1969. This Amendment Act was passed to enable the Parliament to adopt legislation to confer the status of an autonomous state on the hill districts of Assam within the State.

Twenty-third Amendment, 1969. By this Amendment Act, the reservation of seat for the Scheduled Castes, Scheduled Tribes and Anglo-Indians in the Parliament and the State Legislature was extended for a further period of ten years.

Twenty-Fourth Amendment, 1971. This Amendment was brought into effect with the purpose of vesting the Parliament with the power to amend the Fundamental Rights.

1. In Article 13, of the Constitution, after clause (3) the following clause (4) was inserted, namely: "Nothing in this Article shall apply to any amendment of this Constitution made under Article-368".

2. Article 368, was given a new title heading namely: "Power of Parliament to amend the Constitution and the procedure there for". The contention that Article 368, was only a procedural Article and did not vest the Parliament with the power to amend the Constitution was refuted by this new provision.

3. Clause (2), was added to Article 368, which declared the power of the Parliament to amend, repeal or abridge any provision of the Constitution, notwithstanding anything to the contrary.

4. It was made obligatory on the part of the President to give his assent to the Constitution Amendment Bills, duly passed.

Twenty-Fifth Amendment, 1971. By this amendment it was sought to remove the obstacles that had been placed by the Supreme Court through its rulings in the Bank Nationalisation Case and the Privy Purses Case. It gave absolute power to the Parliament to determine compensation for the property acquired for public purpose. Laws giving effect to policies of State towards securing the Directive Principles as embodied in Article-39, of the Constitution were kept outside purview of judicial review by declaring that such a law will not be invalid on the ground that it is inconsistent with or takes away or abridges any of the rights conferred by Article-14, Article-19 or Article-31, and no law containing a declaration that it is for giving effect to such policy shall be called in question in any court on the ground that it does not give effect to such policy. The provisions of this Article in its amendment form shall not apply to any law made by a State Legislature unless such law having been reserved for the consideration of the President, has received his assent.

Twenty-Sixth Amendment, 1971. Through this amendment the privileges and the privy purses enjoyed by the former rulers of Indian States were abolished.

Twenty Seventh Amendment, 1971. It sought to create a new Union Territory of Mizoram and provided for it a Legislature and a Council of Ministers.

Twenty Eighth Amendment, 1972. Article-314, which gave protection to the privileges and conditions of service of the I.C.S. Officers was deleted from the Constitution.

Twenty Ninth Amendment, 1972. Land Reform Acts passed by the Kerala Legislature in 1969 and 1971, and struck down by the Kerala High Court and the Supreme Court were validated by this amendment and these were included in the Ninth Schedule of the Constitution.

Thirtieth Amendment, 1972. Article 133, (1) of the Constitution provided that an appeal could lie to the Supreme Court from any judgment, decree or final order in a civil proceeding of a High Court in the territory of India, if the High Court certifies that the amount or value of the subject matter of the dispute in the court is not less than twenty thousand rupees (this was later on raised to one lakh of rupees). This valuation test was considered irrational by the Central Government as it discriminated between the rich and the poor. The provision that an appeal to the Supreme Court could lie, if the case involved some substantial question of law was also considered unsatisfactory.

Thus, the Article 133, of the Constitution for Clause (1), the following clause was substituted, namely:

"(1) An appeal shall lie to the Supreme Court from any judgment, decree or final order in civil proceeding of a High Court in the territory of India if the High Court certifies:

(a) that the case involves a substantial question of law of general importance; and

(b) that in the opinion of the High Court the said question needs to be decided by the Supreme Court".

Tirty First Amendment, 1973. It sought to increase the strength of the Lok Sabha from 525 to 545. The upper limit of state representation has been increased from 500 to 525 and that of Union Territories decreased from 25 to 20.

Thirty Second Amendment, 1974. It sought to stop the agitation of the Telengana people and some other areas of Andhra Pradesh by providing for equitable opportunities for the people of different areas in matters of admission to educational institutions and public employment.

Thirty Third Amendment, 1974. It sought to prevent the resignation of legislators under duress and coercion and gave the power to the Speakers to decide the genuineness of each case of resignation and to accept or reject it.

Thirty Fourth Amendment, 1974. This was sought to amend the Fifth Schedule of the Constitution. Originally this Schedule had only 13 entries. The entries 14—21 were added in 1951, and 22—64 in 1964. Two more entries were added later on. Now the number of those entries went upto 86 and 20 new entries were added by this amendment.

Thirty Fifth Amendment, 1974. By this amendment the "protectorate" status of Sikkim was abolished and the status of an "Associate state conferred on it. A new Schedule (10th) was added to the Constitution and the terms and conditions of association of Sikkim with the Union of India, were laid down.

Thirty Sixth Amendment, 1975. Sikkim was made the 22nd State of India and a Legislative Assembly was provided consisting of not less than thirty members. It was to have the same powers as the legislative assemblies of other states. Sikkim was allotted one seat in the Lok Sabha.

Thirty Seventh Amendment, 1975. By this amendment, in addition to Pondicherry and Mizoram a Legislative Assembly and a Council of Ministers was provided for Arunachal Pradesh. This was done by amending Article 239A, of the Constitution. As a result of this amendment the political aspirations of the people of this Union Territory were satisfied.

Thirty Eighth Amendment, 1975. Prime Minister Indira Gandhi promulgated internal emergency under Article 352, of the Constitution and during the period of emergency drastic and far-teaching changes were made in the Constitution by means of amendments.

The 38th amendment amended Articles 123, 213 and 239B, dealing with the power of the President, Governor and Administrator to promulgate ordinances and thereby sought to provide in the Constitution that the satisfaction of these officers shall be final and conclusive, and shall not be questioned in any court on any ground. Article 352, 356, and 360, dealing with the emergency provisions of the President were amended and the President was authorised to issue on different grounds whether or not there was a proclamation already in existence and in operation.

Thirty Ninth Amendment, 1975. By this amendment two new Articles (Articles 71 and 329A) were introduced in the Constitution and several Acts including the Representation of the Peoples Act, 1974, and the Election Laws (Amendment) Act, 1975, were put in the Ninth Schedule to keep them away from the purview of judicial review. The new Article 71, which replaced the old Article debarred the Supreme Court from hearing disputes concerning the elections of the President and the Vice-President. Parliament was empowered to pass laws regulating their elections, including the making of a provision for the decision of disputes relating to their election. The Article 329A, deprived the courts of their powers to try election petitions in which the election of the Prime Minister or the Speaker of the Lok Sabha is challenged. The Supreme Court declare clause (4) of Article 329A, as unconstitutional. It was the object of this clause to free the disputed elections of the Prime Minister and the Speaker to the Parliament from the restraints of all election laws. It declared such elections. Valid not withstanding any judgment of any court. Clause (5) of Article 329A, asked the Supreme Court to dispose of any appeal pending before it before the commencement of the 39th

Amendment Act, on the assumption that the judgement under appeal is void and that the election declared void by the judgement shall continue to be valid in all respects according to this new Article.

There was only one purpose of this amendment to save the election of the then Prime Minister, Mrs. Gandhi, which had been declared void by the Allahabad High Court.

Fortieth Amendment,1976. It sought to give protection to Article 318, of the Constitution and to 64 Central and State Laws by inserting them in the Ninth Schedule. The purpose of this amendment was to implement the Twenty-point Programme of Mrs. Indira Gandhi.

Forty First Amendment, 1976. Article 316(2), of the Constitution was amended and the age of retirement of the Chairman and Members of the State Public Service Commissions was raised from 60 to 62 years.

Forty Second Amendment, 1976. On the basis of the recommendations of the Swaran Singh Committee, appointed by the President of the Congress Party most extensive and detailed amendments of the Constitution were sought to be made by this amendment.

Besides amending the Preamble, Forty Articles and the Seventy Schedules, it also introduced 14 new Articles. As the relevant amendments are mentioned at appropriate places the only some major features of this amendment are given below:

(a) The Preamble is amended to include the words "Secular" and "Socialist" in the expression "Sovereign Democratic" Republic and to add words and integrity after the word unity in the expression 'Unit of the Nation'.

(b) Directive Principles are given precedence over Fundamental Rights.

(c) A new Part, Part IV-A, dealing with Fundamental Duties is inserged in the Constitution.

(d) It is explicitly stated that the advice given by the Council of Ministers shall be binding on the President.

(e) The duration of the House of the People and the State Legislative Assemblies was increased from five to six years.

(f) The Supreme Court alone could determine the validity of a Central Law.

(g) High Court's Writ jurisdiction was severely curtailed.

(h) Special tribunals are to set-up far administrative industrial and other specified matters.

(i) An Emergency could be proclaimed in respect of a part of the country.

(j) By amending Article 368, it was declared that the Parliament's power to amend the Constitution under this Article was without any limit.

Forty Third Amendment, 1977. This amendment was introduced by the Janata Party an 16th December, 1977. The Janata Party was of the opinion that the 42nd Amendment was unconstitutional and it deserved to be repealed, The 43rd Amendment was a 10 Clause Act and it sought to repeal Articles 31D, 32A, 313A, 144A, 226A and to amend Articles 145, 226, 228, and 366. The concept of anti-national activity as sneaked into the Constitution by Article 31D was sought to be deleted completely in order to restore the democratic content of the Constitution. The powers lost by the judiciary during the Emergency were restored back The Supreme Court regained its power to invalidate a State Law and High Courts got back the power to examine the validity of Central Laws.

Forty Fourth Amendment, 1978. Some of the main provisions of the 44th Amendment are given below:

(a) It took away the right to property from the category of Fundamental Rights and made it legal right which could be regulated by ordinary laws. However, Clause 34 sought to insert a new Article 300A in Part XII of the Constitution to provide that no person shall be deprived of his property save by authority of law.

(b) Article 22, dealing with preventive detention was amended. The maximum period far which a person may be detained without obtaining the opinion of the Advisory Board was reduced from three months to two-months, The system of preventive detention without referring to any Advisory Board was abolished.

(c) Article 71, was amended and brought to its original form (as it was before the 39th Amendment) and gave the Jurisdiction to the Supreme Court to inquire into all doubts and disputes arising out of or in connection with the election of the President or Vice-President.

(d) The term of the Lok Sabha and the State Legislative Assemblies were again reduced from six to five years with necessary saving provisions.

(e) It provided that decisions on questions as to disqualification of Members of Parliament and State Legislatures shall be in accordance with the opinion of the Election Commission. It thus restored the position as it obtained prior to the 42nd Amendment of the Constitution.

(f) Clause 21, of the new Amending Act provided for the amendment of Article 139A, that was inserted in the Constitution by the 42nd Amendment Act. The Supreme Court's power to grant Special Leave to case for appeal was to be exclusively regulated by Article 136, of the Constitution.

(g) Clause 30, provided for the amendment of Article 226. Article 226, was restored to its earlier position as it was prior to its amendment by the 42nd Constitution Amendment Act.

(h) Article 329A, which related to special provisions as to elections of Parliament in the case of Prime Minister and Speaker (as inserted by the 42nd Amendment Act) was deleted.

(i) Clause 38 of the 44th Amendment Act, sought to amend Article 352, relating to proclamation of Emergency to check the abuse of powers under this Article. The ground of internal disturbance was substituted by the ground of armed rebellion. It was also provided that the President shall not issue Proclamation of Emergency unless the decision of the Cabinet in favour of it had been communicated to him in writing. If further provided that a proclamation of Emergency would require to be approved within a period of one month (instead of two months as hitherto provided) by resolution of both House of Parliament, Clause (5) of Article 352, which was inserted into the Constitution by the 38th Amendment Act was deleted. By this provision the satisfaction of the President as to the existence of a grave emergency necessitating the issue of a Proclamation of Emergency was final.

(j) Article 356, was amended to specify that a Proclamation of Emergency under this Article can be made only after its approval by resolutions by both Houses of Parliament and shall continue for six months from the date of issue of the Proclamation. It can further continue for a period of six months upon its being approved by both Houses of the Parliament. This amendment restored the above provision to its original position and the duration of one year which had been inserted by the Forty-second Amendment Act was reduced to six months. The extension beyond the period of one year of this type of Emergency Proclamation could be possible only when a Proclamation of Emergency was in operation in whole of India or in whole or any part of the State or when the Election Commission certified that the continuance of the Proclamation was necessary on account of difficulties in holding General Elections to the Legislative Assembly of the State concerned.

(k) The amendment provided that Article 19, would become suspended only in the case of Proclamation of Emergency issued on the ground of war or external aggression and not in case of a Proclamation issued on the ground of armed rebellion.

(l) Clause 40, of the 44th Amendment Act sought to amend Article 359, relating to the suspension of the enforcement of the rights conferred by Part III of the Constitution during emergencies. It provided that the right to life and personal liberty under Article 21, could not be suspended.

(m) A new Article-361A, was inserted in the Constitution by Clause-42 of the 44th Amendment Act. Publication of the proceedings of the Parliament and State Legislatures were given constitutional protection.

(n) The Ninth Schedule of the Constitution was amended to omit Entry-87, [the Representation of the People Act, 1951 the Representation of the People (Amendment) Act, 1974 and the Election Law (Amendment) Act, 1975]. Entry-92 (the Maintenance of Internal Security Act, 1971) and Entry-130 (the Prevention of Publication of Objectionable Matter Act, 1976).

(o) Clause-45, sought to amend the Forty-second Amendment Act to the effect that its Sections 18, 19, 21, 22, 31, 32, 34, 35, 58 and 59 would be omitted from the Constitution.

Forty-Fifth Amendment, 1980. The constitutional provision for the reservation of seats in the Parliament and the State Legislatures for the Scheduled Caste and Scheduled Tribe Member was to lapse on 25th January, 1980. Mrs. Gandhi immediately after coming to power amended Articles-330 and 332, to extend the above mentioned reservations for a further period of ten years.

The provision for the nomination of Anglo-Indians to the Lok Sabha and certain State Assemblies was also extended for the same period of ten years.

The Fiftieth Amendment, was carried out in 1984 and authorised parliament to modify rights of person engaged in collection of intelligence and transmission and receipt of messages, etc.

The Fifty-Second Amendment, was carried out in 1985 to curb political defections. It specified the disqualifications in the Tenth Schedule which could lead to loss of membership by members of Parliament or State Legislatures.

The Fifty-Fourth Amendment, carried out in 1986 amended Part D of the Second Schedule of the Constitution and raised the salaries of Chief justice of India from Rs. 5,000 to Rs. 10,000; Supreme Court judges and Chief justices of High Courts, from Rs. 4,000 to Rs. 9,000 and High Court judges from Rs. 3,500 to Rs. 8,000.

The Fifty-Fifth Amendment, Act (1986) granted special powers to the Governor of Arunachal Pradesh and provided for a 30-member State Assembly for the State.

The Fifty-Sixth Amendment, carried out in May 1987, accorded the status of a State to the Goa district of the existing Union Territory of Goa, Daman and Diu and provided for a 40-member Legislative Assembly for the new State.

The Fifty-Seventh Amendment, was carried out in August 1987, it provided for reservation of seats for Scheduled tribes in Nagaland, Meghalaya, Mizoram and Arunchal Pradesh in Parliament and in the State Assemblies of Nagaland and Meghalaya.

The Fifty-Eighth Amendment, Act (1987) provided for an authoritative text of the Constitution in Hindi and asserted that the translation of this Constitution shall have the same meaning as the original Constitution thereof.

The Fifty-Ninth Amendment, carried out in March 1988, authorised the Government to proclaim Emergency in Punjab on grounds of internal disturbances. It also provided for the extension of President's Rule for a further of two years.

The Sixtieth Amendment, was carried out in December 1988. It increased the ceiling of profession tax from Rs. 250 per person per annum to Rs. 2500 per person per annum.

The Sixty-First Amendment, carried out in 1989, reduced the voting age from 21 years to 18 years for the Lok Sabha as well as for Assembly elections.

The Sixty-Second Amendment, Act (1989) extended the reservation of Scheduled Castes and Scheduled tribes in the Lok Sabha and the State Assemblies for a further period of 10 years beyond 1990, *viz.*, up to the year 2000. It also extended reservation for the Anglo-Indians in the Lok Sabha through nomination.

The Sixty-Third Amendment, Act (1990) repealed the 59th Constitutional Amendment under which the Government was empowered to impose Emergency in Punjab.

The Sixty-Fourth Amendment, Act (1990) sought to extend the President's Rule in Punjab by six months beyond May 11, 1990.

The Sixty-Fifth Amendment, Act (1990) accorded statutory status to the Commission for Scheduled Castes and Scheduled Tribes and designated it as the National Commission for the Scheduled Castes and Scheduled Tribes. The Commission is to consist of a chairperson, vice-chairperson and five other members appointed by the President.

The Sixty-Sixth Amendment, Act (1990) included 55 new land reform Acts, passed by various States, in the Ninth Schedule.

The Sixty-Seventh Amendment, Act (1990) extended President's Rule in Punjab for a further period of six months beyond November 11, 1990.

The Sixty-Eighth Amendment, Act (1991) inserted in the Constitution Articles 239-AA and 239-AB comprising special provisions with respect to Delhi, to the called National Capital Territory of Delhi, providing for a Legislative Assembly and Council of Ministers.

The Seventieth Amendment, Act (1992) amended Articles 54 and 368 to include members of the Legislative Assemblies of Delhi and Pondicherry in the electoral college (for presidential elections).

The Seventy-First Amendment, Act (1992) included Konkani, Manipuri and Neplese languages in the Eighth Schedule, thus raising the numbers of languages in that schedule from 15 to 18.

The Seventy-Second Amendment, Act (1992) related to inserting clause 3B in Article 332 with regard to reservation of seats for Scheduled Castes/Tribes in States' legislature.

The Seventy-Third Amendment, Act (1992) which got presidential assent on April 25, 1993 after ratification of the required number of States, provided constitutional guarantee for formation of Panchayats, inserted Part IX and the Eleventh Schedule in the Constitution.

The Seventy-Fourth Amendment, Act (1992) which got the President's assent on June 6, 1993 after ratification of the required number of States, inserted Part IX A containing Articles 243P to 243ZG, and the Twelfth Schedule. It provided for three types of Municipalities with devolution of powers and responsibilities by the State legislatures regarding levy of taxes and duties to be performed by them.

The Seventy-Fifth Amendment, Act (1994) made some changes regarding rent laws in Article 223B of the Constitution.

The Seventy-Sixth Amendment, Act (1994) sought to include the Tamil Nadu Reservation Act (providing for 69 per cent reservation for educational institutions and jobs in the State) in the Ninth Schedule, so that it will be outside judicial law.

The Seventy-Seventh Amendment, Act (1995) added a new clause 4(a) to Article 16 of the Constitution by which the State a authorised to make provisions for reservation in promotions in Government jobs in favour of scheduled Castes and Scheduled Tribes.

The Seventy-Eighth Amendment, Act (1995) placed 27 land reforms acts of various States under the Ninth Schedule of the Constitution. There are now 284 Acts included in this Schedule.

The Seventy-Ninth Amendment, Act (1999) extended the reservation for the Scheduled Castes and Scheduled Tribes and the representation of the Anglo-Indian community by nomination in the Lok Sabha and the State Assemblies to another ten years (i.e., till January 2010.)

The Eightieth Amendment, Act (2000) sought to carry out changes in tax distribution between Centre and States as per Articles 269, 270 and 272.

The Eighty-First Amendment, Act (2000) removed limitation of 50 per cent reservation on total reservation imposed by the

Supreme Court to enable the Government to fill the backlog in vacancies for Scheduled Castes and Scheduled Tribes.

The Eighty-Second Amendment, Act (2000) sought to ensure status quo in terms in relaxation of qualifying and standards of evaluation for Scheduled Castes and Scheduled Tribes in promotions both in Central and State Government services.

The Eighty-Third Amendment, Act (2000) related to Article 273D, sought exemption of the State of Arunachal Pradesh from reservation of seats for the Scheduled Castes in Panchayati Raj system in the State (as on Scheduled Caste population exists in Arunachal Pradesh).

The Eighty-Fourth Amendment, Act (2002) lifted the freeze on the delimitation of constituencies imposed by the 42nd Amendment and allowed delimitation within states on the basis of the 1991 census. However, the allocation of seats in Lok Sabha and State Assemblies have been frozen up to 2026.

The Eighty-Fifth Amendment, Act (2002) allows government employees belonging to the Scheduled Castes and the Scheduled Tribes (SCs/STs) to accelerated seniority consequent upon their elevation under the reservation rules with effect from June 1995. The amendment provides for "consequential seniority" to the SCs/STs for promotion in government service by virtue of the rule of reservation.

The Eighty-Sixth Amendment, Act (2002) made free and compulsory primary education a fundamental right. As per the amendment to Article 21 of the Constitution, the "Government shall provide free and compulsory education to all children from the age of six to 14 in such a manner as the State may by law determine..." The Act also seeks to compel parents to send their children to school by including it as a Fundamental Duty (Article 51A); and amends Article 45 of the Constitution to make the state "endeavour to provide early childhood care and education for all children until they complete six years of age."

❒

4

Structure and Process

THE PRESIDENT OF INDIA

Article 53(1), of the Constitution states: "The executive power of the Union shall be vested in the President and shall be exercised by him either directly or through officers subordinate to him in accordance with this Constitution." The Union Executive consists of the President, the Vice-President, the Prime Minister and the members of he Council of Ministers. The Indian Constitution provides for a parliamentary form of Government and therefore unlike the American President, the Indian President enjoys only nominal powers. The Government runs in his name and formally all works of the government are carried in the name of the President. But the real powers are vested in the Prime Minister and the Council of Ministers.

Eligibility for Election and Term of Office. The Constitution provides that to be eligible for election as President, a person must be a citizen of India, must have completed the age of 35 years, and must be eligible for election as a member of the Lok Sabha. A person who holds any office under the Government of India, or any State Government or any local authority subject to the control of these Governments, is not eligible for election as President. However, a person will not be deemed to hold any office of profit, for the purpose of this provision, if he is the President or the Vice-President of the Union or the Governor of any State or is a Minister of any State or the Union.

The term of office of the President is for five years. He is entitled for re-election. However, there is the tendency towards the development of a convention that no President shall continue in office for a third term. The President cannot hold any other office of profit.

If a member of Parliament or a State Legislature is elected as President, his seat will be deemed to have been vacated and fresh election will be held to fill-up that vacancy. The President may resign from his office by writing under his hand to the Vice-President of India.

Emoluments and Privileges. The Parliament has recently enhanced the salary from Rs. 10,000 to Rs. 15,000 per month and the pension has been enhanced to Rs. 30,000 a year, after retirement.

The Constitution grants certain privileges to the President. He is not answerable to any court for the exercise of the powers, functions and duties of his office. No criminal proceeding can be initiated against the President. He cannot be arrested or imprisoned during the term of his office. A prior notice of at least two months has to be issued in order to start a civil suit against the President.

Election of the President. The Indian President is indirectly elected through an electoral college consisting of, *(a)* the elected members of both the Houses or Parliament, and *(b)* elected members of the Legislative Assemblies of the States. The election of the President will be by the method of proportional representation and single transferable vote and the voting is by secret ballot.

The indirect election of the President was opposed by some members of the Constituent Assembly. The advocated for the direct election of the President by the people, because it would be more democratic. The President would be in a position to check the autocratic powers of the Cabinet. But this was not accepted. In a parliamentary set-up like India's there is no necessity of a powerful President like the President of the U.S.A. The President of India will act as the constitutional head and a direct election for electing the 'figure head' of the State was considered superfluous. Moreover, the huge size of the electorate would be too unwieldy and put great strains on the administrative machinery. A President directly elected by the people would become powerful and this would be incompatible with the parliamentary system of government followed in India. While justifying the provision of the indirect election of the President.

Procedure of the Election. The President is elected by a complicated method. The votes of the different-members of the electoral college differ in value. The value of the vote of a particular member is determined by the proportionate size of the population by represents. The value of the vote of a member is determined by the following formula:

(1) The number of votes which each elected members of the Legislative Assembly of a State has	Population of the State × 100 Total number of elected members of the State Legislative Assembly.
(2) The number of votes which each elected members of either House of Parliament has	Total number of votes assigned to members of all the Legislative Assemblies of the States Total number of elected members of both the House of Parliament.

This procedure, as determined by the above formula secures uniformity among the States inter se and maintains parity between the Union and the States as a whole in their influence over the presidential election. As far as the States are concerned, due weightage is given to the population of the State. The second formula secures the parity between the votes of all the MLAs and the votes of the MPs. The MLAs of all the State put together represent the total population of India and so do the elected members of the two Houses of Parliament. It is, therefore justified that the two groups of electors should have equal voice in the election of the President. In determining the number of votes to be given to a member, fractions less than half in the final result are ignored, while those equal to or exceeding half count as one.

Polling for the Presidential election is held in Delhi and also in the different States capitals. Members of Legislative Assemblies vote in the premises of their respective Assemblies, whereas the MPs may vote either in Delhi or in their respective States. There is also the provision, for electors under preventive detentions, to vote by postal ballot for the Presidential (but not the Vice-Presidential) elections. After the polling, the ballot boxes are sealed and sent to the Returning Officer, at Delhi, for counting.

Impeachment Process. The Constitution provides for the impeachment of the President for the violation of the Constitution. The President may be removed from office by impeachment. The charge of impeachment may be preferred by either House of the Parliament, subject to at least 14 days written notice, signed by not less than one-fourth of its total members. But this must be passed in the form of a resolution by a majority of not less than two-third of the total membership of the House. These charges are to be investigated by House other than the one framing them. If after the investigation the charges are sustained by a majority of not less than two-thirds of the total membership of the House, it will have the effect of removing the President from his office forthwith.

An election to fill-up the vacancy of the President shall be held as soon as possible and in no case later than six months from the date of the occurrence of the vacancy. Till it is filled-up, the Vice-President acts as the President and if the Vice-President is not available for the purpose, then the Chief Justice of the Supreme Court shall act as the President.

Oath of Office. Every President and every acting President has to take an oath, as prescribed by the Constitution, before assuming his office. The President takes the oath to preserve, protect and defend the Constitution and the law of the country and devote himself to the service and well-being of the people of India. The Chief Justice of India and in his absence senior-most Judge of the Supreme Court available, administers the oath of office to the President.

POWERS OF THE PRESIDENT

The President as head of the State is entitled to exercise certain powers. The Public powers of the President can be broadly classified under five heads: *(a)* legislative powers, *(b)* executive powers, *(c)* financial powers, *(d)* judicial powers, and *(e)* emergency powers. These powers, excepting the emergency powers, are exercised by the President in the ordinary course of the administration of the country. He exercises the emergency powers during the abnormal situations of war, internal disorders, serious financial deficit or constitutional breakdown in a State in order to protect the country from the impending danger.

Legislative Powers. Even though the President is not a member of anyone House of the Union Parliament, he exercises several legislative powers. He has the power to nominate to the Rajya Sabha 12 members who have distinguished themselves in the field of arts, literature, science and social services etc., may nominate two Anglo-Indians to the House of the People (the Lok Sabha) if he thinks that the Anglo-Indian community is not properly represented in that House. He also decides about the disqualification of any member of either House, on the advice of the Election Commission. The President summons each House of Parliament to meet at such time and place as he thinks fit. But there should not be a gap of more than six months between its last sitting in one session and the date fixed for its first sitting in the next session. The President is empowered to prorogue the Houses or either House and to dissolve the Lok Sabha. He can call joint sittings of the two Houses to resolve their differences. The President can address both the Houses of Parliament assembled together or either House and can send messages to either House of the Parliament. At the commencement of the first session of each year and also at the commencement of the first session of the Lok Sabha, after every general election, the President shall address both Houses of Parliament assembled together and inform them the cause of summon.

As regards legislation, the prior recommendation or the sanction of the President is required for the introduction in the Parliament of certain bills, such as a bill to redistribute territory of States or alter their names, boundaries, or areas or a money bill. President's authorisation is necessary for the introduction of certain bills in State Legislature also, *e.g.*, a bill for the purpose of imposing certain restrictions on freedom of trade, commerce or intercourse within the State. All state bills, dealing with subjects of the Concurrent List, if in conflict with any Union law, are to be reserved by the concerned Governors for the assent of the President. State bills providing for the compulsory acquisition of property by the state or imposing certain specified taxes require the assent of the President. In the case of the specified kinds of bills of the states, the President's power to refuse assent is real and absolute.

All bills after having been passed by both the Houses of Parliament must be presented to the President for his assent. Bills become Acts only after receiving the assent of the President. He cannot return the bill to the Parliament for reconsideration. The President, now, is under a constitutional obligation to assent to it. The Constitutional amendment bills passed by the Parliament are also sent to the President for his assent. Whether such a bill could be voted by the President was subject to controversy. But the constitution's Twenty-fourth Amendment Act, 1971 has made it obligatory on the part of the President to give his consent.

The President, has the power to issue ordinances, to meet with certain exigencies, during the period when the Parliament is not in session. The ordinances have got the force of Acts passed by Parliament. All such ordinances must be laid before both Houses of Parliament when they meet in session and will have no validity at the expiration of six weeks from the date on which Parliament reassembled, unless withdrawn earlier. Ordinances can be withdrawn by the President or by resolutions passed by both Houses of Parliament disapproving them. Such ordinances must be within the legislative competence of the Union Parliament, otherwise they are void.

Executive Powers. The President is the chief executive head of the Indian Union. All the executive powers are vested in him and he shall exercise these powers either directly or through the officers subordinate to him. The entire administration of the Government of India is conducted in the President's name and all actions and decisions of the Union Government are, formally speaking, his.

The President as executive head enjoys vast powers of appointment. He appoints the leader of the majority party as the Prime Minister and according to the latter's advice, he appoints the other Ministers. He also appoints the Governors, Judges of the Supreme Court and High Courts, the Attorney-General, the Comptroller and Auditor-General, the Chairman and members of the Union Public Service Commission, the Election Commission, the Finance Commission, the Official Languages Commission and a number of other commissions.

The President is empowered to enter into treaties with foreign countries and to ratify them. He appoints the Indian Ambassadors and High Commissioners in the different foreign countries and receives the Ambassadors and High Commissioners accredited to India. The President has the Supreme Command of the defence forces of the country. Declaration of war and conclusion of peace treaty are to be made in the name of the President.

The President has the power of direction, co-ordination and control of certain functions in relation to State governments. He can issue directions to State governments for the unimpeded operation of the Union executive power and to ensure due compliance of the States with Union laws. Directions may be issued by the President to the State governments as regards the construction and maintenance of communications of national or military importance and for the protection of the railways. Functions relating to Union matters may be submitted by the President to the government of the States and their officers, with the consent of the states concerned. He has the power to appoint an interstate council in order to maintain good relations between the States and also between the States and the Union.

The Indian Constitution provides that every Union Territory shall be administered by the President acting through the administrator to be appointed by him.

Financial Powers. At the commencement of every financial year, the President shall cause to be laid before both the Houses of Parliament a statement of the estimated receipts and expenditures of the Government of India for the particular year. The various items of expenditure and income shall be separately shown in the annual financial statement. No demand for grant can be made except on the recommendation of the President. The President is also authorised to ask for additional or excess grants. The Contingency Fund of India is at his disposal and he can make advances out it to meet unforeseen expenditure pending its authorisation by Parliament.

Judicial Powers. The Indian President like other heads of State enjoys certain semi-judicial powers. He enjoys the power to grant pardons, remissions of punishment. He can also suspend remit or commute a sentence of any person convicted of an offence where the punishment or the sentence is by a Court Martial, and in all cases where the punishment is for an offence against any law relating to a matter to which the executive power of the Centre extends or where the punishment is a sentence of death.

EMERGENCY POWER

The Constitution confers wide powers upon the President to meet emergencies. It contemplated three kinds of emergencies, namely, *(1)* emergency arising out of war or internal disturbances or the threat of the same, *(2)* emergency arising out of the failure of constitutional machinery in the states, and *(3)* financial emergency.

Emergency Caused by War or Internal Disturbances. Article 352, of the Constitution provides that if the President is satisfied that the security of India or any part thereof is threatened by war or external aggression or internal disturbances, he may proclaim an emergency. Proclamation of emergency may also be issued in anticipation of war, external aggression or disturbance. Such a proclamation will have the following consequences:

(1) The federal constitution of India works as a unitary one.

(2) The Union Parliament will have unrestricted power of making laws for the whole of India or any part thereof and any state law which is in conflict with such laws will be void.

(3) The Union Government can give directions to any State Government regarding the exercise of the latter's executive powers.

(4) The distribution of revenues between the Union and the States may be modified by the order of the President. Such an order must be laid before the two Houses of Parliament.

(5) There is a temporary suspension of the citizen's Fundamental Right to Freedom (Art. 19).

(6) The Fundamental Right to constitutional remedies (Art. 32), may be suspended by the order of the President.

Emergency Caused by a Constitutional Crisis in a State. Article 356, provides that if the President on receipt of report from the Governor of a State or otherwise is satisfied that a situation has arisen in which the Government of a State cannot be carried on in accordance with the provisions of the Constitution or when it has failed to carry out a direction issued to it by the Union Government in respect of the administration of Union matters, he shall issue a proclamation of the failure of constitutional machinery in the State. The effect of such a proclamation will be as follows: -

(1) The President may assume to himself all or any of the functions of the Government of the State and all or any of the functions vested in or exercisable by the Governor of the State or any other authority, other than the State Legislature and High Court.

(2) He may transfer the powers of the State Legislature to the Union Parliament and may take any other incidental action.

(3) The Parliament, however, may confer the legislative powers of the State Legislative upon the President who may delegate it to any other authority he thinks fit.

(4) When the House of People is not in session, the President may authorise any expenditure from the Consolidated Fund of the State.

Emergency Caused by Financial Crisis. Article 360, states that if the President is satisfied that a situation has arisen where by the financial stability or the credit of India or of any part of the territory thereof is threatened, he may make a proclamation to that effect. Such a proclamation will have the following effects:

(1) The executive authority of the Union extends to the giving of necessary directions to any State to observe such canons of financial propriety as may be directed by the President.

(2) The President will have power to issue directions requiring the reduction of salaries and allowances of any class of persons in the service of the State or the Union, including the judges of the Supreme Court and the High Courts.

(3) After the money bills are passed by the State Legislatures, they may be reserved for the consideration of the President.

(4) The President may alter the allocation of revenue between the Union and the State.

All these three kinds of proclamations of emergency must be laid before each House of Parliament and will cease to operate at the expiration of two months, unless before the end of that period they have been approved by both Houses of Parliament. However, if the Lok Sabha is dissolved at the time of the issue of such a proclamation or during .the period of two months from the date of its issue, the proclamation continues to operate till 30 days after the re-assemble of the new Lok Sabha, provided that the Rajya Sabha has approved it within the prescribed time of two months. In accordance with the Forty-Second Amendment, proclamation of emergency for the failure of the constitutional machinery in the State, even if approved by the Parliament, shall continue for a period of one year from the date of approval, but Parliament has the power to further renew it by periods of one year upto a maximum period of three years. But no maximum time limit has been laid down for the two other kinds of proclamations of emergency. A proclamation of emergency may be revoked by a subsequent proclamation of the President.

Change in Emergency provisions introduced by the Forty-second Amendment Act, 1976:

Art. 352, is amended so as to enable the President to make a declaration of emergency in the country as a whole or any part thereof as may be specified in his proclamation. The President shall also have the power to revoke or very his declaration and with it he may make necessary modification in his orders issued earlier in this regard. The powers of the Parliament to ranke laws shall also extend to any state other than the States in which or in any part of which the proclamation of emergency is in operation if and insofar as the security of India or any part of the territory thereof is threatened by activities in or in relation to the part of the territory of India in which the proclamation of emergency is in operation. In Article 356, relating to the emergency in a State the words 'six months' shall be substituted by the words 'one year'. Art 357, is modified so as to mean that any law made by the Parliament in exercise of powers granted to it vide Art. 352, or Art. 356, continue inforce until altered or repealed or amended by a competent legislature or other authority.

Appraisal of Emergency Powers. The emergency powers of the Indian President evoked severe controversy. The defenders of these powers point out that there is no antithesis between the rights and the liberties of the people and the emergency powers, which are intended to safeguard the State against foreign aggression and other kinds of insecurity. The enjoyment of the rights and the liberties by the people can only be possible when the States is able to maintain its security. Thus, any sacrifice made by the people for this purpose would be justified. Moreover, the suspension of the Right to Constitutional Remedies, during the emergency, is only temporary and should not be considered as the permanent denial of this right.

The tone of criticism against the emergency powers of the Indian President is also equally vigorous. Prior to the Forty-second Amendment there was no specific provision in the Constitution that the President shall use these powers on the advice of the Cabinet. It was believed that a popular President, with ambitious designs and a large following in the army, of which incidentally he happens to be the head, may very well use the powers without any regard for the Cabinet and may establish himself as a dictator.

As emergency can be proclaimed in anticipation of its real occurrence, there is the possibility of a cooked up emergency to satisfy personal designs of power, either of the President or the Council of Ministers. The President is not bound to place the proclamation immediately before the Parliament. Thus, he would be in a position to strengthen himself by concentrating all powers in his hands, so that he will be able to wipe out all opposition to his authority or reduce the Parliament to abject submission.

The Constitution has not provided for any specific safeguards against the misuse or the abuse of the emergency powers of the President. As the Right to Constitutional Remedies is suspended during the time of emergency, even courts cannot enquire about the excess of authority during the period of emergency. Interference with the fundamental rights of the individual also cannot be challenged. Like the Governor-General under the Act of 1935, the President is all powerful during this period and he alone is competent to decide when the emergency has occurred and how his powers are to be exercised.

But the most controversial Forty-second Amendment Act has left no doubts regarding the powers and the position of the Indian President. It provides in very specific terms that the President is bound to act on the advice of the Council of Ministers in the exercise of his functions.

In spite of this fact, it may be emphasised that the Indian President was not intended to be a weak one like the French President under the Constitution, of the Third Republic or the Fourth Republic. The powers of the President in India will greatly depend upon his personality. How far he will be able to influence the decisions of the Government, will largely depend upon his own ability and experience, and the personal equation between him and his Prime Minister. But it can be said now without the fear of contradiction that the Forty-second Amendment of the Constitution has solved the controversy regarding the powers of the President for all times to come. He is now bound by the advice of the Council of Ministers.

THE VICE-PRESIDENT

On the pattern of the Constitution of U.S.A, the Indian Constitution also provides for the Vice-President. In America the term of office of the Vice-President is for four years and he succeeds to the Presidency if there is a vacancy in the office and remains as President for the unexpired term of his predecessor. But under the Indian Constitution there is no such provision of the Vice-President continuing for the unexpired period of the predecessor.

Election. The Vice-President of India is elected by the elected members of both Houses of Parliament by secret ballot on the basis of the system of proportional representation by means of the single transferable vote. The members of the State Legislatures do not participate in the election of Vice-President.

Qualification. To be eligible for election to the office of the Vice-President, *(a)* candidate must be a citizen of India, *(b)* must have completed the age of thirty-five years, *(c)* must be eligible for election as a member of the Rajya Sabha, and *(d)* must not hold any office of profit. In this connection provisions similar to those relating to the President apply.

Terms of Office. The Vice-President is elected a term of five years. He can voluntary resign from his office before the completion of his term of his office, by writing to the President under his hand. The Vice-President may also be removed from his office, if a resolution to that effect is passed by the Rajya Sabha by an absolute majority of its members and agreed to by the Lok Sabha. However, a resolution for this purpose can only be moved after fourteen days notice has been given to this effect. Thus, no impeachment is necessary to remove the Vice-President from his office before the end of his term.

Functions and Duties. The Vice-President is the ex-officio Chairman of the Rajya Sabha and in this respect he resembles the Vice-President of the United-States who also acts as the Chairman of the Senate. The Vice-President draws his salary as the. Chairman of the Rajya Sabha, because the Vice-President's office itself carries no salary. In the event of the occurrence of any vacancy in the office of the President by reason of his death, resignation or removal, or otherwise, the Vice-President shall act as President until the date on which a new President enters upon his office. This period must not exceed six months. While acting as President the Vice-President gets the salary, allowance etc., as may be fixed by Parliament by law, and he no longer performs the duties of the Chairman of the Rajya Sabha.

PRIME MINISTER AND COUNCIL OF MINISTERS

The Constituent Assembly came to the conclusion that the British system of government would be more suitable for our country in view of our familiarity with it. But one may feel surprise at the fact that while our Constitution has detailed provisions about many things, the principles of the cabinet system of government have been inexhaustively specified in articles 74, 75 and 78. It shows that while some essential features have been reduced to writing, many things have been left to the established conventions. Art. 74 says: "*(1)* There shall be a Council of Ministers with the Prime Minister at the head to aid and advise the President who shall, in the exercise of his functions, .act in accordance with such advice. Provided that the President may require the Council of Ministers to consider such advice, either generally or otherwise, and the President shall act in accordance with the advice tendered after such reconsideration. *(2)* The question whether any, and if so what, advice was tendered by Ministers to the President shall not be inquired into any court."

Then, Art. 75, says: "*(1)* The Prime Minister shall be appointed by the President and the other Ministers shall be appointed by the President on the advice of the Prime Minister. *(2)* The Ministers shall hold office during the pleasure of the President. *(3)* The Council of Ministers shall be collectively responsible to the House of People. *(4)* Before a Minister enters upon his office, the President shall administer to him the oaths of office and secrecy according to the forms set out for the purpose in the Third Schedule. *(5)* A Minister who for any period of six consecutive months is not a member of either House of Parliament shall at the expiration of that period cease to be a Minister. *(6)* The salaries and allowances of Ministers shall be such as Parliament may from time to time by law determine and, until Parliament so determines, shall be as specified in the Second Schedule."

Finally, Art 78, says: "It shall be the duty of the Prime Minister— *(a)* to communicate to the President all decision of the Council of Ministers relating to the administration of the affairs of the Union and proposals for legislation; *(b)* to furnish such information relating to the administration of the affairs of the Union and proposals for legislation as the President may call for, and *(c)* if the President so required, to submit for the consideration of the Council of Ministers any matter on which a decision has been taken by a Minister but which has not been considered by the Council."

Appointment of Prime Minister. We may well take note of the fact that the provisions of our Constitution in regard to the system of parliamentary government are sketchy. All possible situations have not been covered by the written words of the Constitution. Obviously, much has been left to the well-established conventions. The Prime Minister is the head of the Council of Ministers. He is pointed by the President by virtue of being the leader of the party having clear majority in the Lok Sabha. In case no party has absolute majority in the Lok Sabha, the President may invite the leader of the majority party to form the government. Nehru was appointed as the Prime Minister in 1952, 1957 and 1962 for being the leader of the Congress party having clear majority in the Lok Sabha. So was the case with Mrs. Gandhi who was the leader of the Corgress party after the General Elections of 1967, 1971 and 1980. Since the Congress (I) secured absolute majority in the elections of 1984, its leader (Rajiv Gandhi) was appointed as the Prime Minister.

In case no party is in cleat majority in the Lok Sabha, the President may study the situation and then invite the leader of the largest party banking upon the support of other parties so as to be in a position of majority in the Lok Sabha. In 1977, Morarji Desai was appointed as the Prime Minister, for the Janata Party had been able to establish its chum as the majority party. In 1989, this post was given to V.P. Singh of the Janata Dal as he could prove majority of the National Front (combination of Janata Dal, Congress (S), Telugu Desam, DMK and Assam Gana Parishad) supported from outside by the BJP and the two Communist Parties. The Janata Dal suffered a split in November 1990. A break-away wing under the leadership of Chandra Shekhar (called Janata Dal—Socialist) formed government with the support of Congress (I) led by Rajiv Gandhi. In case the Prime Minister resigns and there is a serious rift in the ranks of the majority party, the President may wait for some time and then on the be is of his own assessment may invite a leader to form the government who may prove his majority in the House and then run a 'stable government'. It happened in July 1979 when President Reddy invited Choudhary Charan Singh to form the government.

The appointment of Prime Minister pertains to the discretionary power of the President, but this discretion must be used with great caution so that his action does not invite the stigma of partisanship. It should not become a matter of public controversy. The President must wait and watch the situation very carefully and then take a decision that wins the confidence of the nation. After the death of Nehru in May, 1964 the President (Radhakrishnan) appointed Gulzarilal Nanda as the acting Prime Minister, but he invited Shastri to form the government after his name was cleared by the Congress Parliamentary Party. Similarly, in January 1966, he appointed Nanda as the acting Prime Minister after the death of Shastri and invited Indira Gandhi to form the government after her name was cleared by the CPP. But in August 1979, President Reddy did not invite Jagjivan Ram to form the government and instead dissolved the Lok Sabha on the advice of the outgoing Prime Minister (Charan Singh) and thereby faced the criticism of the leaders of the then Janata Party.

Functions and Position. The first and foremost function of the Prime Minister is the prepare the list of his ministers. He meets the President with this list and then the Council of Ministers is formed. Very important ministers are designated as Ministers of the Cabinet rank, others are called the Ministers of State, while ministers belonging to third rank are known as Deputy Ministers. It is one of the discretionary powers of the Prime Minister to designate a minister as Deputy Prime Minister as Nehru did for Sardar Patel and Indira Gandhi for Morarji Desai. In a very critical situation the Prime Minister may be forced to have two Deputy Prime Ministers. The Janata Prime Minister (Morarji Desaij had to keep Charan Singh and Jagjivan Rara as his Deputy Prime Ministers. V.P. Singh and Chandra Shekhar did it for Devi Lal. If we go by the facts, we may say that no Prime Minister desires to keep a Deputy Prime Minister until he/she is forced to do so by the compulsions of party politics. It is also one of the discretionary powers chief the Prime Ministers to keep some ministers of the fourth rank known as Parliamentary Secretaries. The President has hardly any say in the selection of the ministers. It is a different matter that a wise and sagacious President may gently advise the Prime Minister to include or not to exclude a particular name in his list of ministers. For instance, Prime Minister Nehru obliged President Prasad by keeping Jagjivan Ram in 1952, 1957 and 1962 and Prime Minister Indira Gandhi honoured the advice of

President Radhakrishnan in not omitting the name of Nanda in 1966. But Prime Minister Rajiv Gandhi did not like to drop K.K. Tewary so as to oblige President Zail Singh.

The President allocates portfolios among the Ministers on the advice of the Prime Minister. The Prime Minister may keep any department or departments under his control; he may also advise the President to reshuffle the portfolios of his ministers from time to time; he may bifurcate or trifurcate a department or have different departments amalgamated into one department. The Cabinet is the policy-making body and all ministers have to sink and swim together. In case a minister disagrees with the policy of the cabinet or with the views of the Prime Minister, he should resign. For instance, ministers like C.D. Deshmukh, Asoka Mehta and Morarji Desai resigned. It is also possible that the Prime Minister may ask a minister to resign or may advise the President to dismiss a member of his ministry. So Devi Lal was dismissed in August, 1990.

The decisions of the Cabinet are virtually the decisions of the Prime Minister. The proposals about appointments of persons to high posts, the determination of home and foreign policies of the government, preparation of budget and introduction of bills in the Parliament, summoning and proroguing the session of the Parliament, and a host of other decisions are taken by the Prime Minister in consultation with his close confidants having important position in the Council of Ministers. In short, in the words of Ramsay Muir, the Cabinet is the steering wheel of the ship of the state and the Prime Minister is its steersman. However, the astonishing feature of cabinet government in our country is that the Prime Minister has 'Presidentialised' his office. Once the Cabinet Secretariat and now the Prime Minister's Office (PMO) has become the real centre of power with the result that the phrase of Prime Minister's being first among equals has lost its significance.

Theoretically, the Prime Minister is *primus inter pares* (first among equals); in practice, the case is quite different. His pre-eminent position, like his Blitish counterpart, is evident from these facts:

State Structure in India

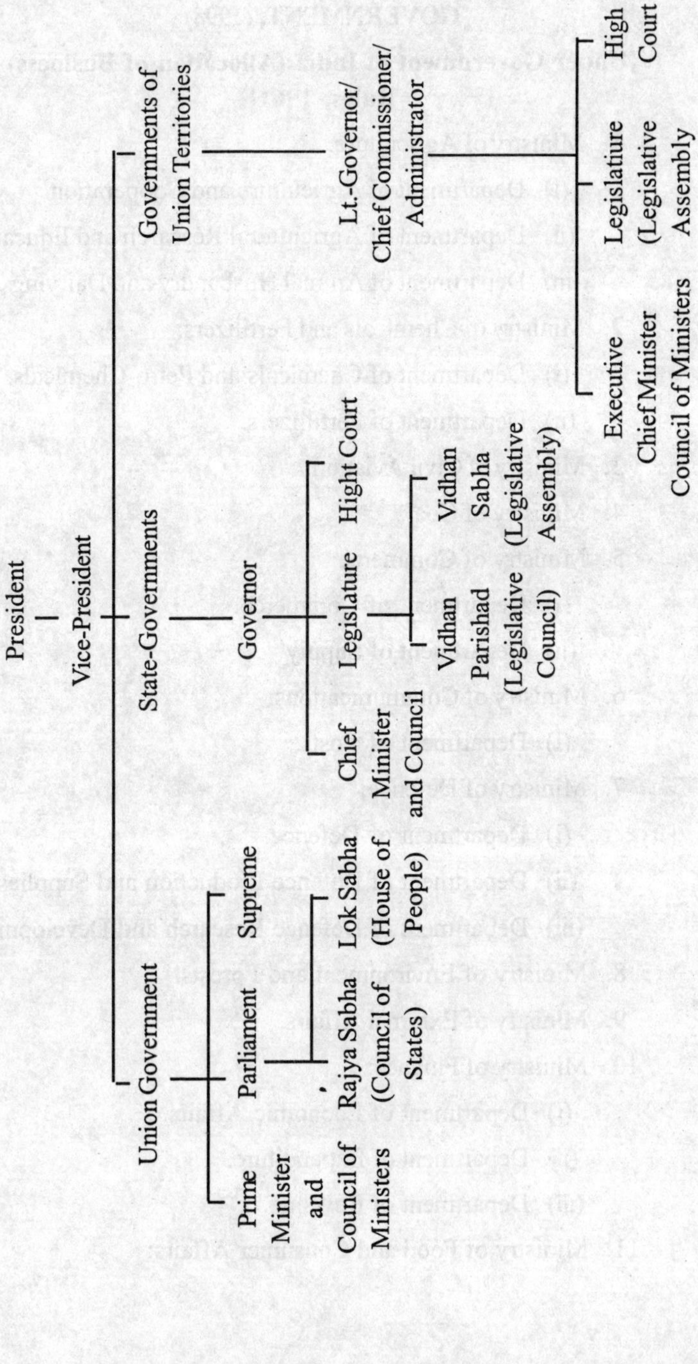

MINISTRIESDEPARTMENTS OF THE UNION GOVERNMENT, (1998)

[Under Government of India (Allocation of Business) Rules, 1961]

1. Ministry of Agriculture:
   - (i) Department of Agriculture and Cooperation.
   - (ii) Department of Agricultural Research and Education.
   - (iii) Department of Animal Husbandry and Dairying
2. Ministry of Chemicals and Fertilizers:
   - (i) Department of Chemicals and Petro-Chemicals.
   - (ii) Department of Fertillizers.
3. Ministry of Civil Aviation:
4. Ministry of Coal.
5. Ministry of Commerce:
   - (i) Department of Commerce.
   - (ii) Department of Supply
6. Ministry of Communications:
   - (i) Department of Posts.
7. Ministry of Defence:
   - (i) Department of Defence.
   - (ii) Department of Defence Production and Supplies.
   - (iii) Department of Defence Research and Development.
8. Ministry of Environment and Forests.
9. Ministry of External Affairs.
10. Ministry of Finance:
    - (i) Department of Economic Affairs.
    - (ii) Department of Expenditure.
    - (iii) Department of Revenue.
11. Ministry of Food and Consumer Affairs:

(i) Department of Food and Civil Supplies.

(ii) Department of Consumer Affairs.

(iii) Department of Sugar and Edible Oils.

12. Ministry of Food Processing Industries.

13. Ministry of Health and Family Welfare:

(i) Department of Health.

(ii) Department of Family Welfare.

(iii) Department of Indian Systems of Medicine and Homoeopathy.

14. Ministry of Home Affairs:

(i) Department of Internal Security.

(ii) Department of States.

(iii) Department of Official Language

(iv) Department of Home.

(v) Department of Jammu and Kashmir Affairs.

15. Ministry of Human Resource Development:

(i) Department of Education.

(ii) Department of Youth Affairs and Sports.

(iii) Department of Culture.

(iv) Department of Women and Child Development.

16. Ministry of Industry:

(i) Department of Industrial Development.

(ii) Department of Telecommunications.

(ii) Department of Public Enterprises.

(iii) Department of Heavy Industry.

(iv) Department of Small Scale Industries and Agro and Rural Industries.

(v) Department of Industrial Policy and Promotion.

17. Ministry of Information and Broadcasting.

18. Ministry of Labour.
19. Ministry of Law, Justice and Company Affairs:
    - (i) Department of Legal Affairs.
    - (ii) Legislative Department.
    - (iii) Department of Justice.
    - (iv) Department of company Affairs.
20. Ministry of Non-conventional Energy Sources.
21. Ministry of Parliamentary Affairs.
22. Ministry of Personnel, Public Grievances and Pensions:
    - (i) Department of Personnel and Training.
    - (ii) Department of Administrative Reforms and Public Grievances.
    - (iii) Department of Pensions and Pensioners' Welfare.
23. Ministry of Petroleum and Natural Gas.
24. Ministry of Planning and Programme Implementation:
    - (i) Department of Planning.
    - (ii) Department of Statistics.
    - (iii) Department of Programme Implementation.
25. Ministry of Power
26. Ministry of Railways
27. Ministry of Rural Areas and Employment:
    - (i) Department of Rural Development.
    - (ii) Department of Wastelands Development.
    - (iii) Department of Rural Employment and Poverty Alleviation.
28. Ministry of Science and Technology:
    - (i) Department of Science and Technology.
    - (ii) Department of Scientific and Industrial Research.
    - (iii) Department of Bio- Technology.

29. Ministry of Steel and Mines:
    (i) Department of Steel
30. Ministry of Surface Transport.
31. Ministry of Textiles.
32. Ministry of Tourism.
33. Ministry of Urban Affairs and Employment:
    (i) Department of Urban Development.
    (ii) Department of Urban Employment and Poverty Alleviation
34. Ministry of Water Resources.
35. Ministry of Social Justice and Employment:
    (i) Department of Urban Development.
    (ii) Department of Uraban Employment and Poverty Alleviation.
36. Ministry of Water Resources.
37. Ministry of Social Justice and Empowerment.
38. Department of Atomic Energy.
39. Department of Electronics.
40. Department of Ocean Development.
41. Department of Space.
42. Cabinet Secretariat.
43. President's Secretariat.
44. Prime Minister's Office.
45. Planning Commission.

"1. He is the leader of the party in majority in the popular House of the legislature.

2. He has the power of selecting other Ministers and also advising the President to dismiss any of them individually, or require any of them to resign. Virtually, the other Ministers hold office at the pleasure of the Prime Minister.

3. The allocation of business amongst the Ministers is a function of the Prime Minister. He can also transfer a Minister from one Department to another.
4. He is the Chairman of the Cabinet, summons its meetings and presides over them.
5. While the resignation of other Ministers merely creates a vacancy, the resignation or death of the Prime Minister dissolves the Cabinet.
6. The Prime Minister stands between the President and the Cabinet. Though individual Ministers have the right of access to the Crown on matters concerning their own Departments, any important communication, particularly relating to policy, can be made only through the Prime Minister.
7. He is in charge of coordinating the policy of the Government and has accordingly a fight of supervision over all the Departments.

In India all these special powers will belong to the Prime Minister in as much as the conventions relating to Cabinet Government are, in general, applicable."

Venkataraman's Refined Version of National Government. The elections held in 1989, for the first time, created a House in which no political party had clear majority. As such, it was given the nickname of a 'hung Parliament'. Since Rajiv Gandhi, the leader of the Congress (I) having largest number of seats in the House declined the offer of the President to form government, the chance was given to V.P. Singh, the leader of the Janata Dal having second position in respect of numerical strength. But this experiment of coalition government failed after 11 months and then a new coalition government under the leadership of Chandra Shekhar came into being that had a life of about seven months. This experiment had the same fate. The Lok Sabha was dissolved and after the general election held in June, 1991 Narsimha Rao of the Congress (I) formed the government by virtue of being the leader of the largest party. It was a minority government that could survive on the support of some other parties.

In course of time, it managed to muster clear majority and Rao, who was not a member of Parliament at the time of his appointment, could get the membership of the Lok Sabha after getting success in a by-election.

However, the spectre of a hung Parliament continued to survive. Hence, some leaders and intellectuals like Vasant Sathe and Nani A. Palkhivala preferred to switch over to the Presidential system as obtaining in America or to a peculiar combination of the Parliamentary and Presidential systems as prevailing in France. Atal Behari Vajpayee, the Leader of the Opposition in the House, came forward with a suggestion to follow the case of Iceland for the installation of a coalition government. He said: "We may have a Presidential system, or we have a constitutional sanction for the formation of coalition governments. If the largest party in the House fails to have a simple majority, as is the case with the Congress after the last General Election, the Constitution may have provisions for the formation of a coalition government, provided all those joining the government would account for two-thirds majority in the Lok Sabha. Of course, this kind of arrangement does not exist in any other country, but we have to devise an apparatus that meets our requirements. What is happening now clearly shows that accountability and stability of the government do not mix well in our political system. We have to devise another system, otherwise crises of the nature, which have erupted now, would go on jolting our political system every now and then."

Since former President R. Venkataraman had the unpleasant experience of such developments, he thought in terms of having a 'national government' or a government of all talents. After retirement he gave expression to his feelings. He could find out points of strength and weakness in both the Presidential and Parliamentary systems as prevailing in other countries of the world and sought to synthesise their merits after keeping in view the glorious traditions of our own country. In an address at Tirpati, on 22 April, 1995 he said: "Modern democracy is based on the rule by majority which means that 51 per cent rule to the exclusion of 49 per cent. It rests on confrontation between the Government and the Opposition. It excludes a large section of the nation from participation in the Government. It breeds jealously in the deprived and arrogance in the rulers. It leads to abuse of the Government machinery for strengthening the party in power. In mature democracies the 49 per cent is reconciled to bide its time till the next general election. In nascent democracies the destabilisation of the Government starts on the very next day after the formation of the Government."

Thus, the former President proposed to devise a system in which there would be adequate participation of all sections rather than the rule of the majority party. He hoped that such a system would replace confrontational politics by cooperative politics and a truly democratic alternative to the present Constitution. He made it clear that his scheme did not envisage total scrapping of the Indian Constitution which in his view was still good, but not good enough to ensure stability and acceptability of all sections. He, therefore, proposed a stable national executive as an alternative to the present form of parliamentary government in our country. His proposals are:

1. There shall be a President to be elected in the same manner as at present or otherwise. The Prime Minister shall be elected as soon as may be after a General Election or on the occurrence of a vacancy in that office by death, resignation or otherwise, by the Lok Sabha by means of the single transferable vote. The Prime Minister shall secure the support of more than 50 per cent of the members of the House, present and voting. The Prime Minister need not be a member of any House of Parliament at the time of his appointment, but he must be an elected member of any House within next six months.

2. The same provision shall apply to the members of the Council of Ministers. The strength of the ministry shall be fixed at 10 per cent of the strength of the Lok Sabha, but the strength of the ministers from the Rajya Sabha shall be anywhere between 25 and $33\frac{1}{3}$ of the strength of the House. The entire body shall be elected by means of single transferable vote in each House of Parliament as is now done in the case of Parliamentary Committees.

3. The Prime Minister and the Council of Ministers shall hold office for the term of Parliament and shall continue till the new Council is appointed in the manner given above. All decisions of the Council of Ministers shall be made by a majority of the members, present and voting. All the ministers shall be removed by a vote of no-confidence or on the failure of any of their proposals in Parliament. If a vacancy arises in the Council of Ministers, it shall be filled in a manner in which vacancies in Parliamentary Committees are filled at present.

4. The decision of the Parliament shall be binding on the Council of Ministers. The Council of Ministers may, however, return for "reconsideration a part or whole of the measure and the decision of the Parliament on such re-consideration shall be final and binding. The validity of the decisions of Parliament shall not be questioned except before the judicial authority competent to decide the same. Since the defeat of a Government measure would not cause its fall, the freedom to vote would cause no instability. As the Council of Ministers would be elected by the whole House, and not nominated by the ruling party, the anti-defection law would automatically be irrelevant.

5. The nation has to be protected against corruption and abuse by irreconcilable executive, namely the Council of Ministers. It is, therefore, necessary to provide for a constitutional authority at the Centre to handle such cases. The authority shall have the same immunity as the judges of the Supreme Court. It may be called 'Lokpal' and have jurisdiction over the Council of Ministers, including Prime Minister and other elected functionaries of the Government. A similar authority may be set-up to deal with the services. Likewise, the States should have a similar constitutional authority to deal with cases under this category. Venkataraman hoped that the net result of the implementation of such proposals would be stability of administration during the term of Parliament, cooperation of all parties in the administration and elimination of rancour and bitterness in the governance of the country.

No doubt, the above proposals have their own merit and the former President has applied his head and heart before presenting his bare outline as a national alternative to Party Government. But a critic may not accept such proposals in view of their impracticable nature. It may be said that a Prime Minister cannot function unless he is able to select and control his ministerial colleagues. If this is left to the Parliament, obviously the position of the Prime Minister would become very weak. If the above proposals be put into operation, it may be feared in advance that the Prime Minister would have colleagues who may not agree with him in policy matters and thus the administration would suffer. It would certainly lead to tensions and conflicts within the Council of Ministers. P.C. Alexander, the Governor of Maharashtra, is, therefore, right in his assertion: "In the last 70 years the Parliamentary form of government has become Prime Ministerial form of government. The key to the whole system is the Prime Minister. The Prime Minister would have the power to nominate and dismiss his colleagues. He should have confidence in his colleagues. They should be on the same wavelength on major issues, otherwise the Government will become weak and this will result in a weak Centre."

COUNCIL OF MINISTERS

The cabinet system of government as evolved in England is largely the product of conventions. The main principles of British cabinet system are followed in India. The Indian Constitution has not provided detailed and positive statutory measures regarding the cabinet system of government but certain constitutional conventions regarding the cabinet government have been incorporated in it. The important principles of cabinet government have been provided by Articles 74 and 75, of the Indian Constitution. Those are analysed below:

It is obligatory on the part of President to appoint a Council of Ministers with the Prime Ministers at its head to aid and advice him in discharging his constitutional functions. The President should not rule, even for a very short period, without the existence of the Council to Ministers. It is the duty of the Council of Ministers to advice the President on State matters. The President has only nominal executive powers and he has the powers to be informed, to advice and to warn the Council of Ministers. But the Council of Ministers is free to accept or reject the advice of the President. The Provision that no Court can enquire into the nature of advice given by the Council of Ministers to the President, emphasises the intimate and the confidential relationship between the President and his Council.

The Ministers hold office during the pleasure of the President. But as long as the Council of Ministers is supported by a majority in the Lok Sabha, the President, even if he is displeased with his Council, cannot dissolve it because that would precipitate a first class constitutional crisis. So in this case the pleasure of the President would be interpreted as enjoying the confidence of the Lok Sabha. The Council of Ministers shall be collectively responsible to the Lok Sabha.

An oath of office and of secrecy is administered by the President to each Minister before he enters upon his office. The Ministers must be members of either House of Parliament and if any of them is not a member of Parliament at the time of his appointment. He must became a member within a period of six months, failing which at the expiration of that period, he shall cease to be a minister. The salaries and the allowances of the Ministers shall be determined by Parliament from time to time. The dependence of the Minister on Parliament is stressed by their salaries being made votable by the Lok Sabha.

Formation of the Council of Ministers. The leader of the majority party in the Parliament is appointed by the President as Prime Minister. So the President's choice is restricted in the appointment of the Prime Minister. However, if on political party has clear majority, them the President may play some independent role in the selection of the Prime Minister and his influence in the composition of the Council of Ministers will be equally proportionate to his personality. The other Ministers are appointed by the President on the advice of the Prime Ministers. This gives the Council of Ministers its unity, and the Prime Minister his pre-position in the Council of Ministers.

It must be noted here that the Constitution does not mention the Cabinet, but only provides for a Council of Ministers, However, as the Council of Ministers is a very large body, it would have been too unwieldy for any serious discussions. Thus, there has developed a Cabinet consisting of the Prime Minister and the more important members of the Council of Ministers. The Council of Ministers is a large body consisting of the Prime Minister, the Cabinet Ministers, Ministers of State and the Deputy Ministers, But the Cabinet is a small body inside the Council of Ministers and consists of the members who hold important portfolios. Finally, to explain the difference between the Cabinet and the Council of Ministers, it may be said that while all members of the Cabinet are members of the Council of Ministers, all the members of the Council of Ministers are not necessarily members of the Cabinet.

Ministerial Responsibility. Ministerial responsibility is the fundamental principle of parliamentary government. The Ministers are collectively responsible to the Lok Sabha for their work. They will continue in office as long as they enjoy the support of the majority of members of the Lok Sabha. Secondly, the Ministers are responsible to the President and enjoy their office during his pleasure. As pointed out earlier, the pleasure of the President would mean the confidence of the Lok Sabha in the Council of Ministers. Finally, the Ministers are also responsible to each other. This is implied from the Principle of collective responsibility, which forms the core of parliamentary system of government. They should consult each other before taking any decision on an important matter and should not behave in manner which would embarrass their colleagues.

Powers and Functions of the Council of Ministers. The Constitution provides that there shall be a Council of Ministers to aid and advise the President in the exercise of his functions. But in practice, it is the Council of Ministers which does everything which the President is supposed to do under the Constitution. Thus the powers and functions which are attributed to the President are in reality the powers and functions of the Council of Ministers. The important functions of the Council of Ministers are discussed below:

(1) ***Policy Making.*** The Council of Ministers formulates the policy of the country for its political and economic administration. The Ministry also decides the foreign polity of the country. It is responsible to decide the policy of the state for the maintenance of internal peace and order and for increasing the standard of living of the people.

(2) ***Administration.*** The Ministry is solely responsible for the administration of the country. It is in accordance with the principles laid down by the Council of Ministers that the administration is run by the civil servants. But the ultimate responsibility is that of the Ministers. They are responsible to the Parliament for the work of the department entrusted to them. The members of the Parliament have the right to ask questions concerning the administration of the country, and in their own interest the Ministers are expected to give satisfactory replies.

(3) ***Legislative Functions.*** The Council of Ministers has a direct hand in the framing of the laws of the country. It determines the legislative programme of the Parliament. The Ministry is the main steering wheel of the Parliament and it introduces almost all the important Bills. Bills introduced by private members of the Parliament have little chance of passage without the support of the Ministry. After the Bill is passed by the Parliament it is sent to the President for his assent on getting which it becomes a law.

(4) ***Budget Preparation.*** The budget is also prepared and introduced in the Parliament by the Cabinet. The Finance Minister prepares the budget in consultation with the other Minister. After the introduction of the Budget in the Parliament, different Ministers present their respective demands. The Parliament is free either to accept or reject the demands. Rejection of the demand would tantamount to the lack of confidence in the Minister. But normally such a situation would never arise as the Government has the support of the majority in the Lok Sabha.

Secretariat of the Cabinet. The Cabinet has a Secretariat of its own. It consists of a Joint and two Deputy Secretaries, two Under Secretaries, one Assistant Secretary, five Staff Officers, four Superintendents, three Economic and Statistical Adviser and the necessary lower staff. The Secretariat prepares the agenda for the Cabinet meeting under the direction of the Prime Minister. It keeps a record of the proceedings of the meetings and the decisions of the

Cabinet. The necessary statistics and information needed by the Cabinet are provided by the Cabinet Secretariat.

WORKING OF PARLIAMENTARY SYSTEM

Art. 79, of Chapter II headlined 'Parliament' contained in Part V titled 'The Union' provide for the constitution of the Union legislature called Parliament (Sansad) consisting of the President, the Rajya Sabha (Council of States) and the Lok Sabha (House of People) respectively—as the upper and lower chambers. The President is an integral part of the Parliament, though he is not a member of any House, for the reason that he summons and prorogues the sessions, may dissolve Lok Sabha, delivers inaugural address and may send messages and, finally, places his signatures to authenticate the bills passed by the Parliament. However, the peculiar thing about our Parliament is that while its general pattern is like that of the English Parliament, it is a non-sovereign lawmaking body like the American Congress. Its legislative power is circumscribed by the written provisions of the Constitution that provide for a federal system of government with power of judicial review vested in the Supreme Court and the High Courts to strike down any law or executive action, in part or full, if it is inconsistent with the Fundamental Rights given in Part Ill or with the basic frame-work of the Constitution.

Rajya Sabha

The Indian Parliament is a bicameral body. Its upper chamber is the Rajya Sabha. It consists of 250 members at the most. Out of this 12 members are nominated by the President from amongst persons distinguished in the field of art, literature, science and social service. The remaining members are the representatives of the States and Union Territories. The number of representatives, as determined by a law of Parliament and specified in Schedule IV of the Constitution, varies from State to State as the number of seats allocated to them is based on the factor of population. It is due to this that while a small State like Nagaland has only one seat, a very big State like the UP has 34 seats. The members are elected by the members of the State Legislative Assemblies in accordance with proportional representation with single transferable vote system. The Parliament may make some other arrangement for the representation of Union Territories. It is due to this that the party-wise composition of the Rajya Sabha reflects the party-wise composition of Vidhan Sabhas in the country.

A member of the Rajya Sabha must possess three qualifications. First, he must be a citizen of India. Second, he must have completed the age of 30 years. Last, he must possess all other qualifications laid down in an act of Parliament. The Representation of the People Act, 1951 says that a person to be chosen as a member of this House from any State, excluding Jammu-Kashmir, must be an elector for a Parliamentary constituency in that State. The disqualifications for the membership of this House are: holding an office of profit under the Government of India or any State except that of a Minister or any other exempted by a law of Parliament, being of unsound mind or an undischarged insolvent as declared by a competent court, being an alien or a non-citizen, and being disqualified under any law of the Parliament.

The Rajya Sabha is a continuing chamber. Its one-third members retire after every second year and elections are held for the vacant seats. Thus, a member of the Rajya Sabha has six years to serve, but he may be re-elected any number of times. (It applies to the nominated members as well). A member of the Rajya Sabha may tender his resignation or cease to be its member in case he incurs some disqualification as provided in Art. 101, of the Constitution. That is, a member of this House shall forfeit his membership in case he becomes a member of the Lok Sabha or of any State legislature, or has voluntarily acquired the citizenship of a foreign State, or is under any acknowledgment of allegiance or adherence to a foreign State, or remains absent from all meetings of the House for a period of 60 days without any reason communicated to the House, or he is expelled from the membership of the House, or is held a political defector by the Chairman of the House.

Though a House of the Elders, the Rajya Sabha is regarded as a weak chamber in comparison to the Lok Sabha. A money bill cannot be introduced in the Rajya Sabha and when such a bill is referred to it after it is passed by the Lok Sabha, it has to pass it within a period of 14 days. The Rajya Sabha may return a money bill with some recommendations, but the Lok Sabha may accept them or not while reconsidering the same bill. A non-money bill may be introduced in any House of Parliament and here the Rajya Sabha is again a weak, though not very weak (as in the case of passing a money bill) chamber. In case there is disagreement between the two chambers, the President may convene a joint session of Parliament. Such a session [as occurred in 1961, in the case of Dowry Prohibition Bill and in 1978, in the case of Banking Service Commission (Repeal) Bill shall be held under the chairmanship of the Presiding Officer of Lok Sabha (Speaker) and the matter shall be decided by majority of votes.] The Speaker alone has the power to decide whether a bill is money bill or not. It is also provided that the Rajya Sabha must pass a bill already passed by the Lok Sabha or return it to Lok Sabha for consideration within six months. There is no such limitation in the case of a bill first passed by the Rajya Sabha and then referred to the Lok Sabha. Then, the Rajya Sabha cannot pass a motion of no-confidence against the government. Its members cannot put adjournment motion which, indeed, amounts to censure motion. At the most, they may criticise and thereby embarrass the government.

But in some other directions, the Rajya Sabha has powers equal to those of the Lok Sabha and in that respect, it cannot be termed as a weak chamber. For instance, a bill of constitutional amendment requiring special majority (absolute majority of the whole House coupled with two-thirds majority of the members, present and voting) for its adoption must be passed by both the Houses. If there is disagreement between the two chambers in passing such a bill, joint session of the Parliament cannot be held. Thus the Rajya Sabha could show its 'teeth' by rejecting the 24th Constitution Amendment Bill (seeking abolition of the privy purses and privileges of the former rulers of princely States) in 1970 and the 64th Constitution Amendment Bill (seeking reorganisation of Panchayati Raj) and the 65th Constitution Amendment Bill (seeking restructuring of urban municipal boards) in 1989. The Rajya Sabha has equal powers with Lok Sabha in matters like electing the President and Vice-President, impeaching the President, judges of the Supreme Court and High Courts and other high officers, approving a proclamation of emergency and extending its

ALLOCATION OF SEATS IN PARLIAMENT

States and Union Territories	*Rajya Sabha*	*Lok Sabha*
States		
1. Andhra Pradesh	18	42
2. Arunachal Pradesh	1	2
3. Assam	7	14
4. Bihar	22	54
5. Goa	1	2
6. Gujarat	11	26
7. Haryana	5	10
8. Himachal Pradesh	3	4
9. Jammu and Kashmir	4	6
10. Karnataka	12	28
11. Kerala	9	20
12. Madhya Pradesh	16	40
13. Maharashtra	19	48
14. Manipur	1	2
15. Meghalaya	1	2
16. Mizoram	1	1
17. Nagaland	1	1
18. Orissa	10	21
19. Punjab	7	13
20. Rajasthan	10	25
21. Sikkim	1	1
22. Tamil Nadu	18	39
23. Tripura	1	2
24. Uttar Pradesh	34	85
25. West Bengal	16	42

Contd.

States and Union Territories	*Rajya Sabha*	*Lok Sabha*
Union Territories		
1. Andaman and Nicobar Islands	-	*1*
2. Chandigarh	-	*1*
3. Dadra and Nagar Haveli	-	*1*
4. Daman and Diu	-	*1*
5. Delhi	*3*	*7*
6. Lakshadweep	-	*1*
7. Pondicherry	*1*	*1*
Nominated	*12*	*2*
Total	245	545

duration, considering the reports of various commissions and autonomous bodies, setting-up martial law courts dining national emergency for dealing with the offences comminuted by the civilians and indemnifying officers for their acts done in good faith, taking away an item from the purview of the Union Public Service Commission, and exercising control over delegated legislation.

But there are some areas in which the Rajya Sabha has special powers and thereby appears more important than the Lok Sabha. For instance, vide Art. 249, it may pass a resolution by its two-thirds majority so as to shift an item of the State List to the Union List or the Concurrent List on the plea of its 'expediency' in the national interest. Such a resolution shall remain in force for one year, but it may renew it again and again. Vide Art. 312, it may pass a resolution by its two-thirds majority so as to propose the creation of an all-India public service to be regularised by a law of Parliament in time to come. Then, it may initiate a move for the removal of the Vice-President. Such a resolution is to be passed by the Rajya Sabha by its absolute majority and then agreed to by the Lok Sabha. Last, in case the Lok Sabha stands dissolved the Rajya Sabha may permit extension of time in the case of 'emergency' declared by the President.

It shows that the Rajya Sabha is neither a weak chamber like the British House of Lords, nor is it a powerful chamber like the

American Senate. It is expected to be a house of the seasoned and elderly leaders. It is true that the Rajya Sabha has failed in living like a 'house of angels it has certainly not been a gathering of reactionary and raw elements. Though its members are drawn by indirect election in which State Legislative Assemblies play their part, it "does not seem to have made the floor of the Council a battleground between Centre and States a defence of States rights, an expression of the regional demands, that is just likely to be heard in the other House."

Lok Sabha

The Lok Sabha is the popular chamber having at the most 550 elected members (530 from the States and 20 from the Union Territories). The President may nominate at the most two members of the Anglo-Indian community in case he finds it not adequately represented therein. The members of this chamber are elected directly by the voters. The whole country is divided into territorial constituencies in a manner that the ratio between the number of the representatives and the size of the population is, as far as practicable, the same throughout the State. Moreover, under the Delimitation Commission Act of 1962, the Election Commission is authorised to determine forthwith the number of seats in the Lok Sabha on the basis of the latest census figures having regard to the constitutional provisions on the subject. Some seats are reserved for Scheduled Castes and Scheduled Tribes.

A member of the Lok Sabha must be a citizen of India and that he must be above 25 years age. He should not be holding an office of profit, nor should he meet any disqualification as already pointed out in the case of a member of the Rajya Sabha. The normal term of the House is five years to be computed from the date of its first sitting. The President may dissolve this House at any time. In case Art. 352, (national emergency) is in force, the Parliament may make a law to extend the life of the Lok Sabha (as happened in 1976). Such a law shall remain in force for one year in one instance, but it may be re-adopted.

Speaker. The Speaker occupies a very dignified position in the order of precedence. He is the Presiding Officer of the Lok Sabha. He is elected by the House and may be removed by it on some charge if a resolution, after 14 days' notice, is passed by its absolute majority. The House also elects a Deputy Speaker who, according to a practice, must belong to a party in the Opposition. The Speaker conducts the session of the House, recognises the members and permits them to speak in the House. He puts matters to vote and then declares the result. He does not vote, but he may exercise his casting vote in order to break the tie. He may give his ruling to settle a dispute. He may admit a question of a motion or reject it if found out of order. In the event of grave disorder, he may adjourn the sitting of the House. He may ask a member to withdraw an unparliamentary expression or may expunge any objectionable portion from the proceedings of the House. He may also 'name' a member and order his police staff to take him out of the House in the event of his serious misbehavior. He may accept the resignation of any member or may rejection the ground of its submission under 'duress'. He certifies that a bill is passed by the House. He may correct a patent error in a bill after it is passed by the House. He may disqualify a member in the event of his political defection. Indeed, the Speaker occupies a position of great prestige and honour. As former Secretary (Lok Sabha) testifies : "The Speaker is the all-important conventional head of the House of the People. Any question which relates to the well-being of the House is always a matter on which the Speaker is consulted and he naturally takes a very direct interest in it...The Speaker is the symbol of impartiality. He is the principal spokesman of the House and represents its collective voice."

Functions and Powers. The Constitution provides that the sessions of the Parliament should be held in a way that the intervening period is of not more than six months. It means that the Parliament must meet at least twice a year. Both the Houses hold their session normally thrice a year known as the Budget Session, Monsoon Session, and Winter Session. In each House the quorum is one-tenth of its total membership. Any member may raise the issue of quorum. If there is no quorum, the Chairman/Speaker may ring the quorum bell to ensure minimum attendance of the members or adjourn the sitting for some time.

The functions and powers of the Lok Sabha must be understood in the light of what we have already said about the functions and powers of the Rajya Sabha. The Lok Sabha is known as the powerful chamber of the Indian Parliament for these reasons. First, it has control over the government. The Council of Ministers is collectively responsible to the Lok Sabha. As such, the ministry may be thrown out in case this House passes a motion of censure or no-confidence or makes a cut in the budget, or disapproves of the policy of the government. For instance, on 7th November 1990, the Lok Sabha created history by rejecting confidence motion put by Prime Minister V.P. Singh. The members may put the ministers to gruelling tests by asking questions, tabling motions (calling attention and adjournment), demanding, half-hour discussion etc. Second, the Lok Sabha has a better position in the joint session by virtue of its numerical strength. Third, the Lok Sabha has control over the purse of the nation. A money bill (and so a budget) can be introduced in the Lok Sabha with the recommendation of the President and, when passed by it, it has to be passed by the Rajya Sabha within 14 days.

However, a comparatively study of the functions and powers of the two Houses leads to this unmistakable impression that the Lok Sabha is a powerful chamber as compared to the Rajya Sabha. There should be no doubt about Rajya Sabha being the upper and Lok Sabha being the lower chamber of the Parliament. However, the two chambers should not be designated as such with a mind to exalt one and denigrate the other that goes to intensify the bitter tradition of rivalry. What should prevail is the convention of harmony and cooperation between the two. Prime Minister Nehru well counselled on 6th May, 1953 that we must not blindly follow the English practice in every way. As he said: "Our guide must, therefore, be our own Constitution which has clearly specified the functions of the Council of States (Rajya Sabha) and the House of the People (Lok Sabha). To call either of these Houses an upper house or a lower is not correct. Each House has full authority to regulate its own procedure within the limits of the Constitution....That the Constitution treats the two Houses equally except in certain financial matters which are to be within the sole purview of the House of People."

No doubt, the Parliament is the pivot around which the whole structure of democratic government revolves. It may be lauded as our nation in miniature. As a learned writer comments: "Parliament of India, representing as it does all constitutional organised shades of public opinion at the national level, occupies a preeminent and central position in Indian polity. It embodies and epitomises the sovereign will of the people; it is the mirror and voice of the nation. The Preamble to the Constitution makes it abundantly clear that the ultimate source of all power are the people of India in whom sovereignty vests. The Constitution, which is the fundamental law of the land, has been 'adopted, enacted and given to ourselves' by 'We, the People of India'. It is, therefore, one of the over-riding concerns of the Parliament to see that the will and the aspirations of the people as reflected in its chambers are best fulfilled in the best manner possible. Members of Parliament, as elected representatives of the people, ventilate the people's grievances and opinions on various issues, scrutinise the functioning of the government on the floor of the Houses of Parliament and enact laws. Parliament functions as the grand inquest and watchdog of the nation."

Conduct of Business and Powers, Privileges and Immunities

The members take their seats in the House after taking an oath before the President or some person appointed by him in that behalf. The oath of affirmation is set out in Schedule III of the Constitution. Save as otherwise provided in this Constitution, all matters in either House of Parliament or in the joint session of both the Houses shall be decided by the majority of votes of the members present and voting. The presiding officer shall have no vote in the first instance, but shall have the right to vote so as to break the tie. Either House of Parliament shall have the power to act notwithstanding in any vacancy in the membership thereof, and any proceedings in the Parliament shall be held valid notwithstanding that it is discovered subsequently that some person who was not entitled so to do sat or voted or otherwise took part in the proceedings. The quorum of each House shall be one-tenth of the total number of the members of the House. In the absence of quorum, the Presiding Officer shall have the power either to adjourn the House, or suspend the meeting until there is quorum.

The members of Parliament have certain privileges without which they cannot discharge their duties properly. The members have a set of special rights and immunities which "exceed those possessed by other bodies or individuals." Thus, Art 105, lays down:

"1. Subject to the provisions of his Constitution and to the rules and standing orders regulating the procedure of Parliament, there shall be freedom of speech in Parliament.

2. No Member of Parliament shall be liable to any proceedings in any court in respect of anything said or any vote given by him in Parliament or any committee thereof, and no person shall be so liable in respect of the publication by or under the authority of either House of Parliament of any report, paper, votes or proceedings.

3. In other respects, the powers, privileges and immunities of each House of Parliament, and the members of the committees of each House, shall be, as may from time to time, be defined by Parliament by law, and, until so defined, shall be those of that House and of its members and committees immediately before the coming into force of Section 15 of the Forty-second Amendment Act of 1978.

4. The above provisions shall apply in relation to persons who by virtue of this Constitution have the right to speak in, and otherwise to take part in the proceedings of a House of Parliament or any Committee thereof as they apply in relation to Members of Parliament."

It is obvious that the powers, privileges and immunities of the members of Parliament have been inexhaustively specified in Art. 105. (Art 194, has the same provision for the members of State Legislatures.) The Forty-fourth Constitution Amendment Act has deleted the phrase that 'until defined by an Act of Parliament, the privileges of the members of Parliament would be the same as those of the British House of Commons'. What is still a matter of difficulty in this connection is that the privileges of the members of Parliament have not yet been exhaustively enumerated in a code. They have their source in some of the provisions of the Constitution, in some legal measures of the country, as well as in the various reports of the Parliamentary Committees and the interpretations of the Courts. The important privileges of the members of Parliament as well as of its committees may be enumerated as under:

1. Freedom to speak in the House and its Committees.
2. Immunity from any proceedings in any court in respect of anything said or vote given by them in the House or its Committees.
3. Immunity from proceedings in any court in respect of the publication by or under the authority of the House of any report, paper, notes or proceedings.
4. Prohibition on the courts to inquire into the proceedings of Parliament and its Committees.
5. Freedom from arrest in civil cases during the continuance of the session of the House and 40 days before its commencement and 40 days after its conclusion.
6. Exemption from liability to serve as jurors.
7. Right of the House to receive immediate information of the arrest, detention, conviction, imprisonment and release of a member.
8. Prohibition of arrest and service of legal process on the members within the precincts of the House without the permission of the presiding officer.
9. Prohibition of disclosure of the proceedings or decisions of a secret sitting of House by the members.
10. Right to refuse to give evidence or produce documents in the courts of law relating to the proceedings of the House without the permission of the presiding officer.
11. Right not to attend as witnesses before the other House or of a House of the State Legislature or its Committee without the permission of the House, nor can a member be compelled to do so without his consent.

12. Power of the House and its Committees to send for persons, papers, records and other relevant material, including witnesses.
13. Administration of oath of affirmation by a Committee of the House before examining a witness.
14. Prohibition of publishing any evidence or statement relating to the reports and proceedings of a Committee before it tabling in the House.
15. Right of the House to regulate its proceedings, its own procedure and conduct of business, and
16. Right of the House to exclude strangers from the House and to a person, whether a member of the House or not, for a breach of privilege or contempt of the House.

It is true that the privileges of the members of Parliament and of State Legislatures are not yet codified. But the dominant view, all along, has been that any codification "is more likely to harm the sovereignty and prestige of Parliament/State Legislatures without any benefit being conferred on the Press and that in the present circumstances, codification of Parliamentary privileges is neither necessary nor desirable."

Critical Appreciation

Our Parliament is a non-sovereign law-making body like the legislature of other countries excluding Britain. While the Constitution has accepted the principle of separation of powers and placed the Parliament in a position of its own, its powers have been circumscribed by the written provisions of the Constitution, by the norms of a federal polity, land above all, by the provision of judicial review. The Supreme Court and the High Courts have the power to declare any law of Parliament void, in part or full, if it is inconsistent with the provisions of the Constitution. Not only this, the Courts have invented some other grounds to strike down a law of a Parliament as the doctrines of 'competence' and of 'basic structure of the Constitution'. We know that in a parliamentary system, the executive usurps the inherent functions of the Parliament. All official bills are carried through and a bill moved by a private member has hardly any chance of adoption unless it receives the blessings of the Ministers. The Parliament discusses matters included in the agenda prepared by the Business Advisory Committee in which the Prime Minister, Minister for Parliamentary Affairs and the Speaker of the Lok Sabha play the decisive part. The voice of the Leader of the Opposition is given some weight of course, but it is the leaders of the party in power who dominate it. Consequently, what the Parliament discusses or may discuss is determined by the policy of the executive.

The Cabinet decides about the duration of the sessions of Parliament. Above all, the Prime Minister may advise the President to dissolve the Lok Sabha at any time. As such, the Parliament looks like a tool in the hands of the Ministers.

It, however, does not mean that in our political set-up the Parliament has become either like an ornamental institution or virtually redundant. It is true that the members of both the Houses have lost their autonomy in the name of discipline in the ranks of the party and they have to vote in the House according to the whip issued by the party leader so as to avoid the penalty of defection amounting to the loss of their membership of the House, it should not be lost sight of that the deliberations of the Parliament have their own impact on the administration of the country. The criticism of the ministry compels the administration to stick to the right side or to face a situation of exit. In case no party commands clear majority in the Lok Sabha, the ministry has to behave in a very responsible way so as to survive in the struggle for existence. The events of the last few years testify to this fact. Some Prime Ministers (like Nehru, Shastri, Indira and Rajiv) could behave like powerful rulers of the country just on account of the overwhelming strength of their party in both Houses of Parliament. But other Prime Ministers (like Morarji Desai, Choudhry Charan Singh, V.P. Singh and Chandra Shekhar) could not complete their term for want of support in the Lok Sabha. Happily, the recent developments indicate that our Parliament "is becoming more representative of the people of India, of the level of their political awareness, or their lack of sophistication, and of their problems, hopes and aspirations."

POWERS OF THE PARLIAMENT

The Indian Parliament is a sovereign body and it is independent of the control of any external authority. But it cannot be called sovereign in the sense the British Parliament is called a sovereign body. The Indian Parliament is internally limited by the division of powers made by the Constitution between the Union and States. There are certain other constitutional limitations on its powers and the Judiciary has been vested with the power to check any encroachment made by the Parliament in the constitutional jurisdiction of the State and the fundamental rights of the individuals. Laws passed by the Indian Parliament are subject to judicial review. The Supreme Court of India is empowered to declare a law passed by the Indian Parliament as unconstitutional or *ultra vires*, if it violates the provisions of the Constitution.

Legislative Powers. Both the Houses of Parliament have almost equal legislative powers with the exception of Money Bills. Ordinary bills must be passed by both the Houses of Parliament before they are presented to the President for his assent. In case of difference of opinion between the two Houses over a bill, there is provision of joint sitting of both the Houses. Such joint sittings are summoned by the President. A bill passed in a joint sitting shall be considered to have been passed by both the Houses of Parliament and may by sent to the President in order to have the force of law.

The Parliament can make laws on all subjects in Union List. It can also legislative on topics included in Concurrent List and the laws of the Parliament shall supersede the State laws in case of conflict. In India the residuary powers are also vested in the Union Parliament which can make laws on topics which are not mentioned in any List of powers under the Constitution. Moreover, the Indian Parliament can also legislate on the subjects given in the State List if there is a proclamation of emergency, or if the Rajya Sabha has passed a resolution to this effect by not less than two-thirds of the members present and voting, or if two or more than two State legislatures have made such a request, or if it is needed in the interests of India's obligations in the international sphere.

Executive Powers. In a Parliamentary System of government the members of the executive are also the members of the legislature. The Executive is a committee of the Parliament and is subject to the control of the Parliament in general and the Lok Sabha in particular. Even though, normally the Council of Ministers is appointed for a term of five years, it may be turned out earlier by the Lok Sabha. The Council of Ministers shall remain in office as long as it enjoys the confidence of the Lok Sabha. There are many ways through which the Parliament controls the executive. The members have the right to put questions and supplementary questions. They may refuse to pass a bill introduced by the Cabinet. They may reject the budget proposal or insist for cut in the demands of a particular department. They may insist on moving an adjournment motion to discuss administrative lapses. Finally, the Lok Sabha has the power to pass the no-confidence motion against the Cabinet. There are special rules regarding the introduction of the no-confidence motion, Fifty members have to rise in their places to signify their support to a motion of no confidence.

In addition to the above methods, the House has several committees through which it exercises control over the executive. There are four such Committees: *(1)* Committee on Subordinate Legislation, *(2)* Committee on Government Assurances, *(3)* Public Accounts Committee, *(4)* Estimates Committee.

Financial Powers. The Parliament exercises full control over the finances of the country and the Government has no power to spend even a single paisa without the sanction of the Parliament. Though the budget is prepared and introduced in the Lok Sabha by the Cabinet, yet it is subject to the approval of the Parliament. The Parliament's approval is also necessary for levying new taxes or revising the rates of the existing taxes and also for incurring any expenditure. It may be noted here that the items chargeable to the Consolidated Fund of India are not votable by Parliament, though discussions can be held on such items of expenditure.

In this context it may be mentioned that like every democratic state, in India the power to control the finances of the country is vested in the Lok Sabha. The Rajya Sabha has very little or practically no role to play as far as the financial administration is concerned. A Money Bill can be introduced only in the Lok Sabha. After it is passed in the Lok Sabha it is sent to the Rajya Sabha which must return the Bill either with approval or with fresh recommendations, within a period of 14 days. The Lok Sabha may or may not accept these recommendations. But in either case it will be deemed to have been passed by both the Houses. The President has no power to return a Money Bill for reconsideration.

Miscellaneous Powers. (a) Parliament has the power to amend the Constitution with the exception of certain provisions for which ratification of not less than half of the state legislatures is required.

(b) Parliament is the most powerful form for ventilating the grievances of the people. Through short notice questions, adjournment motions, questions and supplementary questions and the motion of no-confidence, different public problems are high-lighted on the floor of the Parliament.

(c) It has the power to remove the President of India by impeachment. It can also make an address for the removal of a Judge of the Supreme Court or a High Court, the Chief Election Commissioner and the Comptroller and Auditor-General of India. For this, however, a special procedure is to be adopted as prescribed by the Constitution.

(d) The elected members of the Union Parliament along with the elected members of the State Legislative Assemblies constitute the electoral college for the election of the President of India. The Vice-President is elected by the members of both the Houses of the Parliament.

(e) The Parliament has the power to Punish the members and the outsiders for its contempt.

(f) Parliament has power to increase the number of Judges of the Supreme Court.

(g) It his the power to create or abolish the State Legislative Council on recommendations of the State concerned.

(h) It can create new states or alter the boundaries or names of existing States. However, this can only be done on the recommendations of the President.

RELATIONS BETWEEN THE TWO HOUSES

The Rajya Sabha is definitely a weak partner of the Lok Sabha. This would become amply clear from the analysis of the respective powers of both the Houses. Both the Houses have more or less men of same age group, same qualifications and same bent of mind and they are called to perform the same type of work in similar ways. Thus, the Rajya Sabha has no distinct role to play. It is, natural on the part of the Rajya Sabha to demand a position of equality with the Lok Sabha. This has resulted in quarrels between the two Houses.

As far as the powers of both the Houses are concerned, they have almost the same powers in matters of ordinary law making. An ordinary bill may originate in either House of the Parliament and requires the concurrence of both the Houses for its passage. In case of disagreement between the two Houses, the President shall call a joint sitting of the two Houses where the matter will be decided by a simple majority of votes. In such a meeting due to its numerical superiority, the Lok Sabha can easily outweight the Rajya Sabha.

As regards financial legislation, the Lok Sabha has a definite superiority over the Rajya Sabha. Money bills can only be introduced in the Lok Sabha and they are sent to the Rajya Sabha after their passage in the former House. The Rajya Sabha must return the Bill within 14 days, and it shall be deemed to have been passed by both the Houses whether the Rajya Sabha approves it or not. If there is any dispute on the matter whether a bill is a Money Bill or not, the decision of The Speaker shall be final.

The executive is responsible to the Lok Sabha. The Lok Sabha alone has the ultimate power to control the executive. The Cabinet shall remain in power as long as it enjoys the confidence of the Lok Sabha. If a no-confidence motion is passed against the executive in the Lok Sabha, it is bound to resign. The Lok Sabha has many other methods of controlling the executive. The members of the Rajya Sabha have the power to criticise the work of a Minister in particular, or the Government in general. They have also the right to demand answers to their questions and necessary informations from the Ministers. But the Cabinet is not bound to honour a vote of no-confidence passed against it in the Rajya Sabha and it may resign from office. Thus, in matters of controlling the executive also, the Lok Sabha enjoys more powers than the Rajya Sabha.

The Legislative Procedure

Ariticles 107 to 122, deal with the provisions relating to the passing of bills in Parliament. The bills may be classified as Ordinary Bills and Money Bills. Ordinary Bills can be introduced in either House of the Parliament. But a Money Bill can only be introduced in the Lok Sabha. However, an Ordinary Bill in order to be finally passed requires the concurrence of both the Houses of Parliament. If there is any difference of opinion between the two Houses, that can be solved by a joint committee consisting of members from both the Houses. If the committee fails to solve the differences and the bill is returned by the Rajya Sabha with recommendation, which are not acceptable to the Lok Sabha, a joint sitting of both the Houses may be called by an order of the President. The Speaker of the Lok Sabha presides in such a joint sitting and the decision is made is by a simple majority of votes.

After a bill is passed by both the Houses, it is sent to the President for his assent. The President may either give his assent, or refuse his assent, or delay his assent, or return the bill for reconsideration by Parliament. If a bill which is returned by the President with amendments, for the reconsideration of the Parliament, is repassed by the Parliament with or without amendments, the President shall not withhold his assent from such a bill.

Every bill has to go through different stages before it is finally passed by the Parliament. Similar procedure is follows in both the Houses of Parliament for the passage of a bill. The different stages are discussed below:

Introduction and First Reading. An ordinary bill can he introduced in any House of the Parliament. An ordinary bill may be introduced by a member by giving a notice of one month. The notice has to be accompanied by a text of the but a statement of its objects and a memorandum showing separately the recurring and non-recurring expenditure. A member who wants to introduce a bill first seeks the leave of the House of do so. Usually such leave is not refused, but the Houses reserves the right to exercise this power of refusing the leave for the introduction of bill. If the introduction of the bill is opposed by any member, than the Speaker may ask the mover of the bill and the member opposing it to made explanatory statements. Such speeches are, usually, very brief. Then a vote is taken and if the majority is in favour of the bill it is considered to have been moved. After the introduction of the bill is over, it is published in the Gazette of India.

Second Reading. As regards the second reading stage, the mover of the bill may follow one of the three alternatives. He may move that the bill be taken up for consideration at once or at some future date, as may be specified in the motion. He may move that the bill be circulated among the people for eliciting public opinion on the desirability or otherwise of the bill. Immediate consideration of the bill by House of rare except when it is very urgent and non-controversial and is introduced by the Government. Lastly, he may move that the bill be submitted to a select committee. The usual procedure is to submit the bill to a select committee. Bills of controversial nature are circulated among the people for eliciting their views on the subject. After one of the above three motions has been moved the House than proceeds to discuss the underlying principles of the bill. During this stage, there is no detailed discussions about the provisions of the bill and no amendments are moved. Those who support the bill analyse its merits and those who oppose point out its short-comings. Thus, during the second reading the bill is discussed as a whole.

Committee Stage. The second reading stage of the bill comes to end when its fundamentals are approved. After this stage the bill comes to the third stage which is known as the committee stage. During this stage the bill is usually referred to a select committee which consists, among other members of the House, the sponsor of the bill or those who are incharge of the bill. The Chairman of this committee is nominated by the Speaker and if the Deputy Speaker is the member of any select committee he becomes its Chairman. The committee also includes the Law Members who is an ex-officio member. There is a thorough and clause by clause discussion of the bill during the committee stage. The committee collects all information regarding the bill and its pros and cons are critically examined. After a thorough examination of the bill, the committee proposes such amendments as it thinks necessary.

Report Stage. The members of the Committee are free to express any opinion on the bill and every individual member may give his own separate report. Usually there is a majority report and a minority report. When the report is received in the House, the Secretary of the House publishes the report of the committee along with the minutes of the same. When the report is finally presented to the House, the member incharge of the bill may move for the consideration of the report on the appointed day. The House proceeds to consider the bill clause by clause, as it has emerged from the Select Committee. During this stage members are free to move amendments, the Speaker shall decide as to which amendments are to be considered and which not. Finally, the clause with such amendments as may have been accepted by the House is put to vote. Votes may be taken after every clause or many clauses are discussed together and one may be taken on all of them at one time.

Third Reading. Then the bill comes to the fifth stage, known as the third reading. The bill as a whole is discussed and arguments in favour and against it are expressed by the different members. The third reading stage is a formal one and no substantial change are allowed at this stage. However, certain verbal amendments may be suggested by the members to clear certain ambiguities or defect in the form of the bill and the suggestion may be accepted by the House. If the bill is passed by a majority of the members present and voting, then it shall be deemed to have been passed by the House of its origin and after receiving a certificate to this effect from the presiding officer of the House (the Speaker or the Chairman, as the case may be) the bill goes to the other House. The same procedure is also followed in the other House and the bill goes through the five different stages. It passed in the same form in which it came from the House of its origin, it is sent to the President for his assent, on receipt of which it becomes law.

Financial Procedure. Ariticle 122, of the Constitution provides that in every financial year, the President shall cause to be laid before both the Houses of Parliament a statement of the estimated receipts and expenditure of the Government of India for that year financial of Money Bills are governed by a different set of rules of procedure mentioned in the Constitution.

The budget may be divided into two parts : *(i)* expenditure charged on the Consolidated Fund of India, and *(ii)* other expenditures. The expenditure chargeable on the Consolidated Fund includes the salaries of the President, Presiding Officers of the Parliament, the Auditor-General and the Judges of the Supreme Court, the Federal and the High Courts of India, sums required to satisfy any judgement, decree or award of any court or arbitral tribunal and any other expenditure declared by the Constitution or by Parliament by law to by so charged. This part of the budget is not subject to the vote of the Parliament, though there may be discussion on it. The second part of the budget is submitted to the Lok Sabha in the form of Demands for Grants. It may be discussed, reduced or rejected by the House. But it his no power to enhance it. When grants have been made by the Lok Sabha, an Appropriation Bill is introduced which provides for expenditure out of the Consolidated Fund for both kinds of expenditure. If the amount sanctioned by the Appropriate Act is found to be insufficient, the President has the power to lay before the Parliament another statement showing the estimated amount of expenditure. Similar procedure is followed in respect of Supplementary Grants. Finally, the Lok Sabha has the power to make any grant in advance in respect of the estimated expenditure for a part of any financial year pending the passing of the Appropriation Act. It can also make a grant for meeting an unexpected demand upon the resources of India. It is also empowered to make an exceptional grant.

The Budget introduced in the Lok Sabha by the Finance Minister usually at 5 P.M. on the last day of February. The Budget is also laid before the Rajya Sabha. Before it is finally passed, the Budget goes through five stages: *(i)* Introduction, *(ii)* discussion, *(iii)* voting of demand, *(iv)* consideration and passing of the Appropriation Bill, and *(v)* consideration and passing of the taxation proposals, *i.e.* the Finance Bill.

The general discussion on the Budget follows after two or three days of its introduction. The general principles underlying the Budget are discussed. No discussion of details or cut motion are in order at this stage. After the general discussion is over, the Lok Sabha proceeds to vote the demands. When the demands for Grants are under discussion, the members of Lok Sabha have the right to move 'cut motions.' If a 'cut motion' is approved by the House then it will tantamount to be a vote of no-confidence against the Government. As has been stated earlier, the House can refuse or reduce the grants but it cannot increase them. The demands of each Ministry are taken up in turn. A definite period of time is allotted for this purpose and on the expiry of this time, the Speaker shall put all the demands before the House regardless of the fact whether all of them have been discussed or not.

Another important stage of the Budget is the acceptance by the Lok Sabha of the Appropriation Bill, seeking power to authorise expenditure out of the Consolidated Fund of India. The Finance Bill, incorporating the tax proposals and the allied matters, is also transmitted to the Rajya Sabha like the Appropriation Bill. The Rajya Sabha must return the Bill with its recommendations, if any, within 14 days. The Lok Sabha may accept the recommendations or may turn them down. But in any case, the Bill shall deemed to have been passed by both the Houses, and it shall be presented to the President for his assent. He must give his assent because Presidential veto does not apply to the Appropriation Bill.

GOVERNOR

The Governor is the constitutional head of the State government, but he is not elected, he is appointed by the President and may be recalled or reappointed or transferred by him from one State to another. The Governor performs the same functions what the President does at the Centre with this difference that he has no 'emergency' powers. Each State has a Vidhan Sabha, but in some States the legislature is bicameral having Vidhan Parishad and Vidhan Sabha respectively as upper and lower chambers. All Vidhan Sabhas have a normal term of five years, but the Vidhan Sabha of Jammu-Kashmir has a term of six years. Since we have a unified judiciary, the High Courts are not the third organ of the State governments in the correct sense of the term, they constitute the sub-part of the Union judiciary. Above all, since we have a federal system with a strong Centre, the State governments do not have autonomy that is enjoyed by the states of the USA or the cantons of Switzerland due to the over-riding and over-arching control and interference of the Centre in many areas of the administration of the States.

Appointment. Each State has a Governor. There may be a common Governor for two or more States. He is appointed by the President on the advice of the Union Council of Ministers for five years. A person to be appointed for this post must be a citizen of India; he must be above 35 years of age; and he must not be holding an office of profit. Two usages have developed in this direction. First, the person to be chosen for this post must not be a domicile of that State. For instance, a Maharashtrian should not be appointed as the Governor of Maharashtra. Second, before making this appointment, the Union Government must consult the Chief Minister of the concerned State just for the sake of Courtesy. It does not mean that the Chief Minister may dictate his will in this matter; it is simply a gesture of goodwill that the Centre should show to the real head of the State government. Unfortunately, the second usage has not been observed scrupulously on several occasions. Not only that the Centre has failed to evolve a clear-cut-policy about the selection of persons for this post. Facts illustrate that this post has been given to persons ranging from eminent public figures and seasoned bureaucrats to burnt out politicians and fallen horses. A noted jurist like M.C. Setalved regretted that since the advent of independence, many of those selected for the post "have fallen short of the required standard, largely due to the lowly place given to the office which has come to be treated as a sinecure for mediocrities or as a consolation prize for burnt out politicians."

Functions and Powers. The functions and power of the Governor cover executive, legislative, judicial financial and other spheres. In the executive sphere, his functions are as under:

1. He is the executive head of the State government. The executive power of the state is vested in him that he has to exercise directly or through officers subordinate to him. All executive actions of the State government are taken in his name. He makes rules for the transaction of business of the government and for the allocation of work among his ministers.
2. He appoints the Chief Minister and on his advice appoints other ministers. He administers to them the oaths of office and secrecy. He accepts their resignations. He may dismiss the Chief Minister or any minister on the advice of the Chief Minister. He makes appointment of high officers of the State like Advocate-General, Chairman and members of the State Public Service Commission, Election Commissioner of State, Chairman and members of State Finance Commission etc. and is consulted by the President in the appointment of the judges and Chief Justice of the High Court of his State.
3. He may call for information from the Chief Minister relating to the affairs of administration and proposals for legislation.
4. He may refer any important matter for the consideration of the Council of Ministers.
5. He acts as the Chancellor of State Universities.
6. In case he is satisfied that constitutional machinery in his State has broken down, he may write to the President recommending invocation of Art. 356 of the Constitution. If it happens, he acts as the 'agent' of the President in running the administration of the State.

Then, he performs important functions in the legislative sphere as under:

1. He is an integral part of the State legislature without being its member. He summons the session of the legislature and prorogues it. He may dissolve the Vidhan Sabha at any time on or against the advice of the Chief Minister.
2. He may nominate one member of the Anglo-Indian community to the Vidhan Sabha in case he finds it not adequately represented in it. If the State legislature is bicameral, he nominates about one-sixth of its members from amongst persons distinguished in the fields of art, literature, science, social service and cooperative movement.
3. On the advice of the Election Commission, he can decide a matter relating to the disqualification of a legislator of his State.
4. The first session of the legislature of a new year and a session after a general election begins with his inaugural address.
5. He may send messages to the legislature for consideration.
6. In case the legislature is not in session and some law is necessarily to be put into force, he may promulgate an ordinance having the force of law. It may be withdrawn at any time by him, but it can remain in force at the most for six weeks after the reassembling of the State legislature.
7. The annual reports of various bodies like Public Service Commission and Auditor-General are submitted to him that he causes to be laid before the legislature for consideration.
8. He has veto power. As such, he may give assent to a non-money bill, or withhold his assent, or return it for the reconsideration of the legislature.
9. In case he finds that a bill passed by the State legislature seeks abolition of private property, or derogates the jurisdiction of the High Court, or seeks taxation on an item declared 'essential' by a law of the Parliament, or is likely to be in conflict with any law or policy of the Union Government, he may 'reserve' it for the consideration of the President of India.

Like the President, in the judicial sphere, he has 'prerogative of mercy'. He may grant pardon to a person convicted by the Court or may remit or commute the sentence provided all judicial remedies have been exhausted and the matter falls within the executive authority of the State government. He can decide matters relating to the appointments, postings and promotion of district judges and other judicial officers. He enjoys personal immunity from all civil and criminal proceedings during his term of office.

In the financial sphere, he has these powers. A money bill can be introduced in the Vidhan Sabha with his recommendation. He causes the annual financial statement or budget of the State government laid before the Vidhan Sabha. The Contingency Fund of the State is at his disposal and he can make advances our of it to meet an unforeseen expenditure pending its authorisation by the State legislature.

Besides, the Governor has some discretionary powers. He may study the situation prevailing in his State and on the basis of his 'satisfaction' may advise the President to invoke Art. 356 of the Constitution. The Governor of Assam, Arunachal Pradesh and Nagaland have special powers to deal with anti-national elements. In case a Governor is entrusted with the charge of an adjoining Union Territory, there he may act independently in the capacity of its Lt.-Governor or Administrator. He may permit initiation of legal proceedings against the serving or ex-Chief Minister involved in some alleged scandal or criminal wrong. In case he is satisfied that the Chief Minister has lost majority in the Vidhan Sabha, he may either dismiss him or ask him to prove majority in the House at an early date.

Position. The Governor acts in a dual capacity. On the one hand, he acts as the constitutional head of the State government. As such, he is expected to act on the advice of the Chief Minister. Here his position may be identified with the British monarch. But a critic may go to the extent of calling this post as a sinecure job or a gubernatorial assignment. Since the Governor has to act invariably on the advice of the Chief Minister, his position may be compared, in the words of a former Governor of U.P. (Mrs. Sarojini Naidu), with 'a bird in the golden cage'. On the other hand, the Governor acts like the agent or the eyes and the ears of the Centre. Since he can live in office during the 'pleasure' of the President, he must look towards the Centre in each and every delicate or sensitive situation. Whenever a critical situation arises, the Governors rush to New Delhi and try to settle it in a way appreciable to the Central leaders.

It is for this reason that the office of the Governor becomes the subject of criticism particularly when State government is run by a party which is not in power at the Centre. It is a fact that a person may live as a Governor only when he manages to keep both the Prime Minister and the Chief Minister in good humour. A Governor has to go in case he forfeits the pleasure of the Prime Minister as happened with Prabhu Das Patwari of Tamil Nadu, Raghukul Tilak of Rajasthan and Jagmohan of Jammu-Kashmir. It is also possible that sensing the mood of the Council of Ministers, the President may tacitly or indirectly advise the Governors to resign instead of facing premature exit. It is also a fact that a person in the good books of the Prime Minister may continue as a Governor either in a particular State or be shifted to another State with every prospect of re-appointment. Keeping it all in view, this fact "must be accepted that the Governor today is the hare in a puppet show—his role depends upon what the behind is doing with the strings."

Chief Ministers and Council of Ministers

Appointment. The Chief Minister is the real head of the State government. He is appointed by the Governor. In accordance with the principle of parliamentary government, the Chief Minister must be the leader of the party having majority in the Vidhan Sabha. In case a political party manages to secure clear majority in the Vidhan Sabha, its leader is invited by the Governor to form the government. In case no party gets absolute majority in the Vidhan Sabha, then a coalition government is formed. Two or more parties may form a coalition and then their chosen leader is invited by the Governor to form the government. If no party gets clears majority and there is no chance of the formation of a coalition government either, the Governor may advise the President to invoke Art. 356. The Governor appoints ministers on the advice of the Chief Minister. Since the ministry lives in office during the 'pleasure' of the Governor, he may dismiss a Chief Minister in case he forfeits the claim of being the leader of the party having majority in the Vidhan Sabha, or when there is a serious split in the ranks of the party having clear majority there.

Functions and Powers. Like the Prime Minister at the Centre, the Chief Minister is the real head of the State government. He advises the Governor to appoint ministers and deputy ministers and distribute portfolios among them. He may advise the Governor to dismiss a minister in case the differs from the policy and working of the Council of Ministers. He acts as the channel of communication between the Governor and the Council of Ministers and also between the Council of Ministers and the State legislature. He advises the Governor to make high appointments, to summon the session of the State legislature, and to dissolve the Vidhan Sabha. However, his actual position depends upon three situational variables. In case he is a powerful leader of the party having comfortable majority in the Vidhan Sabha and is also in the good books of the Prime Minister, he behaves like a 'showman' of his government. All ministers work under his leadership and the Vidhan Sabha cannot present to him a formidable challenge. In case he is a strong leader of the party having comfortable majority in the Vidhan Sabha but in opposition at the Centre, his position becomes weak owing to the hostile attitude of the Central government. In such a situation, he manages to act like a 'spokesman' of his party. With tact as well as with worldly wisdom he may prove his strong hold over the government of the State. But in case he is the leader of a coalition government with different constituents pulling in different directions coupled with the hostile attitude of the Centre, his position is quite vulnerable on every front and thus he plays, in the words of Jyoti Basu, the role of a 'postman'. The experiences of the days of Congress hegemony show that most of the Chief Ministers happily devalued themselves as 'chief messengers' of the supreme leader of their party and the Prime Minister of the country.

The Council of Ministers is the team headed by a Chief Minister to aid and advise the Governor in the exercise of his functions, except where he has the power to act in his discretion, and is collectively responsible to the Vidhan Sabha. It is necessary that all ministers must be the member of the State legislature. In case a Chief Minister or any of the ministers is not a member of the legislature, he must secure its membership within a period of 6 months. It is also given that in the States of Bihar, Orissa and Madhya Pradesh, there shall be a minister in charge of tribal welfare who may in addition be in charge of the welfare of the Scheduled Castes and backward classes or any other work.

The Council of Ministers is the policy-making body. The Chief Minister presides over the meetings of the cabinet and every member is bound to honour the decisions taken therein. In the event of difference of views, the minister should resign. The Governor may refer any important matter for the consideration of the Council of Ministers. If a question arises whether there is any matter in respect of which the Governor is required to act in his discretion, the decision of the Governor shall be final and the validity of anything done by the Governor shall not be called in question on the ground that he ought to have acted in his discretion. The question whether any, and if so what, advice was tendered by the ministers to the Governor shall not be inquired into any court. In case the Governor asks for any information relating to the affairs of administration or proposals for legislation, the Chief Minister is duty bound to supply it to him. However, the 'pleasure' of the Governor does not involve the element of arbitrariness or anything like subjective assessment, because it is for the Legislative Assembly to enforce the principle of collective responsibility.

Legislature

Each State of the Indian Union has a Vidhan Sabha, but five States (Bihar, UP, Karnataka, Maharashtra and Jammu-Kashmir) have an upper chamber (Vidhan Parished) as well. As power Art. 169, the Centre has the power to create or abolish Vidhan Parished in case a resolution to this effect is passed by the Vidhan Sabha of that by special majority (absolute majority of the whole House as well as 2/3 majority of the members, present and voting). Hence, the

Parliament made laws to abolish the Vidhan Parishads of West Bengal, Punjab, Andhra Pradesh and Tamil Nadu. It is also possible that the Centre any adopt a dilatory attitude and in the meantime a newly constituted Vidhan Sabha may rescind the earlier resolution and thereby save the Vidhan Parishad as happened in the cases of UP and Bihar. It is also possible that a Vidhan Parishad may not be created in a State in spite of its provision in the Constitution as we may note in the case of Madhya Pradesh.

Vidhan Parishad

The strength of a Vidhan Parishad varies from State to State. It is provided that the strength of the Vidhan Parishad may be at least 40 and at most not more than one-third strength of the Vidhan Sabha of the State. The composition of this chamber is determined by a formula involving the method of indirect election in some and direct election in some other categories, leaving the case of some members nominated by the Governor. It is as under:

1. About one-third members are elected by the Vidhan Sabha from amongst persons who are not its members.
2. About one-third members are elected by the local bodies of the State (like Municipal Boards, Zila Prishads or any other authority as specified in a law of Parliament).
3. About one-twelfth members are elected by persons of at least 3 years' standing as teachers in educational institutions not lower in standard than that of a secondary school.
4. About one-twelfth member are elected by the University graduates of at least 3 years' standing in the State.
5. About one-sixth members are nominated by the Governor from amongst persons possessing special knowledge of or experience in the fields of art, literature, science, social service and cooperative movement.

A member of the Vidhan Parishad must have three qualifications. First, he must be a citizen of India. Second, he must be above 30 years of age. Last, he must posses all other qualifications as laid

COMPOSITION OF VIDHAN PARISHADS

States	*Total Seats*	*Nom. by Governor*	*Elections by Assembly*	*by Local Bodies*	*by Teachers*	*by Graduates*
1. Bihar	96	12	34	34	8	8
2. Uttar Pradesh	108	12	39	39	9	9
3. Karantaka	63	9	21	21	6	6
4. Maharashtra	78	12	31	21	7	7
5. Jammu-Kaskmir	36	6	21	7	2	–

down in a law of Parliament. A person cannot be a member of both the Houses of Parliament, or of both the Houses of State legislature, or of a House of a State legislature and a House of Parliament at one and the same time. The Vidhan Parishad is a permanent chamber. Its one-third members retire after every second year. As such a member enjoys a tenure of six years. He may be re-elected nay number of times. The Parishad elects its Chairman and Deputy Chairman.

The Vidhan Parishad has no effective powers. It has to pass a Money Bill passed by the Vidhan Sabha within 14 days and a non-money bill passed by the Vidhan Sabha within 3 months. In case the Vidhan Parishad rejects or returns a non-money bill, be Vidhan Sabha may re-adopt it and the Vidhan Parishad has to pass it within a period of one month. There is no provision for joint sitting in such a matter. A returns a Money Bill to the Vidhan Sabha, the latter may pass it again after accepting or rejecting the recommendations of the former. The Council of Ministers is collectively responsible to the Vidhan Sabha. As such, it may put the government to some inconvenience at the most by thrown critical light on its acts of commission and omission. The members of this House do not take part in the election of the President and of the members of the Rajya Sabha. In short, the Vidhan Parishad cannot over-ride the will of the Vidhan Sabha. Keeping in view is insignificant position and condemning it as a rendezvous of retired and burnt-out politicians, it is said that the Vidhan Parishads are not even like an ornamental chamber. "Should they prove inoffensive, they might be retained. If not, they can be abolished without much trouble."

Vidhan Sabha

But the Vidhan Sabha is the popular and powerful chamber of the State legislature. The Vidhan Sabha of a State may have at the most 500 members and at the least 60 members depending upon the demorgraphic composition of the State. (The strength of a Vidhan Sabhas is specified in a law of the Parliament that may fix a strength of even less than 60.) The members are elected directly by the voters of the State, but the Governor may nominate one Anglo-Indian as a member in order to give representation to this community. Some seats of Assam where special provisions have been made for the sake of Scheduled Tribes. After each census the total number of seats in each State and the division of seats into territorial constituencies is re-adjusted by the Election Commission in accordance with the law of Parliament. It is essential that the ratio between the population of each constituency and the number of seats allotted to it must be, as far as practicable, same throughout the State.

A member of the Vidhan Sabha must be citizen of India; he must be above 25 years of age; and that he must fulfil all other qualifications as laid down in an act of Parliament. No person can be a member of the two Houses, including the Parliament, or some other State legislature at the same time. The normal term of the Vidhan Sabha is five years. It begins from the date of its first meeting. In case national emergency (under Art. 352), is in force, the Parliament may extend the life of Vidhan Sabha by on year by making a law in this regard. Such a law may be renewed again and again. But within 6 months of the termination of emergency, elections must take place. The Governor has the power to dissolve the Vidhan Sabha at any time. In case Art. 356, of the Constitution is invoked, it depends upon the text of the proclamation of emergency to dissolution. The House elects its Speaker and Deputy Speaker who are accountable to it. That is the Vidhan Sabha may remove is Presiding Officer by passing a vote of no-confidence against him by its absolute majority.

ALLOCATION OF SEATS IN STATE LEGISLATIVE ASSEMBLIES

States	Seats	States	Seats
1. Andhra Pradesh	294	2. Auranchal pradesh	60
3. Assam	126	4. Bihar	324
5. Goa	40	6. Gujarat	182
7. Haryana	90	8. Himachal Pradesh	68
9. Jammu-Kashmir	76*	10. Karnataka	226
11. Kerala	140	12. Madhya Pradesh	320
13. Maharashtra	288	14. Manipur	60
15. Meghalaya	60	16. Mizoram	40
17. Nagaland	60	18. Orissa	147
19. Punjab	117	20. Rajasthan	200
21. Sikkim	32	22. Tamil Nadu	234
23. Tripura	60	24. Uttar Pradesh	425
25. West Bengal	294		

*The total number of seats is 100; remaining seats have been earmarked for the area now under the illegal occupation of Pakistan.

As already pointed out, the Vidhan Sabha is a powerful chamber. A money bill and a budget are introduced in it. Its members take part in the election of the President of India and of the members of the Rajya Sabha and Vidhan Parishad (if it is there) in accordance with proportional representation with single transferable vote system. Since the ministry is accountable to the Vidhan Sabha, it may throw out the government by passing a vote of no-confidence against it. It may express its lack of confidence in the government by rejecting an official bill, or by making a cut in the budget, or by disapproving the policy of the cabinet, or by passing the motion of censure. It considers reports submitted by the State Public Service Commission, Auditor-General etc. In case the Centre desires to make alteration in the name, area or boundary lines of a State, the President shall refer that proposal to know the view of its Vidhan Sabha before recommending is introduction in the Parliament. He may also fix a time limit within which the Vidhan Sabha has to give its view. The Vidhan Sabha gives its view on such a proposal, but the Center is not bound to honour it. In case of a constitutional amendment bill referred to it for ratification under Art. 368, it passes a resolution by simple majority to endorse it or not.

On the whole, the position of the State legislatures is very weak. They can make a law on a subject of the State List. They can make a law on a subject of the Concurrent List also. In case a law on a subject of the Concurrent List has already been made by the Centre, then the bill passed by the State legislature shall be 'reserved' by the Governor for the consideration of the President of India. Moreover, in the event of any conflict between the Central law and the State law on matter of Concurrent List, the former shall prevail and the latter shall remain inoperative to the extent of being repugnant to the former. We have also seen conditions in which the Centre can make a law on a subject of the State List and here in the event of any conflict between the Central law and State law, the latter shall remain 'suspended' to the extend of being repugnant to the former and be effective again after the revocation of the former. It may also be kept in view that the Governor is duty bound to keep any bill passed by the State legislature 'reserved' for the consideration of the President in case he finds it likely to be in conflict with any law or policy of the Centre. Thus, the operation of the legislative process at the Central as well as at the State levels "reinforces the Union predominance in the legislative field."

Critical Appreciation

Though the component units of federal system, the State governments do not have the type of autonomy that is enjoyed by the States of America or the Cantons of Switzerland. There are many inroads through which the Centre may exercise its dominance over the States in normal as well as abnormal times. Not only this, the States must carry out the directives sent to them by Centre, otherwise it would be taken as the 'breakdown of constitutional machinery' there and then the Centre shall have the power to dismiss a State government under Art. 356. The President is the head of the Indian

Republic and the Governor, while being the constitutional head of the State government, acts as the 'eyes and the ears' of the Centre. Despite this all, our State government cannot be identified with the provinces of Canada which, in the words of Dawson, 'are like glorified municipalities'. It is true that such a statement has now become outdated as the Canadian provinces have gained more power, still they have no autonomy as is available to the Sates of America, Australia and Germany. In fine, the position of the States of the Indian Union falls somewhere between the States of Aermica on the one side and of the Provinces of Canada on the other.

UNION-STATE RELATIONS

The Constitution has elaborate provisions to specify relations between the Union and the States in three important directions. While Part XI specifies legislative and administration relations, Part XII specifies financial relations between the Centre and the States. We may have a brief study of the Union-State relations in the following manners :

Legislative. Both the Centre and the States have been given power to make laws. The Centre can made a law on any item of the Union List. The States can take up any item of the State List for a legislative purpose. Both the Centre and the States can make a law on an item of the Concurrent List with this provision that in the event of any conflict between the Central and State laws, the law of the Centre shall prevail and the law of the State shall be void to the extent of being repugnant to that. It shows that while the Centre has direct control over the items of the Union List, it has the same kind of control over the items of the Concurrent List as well. However, the important point to be noted here is that under some conditions, the Centre can make a law on an item of the State List as well under these conditions:

1. Art. 249, Says that the Rajya Sabha may adopt a special resolution by two-thirds majority of its members, present and voting, and thereby shift an item of the State List to the Union List or to the Concurrent List on the ground that it has become expedient in the national interest. Such a resolution shall remain in force for a period of one year, but

the Rajya Sabha may re-adopt this resolution again and again. So long as this resolution stands, the Centre shall have the power to make a law on that item of the State List. Such a law of the Centre shall remain in force and the law of the State or States shall remain 'suspended' to the extent of being repugnant to the Central law, but it shall come into effect when the law of the Centre is revoked. Such a law of the Centre, unless revoked earlier, shall remain in force at the most for a period of 6 months after the lapsing of the resolution.

2. Art. 250, says that the centre shall have the power to make a law on an item of the State List during the period of 'emergency'. It should be noted here that Parliament's power in this regard shall cover the whole country in case of emergency under Art. 352, and to some State in the case of emergency under Art. 356, in force. It should be repeated here that the State Law shall remain 'suspended' to the extent it is repugnant to the Union law. However, the Union law, unless revoked earlier, shall remain in operation at the most for six months after the termination of emergency.
3. Art. 252, says that the Parliament shall have the power to make a law on an item of the State List when there is a request to this effect by two or more States. Such a law shall apply to the States that make such a request, or it may apply to some other State if it becomes a party to the request afterwards. It has also been made clear that such a law can be amended or repealed only by the Parliament at the request of the concerned State legislatures.
4. Art. 253, says that the Parliament can make law on any item of the State List to implement some international treaty, agreement or convention.

A student of the Indian constitutional system may thus form this impression that the Centre has exclusive control over the items of the Union List and over-riding control over the items of the Concurrent

List, but there are some inroads through which it may exercise it control over the items of the State List as well in normal as well as abnormal times.

Administrative. The strong and over-riding position of the Centre may be noted in the administrative sphere as well. Here the following points should be noted :

1. Art. 256, says that the executive power of every State shall be so exercised as to ensure compliance with the laws made by the Parliament and any existing laws which apply in that State, and the executive power of the Union shall extend to the giving of such directions to a State as may appear to the Government of India necessary for that purpose.
2. Art. 257, says that the executive power of every State shall be so exercised as not to impede or prejudice the executive power of the Union, and the executive power of the Union shall extend to the giving of such directions to a State as many appear to the Government of India necessary for that purpose. The executive power of the Union shall also extend to the giving of directions of State as to the construction and maintenance of the means of communication declared in this direction to be of national and military importance.
3. Art. 258, says that the President may, with the consent of the government of a State, entrust either conditionally or unconditionally to it or to its officers function in respect of any matter to which the executive power of the Union extends. A law made by the Parliament which applies in any State may, notwithstanding that it relates to a matter with respect to which the legislature of the State has no power to make law, confer powers and impose duties, or authorise the conferment of power and the imposition of duties, upon the State of officers and authorities thereof. Likewise, the Governor of a State may, with the consent of the Government of India, entrust either conditionally or

unconditionally to that government or its officers functions in relation to any matter to which the executive power of the State extends.

4. Art. 260, lays down that the Government of India may by agreement with the government of any territory not being a part of the territory of India, undertake any executive, legislative or judicial functions vested in the government of such territory, but every such agreement shall be subject to, and governed by, any law relating to the exercise of foreign jurisdiction for the time being in force.
5. Art. 261, says that full faith and credit shall be given throughout the territory of India to public acts, records and judicial proceedings of the Union and of every State.
6. Art. 262, says that the Parliament may by law provide for the adjudication of any dispute or complaint with respect to the use, distribution and control of the waters or in any Inter-State river valley.
7. Art. 263, says about the establishment of an Inter-State Council. If at any time it appears to the President of India that the public interest would be served by the establishment of an Inter-State Council charged with the duty of, *(a)* inquiring into and advising upon disputes which may have arisen between States, *(b)* investigating and discussing subjects in which some or all of the States, or the Union and one or more of the States have a common interest, or *(c)* making recommendations upon any such subject, and in particular, recommendations for the better coordination of policy and action with respect to that subject, it shall be lawful for the President to establish by order such a Council and to define the nature and duties to be performed by it and its organisation and procedure.

A look at these provisions of the Constitution confirms the same critical impression that as in the legislative sphere so here the position of the Centre is very strong and compared to that the position of the State government is very weak.

Financial. Finally, we come to financial relations between the Union and the State. Here following points should be noted :

1. Art. 268, says about duties to be lived by the Union but collected and appropriated by the States. In includes duties on medicinal and toilet preparations, excise on tobacco, corporation tax, customs and import duties, estate duty, terminal taxes on goods and passengers, tax on goods for Inter-State trade etc.
2. Art. 269, says about taxes to be levied and collected by the Union but assigned to the States. It includes duties in respect of succession to property other than agricultural land, estate duty in respect of property other than agricultural, terminal taxes on goods and passengers carried by rail, sea or air, taxes on railway fares and freights, taxes on the sale and purchase of newspapers and advertisements given therein etc.
3. Art. 270, says about taxes to be levied and collected by the Union and distributed between the Union and the States. It includes tax on income other than agricultural.
4. Art. 271, says about the taxes to be levied and collected by the Union and which may be distributed between the Union and the States. It includes many items given in the Union List as railways, post and telegraph, telephones, wireless, foreign exchange, foreign loans, customs and export duties etc.
5. Art. 272, says about the grants-in-aid given by the Union to the States for implementing its planning programmes as well as for the development of the Scheduled Castes, Scheduled Tribes and other weaker sections of the Community. It is provided that the President shall determine special grants to some States like Assam, Biher, Orissa and West Bengal in lieu of export duty on jute and jute products.
6. Above all, Art. 280, says about the setting-up of a Finance Commission by the President of India after a gap of every five years, or whenever he so deems necessary, having a

> Chairman and four other members which shall recommendations as to the distribution between the Union and the States of the net proceeds of taxes which are to be or may be divided between them and the allocation between the States of the respective shares of such proceeds and the principles which should govern the grants-in-aid of the revenues of the States out of the Consolidated Fund of India.

Critical Appreciation

A critical study of the provisions of the Constitution relating to Union-State relations in legislative, administrative and financial spheres leaves this impression that India has a federal system 'with strong centralising tendency.' The distribution of powers between the Centre and the States is hardly equitable in view of the fact that all important items are included in the Union List that is under the exclusive authority of the Centre. Since all items of the Concurrent List are subject to the over-riding authority of the Centre, same can be said about this List as well. Even the items of the State List are indirectly under the control of the Centre. Residuary items are also with the Centre. Moreover, under Art. 200, the Governor of a State may reserve a bill passed by the State legislature for the 'consideration' of the President of India if it seeks to abolish private property, or imposes tax on an item already declared 'essential' by law of the Parliament, or derogates the jurisdiction of the High Court, or may create a situation of conflict with some law or administrative action or policy of the Centre. It should be noted here that in such matters the veto power of the President is absolute. There is no time limit within which the President has to return a bill after his 'consideration'. Facts show that some bills passed by the State Legislatures became defunct because of pending in the office of the Union Law Ministry for a period of more than twenty years.

Similarly, in the administrative sphere, the Centre may issue directives to the States which they carry out in order to avoid the invocation of Art. 356. The States cannot initiate a bill of constitutional amendment, nor can they take disciplinary action against the IAS and IPS officers in spite of the fact that they draw salaries and allowances from State exchequer for being in service there. The Governor and the High Court judges serve State governments and draw their salaries and allowances from the State exchequer, but the States cannot initiate impeachment proceedings against them. The Centre can make alteration in the boundary lines of the States as per its own policy after taking the opinion of the concerned State or States just for the sake of courtesy. The States have no power to frame their own constitution. (Jammu-Kashimir is an exception the to political reasons). There is single citizenship in the country. This feature of singleness may also be noted in the system of integrated judiciary and application of civil and criminal law and procedure throughout the country. Financially, the States are too weak and they are bound to exist on the assistance of the Centre. Keeping all this in view, an eminent English writer says that, India "is a unitary state with subsidiary federal features rather than a federal state with subsidiary unitary features."

However, such critical observations should not be accepted without any reservation. As a matter of fact, every country his own typical problems in the light of which its constitutional system grows and lives in operation. It is true that the Indian federal system does not permit the kind of autonomy that is available to the states of the United States of America or the Cantons of Switzerland; but it certainly grants to the units more autonomy than what is available to the Provinces of Canada or the lander of Germany. By following the Australian model of 'cooperative federalism', we have established some agencies of Union-State cooperation and coordination (like Inter-State Council, Finance Commission and Zonal Councils) and also evolved some extra-constitutional devices (like National Development Council and annual meetings of the Governors and Chief Ministers in New Delhi) so as to enable the Union the State governments to consider matters of common interest and iron out their differences within the constitutional framework of the country. A strong Centre is the need of the hour to deal with many fissiparous tendencies and anti-national forces. So, in the words of Dr. Rajendra Prasad, "India is an indissoluble union of indissoluble states."

❐

5

Panchayati Raj Institutions

THE WORKING OF PANCHAYATI RAJ

The evaluation of Panchayati Raj too poses a major problem both in theory and research. The lack of conceptual clarity and the prevailing ambiguity about the objectives of Panchayati Raj makes our enquiry all the more cumbersome. It is a great challenge to fix the boundaries of the system and its environment. The fact that the Panchayati Raj is not autonomous system, but a segment of a larger whole complicates the situation. Further, the multi-dimensional character of the Panchayati Raj as a local self-government institution, as an agency of development administration and as a part of the power structure creates confusion in the minds of those scholars who intend to evaluate its functions.

We have also been the structure of Panchayati Raj as it actually emerged from the discussion that followed the report of Balwant Rai Mehta team and from the various emphasis that different states placed on different aspects of the team's recommendations because the committee did not favour rigidity in regard to the uniform pattern of Panchayati Raj throughout the country. However, it laid down some fundamental principles which underline the spirit of democratic decentralisation. These were:

(a) There should be three-tiered structure of local self-government bodies from village to the district level and these bodies should be linked together;

(b) There should be genuine transfer of power and responsibilities of these bodies to enable them to discharge their responsibilities;

(c) All welfare and development schemes and programmes at the three levels should be channelled through these bodies only;

(d) Adequate resources be tranformed to these bodies; and

(e) The three-tiered system should facilitate further devolution and dispersal of power and responsibility in the future.

The Panchayati Raj movement started with all funfare, enthusiasm, laudable objectives and hopes. A new democratic structure was devised which would not only put the Community Development Programme back on its track out, would also (as a long measure) help accelerate the process of development. It was based on the assumption that the establishment of a chain of new democratic institutions at the grass-root level would bring democracy at the doors of the people, that it would evoke people's participation and open many more avenues to the rural community for their participation in the political process of the country.

It would be useful to examine how far Panchayati Raj has succeeded in achieving the above aims. But to assess to what extent the present structures of Panchayati Raj have been able to achieve the development goals on the one hand and the tempo of political development on the other is a difficult exercise. Here, in this chapter, an attempt has been made to discuss the performance of Panchayati Raj Institutions on the political and development fronts.

I. Political Impact of Panchayati Raj. The introduction of the Panchayati Raj Institutions has undoubtedly started the process of politicisation. The people have acquired a great deal of political consciousness. The decentralised democratic system with "universal adult franchise, secret ballot and activities of political parties has brought a political awakening among the people in the rural areas."

The various studies show that political offices are keenly contested unlike in the past when the members could get elected without any opposition. It may pointed out that in spite of this awareness amongst the rural masses, the ultimate goal of making them politically articulate citizens of a democratic order seems to be a distant dream. However, the fact remains that they are very much aware and convinced that their vote has a value and they can influence the decision making process. In the words of Rajni Kothari, "largely as a result of the operation of adult franchise, considerable shift has occurred in social base of politics. Sections of the people who had been hiterto denied access to the political power and who had considered politics as the legitimate concern of the martial and learned classes, have been exposed to the new ideology, have realised the power of numbers and have started organising themselves through their own associations and leaders.

Similarly, it has been felt by some that one of the direct and perhaps the most significant consequences of this introduction is some kind of loosening up the conventionally established political relationship on the one hand, and an ever-growing awareness that public policy decisions and their implementation can be influenced on the other. Some studies have indicated that political awareness of the people in the villages is not confined to this realisation only, but they have even effectively asserted their political claims and have judiciously exercised their right to vote. But it cannot be said to be a general trend. It is just a beginning. It must be pointed out here that increased political consciousness has also resulted in a struggle for status and power among individuals and social groups and it has paved the way for the entry of political parties. But unfortunately, the political parties have failed in making the rural masses identify them with their policies and programmes. The studies have shown that the village elections are still based on individual or caste loyalties.

Regarding the Leadership Pattern. It is being pointed out that the leadership pattern has been secularised at the various levels of Panchayati Raj. The new emerging elite is less ascription based and more performance oriented. They are less orthodox in approach and better educated and younger in years. Although it is significant trend yet it cannot be considered as a general rule. For instance, some studies in Karnataka, Punjab and Rajasthan have indicated that the power structure in Panchayats is found to be still in favour of the order age. On the whole, the Panchayati Raj has brought about a revolutionary change in the social psychology and political approach of the village masses. Even if we examine the role of Panchayati Raj

Institutions in terms of legitimacy, mobilisation and communication, which are the main determinants of the effectiveness of a political system some positive signs are visible. To be more specific, the Panchayati Raj Institutions are on the road of political development. The need of the hour is to bring greater dynamism in rural areas.

II. Development Role of Panchayati Raj. As we know, a viable infrastructure has been established in the rural areas right from the village level upto district and state levels with a happy mix of government paid block organisation and elected Panchayati Raj Institutions in most of the states. The founding fathers of Panchayati Raj were confident that once the institutions of rural local government were structured on democratic lines and were given the needed initiative and resources, they would facilitate the work of rural social and economic development. Now let us evaluate the development impact of Panchayati Raj which has come to stay as stated above.

In this regard, the Government of India clearly brought out the pivotal position of Panchayati Raj in development activities for the rural area in the First Plan Document and in the subsequent plans thereafter. The Second Five Year Plan wanted the village institution to be placed on sound footing and to be entrusted with a great deal of the responsibility for carrying out local programmes. The All India Panchayat Parishad in 1973, too observed and appealed to the Planning Commission to recognise Panchayati Raj Institutions as the proper instrument for implementation of the Five Year Plans.

(1) Many have Emphasised that Panchayati Raj Bodies at Different Levels can Play a Vital Role in Agricultural Production. Balwant Rai Metha's Report observed that the "material progress in the agricultural sector can be judged only by the total increase in agricultural production. The Annual Conference of Development Commissioners and Ministers of Community Development and Panchayati Raj (1966), too recommended some measures. In fact, the real contribution of Panchayati Raj bodies to agricultural development has remained a debatable issue. It has been pointed out by same that the leadership at the block and village level had not shown enough awareness and capacity to get priority to development work and suggested the establishment of separate agency. Rudramurthy has observed that the village Panchayats have not yet come up to expectations. However, R.N. Chopra is emphatic that Panchayati Raj bodies cannot handle agricultural production and it can be handled successfully only under a system of single-line control and responsibility. But K.N. Raj, who is critical of the acitivites pertaining to agriculture has very rightly suggested that the "States should experiment with planning from below by concentrating initially on district, block and village levels and thereby, take full advantage of the existing institutional structure." It would not be out of place if we mention the views of an Expert Committee on Assessment and Evaluation appointed by the Central Government. The Committee observed, "Involvement of local leadership in agricultural development is, no doubt, necessary, but, such a leadership has to be functional and trained. The Committee found that popularly elected Panchayati Raj Institutions were of some help in creating awareness of the need for agricultural practices, but in regard to agricultural modernisation they have not played a significant part. It is, therefore, necessary to consider the policies regarding the role that should be assigned to the Panchayati Raj Institutions in agricultural development.

The studies conducted by some scholars to assess certain aspects of the functioning of the diffferent tiers of Panchayati Raj in the states of Tamil Nadu, Gujarat, Andhra Pradesh and Madhya Pradesh have revealed that significant role has been played by the Panchayati Raj Institutions in agricultural production. For instance, in Gujarat and Andhra Pradesh, these institutions have been able to make improvements with respect to roads, implments and loans for irrigation, distribution of fertilizers, seeds and insecticides and guidance in cropping patterns. Similarly, in Tamil Nadu the Panchayati Raj bodies seem to have made all round impact on different Community Services, and that almost all services connected with agriculture. However, in Madhya Pradesh, the impact of Panchayati Raj Institutions has been negligible.

(2) Panchayati Raj Institutions can Play a Significant Role in Looking After the Interests of Weaker Sections. Various committees have stressed the need for such a role. That is why the various Panchayati Raj legislations have incorporated provisions for representing the members of the scheduled castes and tribes on Panchayati Raj Institutions. The Constitutional Amendment Act, 1992, has made it obligatory for all the State Governments to fill up the membership of scheduled castes on the basis of population. In all states except Punjab and U.P., the Panchayati Raj Institutions have appointed committees to look after the interests of the weaker sections. The Committee on Plan Projects appointed by the Planning Commission on the role and functions of Panchayati Raj Institutions in planning development considered it necessary to associate the weaker sections with the Panchayati Raj Institutions.

Darji Committee in Gujarat and Sadiqu Ali Committee in Rajasthan too stressed the need for raising the status of the weaker sections, but the committee further opined that by the large, the Panchayati Raj Institutions have not been able to devote any specific attention and render any significant help to weaker sections.

(3) In the Field of Education also Panchayati Raj Institutions can Play a Pivotal Role in the Development of the Community. In many states education, at the primary and secondary levels has been transferred to the Panchayati Raj bodies but, the progress has been uneven. In this regard, the various states have incorporated certain provisions in the controlling Act. For instance in Tamil Nadu, The Madras Panchayats Act, 1938, has provided that the Panchayat should levy a local tax to cover a specific proportion of increased expenditure on elementary education. Similarly, the Act gives the responsibility to the Panchayats for ensuring enrolment and regular attendance at the primary classes. However, in Punjab, the Punjab Gram Panchayat Act, 1952 provided that where a group of neighbouring gram Panchayat areas have no primary school, hospital or Ayurvedic dispensary, the Panchayat samiti or the state government shall place such funds as may be necessary for the purpose, at the disposal of the gram Panchayats concerned.

(4) The Evaluation of Panchayati Raj Institutions can be Judged in Terms of Land Reforms Measures Implemented in the Various States. In fact, because of the inadequacy of revenue machinery in different states to enforce different aspects of land reforms measures, suggestions for associating the democratic institutions or Panchayati Raj Institutions in their implementation were first made during the Second Five Year Plan. The Plan suggested that "in carrying out various tasks, the official machinery can and should derive a great deal of assistance from the agencies of district development administration, namely village Panchayats, development committees in talukas and development councils". The Second Plan further opined that village Panchayats can play a significant role in the achievement of high standards of management and efficiency and in assiting the progress of consolidation of holdings.

The various committees both at the central and state level have examined the issue of associating Panchayati Raj bodies in implementing the land reform revenues. For instance Ramanadhan Study Team (1968), appointed by the Government of India examined this issue intensively and as many as 9 states expressed their opinion on the issue of associating Panchayats and other levels of rural local government in the task of implementing land reforms.

The general consensus was that the Panchayats were not adequately equipped for this purpose as it involved an intricate knowledge to revenue laws and rules made their-under.

From the preceding analysis of the political and development role of Panchayati Raj Institutions, it becomes amply clear that it is accepted by almost all that the Panchayati Raj has strengthened a participatory democratic culture. Undoubtedly, there is a lot of political awareness in the rural India and it is the Panchayati Raj which has made rural masses more articulated. Some of the thinkers opine that it has been useful as a socialising agent by imparting the values of democracy in the rural masses. Critics, however, may say that such awareness is exhibited only at the time of elections, but, this is no mean achievement in a country where the rural people suffer from political apathy.

FACTORS LEADINGS TO POOR PERFORMANCE OF PANCHAYATI RAJ INSTITUTIONS

We have seen the Panchayati Raj system has been working for over four decades now. However, the system has failed to sustain its initial charm or support. A number of factors may be pointed out leading to the dismal picture of Panchayati Raj. Panchayati Raj Institutions have always been suffering from the lack of faith on the part of political leaders and administrators.

1. Lack of Faith and Constitutional Support. Till recently the Panchayati Raj institutions have been suffering from the lack of constitutional recognition. The intention of the constitution makers was to see the village Panchayats as the units of self-government and not as agents of state governments, but because of the insufficient constitutional support, the state governments continued to tamper with these institutions for their own advantage. Much of the state legislation was directed towards making these institutions as state agents only and not the real grass-root institutions. However, with the implementation of the various provisions of the Constitutional Amendment Act, 1992 by all the States, a congenial environment has been created. The future of these institutions is bright.

2. Gram Sabha has not Proved to be Effective Embodiment and Instrument of Grass-Roots Democracy. The Gram Sabha is the general body of the village Panchayat and consists of all eligible voters in the jurisdiction of a Gram Panchayat. The Sabha is established as a statutory body in most states. The Gram Sabha comes closest to the team's concept of 'participating democracy' and constitutes the base of the Panchayati Raj system. The Gram Sabha has been conceived as an only institution wherein we catch the glimpse of direct democracy. The institutions reflects the idea of Prof. Maddick who says, "for long term success, there can be no alternative to popular participation and ultimately popular control."

It is rather unfortunate that Gram Sabha has failed to act as an effective embodiment and instrument of grass-root democracy. Many Gram Sabhas have not been able to summon up enough interest in their own responsibilities to justify even the minimum of two meetings in a year that legislation has generally prescribed and it has been suggested that, "In almost every state, the role of the Gram Sabha is only ceremonial and formal". Reviewing the progress of Gram Sabha, Shri S.K. Dey had to confess publically that in spite of statutory provisions, members of Gram Sabha are not taking interest in the deliberations of this body.

3. Attitude of Government Towards Panchayati Raj. All the State governments have shown lukewarm attitude towards their development. There has been widespread arbitrariness in superseding Panchayati Raj Institutions and elections have in many states not been held for years. Till 1992, when 73rd Constitutional Amendment Act was passed by the Parliament, power jealous state politicians had been using the absence of a constitutional guarantee to cripple Panchayati Raj. By providing constitutional hurdle to the Panchayati Raj Institutions a major guarantee is over. Even than they may not desist from doing a mischief in the future. Thus, local leaders will have to resist any such move in the future.

4. Lack of Capacity of Panchayats to Perform a Wide Range of Functions. The Gram Panchayat, under the various Acts, has been entrusted with a wide range of functions, which are well beyond the capacity of the great majority of the Panchayats. The lack of capacity has two facets, financial and managerial. The Panchayats have been empowered to levy certain taxes such as taxes on the dwellings, vehicles and professions, realization of fees from the periodical markets, if the village is large enough and sometimes a cess on the land revenue collected from the village. But there are problems regarding the evaluation of dwellings for the purpose of taxing. The local pressures have generally ensured that the rate of the tax is close to the minimum. The share of land revenue made available to the Panchayats by the state government has also not proved substantial in absolute terms. This is largely due to the multiplicity of tiers. There is also no end to the number of grants and channels through which these are received. For instance the Narsimhan Committee in Andhra Pradesh (1970-71), observed that although the list of functions under gram Panchayats is very large, but the per capita income for all the notified and non-notified gram Panchayats was just Rs. 2.75. The Study team on Panchayati Raj in Punjab has also observed that in so far as the Panchayats are concerned, it may be pointed out that these bodies have hardly any finance worth the name through which they can undertake development activities. Similar views are given by Rajindra Singh Team.

5. Inadequacy of Panchayat Samiti as an Organ of Economic Planning. As we are very much aware, almost all the states have made the samiti a powerful and effective instrument of economic and social progress. Despite the competence given to them by law, few samities have shown a readiness to levy tax to the extent that will result in the availability of funds adequate for the proper discharge of the functions they are expected to perform. The reluctance to levy tax is mainly a reflection of local pressure which the samitis have, by and large, so far proved unable to resist. The process by which the Five Year Plans have come to be formulated has been the central government vast powers both in the spheres of programming and in the matter of financial resources.

As a result of these trends, some observers of Panchayati Raj have pointed out that the sphere in which the influence of Panchayat samiti has been most marked is political rather than economic. "It had been expected that Panchayati Raj would primarily be a development mechanism and make up the shortfalls of the community development programme... In practice it has emerged primarily as a power mechanism. The local leader is developing strong links with the state leaders, particularly ministers who patronize him because they know he is more or less to serve as a vote bank for his area. The Panchayati Raj has brought about a political frame-work for the development of pattern of closer contact between the local and state leadership.

6. Panchayati Raj has been Seen as Rival Centre of Power. The major reason for decline of Panchayati Raj has been seen by the political leadership at the state level as a rival centre of power. Panchayati Raj Institution enactments by the large created weak institutions, and the manner in which the enactments were applied made the institutions weaker. Thus Haryana had Zila Parishads which were merely supervisory bodies, but presumably because they had the potential of being politically troublesome they were suddenly abolished in 1973.

7. Relationship Between Non-Officials and Officials. Ineffective performance of Panchayati Raj Institutions can also be attributed to the absence of cordial relationship between non-officials and officials. In fact, one of the most difficult problems of Panchayati Raj is the relationship between non-officials. Writing on the leadership between the non-officials, Henry Maddick observed : "One of the most difficult questions in connection with local government and, in particular, a new local government system is what relationship should exist between officials and non-officials. Ideally the relationship should be one of popular leadership and the interpretation of the popular will by the elected or co-opted representatives, advising and counselling the officials with whom must rest the execution of the policy finally adopted. This is well established pattern in a number of systems, but is appreciated in India better in state government than in local". At the state and central levels, the civil servants are not expected to come in close contact with the politicians except at committee sessions. Largely their dealing is with the minister in day-to-day working and are somewhat insulated from political pressures such as those to which the secretary of the Zila Parishad or the block development officer of a Panchayati Samiti is normally exposed to at the district and samiti levels.

On the whole, the situation does not seem to be satisfactory in most of the states because different opinions prevail amongst the officials and non-officials about their respective roles and responsibilities and each of these groups has stereotyped images of the other which has affected the proper functioning of Panchayati Raj Institutions. Such a state of affairs can be corrected if we are able to bring about a change of out-look among the officials and non-officials. Raghubir Sahai opines that the elaborate machinery of supervision, a well thought out training programme would be necessary to restructure some of the personal habits in thinking and behaving. Similar views have been given by Ram K. Vepa and C.V.H. Rao. Ram K. Vepa thinks that in the success of attempts to train the corps of rural leadership lies the hope of the future.

Leadership Training Programmes should be geared to the task of preparing the leaders in accordance with the goals of democratic decentralisation. However, C.V.H. Rao opines that the need for holding orientation courses for the benefit of the members and

Presidents of Panchayats in training institutes would enable them to perform their duties efficiently and effectively. The assertion of Raghubir Sahai is that a non-official with a will and requisite ability would be able to play his part very well and make the officials move in the right direction.

8. Lack of Commitment on the Part of Officials and Non-Officials. The various studies have clearly demonstrated that there is a lack of commitment in these institutions. Uncertainty seems to loom large with regard to these institutions. It has been pointed out that in spite of the sympathy shown to them, there is still no conviction about the utility of these bodies in rural development. So long this wavering approach continues, the performance of these institutions is bound to be ineffective. The initiative taken by the late Prime Minister Rajiv Gandhi to strengthen these institutions was noteworthy. He asked all the chief ministers to hold regular elections to Panchayati Raj Institutions and to support them administratively and financially to make them "vibrant instruments of popular participation in the development process". These proved to be encouraging signs for the future leadership.

9. Casteism and Communalism. The various studies have indicated that casteism and communalism stand in the way of the proper operation of Panchayati Raj administration. The influence of these factors has been banefual to development. One important and serious aspect of Panchayati Raj Institutions is the interference of the political parties in their administration. To avoid this, the political parties should be recognised at the Panchayat level, but, at the same time every thing possible should be done to eliminate the evil consequences of the petty party politics in the administration of Panchayati Raj Institutions. Ashok Mehta Committee too opined that participation of political parties in Panchayati Raj elections would ensure clear orientation towards development programmes and facilitate healthier linkages with higher level political process.

Besides, the above mentioned factors affecting the performance of Panchayati Raj Institutions, the Panchayati Raj Institutions have been under constant review in some of the states. For instance, The Administrative Reforms Commission (1966), and subsequent committees thereafter, reported that the following factors have contributed to the ineffective performance of the Panchayati Raj Institutions.

Panchayats

(i) limited financial resources for a vigorous and constructive role;

(ii) local functions;

(iii) too much political intereference;

(iv) defective methods of elections;

(v) too many elections;

(vi) inadequate cooperation between the officials and non-officials.

(vii) police hostility;

Panchayat Samitis and Zila Parishads

(i) inadequate finances;

(ii) element of dual control and lack of coordination at the block level;

(iii) non-cooperation from the departments placed at the disposal of Panchayati Samiti;

(iv) Three tier system adopted by the state government had no practical and effective administrative links;

(v) government's lack of faith in these institutions;

(vi) policy hostility; and

(vii) faulty methods of elections.

From the above discussions and available studies it is evident that the performance of Panchayati Raj bodies has not been encouraging. The causes mentioned above are known, but the same have never been looked into seriously. There is no doubt that the developmental programmes have not been channelled through them fully, but it must be understood that it has many achievements to its credit in introducing a process of democratic seed drilling in the Indian soil, in breaking the gulf between the bureaucratic elite and the people and in generating a new leadership, not relatively young, in age but pro-social change in outlook.

URBANISATION : INDIAN SCENARIO

Urbanisation is characterised by movement of people from rural communities concerned chiefly or solely with agriculture (rural communities) to other communities where activities are primarily centred in management, trade, manufacture or allied interests (urban communities). In short, urbanisation is a multifaceted phenomenon—a process which reveals itself through temporal, spacial and sectoral and sectoral changes in the demographic, soico-economic, technological and environmental aspects of life in a given society. These changes manifest themselves in the increasing concentration of population in human settlements larger than villages, in the increasing involvement of the people in the secondary the teritary production functions and in the progressive adoption of certain social traits which are a typical of traditional rural societies.

Urbanisation is a world-wide phenomenon. It has been going on at a very accelerated pace in recent years. According to the estimates and projections of the United Nations Population Division, the urban population in the world had risen from 1361 million in 1970 to 2,286 million in 1990, and is likely to be about 5 billion in 2025. In terms of population urban population in the total world population, it implies an increase from 36.9 per cent in 1970 to 43.6 per cent in 1990, and 62.5 per cent in 2025. By the turn of the century over 50 per cent of the world population will be urban as against 29 per cent in 1950, 39 per cent in 1975, and 43 per cent in 1985. In other words, the urban population of the world which doubled between 1850 and 1975, will further double between 1975, and 2000. Massive urbanisation is engulfing the Third World. Within the span of the last two decades, towns and cities all over Asia, Africa and Latin America have been doubling and tripling in size. The developing countries are urbanising not only more rapidly than the industrial nations are now but also more rapidly than the industrial nations did in the heyday of their urban growth. U.N. forecasts that by the end of this century, 41 per cent of the population in the developing countries will be living in towns and about 80 per cent in Latin America, the most urbanised region. In keeping with the global trend, there has been a accelerated growth of urbanisation in India. In 1951, the urban population was 62.28 million, thirty years later (1981) it had gone up by 2½ times to 160 millions and was estimated authoritatively in 1988, to have reached 200 million and is expected to touch about 350 million by the end of the century.

In the context of India, the census reports of 1961, todate have defined those places as urban areas which have a local authority like municipality, contonment broad, notified are committees, and all other places which satisfy the requirements of a minimum population of 5,000, at least 75 per cent of the male working population engaged in non-agricultural pursuits and a density of population of atleast 400 persons per square km. Apart from above criterion, the state government can declare a place as an urban area if it has a pronounced urban characteristic and amenities as the newly founded industrial areas, large housing settlements or places of tourist importance usually have.

SALIENT FEATURES OF URBANISATION IN INDIA

The salient features of the urbanisation process in India may be described as follows:

1. Tremendous Increase in Urban Population. India has witnessed tremendous increase in its urban population since independence. The total population of the country had doubled from 350 million in 1947 to 800 millions in 1988, and it stood at 84-94 million on March 1, 1991. During 1947-1988, urban population had increased four-fold from 50 million to 200 million. By the end of the century (24th Oct., 1999), the total population is projected to touch 1000 million and urban population 350 million. Expert Committee of the Registrar General (Census), however, projects urban population of 32.6 crores in 2001. National Commission on Urbanisation is of the view that the total population of India in 2001 will exceed 100 crores and the urban population will be in the range of 34 to 35 crores 35% of the total. According to the latest projections made by the United Nations, India's urban population is expected to be 33 crores in 2001, 45.4 crores in 2010, 59.1 crores in 2020 and 65.8 crores in

2025 when the total population of India is expected to be 122.9 crores.

2. Rise in the Number of Urban Areas. The country is becoming urbanised at an alarming rate. Consequently the number of urban areas is increasing. According to the Census Report of 1971, urban India comprised 1921 towns including 69 urban agglomerations. In 1989, there were 3301 urban settlements. Their number is to increase inevitably with the anticipated increase in urban population.

3. Uneven Distribution of Urban Population in Various States/UT's. Urban population is unevenly distributed in different States and Union Territories in the country. At the end of the spectrum, we have Arunachal Pradesh and Himachal Pradesh with 6.6 per cent and 7.6 per cent urban population respectively, at the other end are Maharashtra and Tamil Nadu with 35 per cent and 33 per cent urban population respectively. In between, we have states with proportion of urban population ranging from 11 to 32 per cent. The Union Territory of Chandigarh is 93.6 per cent urban while Dadra and Nagar Haveli Union Territory is only 6.7 per cent urban.

4. Rise in Urban India and Decline in Rural Growth to Continue. In the last five years of this century (1996-2001), the annual exponential growth rate in urban India as a whole is expected to be of the order of 3.4 per cent and for rural India 0.7 per cent. In economially backward states and high urban states the urban and rural growth rates are estimated to be as follows :

Economically Backward States

	Urban Growth Rate	*Rural Growth Rate*
Uttar Pradesh	5.1	0.5
Orissa	4.7	0.4
Rajasthan	4.4	1.1
Bihar	4.4	1.4
Madhya Pradesh	3.9	1.4
Andhra Pradesh	2.9	0.5

In Punjab and Haryana the rural and urban growth rates are estimated to be 0.3 and 0.4 (rural) and 3.2 and 4.3 (urban) respectively.

5. Even Balance Between Natural Increase in the Population of Urban Centres and Growth Through Migration. There are three components of urban growth in our country namely : (i) Natural increase in population in urban areas *i.e.,* increase in urban population as a result of natural growth through births in urban areas; (ii) Net increase through migration to urban areas, and (iii) The Impact of reclassification or rural areas as urban. According to estimates made by the National Institute of Urban Affairs in 1988, during the decade (197-81) natural increase accounted for a little over 41 per cent of the total urban growth, immigration for a little over 40 per cent and reclassification for about 19 per cent. It is thus evident that there is almost even balance between the natural increase in the population of the urban centres and growth through migration, each accounting for approximately 40 per cent of the increase with a less than 20 per cent accounting from reclassification. It is to be noted that while the natural increase of large cities tends to remain within these cities, the migration stream tends to be from village to town and town to large city; the present trend of migration is likely to bring about a massive increase in the size of existing large cities.

6. Classification of Urban Areas. The Indian Census customarily classifies urban areas into six population size groups as follows :

Class	*Range of Population*
I	1,00,000 and above
II	50,000 to 99,991
III	20,000 to 49,999
IV	10,000 to 19,999
V	5,000 to 9,999
VI	below 5000

(According to Census practice, Class I cities denote towns with population of 1 lakh and above).

This classification, which was introduced over hundred years ago, now seems to be obsolete in view of the expanding urban base and the rate of urban growth. The National Commission on Urbanisation has therefore recommended a new criterion for classification of cities and towns as follows :

Class Cities	*Range of Population*
C 1	1 lakh to 5 lakh
C 2	5 lakhs to 10 lakhs
C 3	10 lakhs to 20 lakhs
C 4	20 lakhs to 50 lakhs
C 5	50 lakhs to 100 lakhs
C 6	100 lakhs and above
Towns	
T 1	20,000 to 50,000
T 2	50,000 to 1,00,000

The Commission is also of the view that there is no much point in considering towns with population below 20,000 as urban except in special cases like new factory towns, hill towns etc.

Of the 218 Class I cities in India (excluding Assam) there are 12 with a population of one million (ten lakhs) and more, 30 with a population in the range of 500,000 and 999,9999, 91 in the range of 250,0000 top 499,999 and 135 in the range of 100,000 to 249,999. In 1981, there were 12 million plus (ten lakhs) cities. Their number is expected to increase to 400 by the year 2001. The increase in urban population has resulted not only in increase in the number of urban areas but also in their upgradation from a city of low grade to a city of higher class. This phenomenon is in evidence in almost all the states which can be substantiated by delineating for example, demographic context of the state of Haryana as a representative of the other states of India.

PROBLEMS/CHALLENGES OF URBANISATION

Urbanisation poses several problems of multi-dimentional nature, such as, slums, insanitation, environmental pollution, scarcity of housing, water, electricity, transport and medical aid. The speed with which the urban population is growing, overflowing the boundaries and forming sprawling agglomeration of buildings, has created difficulties and the tasks of city governments have become formidable. With the increasing pace of urbanisation, demands made on municipal bodies have vestly increased which those institutions, presently constituted as they are, are grossly inadequately structured and equipped to meet. They are a hangover of early nineteenth century and are therefore not in a position to meet the demands of the cities standing on the threshold of 21st century. Some of the major problems and challenges posed by urbanisation in India are as follows :

1. Shortage of Housing. The most visible and dehumanising manifestation of urbanisation in a developing country is the large number of squatters and shanty dwellers found in all the major cities. The reason for this state of affair is housing crisis. The reality of the urban housing scene in India is that more than two lakh urban households are without any shelter and as many as 45 per cent are living in just single room houses, nearly 5 persons to a room, in a state of extreme over-crowding. In 1981, nearly 37 per cent were without electricity and about 66 per cent were without latrine.

The urban housing stock which was 14.1 million in 1961, had increased to 18.5 million in 1971, and to 28 million in 1981. Policy statements in successive Plan Documents have continued to emphasise the importance of the housing sector, but in reality, investments in housing as a percentage of total investments have declined.

In 1981, out of a total urban population of nearly 160 million, 32 to 40 millions were estimated to be in slums alone.

The failure to provide adequate, proper and affordable housing manifests itself in many forms: overcrowding, congestion, high prices, formation of slums and squatter settlements, and a sharp decline in the quality of the overall living environment. Rapid population growth, inadequate investment, wide-spread poverty, are some of the principal causes of housing crisis.

The key to success in increasing supply, both quantitatively and qualitatively, *i.e.,* in sheltering the millions and providing need-based, appropriate houses, lies in ensuring success to housing inputs;—land, building material, finance and services : the state facilitating land supply; all city dwellers being served equally in the matter of provision of basic environmental and social services, and strengthening the resource base of the local bodies to ensure this; creating properly designed, structured and staffed housing finance agencies which may effectively reach out to and service the poor; making arrangements that would accelerate production of low-cost building materials; and above all an effective industrial housing policy—providing minimum required accommodation to every employee as a pre-condition.

2. Strain on Civic Amenities. Under Article 47, of the constitutions, it is the duty of the State to improve the standard of living of the people, in particular, to improve public health standards. Water, Sewerage and drainage are three crucial elements for life, without which there can be neither health nor comfort.

A major feature of an urban scene is the misery and serious health hazards cuased by lack of water supply and sanitation. Almost all the urban centres, even those which at one time had reasonably adequate water supply, are now suffering from crippling shortages. It is a matter of national disgrace that in 1988, there were prolonged periods when Hyderabad and Madras received piped water supply for only about 20 minutes a day with many localities going without water for many days. Delhi, too, has had to face servere problems in the summer of 1988.

3. Haphazard Growth of Transportation. All major cities are plagued with traffic congestion. The obvious factors responsible are the concentration of too many people and activites in too small a place, and the inefficient relationship of work-places and residences. In the past two decades, the situation has further deteriorated significantly. In the absence of an integrated policy and coordinated approach, intra-city transportation has grown in a haphazard manner, without any long term perspective, causing congestion and severe crisis in the cities. An urban transportation system can be developed optimally only when transport and land use planning are examined together.

4. Scourage of Urban Poverty. The major demanding of the urban challenges is the challenge posed by urban poverty, the worst pollution of all, manifest in the urban slums which dominate the townscape, and in the mass of beggars, petty hawkers and causal workers struggling to eke out a living. The task of adequately feeding, educating, housing and employing a large and rapidly growing, number of under-nourished, semi-literate, semi-skilled under-employed and impoverished city dwellers, living on pavements, in poorly serviced crawls, in unhygienic slums in illegal squatters colonies and in other forms of degraded and inadequate settlements and struggling to make a living from lowpaying and unstable occupations is the challenge facing urban planners.

5. Growth of Slums. People who migrate from villages to urban areas in search of employment or for other reasons cannot afford to pay the high prices of pucca shelters or are not in a position to buy land at the higher prices charged near their work places. They cannot afford to buy means of transport to reach their destinations. Therefore, they settle on marginal lands near their work places, which are considered unfit for habitation by the non-poor classes. These places are river banks, railway lands, unconstructed residential plots in private colonies, etc. They construct their living places with cheap scrap and material like gunny bags, tarpaulin, tin sheets, wooden planks, mud, etc. These places are always without civic amenities.

6. Scarcity of Urban Land. The most disastrous feature of urbanisation in India has been that urban land has become extremely scarce and expensive beyond the reach of the poor. The shortage of land has forced both sellers and buyers into a disrespect for the law. Black money has profilerated, corruption has become rife and moral values have been eroded. The colonisers are making huge profits by fleecing those who are in dire need of shelters. Inevitably the poor have been affected most of all with legal, institutionalised and simplified access or urban land at affordable prices denied to them, they have had to take to the only option available-illegal occupation of land resulting in squatter colonies deprived of basic municipal services presenting the most brutish abuses of human dignity.

7. Lack of Employment Opportunities. Migrants to the urban areas are hopeful of getting employment as the towns and cities are expected to provide numerous job opportunities but they get frustrated when their hopes are belied as it is not easy to procure an employment commensurate with their qualifications and skills. Graduates and post-graduates working as peons and rickshaw-pullers are a common sight. Although the lower class migrants are mostly absorbed in building or construction work and in the labour force of the factories but the semi-literates form an unstable, excitable mass to the used by anti-social hoodlums for sinister and sadistic designs and diabolical actions of arson and looting during agitations.

8. Menace of Pollution. The gravest challenge to urbanisation is that of pollution of water, air, noise and solid waste. The Environment (Protection) Act, 1986 defines environmental pollutants as any solid, liquid or gasious substance present in such concentration as may or tend to be injurious to the environment. Industrial effluents, municipal sewage and agro-chemicals are the major pollutants of water. According to WHO estimates as much as 80 per cent of the world's diseases are traceable to weather pollution. Long exposure to polluted air caused by industries and vehicles is responsible for a variety of diseases including lung cancer, pneumonia, bronchitis, asthma and even the common cold. Noise pollution causes blood vessels contract leading to high-blood pressure and may affect the brain. Pollution also causes serious damage to animals, birds, aquatic life, crops and vegetation. Solid waste consisting mainly of municipal refuge and garbage is hazardous as it harbours disease carrying organisam and vectors, attracts stray dogs and pollutes the surface and ground water.

9. Ruralisation of Urban Areas. Another problem of urbanisation is the transfer of the phenomenon of ruralisation to urban centres especially those traits of rural living which render the towns and cities bear ugly looks and cause unhygienic conditions enormously straining the municipal administration and civic services. The rural migrants unable to get employment in urban areas continue with their traditional rural occupations such as animal husbandry and their livestock which results in cowdung spreading all over the streets and urban centres being crowded with buffaloes, cows, goats, poultry birds, pigs and stray cattle and the green belts and parks turning into grazing grounds and cattle sheds.

10. Increasing Social Development Problems. Urbanisation, according to Kingsley Davis, represents a revolutionary change in the whole pattern of social life. To quote a United Nations Report, "The explosive nature of urban growth and the dire poverty in which it typically takes place, poses special problems or social development. Illiterate, unskilled and socially bewildered rural migrants fill squatter shack towns and find little work, a bare subsistance and barren opportunities for self-employment. They are nearly a complete burden on the trecherously thin layer of public services. Illegitimacy, disease and crime symbolise demoralising social enzymes at work. Besides many immigrants remain semi-urbanised, for they maintain strong ties with their native culture. The immigrants with the same culture and background usually have a strong tendency to congregate together for various social reasons.

11. Encroachment of Agricultural Lands. The process of urbanisation has also assumed a new dimension of encroachment on agricultural lands at an unprecedented rate. For example, urbanisation in Haryana has swallowed up over five lakhs acres of fertile rival land in the past 23 years since its inception in 1966. The proximity of Faridabad and Gurgaon to Delhi has accelerated the pace of urbanisation in the villages. The areas between Delhi and Faridabad, Delhi and Gurgaon, Delhi and Bahadurgarh, Delhi and Sonepat are all merging into large urban agglomeration and the agricultural land between Delhi and these towns of Haryana has thus been lost for ever.

12. Other Problems of Urbanisation. The urban centres suffer from numerous other evils of city life. The rural migrants feel bewildered when they experience that the city people are most selfish, self-centred and do not bother about what is happening to others; one is totally lost amidst the din and monotony of the rat race, and no one has the time to pause and look around. Most of the city folk are losing touch with the Indian culture and are becoming more and more westernised. Moral values thrive in rural areas even today.

Elders are respected, guests welcome, love and affection for fellow-beings are still found in plenty. In towns and cities there is moral decay. Selfishness and devil-may-care attitudes have made the city the life boring. The migrants are often lone, resentful and most vulnerable to drug-addiction the contaminating influence of city of life.

URBAN AND REGIONAL PLANNING AND DEVELOPMENT

Urban planning has been defined as a technique and method of development that "contributes to the organization, development and evolution of urban areas and their urbanising environs, based on economic, social, legal and aesthetic concepts and conditions in order to promote the welfare of the public and quality of environment."

Need of Urban Development Planning. A rapid rate of urbanisation is visible in India and the problems of urbanization are becoming more and more complex in nature. Acute shortage of housing, snarling traffic jams and delays, difficulties of transport, growing uncleanliness of streets and public places, alarming population densities and erection of sky scrapers to worsen them further, inadequate water supply, protests and protest marches of a highly discontended population, and overall deterioration of the quality of urban living, have made our cities face anxiety, tension and unrest. In some of the largest metropolitan areas problems have become so difficult, and the expenses of satisfying unmet needs are so astronomical, that the civic authorities have come almost paralysed-drift being the order of the day. Deterioration has almost reached a point where further aggravation may result, not in further deterioration but explosion or destruction.

It is obvious that as the size of the urban areas grows, the service functions of the local body get dominated by the development and development promotion functions which are several times more in magnitude and complex in character and this is caused by the rapidity and size of growth which the urban body experiences. The urban body itself cannot grow at that rate and, therefore, the development functions which it should have normally undertaken get neglected. The continues to exercise its service functions, but for carrying out the development functions, bodies like the Improvement Trust have come into being. But with more official element in such bodies they tend to be less responsive and sensitive to the people's needs as compared to the local body. Moreover, in most of the cases it has been found that these bodies have been unable to cope with the mounting problems.

Evaluation of Urban Planning. In India, the evolution of human settlements planning could be traced to Vedic texts. The Vedas, the Puranas and other texts like Vastushastra, Mansara and Mayamatam also lay down the principles of planning and location of towns and villages. Kautilya's Arthshastra written three centuries before the Christian era discussed dimension of fiscal planning and town administration. Earliest examples of Vedic town planning available are Madurai, Srirangam, Kanchipuram, built with the temple as the focal point and concentric square streets all around at some length. The emphasis of Vedic settlement planning was not only on placing and spacing buildings and siting of locations but was also on the organic interdependence of locations with nature of maintain the environmental balance of man.

A good number of planned cities were developed by different rulers during the later periods of history. Shahjahanabad, the walled city of Delhi, constructed in 1640, is one of the finest examples of Mughal town planning showing the growth of city around the main axis between royal palace and mosque. Other examples of Mughal period are Fatehpur Sikri, Agra, Lucknow being the replica of grandeur in architecture and civic design. The city of Jaipur built by Maharaja Sawai Jai Singh II during 1720s is one of the best examples of the revival of Vedic principles of settlement planning on a grid pattern with strict architectural and land-use controls on the main streets—residential areas planned with spatial hierarchy of "chowks" (public squares) being the interjunction of main roads through a gateway leading to the main 'bazaar' of the city.

During the British period, the revival of industry and commerce with the growth of industrial capitalism further aggravated the problems of urban planning. The development of Port towns like Chennai,

Mumbai and Calcutta, well-connected with cantonments and civil lines of Meerut, Ambala, Allahabad, Mathura and Agra took place. Besides there are a number of examples of industrial townships like Ahmedabad, Jamshedpur, Kanpur, etc. and hill stations like Simla, Mussoorie, Dalhausie, etc. However, during the British period there were no specific policies or strategies to guide or influence urban development or urbanization.

The independence of the country brought with it pressing problems of rehabilitation and settlement of displaced people from Pakistan. This initiated certain programmes directed towards urban settlements. A number of refugee townships were built. They were initially conceived as residential suburds, but subsequently planned as a self-contained towanships providing employment opportunities in industry, trade and commerce. With the establishment of Planning Commission in 1950, its Research Programme Committee commissioned detailed studies of the metropolises and more populous cities. Eminent authors produced monographs. In the first two Five Year Plans, overriding priorities of investment were in areas other than urban development. Some emphasis was laid on strengthening urban infra-structure, inter-city communication, and sub-urban commuting facilities.

The Third Plan specifically provided for the preparation of comprehensive development plans for major metropolitan centres, state capitals, port towns, rapidly growing industrial towns and pilgrim/tourist centres. The preparation of regional development plans was advocated for some priority areas, where there was in urgent need for channelizing the development sparked off by major plan projects like the multi-purpose river valley projects, location of steel plants and other large scale industries in the public sector. For urban planning, planning bodies were set up in several large cities. The decade of sixties marked the era when urban planning models and analytical exercises on a wide range of parameters were developed in India, so much so that the work done in Calcutta, Mumbai, Chennai and not the least Delhi became a model for numerous countries. Also, a new impetus was given to the idea of developing a number of self-contained towns with diversified economic base. The

Forth Plan laid emphasis on the need to prevent the unrestricted growth of metropolitan cities and recommended a regional approach to the problem of urban development with the restructuring of local areas and strengthening and reorganization of the local administrative set-ups to enable them to cope with the growing problem.

The prevailing urban planning approach has been dominated by the British town planning tradition of a garden city characterised by shifting of major industries outside the city limits, 'multi-nodal' transportation on the basis of self-contained settlements and segregation of land use through development control. In addition, the colonial heritage of urban planning is also descernible through decongestion of the old city and concentrating on developing the suburds and the civil line. The existing system of urban planning suffers from a number of gaps with inadequacies. The prevailing planning practice is based on western techniques with cumbersome process involving formidable amount of data collection, sophisticated techniques utilised for analysis which are time consuming with very little outcome in the form of a development plan.

The report of the Planning Commission's Task Force (1983), on planning of urban development, marked a departure in delineating the policy perspectives and identifying relevant issues in urban planning in the country. The report was not only technically competent and analytically sharp, but was also remarkably candid in its condemination of the prevalent practices in urban planning that were largely irrelevant and ineffective under Indian conditions. After an exhaustive analysis of the available data the report made the point that the rise in rural population needs to be absorbed through a rapid expansion of non-agricultural livelihoods and employment in the urban and semi-urban nodes.

Administrative Aspects of Urban Planning

It has been noted during various studies that the local bodies, being too much preoccupied with maintenance of civic services and lacking in adequate financial resources and necessary technical, are not generally suitable agencies for undertaking planning and execution of major urban development projects. As has been noted earlier the outcome of this situation is some or the other development agency such as Improvement Trust, Town Planning Trust, or some special planning and development authority. It will be appropriate here to examine the nature of such agencies.

Improvement Trust. The concept of Improvement Trust has already been disucssed earlier. The concept of 'improvement trust' is the oldest and the most widely used concept in our country. These trusts have many points to their credit and many to their debit. Though they have done a lot to improve the situation in a number of cities, it appears that they may have to yield place to a more dynamic concept wherein the emphasis is on overall planning and development rather than merely on improvement.

Town Planning Trust. This type of agency is embodied in the Town Planning Acts of Andhra Pradesh and Kerala. Such a trust has powers to prepare, implement and enforce Master Plan and detailed Town Planning Schemes. The representative nature of governing body of town planning is a good feature though it lacks in adequate independent source income.

Metropolitan Development Authorities. Regarding the planning for the metropolitan areas there are some agencies at work, for instance Calcutta Metropolitan Development Authority, Delhi Development Authority, Madras Metropolitan Development Authority and so on. The Delhi Development Authority, a high powered body, is responsible for preparing, implementing and enforcing the Master Plan and Zonal Development Plans for different areas into which the entire urbanisable areas has been divided. The Madras Metropolitan Development Authority which has been constituted as a distinct and separate Authority by an amendment to the Town and Country Planning Act, 1971 (Tamil Nadu), has the following major functions: carrying out a survey of the Madras Metropolitan Planning Area and preparing reports on the survey so carried out; preparation of a Master Plan or a Detailed Development Plan or a new Town Development Plan, as the care may be; preparation of an existing lands use map and such other maps as may be necessary for the purpose of preparing and development plan; carrying out such works as are contemplated in any development plan; to prepare a New town Development Plan for the area concerned; and to perform such other functions as may be entrusted to it by the Government.

Other Planning Bodies. In Punjab and Haryana, there are Divisional Town Planners each giving technical guidance on planning matters in local bodies and other agencies within one or more districts. In Andhra Pradesh, Tamil Nadju, Gujarat and Maharasthra, the State Town Planning Directorate prepares statutory planning schemes, be they master plans or detailed Town Planning Schemes, on behalf of the local bodies.

We have seen that a variety of urban planning and development authorities are in operation in different states. These bodies are separate from the existing local bodies. Experience has indicated that wherever such authorities have been set up, initially there may have been amity, progressively these bodies have started to fight with one another and appear to general public as having opposite interests. It has been noted that such an authority having mostly the official element is least influnced by community's interests and aspirations. Where protests have been made in this regard, it has been often interpreted, and sometimes rightly too, that it is the interest groups that were bringing pressure on the development authority and these were not in the general interests of the people. While this cannot be altogether ruled out, the fact is that there is no direct communication between the development authority and the communities involved in the development, the responsive character and the sensitivity of the development authority has been seriously jeopardized.

Apart from a suitable planning and development authority, the process and quality of the plan is equally important. As has been noted earlier, many complicated procedures and data are involved which generally cause delays. It is more often, than not, that by the time the data are collected, compiled and analysed the master plan is finalised, the form and picture of he region have altogether changed and the development problems become so much accentuated that they become rather incompatiable with the changed context. Because of the procedural limitations the budget-oriented urban development programme is missing.

Besides the above, some more common problems have been noted during various studies. These include: excessive control of the state government suppressing the initiative and dynamism and causing the delays; absence of penal provisions for violation of the Master Plan proposals; limitation of the jurisdiction of the planning and development authorities; the concerned personnel have no regular organisation pattern like the other development organizations of the government (P.W.D., Electricity Board, etc.), resulting that the personnel is often either under-utilised or over-utilised; lack of power provisions for inter-authority co-ordination which is very much essential for plan formulation as well as implementation; lack of prescribed planning standards; and lack of people's participation.

The review of exising patterns of urban planning and development thus reveals that the exsiting administrative structures is inadequate to meet the growing challenges and complexities of the urban situation. Planning processes are not being supported and backed by the effective administrative machinery for ensuring coordinated development and enforcement of Master Plans.

The Rural Urban Relationship Committee accepted the district as the unit for planning and development purpose except in the cases of metropolitan and industrial complexes. To this effect the committee recommended statutory planning and development authority at the district level and in case of predominantly rural districts, the committee considered it economical and expedient to entrust planning and development to Zila Parishad. For metropolitan areas and large cities, the Commmittee recommended for the setting up of a separate planning deevlopment authority under the chairmanship of the Minister of Local Self-Government and having representatives of Zila Parishad, chief executive officer, and separate members to be incharge of planning, engineering and finance.

The Town and Country Planning Organization prepared a model law on urban development authorities, in 1973, for adoption by the State Governments. This was discussed and consensus seemed to be that for the metropolitan areas, there was a need for a two-tier approach. Metropolitan planning and development could be entrusted with a high-powered metropolitan development authority and local authorities could continue to discharge normal maintenance functions at local level. For the non-metropolitan areas, the local authorities could discharge the planning and development functions within a regional planning strategy to be formulated at the state level.

At the state-level, the Task Force suggests consolidation of fragmented responsibilities for urban development and a reorganised urban planning machinery to inegrate investment allocations for urban development with corresponding physical planning exercises, undertaking regional urban development plans, preparation of physical land use and infrastructure, plans for smaller towns within such regional strategies, advising the metropolitan and urban local planning authorities on physical plan preparation, and finally, undertaking the appraisal-monitoring-evaluation tasks of state-funded urban development projects. At the local level, detailed geographic and economic analyis of the metropolitan regions be initiated under the auspices of the Planning Commission in collaboration with academic and research institutions. Outside of the metropolitan regions, the municipal bodies are to be strengthened for undertaking urban planning for their respective areas within the regional dimensions spelt out by the state-level planning organization.

Regional Planning and Development

In all development countries wherein planning and direction of economic growth is characteristic of governmental administration, a regional approach to planning is becoming increasingly important, particularly in relation to the development of metropolitan areas, under-developed areas, rural and community development and certain sectoral activities like location of industries or distribution of social services to the community.

Regional planning is an approach, a planning philosophy and a strategy, and provides a frame of reference for integrated or complementary development between different sectors of economy, areas and area levels. Regional planning is perspective and provides only broad guidelines of development for the region. It involves basically the preparation of an integrated plan for land use and settlements in the region specified. Regional planning is sometimes regarded as an extended form of town planning. According to this view, regional planning is only as extension of urban planning and its concepts, both in theory and practice. The most accepted and yet the most complex task of regional planning is to prepare a comprehensive regional development plan, an integrated and coordinated plan between the physical, economic and social components in a given region and inter-regional, that is, between different levels of regions.

In India, in the early stages of planning, the problems and issue of regional development did not arise as boldly as they do today. Even though the First and Second Five Year Plans did mention the need for spatial diversification of economic activities, the statements were couched with several *ifs* and buts and were perhaps designed to recognize the problem rather than to attempt regional disaggregation of national plans. During the Third Plan, the regional development policy became more explicit even though it continued to side-track the basic issue of regional development planning on a national scale. Regional balance was treated as a long term issue. Latter, in the light of increasing heterogeneities and complaints of neglect from the states, the Planning Commission's view in respect of regional imbalances in economic development changed from an inter-state to an intra-state search for balance. It has been realised that in order to reach the social and economic goals of development, a greater diffusion and growth of activity and employment at local levels would be needed. Since the acceptance of this idea would require not only larger effort but also changes in planning procedures, some attempts were made to decentralize the planning process to the sub-national and sub-state levels.

Administrative Aspects of Regional Planning

Social and economic planning is the equal and joint responsibility of the centre and the states under the Indian Constitution, but there is no specific reference regarding regional planning. With the growing realization of its importance, a suitable machinery now remains to be evolved out of the present constitutional provisions. Within the constitutional provisions several patterns for regional planning are possible. Any arrangment for effective implementation has, however, to take into account the financial resources, legislative competence and administrative authority required for the purpose. The major responsibility for directing and regulating planned development at regional level has to be undertaken by the administrative bodies at the state or lower levels. Under the provisions of existing town and country planning laws, the function of the State, Town and Country Planning Department is only to give advice on planning standards to local bodies in whom rest the statutory powers of town planning. It is only in a few states that the special arrangements have been made to look after the regional planning. In most of the other states much attention has not been paid towards this direction. Moreover, most of the states are equipped or unprepared for such a task. The administrative machinery and the financial resources of the states have, by and large, proved inadequate to perform the complex functions of regional planning and development.

As has been discussed in the case of urban planning and development some *ad hoc* special purpose body may be appointed at local level for a particular regions in a state. It is possible that within a state, a number of such special *ad hoc* authorities are created to cater to the myriad development needs of various regions each delineated for a special purpose with its own boundaries. In the views of Abhijit Datta this inevitably creates problems of coordination between the *ad hoc* authorities and the States' field administration on the one hand, and the local government units falling within the respective jurisdictions of these authorities on the other, thus, the emergence of *ad hoc* development authorities not only bypasses the traditional government macninery at the field level, in turn these weaken the very system of field administration and local government in their control and coordinated roles. Naturally, the *ad hoc* development authorities are bedevilled by the problems of competitive jurisdictions, inadequacy of regulatory powers, lack of local accountability and participation, and insufficiency of locally raised resources. All these shortcomings bedevil the working of the *ad hoc* development authorities, especially during the operation and maintenance phases.

Metropolitan Regional Planning. In the wake of rapid urbanization, there has been a great awareness of the need for regional planning at the metropolitan level. Past efforts aiming at limited land use control through municipal administration and Improvement Trusts have demonstrated the utility of such an approach and led to a search for greater comprehensiveness in planning. The need for integrating economic planning with physical planning was realised. In metropolitan planning, therefore, it is necessary to consider the hinterland to seek out the growth nodes that can receive some activities and functions and still depend for business and other facilities on the metropolitan city, to delineate the areas which support the metropolis with food and daily supplies, and to ensure that growth in the hinterland is linked efficiently with growth in the metropolis. The present efforts in metropolitan planning are influenced by such an approach.

The problems of metropolitan administration have also come to the force in recent years, for in many of our metropolitan cities the administration has grown on a fragmented base. Since, metropolitan development is multi-functional in its scope and the development authority designed for this purpose must also have such a dimension. Planning does meet this multi-functional requirement, but it is extremely difficult to bring together the various functional threads of such development within a single *ad hoc* authority, except through a process of decentralization from the state to the units of field administration or through a process of devolution of state functional responsibilities to the local governments. Again the metropolitan areas delineated do not conform to the boundaries of the States' field administration or local governments and, consequently, the problems of control and coordination become manifest. The experience in our country shows that along with a proliferation of functional *ad hoc* authorities, there is also *ad hoc* metropolitan development authority charged with the planning and construction roles. These two types of authorities rarely act in unison, while the control and co-ordination powers of the metropolitan development authorities are diluted to transform these into institutions for project monitoring and channelling of external resources to the various public authorities.

Urban and Regional Coordination

The problem of coordination has become of intense importance because of multiplicity of government agencies operating a multiplicity of programmes. For the integrated development of any area coordination is quite important to achieve because a region and its urban centres are closely related to each other. Changes in one affect the position in other. Looking at their interdependence and the need to maintain the developmental and ecological balance a masterplan for whole of the region is required. Such a masterplan should be linked with the plans of the State Government and even national plans. At each level, therefore, there is a need for a strong and well connected administrative machinery at the appropriate levels. The important thing is to coordinate the planning and development efforts being undertaken at different levels. Such a responsibility should be that of national and state governments. To this effect, the urban development division of the Planning Commission has issued directives to states for preparing city development plans and 'five yearly' and 'yearly' programmes so that the masterplans may be dovetailed with the state plans. The Town and Country Planning Organization, Government of India, on the directions of Planning Commission has formulated city development plans for certain towns. However, these plans could serve only as model guidelines because for the state governments these were never implemented. In almost all the states, the old pattern is being followed.

CENTRAL GOVERNMENT AND PANCHAYATI RAJ

Constitution and Central Government. The Panchayati Raj Institutions—which constitute the rural local government in India—come under the direct responsibility of the state governments falling as they do in the state list of the subjects enumerated in the Indian constitution. Nevertheless, the central government cannot afford to permit iself a posture of complete unconcern and aloofness with regard to local government. Even in federally governed countries, the central government finds itself under as inescapable obligation to provide professional leadership, to set up standards of service and generally to assist the states in finding satisfactory solutions of at least the more intractable problems and issues. Secondly, it is customary for the central government to make available to the states funds for support of local government. As a grant-giver, the central government owes it to the tax-payer and to the parliament that it keeps a general watch over the health and progress of local government in the country. Finally, with the increasing complexity of the society and governmentalization of a vast range of its affairs, local government, too, has steadily emerged as an entity central to human welfare : it becomes too important a level of administration to be left solely to the care of the state government. Very correctly does a United Nations report entitled Decentralization for National and Local Development emphasize : "The advisability in a federal system of charging a ministry of department at the federal level with special responsibility for local government matters will depends on the extent of need for coordinating the local government relationships and activities of federal agencies. Where federal agencies have numerous contacts with local authorities, *e.g.*, through grants-in-aid and other forms of financial cooperation, and where their activities have a direct impact on local problems and programmes, such a federal unit may be advisable."

Role of Central Government. The central government in India is called upon to perform several functions with regard to Panchayati Raj even while the latter constitutes undoubtedly the direct responsibility of the state government. The centre has a responsibility for ensuring that the information about important developments and activities in the field of Panchayati Raj in the various states is made available to all of them including other subsidiary formations. Secondly, it must carry out a comparative study of the different systems and models of Panchayati Raj existing in the country and communicate the findings to the states and even to the general public. This is a function which the central government alone is in a position to perform. Thirdly, the central government has the ultimate responsibility of ensuring that the system of Panchayati Raj as accepted as the government conferences is implemented by the states. Ultimately, the central government is the only authority in the country which can point out to the state government and latter's errors and lapses in dealing with Panchayati Raj : no other organization in the country can bring to bear the same degree of moral pressure on the states.

The responsibility of the central government becomes direct and undivided with regard to Panchayati Raj in the union territories in the case of these territories, the central government is to Panchayati Raj what the state is to the latter in its own jurisdiction. Also, the central governments's role in state subjects, such as Panchayati Raj, undergoes an apparently qualitative change consequent upon the enforcement of Article 356 of the constitution, which, it may be recalled, provides for the central take-over of administration of a state in the event of a constitutional breakdown in it and which has been invoked (till the time of writing of the present paper) more than eighty times since the operation of the constitution. When a certain state finds itself placed under the President's rule, the central government's control over the whole range of tis administration becomes in effect, direct and complete. Coming to the subject of Panchayati Raj, parliament becomes constitutionally competent to enact a statute for the state under President's rule. However, as the centre has been interpreting its role under Presidential rule essentially as that of a care-taker, it has not evinced any pronounced interest in the field of Panchayati Raj.

Central Government's Role in Practice. The foregoing discussion does not perhaps highlight sufficiently accurately the central government's contribution to Panchayati Raj institutions in the country. Both the concept of Panchayati Raj, in its modern sense, and its organizational structure have been orginally conceived by a committee set up at the central level—the team for the Study of Community Projects and National Extension Service, popularly known as the Balvant Rai Mehta Committee after the name of its Chairman, Balvant Rai Gopaljee Mehta. Scarcely has a committee in the annals of rural local government in India brought about a more pervasive and fundamental system of reforms. From now onwards untill 1963, or so, the central government provided the main thrust to Panchayati Raj movement in India. The central interest in this field remained at the remarkably high pitch, which owed itself largely to the personality of S.K. Dey, a name only second in importance to Balvant Rai Mehta in the area of Panchayati Raj, and the ideological support given by Jawaharlal Nehru. During this period the central government was busy in securing the states' acceptance of Panchayati Raj, mobilising national public opinion in its favour and creating a support-structure for it. It was regularly holding conferences and meetings of ministers, civil servants and non-officials. It also launched a number of committees to examine the various aspects of Panchayati Raj.

Historical Description. It may be of interest to survey, even if briefly, the history of administrative arrangement at the central level for dealing with rural local government. Until 1959, both rural and local government were being handled by a common organization in the central government, though its exact location was changing over a period of time. Originally, local government—both rural and urban—was the charge of the Home Department (the predecessor of the present Ministry of Home Affairs) first set up in 1843. Consequent upon the enactment of the Government of India Act, 1919, a change in its location was made. In 1923, a new department, called the Department of Education, Health and Land, was created, and local government became the responsibility of this department. It would be more correct to add "indirect" before the word 'responsibility' : local government became a provincial subject under the Montague-Chelmsford Reform of 1919 and was put in the 'transferred list' of subjects. As local government has been the responsibility of the Ministry oif Health in Great Britain, a similar administrative arrangement was designed in India as well.

Around sixties, the central government began considering agriculture as the principal thrust of the community development programme. The device contrived to secure such a purpose was first political and later administrative. It was the Ministry of Food and Agriculture which was assigned in 1963, the task of representing the Ministry of Community Development and Cooperation in the cabinet and of supervising this ministry in regard to its agricultural work and cooperatives in rural areas. In 1966, the separate Ministry of Community Development ceased to exist and was succeeded by the Ministry of Food, Agriculture, Community Development, and

Cooperation. It is this administrative arrangement which prevails since then. The ministry—now bearing the nomenclature of the Ministry of Agriculture—has under it the following four departments : Department of Agriculture and Cooperation, Department of Agricultural Research and Education, Department of Rural Development, and Department of Fertilizers, Department of Cooperation and Department of Community Development since 1955. It is the Ministry of Rural Areas and Employment which is in charge of Panchayati Raj.

Ministry of Rural Areas and Employment. The association of Panchayati Raj with rural development may not look very astonishing, at least, to those conversant with the historical antecedent of Panchayati Raj. The Panchayati Raj has had its origin firmly rooted in the rural, earlier community development programme, and ever since both have been going together—to keep the perspective intact and integrated; Panchayati Raj is the means and the rural development is the ultimate end.

The Ministry looks after the following:

1. Rural Community Development Programme.
2. Panchayati Raj.
3. Training and orientation of personnel, both official and non-official, connected with the community development programmes and Panchayati Raj.
4. Study and research in Community Development Programme and Panchayati Raj.

In regard to Panchayati Raj, the Ministry engages itself in performing the functions given below :

1. It acts as the catalytic agent in the evolution of national policies in the field of Panchayati Raj.
2. It assists the states in formulating legislation as well as in the working of the Panchayati Raj institutions to ensure that certain basic principles are observed.
3. It conducts researches in Panchayat: Raj.
4. It acts as a clearing house of information of Panchayati Raj.

5. It undertakes periodic review of the working of the Panchayati Raj system in the states.

TYPES OF CONTROL OVER PANCHAYATI RAJ INSTITUTIONS

In terms of forms, almost all the state governments exercise four types of control over these institutions.

1. Institutional; 2. Administrative; 3. Technical and 4. Financial.

All the four types of control identified here is statutory, but, there are significant variations with regard to the form of statutory provisions under which they operate.

1. Institutional Control. The term 'institutional control' and 'supervision' is used to connote and cover all those statutory provisions which empower some specific agency, usually the government or the collector, or regulate the formation area and jurisdiction, membership structure and composition, elections, size of the councils, functional jurisdiction, staff, inter-institutional disputes and so on. To be more specific, the various provisions as envisaged in the various Acts, thus, determine the vital components of an institution, *i.e.*, name, area, boundaries and membership.

In fact, institutional control is the cornerstone of the pattern of control and supervision over Panchayati Raj Institutions which relates to the basic structure and fabric of the Panchayati Raj Institutions. It tends to ensure that these statutory bodies in their operation do not violate or vitiate the spirit and the letter of the law that has created the Panchayati Raj bodies. In other words, the institutional control is a multi-dimensional affair which has been discussed in the following manner :

(i) ***Determining the Size and Boundaries of Panchayati Raj Institutions.*** The Panchayati Raj Institions, being an off-spring of the Acts enacted by the state legislatures, not being products of organic evolution of self-government, their jurisdiction is subject to control. The various Panchayati Raj legislations of various states empower the state government to determine the size and boundaries of these

institutions. The study conducted by Iqbal Narain, Sushil Kumar, P.C. Mathur and others on Panchayati Raj administration in the states of Chennai, Rajasthan and Maharashtra indicates that the scope of this form of control is the maximum with regard to the lowest tier—the Panchayat, while in case of over two tiers, the scope is rather limited. Such a variation is because of the fact that the Act authorising the establishment of the Panchayats vests comprehensive powers with regard to delineation and demarcation of the area of Panchayati in the hands of district level functionaries. For instance, in Tamil Nadu, the Collector classifies local areas as Panchayat towns and villages and also gives them their respective names.

In fact, it has been clearly laid down in the law of each state that the jurisdiction of the 'Panchayat Samiti' and the 'Zila Parishad' would respectively be co-terminous with that of either a community development block (as in Punjab and Haryana) or with a 'taluka' (as in Gujarat). Thus, the district/the state government must ultimately follow these directives. It is interesting to point out here that the statutory provisions are so much flexible that the state government can modify the boundaries at will. There are numerous cases where state governments have exercised this power on the grounds which have nothing to do with the twin objectives of economic development or democratic institution building.

(ii) Amendment of Schedule and Delegation of Authority. The various State Acts give the sole authority to the state government to amend the schedule wherein the functions of these bodies are enumerated. The state government has been authorised to delegate all or any of its powers to any officer or authority for carrying out the functions. For instance, The Punjab Gram Panchayat Act of 1952 further authorised the state government to withdraw any of the power so delegated and to impose such restrictions and exercise such control and revision as it may deem fit. The

Punjab Panchayati Raj Act, 1994 replaces the Punjab Gram Panchayat Act, 1952 relating to Gram Panchayat.

(iii) ***Power of the Government to hold General Elections.*** Another important type of institutional control that the state government exercises over Panchayati Raj Institutions is in regard to their elections. For instance, earlier Controlling Act, The Punjab Gram Panchayat Act, 1952 empowered state government to decide the mode of elections; whether these are to be held directly or indirectly; whether the whole village/block is to form one single constituency. The second important aspect relates to the schedule of dates within which the elections are to be held and completed. Similarly, after the elections, the disputes arising out of them are also settled. These provisions have been incorporated in the Punjab Panchayati Raj Act, 1994.

(iv) ***Determining the Size of the Council.*** In regard to the size of the council, the state governments possess a lot of discretionary powers. Similarly, in regard to the mode of elections too, the Panchayati Raj Institutions are subject to government's control. The degree of control is greater in the case of Panchayats as compared to other tiers. In almost all the states, the precise strength and composition of the intermediate and apex tiers, is explicity defined in the Acts governing their establishment. However, in all the states the various statutes establishment the Panchayats merely prescribe the minimum and maximum number of members, empowering the Collector to determine the actual size of the Panchayats. The degree is discretion vested in the state government is quite visible when we look at the relevant sections of the Panchayat law. For instance, The Punjab Panchayati Raj Act, 1994 provides for Panchayats having 5 to 13 members and a Sarpanch on the basis of population. For population exceeding 200 but not exceeding 1,000 number of Panches has been fixed at 5 and for a population exceeding 10,000 the maximum number has been fixed at 13.

(v) ***Control over Panchayati Raj Staff.*** It is important medium of institutional control. Rather it is one of the basic ingredients of the institutional control over Panchayati Raj Institutions. A large section of the staff of these institutions is the personnel borne as State Cadre and deputed to local bodies by the corresponding departments of the State Government. Thus, problem of maintenance of proper control and supervision over both (officials directly recruited by Panchayati Raj Institutions and persons on deputation) is there. The types of officials are the critical importance as far as the operation of Panchayati Raj system is concerned. For instance, the Panchayati Raj statutes in Tamil Nadu, Maharashtra and Rajasthan contain a number of provisions relating to personnel management, but, only those which are mainly related to structural dimensions can be regarded as falling into the category of institutional control. It is interesting to point out that in addition to controlling the conditions of service, strength and status of state cadre officials, the various Acts authorise the state governments to regulate the conditions of service of even those officials whom the Panchayati Raj Institutions recruit on their own, and pay out of their own funds. As opined by Iqbal Narain, "the sole objective of these provisions in the case of Panchayati Raj system is to prevent the occurrence of any disparity between the Panchayati Raj employees. But in practice, the state governments have utilized these provisions to ensure that no Panchayati Raj employee gets better pay or other allowances or amenities, etc., as compared to government servants of the same rank, class and status. The criticism has come from some quarters, but, not very much alive because Panchayati Raj Institutions are, as yet, in no position to offer better service conditions to their employees. The Administrative Reforms Commission has recommended for increasing the staff support by the state government for the rural local government. In recommended that recruitment to class III service may be handed over to

a district selection board. The composition of these selection boards may be decided upon by the state government. The control of the staff is so strong that these institutions must adhere to all the schedules prescribed for appointing the number of officials. Deviations from them are viewed with concern by the state government.

(vi) ***Settlement of Inter-Institutional Disputes.*** The Panchayati Raj system, being a three tiered inter-locked institutional structure, the possibility of conflicts and disputes between institutions at the state level and at different levels are quite high. The disputes may arise between two Panchayat Samitis or between a Panchayat Samiti and municipal board. The various Panchayati Raj Acts have such provisions. For instance, in Maharashtra, Rajasthan and Tamil Nadu as a rule, there are specific provisions which authorise the state government to act as the final arbiter of all disputes and concflicts among the various Panchayati Raj Institutions. In addition to this, the higher level bodies of Panchayati Raj system have been empowered to coordinate the work of the bodies at the power level. The objective of such provisions is to avoid vertical inter-institutional conflicts. In Punjab and in Haryana also The Punjab Panchayat Samities and Zila Parishad Act, 1961, authorised the district and divisional level officers to decide such disputes. The specific provisions in this regard are :

(a) The Deputy Commssioner shall decide the dispute where the dispute is between Panchayat Samities in the same district.

(b) Where the dispute is between Panchayat Samitis situated in different districts of the same division, the Deputy Commissioners concerned shall decide the dispute, and if they fail to arrive at a decision, a reference shall be made jointly by the Deputy Commissioners to the Commissioner of the division, whose decision thereon shall be final.

(c) Where a dispute is been Panchayat Samitis/Zila Parishads in different divisions, the Deputy Com-missioners concerned shall decide the dispute. In the case of disagreement, reference shall be made jointly to the Commissioners of the divisions. Where the Commissioners also fail to arrive at a decision, a reference shall be made jointly by them to the government, whose decision thereon shall be final. However, this Act has been replaced by the Punjab Panchayati Raj Act, 1994.

(vii) Control over Properties, Papers, Premises Records and Documents. Although the Panchayati Raj bodies with the exception of Panchayat Samiti in Maharashtra have been granted corporate status (by the statutes governing the Panchayati Raj institutions) with powers to manage their own affairs and properties, but they are subjected to a variety of institutional controls designed to keep a watch on their properties, papers records and documents. Generally, the media of this type of institutional control are :

(a) Power the state government and its functionaries to call for any record and documents.

(b) Power to call for statements and periodical reports.

(c) Power to authorise officials the attend the meetings of these institutions.

(d) Power to inspect the office and other official premises and properties.

2. Administrative Control. The term administrative control refers to those powers and measures which enable the controlling agency to check and regulate the day-to-day policies and administration of Panchayati Raj Institutions. As already stated, every state has a well knit administrative apparatus from the state level to the block level, to exercise administrative control over Panchayati Raj bodies. It includes both, control over 'policy' and 'administration'. The main objective of administrative control is to prevent the implementation of certain policies and decisions if they run counter to the basic goals and purposes of the institution concerned. It is the duty of the state governments in all the states to continuously keep on eye over them. However, there are specific provisions of supervision or control to be exercised by various government functionaries at the lower levels. The administrative control is primarily directed against the non-official members of the Panchayati Raj Institutions. Although mode and media of control differ from one state to another, yet there is a certain common and somewhat uniform pattern of administrative control, especially in terms of media. The following are the major media of administrative control :

(i) ***Supersession and Dissolution of Panchayati Raj Institutions.*** In all the states, statutory provisions exist for the supersession and dissolution of Panchayati Raj bodies before the expiry of their normal term by the state government. In Punjab, the state is empowered to suspend or supersede the Panchayati Raj Institutions, if in the opinion of government, these bodies are incompetent to form or presistently make default in the performance of the duties imposed on it by the Acts or exceed or abuse their powers. On the suspension or supersession of Gram Panchayat/Panchayat Samiti/Zila Parishad, under the controlling acts, all members will cease to exercise their powers and functions and vacate their sets in case of suspension and supersession respectively. However, the government is fully empowered to review the Panchayati Raj Institutions so suspended and establish another gram Panchayat/Panchayat Samiti/Zila Parishad in place of one so superseded. In Maharashtra, however, the government can dissolve Zila Parishad or Panchayat Samiti if the institution in its opinion exceeds or abuses its powers, or makes persisent defaults in performance of duties, or wilfully disregards any instructions or directives issued by the government. In Tamil Nadu, the Collector has been authorised to dissolve and supersede Panchayat Union Council. However, there is no provision for dissolution or supersession of the District Development Councils.

In Rajasthan, before The 73rd Constitutional Amendment Act, 1992 came into force. The Controlling Act empowered the government to supersede any Panchayati Raj Institution. The maximum period of suspension has been fixed at one year, so as to avoid the atmosphere of uncertainity and curb bureaucratic tendencies. It is heartening to note that the state government has superseded or dissolved Panchayati Raj bodies on rare occasions. In this regard, recommendations given by the Study Team on District Administration of ARC are worth mentioning. The Team recommended that in cases of maladministration, powers of superseding and dissolving Panchayati Raj bodies upto the level of Panchayat Samiti should be vested in the district tribunal. However, for Zila Parishad, the tribunal should be empowered to make enquiries but it should submit its report for final orders to the district board of revenue. "An appeal will be against the orders of the district tribunal to the state board of revenue, and against the orders of the board of revenue, to the state government". Earlier to this attempt in Rajasthan also, The Rajasthan Study Team on Panchayati Raj (1964), felt that, "The system of control and supervision in case of Panchayati Raj Institutions should be such as may ensure continuity on the one hand and prompt corrective action on the other." The committee recommended a two-tier arrangement, one at the district level (by setting up district tribunal) and another at the state level (by setting up state tribunal). However, The report of a syndicate group on. "Supervision and Guidance in Panchayati Raj", (at the National Institute of Community Development) recommended that it would not be desirable to vest the powers of supersession and dissolution of elected bodies directly in the state government. Such powers should be left to an independent high-powered tribunal on whose recommendations the government should act.

(ii) ***Power of Cancel or Suspend Resolution.*** In all the states, relevant legislations empower the state governments to cancel or suspend resolutions by the Panchayati Raj Institutions, direct, or prohibit the execution of any work in the public interest. The power to cancel or suspend a resolution of a Panchayat is in most cases with the government officers, *i.e.*, Deputy Commissioner. In U.P., however, the power vests with the Zila Parishad and in Maharashtra with the standing committee of Zila Parishad. In the cases of Panchayat Samiti and Zila Parishads, however, such powers invariably vest with the government or officers nominated by the government. In Punjab, the Deputy Commissioner or the sub-divisional officer has been authorised by written orders to suspend the execution of any resolution or order of the gram Panchayat other than an order passed in judicial proceedings. However, in case of Panchayat Samitis and Zila Parishads, this power is used by the state government. Panchayat Samiti and Zila Parishad Act, 1961 authorised the state government to cancel any resolution passed by the Panchayat Samiti/Zila Parishad or any standing committee if the resulution is not legally passed, or is in excess of or abuse of the powers conferred by the Act, or is contrary to the interests of the public and on its execution is likely to cause danger to human, life, health or safety or is likely to lead to riot or affray. The formidable power of concellation or suspension of resolutions of the Panchayati Raj Institutions has been by and large exercised springly and judiciously in Tamil Nadu, Maharashtra, and Rajasthan.

(iii) ***Removal of Members of Panchayati Raj Institutions.*** It is also an important medium of administrative control. All the controlling Act of various states make a provision for this type of control. However, the authorities competent to order the removal of members and the grounds as well as the mode of removal is not uniform in all the states. The main purpose of providing for the removal of members and office bearers from the Panchayati Raj institutions is to enable the controlling authority to take adequate disciplinary action against an individual who does not abide by the laws and rules governing these institutions. The common ground and circumstances on which the non-official members or office bearers of Panchayati Raj Institutions can be removed may be :

(a) wilfully violating the provisions of the controlling Act and other rules and regulations;

(b) abusing or exceeding the powers vested in them;

(c) being guilty of wilful misconduct, neglect of duties or being persistently remiss in the discharge of the duties;

(d) continued absence from the meetings;

(e) conviction for an offence involving moral turpitude or election offence, etc.

For instance, in Maharashtra, the Panchayati Raj statutes mention only the ground covered in (c), but, in Rajasthan provisions pertain to (a) to (c). In Punjab and Haryana, the removal is effected on the grounds mention in (c), (d) and (e) whereas in Tamil Nadu for (a) and (b).

The power of removal also differs from state to state. However, in case of Panchayat Samiti and Zila Parishad, it is generally the government itself that orders the removal of the members and office bearers. For instance, in Maharashtra ultimate authority vests with the government, but it is exercised through the Commissioner and the Collector. In Rajasthan, this authority of the government is exercised by the Panchayat and development department, which operates through the Collector. So far the removal of 'panchas' and 'sarpanchas' is concerned. The power has been devolved to the lower level functionaries.

Although state government and the various functionaries have been authorised to remove the office bearers of members, yet procedure of removal seems to be quite complicated. In this context in Rajasthan, and Sadiq Ali Committee observed : "The powers of disciplinary action against the elected representatives vest in the state government at present. Here again prompt action is not taken due to increased volume of work and distances involved. The committee, therefore, separately recommended a single line of control. However, in same states legislation further provides the consent of the Zila Parishad. For instance, in Maharashtra, the member of Zila Parishad and Panchayat Samiti can be removed only with the concurrence of the Zila Parishad council. In Tamil Nadu also legislation makes more or less the same provision. This provision seems to be democratic in character, but the experience in various states indicates that even the government passed orders for the removal of the members, but, at the time of endorsement they failed to be upheld for want of requisite majority of members. This was done on political grounds. It has, therefore, been pointed out by some scholars that such provisions may altogether be deleted. However, the power of removal vested in the state government has come in for a serious criticism. The various studies in the states of Rajasthan, Maharashtra and Tamil Nadu have revealed that quite often decisions have been taken on political considerations.

In this regard the Rajasthan Study Team on Panchayati Raj felt that, "the system of control and supervision in case of Panchayati Raj Institutions should be such as may ensure continuity on the one hand and prompt corrective action on the other. The powers of disciplinery action over elected representatives by the government exposes the government to allegations of partiality and also it delays action. It would, therefore, be proper if the disciplinery powers and powers of control are exercised by an independent body." The committee recommended a two-tier arrangement, one at the district level and another at the state level. The

Administrative Reforms Commission too examined this issue and recommended, "All cases involving an offence tantamount to the removal of members must first be thoroughly investigated by a district tribunal consisting of the Collector and a subordinate judge. In case the removal is recommendated, only then the removal may be affected."

From the above discussion, it is quite clear that before the 73rd Constitutional Amendment Act, 1992 the previous Controlling Acts did possess drastic provisions for removing the members of Panchayati Raj Institutions but the recent legislation are quite significant and significantly control the powers of the State Governments in this regard.

(iv) ***Inspection and Tours.*** The inspections or tours constitute one of the most important media of supervision and control. The main purpose of inspection is to satisfy that the rules and regulations and laws in force are being complied with. Such an exercise is performed through the medium of periodic inspections of their papers, proceedings of Gram Panchayats and its immovable property and also to call for any information. Similar is the position of Zila Parishad *vis-a-vis* the Panchayat Samiti. Before the 73rd Constitutional Amendment came into force in Rajasthan, for instance, sections 27 and 68 of the Rajasthan Panchayat Samiti and Zila Parishad Act, 1959 and Section 77 of the Rajasthan Samiti and Zila Parishad Act, 1959 and Section 77 of the Rajasthan Panchayat Act, 1953 empowered the officials of the state government to inspect any immovable property, records, documents, and works in progress. In Punjab, the Punjab Panchayat Samiti Zila Parishad Act, 1961 under Section 101 authorised the deputy Commissioner concerned to inspect any document and require any Panchayat Samiti and Zila Parishad to furnish any statements and accounts or copies of documents. However, in the state of Maharashtra, the district collector was not authorised to inspect Panchayati Raj Institutions. The divisional

commissioner has been given a definite role. The divisional commissioner in Maharashtra was empowered :

(a) to inspect any immovable property;

(b) to call for any return, statement, account and report;

(c) to call for the meetings of Zila Parishad or its committee;

(d) to give directions to Zila Parishad for increasing its income, and

(e) to order reduction in the establishment of the Zila Parishad. Discussing about the role of the divisional commissioner in the control and supervision of Panchayati Raj Institutions, the Mysore Committee on Panchayati Raj, observed, "The divisional commisssioners may, subject to the control and orders of state government, be the chief controlling authority in respect of all matters relating to the administration of these bodies".

To make the supervision and control worthwhile and effective, the various state governments have laid down the scale of inspections and tours of the heads of the departments, regional, district and block level officers. However, for the officers attached to the headquarters office, it is the discretion of the head of the department to prescribe the scale of inspections and tours. For instance, in Tamil Nadu, regular annual inspections of Panchayat union are performed in the prescribed way. In Punjab also, officers are to do touring in a year for fixed number of days. The performa meant for such inspections lists a number of items of general information; but the casual inspections, on the contrary, are meant to serve a far more useful purpose. They are meant to go directly into the practical problems of Panchayati Raj Institutions. However, the study of casual inspections in Tamil Nadu, Rajasthan and Punjab shows that the causal inspections by and large seem to have fallen into an unseemingly rut of routine.

A general trend is to make the prescribed number of inspections to earn full credit for efficiency, irrespective of the impact of such inspections on the Panchayati Raj Institutions. The notes of inspections, as per prescribed procedures, are fowarded to the Collector for review. The Collector makes such a review in a routing way and sends a memorandum to the concerned block development officer for taking necessary action. Since the files are to be destroyed after one year, the officer concerned does not pursue the matter seriously. In Rajasthan, the experience in this connection by those official has been satisfactory.

(v) ***Miscellaneous Media of Administrative Control.*** In addition to the above mentioned media of administrative control, there are some others. The same have been identified as under :

(a) Performance of duties in default.

(b) Attending the meetings of Panchayati Raj Institutions.

(c) Prescribing the details of organisation.

(d) Types of registers and forms are determined.

(e) Issuance of general directives.

(f) Approval of bye-laws.

(g) Instituting enquiries.

(h) Enforcement of no-confidence motions.

A persual of the method of administrative control and a study of their past performance provides us a sufficient evidence to prove the fact that the comprehensive control of the state government over Panchayati Raj Institutions has crippled the little autonomy that has been granted to them. As a result of bureaucratic control and state interference, the old expections that the Panchayati Raj Institutions imbibing the new spirit and possessing new goals, might work out simply because their initiative stands cramped.

3. Technical Control. Technical supervision refers to the regulation and supervision of the various plans, programmes and projects formulated and implemented by Panchayati Raj Institutions within their statutory functional jurisdiction. Although the distinction between administrative control and technical control is rather tenuous, yet the state government and the technical departments in almost all the states exercise technical control and supervision over Panchayati Raj Institutions. The extent of control and media of control and supervision over Panchayati Raj bodies differ from state to state in accordance with the status and levels of technical functionaries, but the media of control in most of the states can be summed up in the following categories :

(i) Providing technical approval of schemes and projects.

(ii) Inspections, tours and personal visits by the technical functionaries.

(iii) Attendance in meetings of Panchayati Raj Institutions.

(iv) Administrative control over the technical functionaries.

(v) Periodical staff meetings.

(vi) Reports and statements.

Regarding operational level too, no such uniformity is found in the states. For instance, in Maharashtra, where the apex institutions of the Panchayati Raj system (*i.e.*, Zila Parishad) is the Local level in functional terms and the entire district level officers have been placed under the Zila Parishad, there are several departments in each Zila Parishad, *viz*; works, finance, cooperation, education, health and general administration. The controlling act in Maharashtra gave significant power to Zila Parishads. The provisions relating to technical control are mandatory. However, under the Act, "Government has been empowered to authorise its officers to give technical guidance or assistance to any servant of Zila Parishad who is charged with the execution or maintenance of the concerned work or development schemes undertaken by a Zila Parishad or a Panchayat Samiti." Divisional and state level officers visit Zila Parishad and Panchayat Samiti, but the extent and quality of technical advice cannot be considered adequate. In Gujarat, the experience shows that, "The heads of departments at state level are not actively giving technical guidance to Panchayati Raj Institutions and are not keeping proper technical control over them."

The pattern of technical control in Rajasthan, Punjab and Tamil Nadu, for instance, is substantially different from the Maharashtra pattern because in these states, the apex institution, *i.e.*, Zila Parishad, was purely an advisory body and the focal level for the purpose of policy execution was the intermediate tier—Panchayat Samiti in Rajasthan and Punjab and Panchayat union council in Tamil Nadu. In Rajasthan, the state and regional level officers, as mentioned above, through the media of inspections, tours and field visits, have been quite active and successful in maintaining technical supervision. Although there have been serious shortfalls and troubles, yet the net effect of this type of control has been highly beneficial for improving the tone of performance of technical functions at the block and village levels.

4. Financial Control. Financial control and supervision is one of the most effective instruments of control over the Panchayati Raj Institutions. This type of control, more or less, is similar throughout the country. Financial control and supervision relate to regulation of the finances, bedgets, accounts and audit of the Panchayati Raj Institutions. For instance, the Panchayati Raj statutes in Punjab, Haryana, Maharashtra, Rajasthan and Tamil Nadu have a separate chapter devoted to Finances and Taxes, relating to regulation of the finances, budget, account and audit of the Panchayati Raj Institutions. However, the study of the various financial provisions under the Acts shows that those provisions make its entire structure susceptible to state control to a great extent in two ways. In the first place, in all the states, detailed accounting procedures have been laid down by the state government for the Panchayati Raj bodies. These pertain to : *(i)* Itemisation of income and expenditure; *(ii)* custody of and control over funds; *(iii)* periodical scrunity of account by the appropriate authorities; *(iv)* audit of accounts at regular intervals; *(v)* sanctioning of the budget and so on.

Audit is the instrument through which control and supervision is exercised, deficiencies located and loop holes plugged in ensure soundness all round. There is provision for the periodical audit of accounts of the Panchayati Raj bodies by the auditors appointed by the state governments. Generally, the Panchayat accounts are audited by the inspecting officer of Panchayats at the Samiti level on behalf of the block development officer. The responsibility of the audit of accounts of Samitis and parishads has been given to an officer of the state government known as the examiner of local and accounts in Punjab. Harayana, Andhra Pradesh, Assam, Gujarat, Tamil Nadu and Rajasthan. In West Bengal, this responsibility is performed by the extension officer Panchayat, in Orissa by the director of gram Panchayats and by the chief audit officer of co-operative societies and panachayats in Uttar Pradesh. Under the rules, the Panchayati Raj Institutions are expected to comply with the audit objections promptly, "but in actual practice how far they follow this is open to doubt."

In addition to the audit, sanctioning of the budget is also considered to be an important instrument of control. In almost all the states, act and the rules framed there under, prescribed the form and time schedule of budgets to be framed by the Panchayati Raj bodies for submission to higher authorities. In this regard, two patterns are discernible.

In some states, it is the superior tier that has the power to sanction the budget. Usually, for the Panchayat, the panachayat Samiti is the sanctioning authority. In some states, the final authority is officer nominated by the government, while in few others, the Panchayat itself is competent to sanction its own budget.

Secondly, heavy dependence of the Panchayati Raj Institutions on the state assistance automatically makes the whole structure susceptible to state control and supervision. For instance, the Panchayati Raj statutes in Punjab, Tamil Nadu, Rajasthan and Maharashtra contain provisions—mandatory in nature, concerning the size and sources of income, subsidies, grants-in-aid, taxes, receipts from property managements, loans, donations and so on. Various development departments may initiate projects of local benefits or finance schemes undertaken by the local bodies.

In short, the local authorities in all the states have been assured substantial grants by their governments and the general trend seems to be that the higher the tier, the greater is the dependence on state grants, tax allocations and other financial assistance. As the Panchayati Raj bodies do not have adequate finance, the grants received from the government are not mainstay of these rural institutions. Thus, it is quite evident from the above discussion that heavy dependence of Panchayati Raj bodies on state assistance leads to excessive financial control by the government which is whittling down the autonomy of these institutions. However in view of the 73rd Constitutional Amendment Act of 1992, all the States have amended their legislations and new provisions has been incorporated in the amendment acts. State Finance Commissions has been set and in various States in the reports of State Finance Commissions some drastic measures have been recommended for transferring State resources to the Panchayati Raj Institutions and urban local bodies. Depending on the state governments of Panchayati Raj Institutions will come down all the financial devolution takes turn. The Panchayati Raj Institutions in addition to generating their own resources will get funds as recommended by State Finance Commission from time to time.

❐

6

Federalism : Theory and Practice in India

Whether India is a federation or not is a controversial issue. Broadly speaking, there are two different schools. The first school led by Professor K.C. Wheare is not prepared to accept that the Indian Constitution is a federal one. He points out: "The Constitution establishes indeed a system of government which is almost quasi-federal, almost devolutionary in character, a unitary State with subsidiary federal features, rather than a federal State with subsidiary unitary features." On the other hand, Dr. D.N. Banerjee, who represents the other school, is of the opinion that India has a federal system with a pronounced bias for the Centre.

The framers of the Indian Constitution deliberately provided for a centralised federation. In the whole text of the Constitution, India is never called a federation, instead Article 1 of the Constitution says, "India, that is Bharat, shall be a Union of States". The framers of the Constitution were aware of the fissiparous tendencies prevalent in India. The prolonged foreign domination over India may very well be ascribed to the lack of unity in the country. They had not yet forgotten the bitter memories of the partition. So in order to maintain the unity and the integrity of the country a federation with a strong Centre was provided by the framers of the Constitution.

Due to a strong unitary bias of our Constitution some critics have gone to the extent of saying that the Indian Constitution is unitary and not federal. But in this context it may be pointed out that India possesses all the normal requirements of a federation such as *(a)* supremacy of the Constitution, *(b)* division of powers between the Union and the component units, and *(c)* an independent and impartial judiciary.

Thus, there is no doubt about the federal structure. India has followed the Canadian model rather than the American model. The cream of powers have been vested in the Centre. The Union List consists of 97 topics, the State List consists of 66 topics and the Concurrent List consists of 47 topics. The Union Parliament is competent to make laws on the Union List and the Concurrent List. State law on the Concurrent List shall be null and void to the extent of its repugnancy if it comes in conflict with the Union law on the same subject. The residuary powers are vested in the Centre. Thus, the centripetal forces are more powerful in the Indian federation than in any other federation. Unlike the other federations, the Indian federation, is a flexible one. This means that during emergencies the federal Constitution of India can be transformed into a unitary one. This is a unique feature which we do not find in any other federation. The creation of a strong Centre is also due to the fact that the process of formation of the Indian federation is form centralisation, to decentralisation, whereas in other federations normally the process of formation is from decentralisation to centralisation. The centralisation of the Indian federation has been justified by Professor D.N. Banerjee. He observed, "To my mind the strong Central Government is indispensable to the maintenance of unity, solidarity and integrity of India."

There is a very strong note of centralism in our Constitution. In this connection Prof. K.T. Shah observed that the Indian States are just 'glorified municipalities' and nothing else. This remark appears to be exaggerated because municipalities have only delegated power. They do not drive any power directly from the Constitution. Moreover, the federal scheme is not disturbed during normal times and the autonomous status of the State is respected. It is only during an emergency that the Centre interferes with the autonomy of the States and even during this period the separate identity of the States is not altogether lost. The executive and the Legislature of the States continue to function but the Union also acquires concurrent power in the State field.

Centralism is not peculiar to India. It is a feature of all the federations of the world. Even in the American federation there are evident signs of centralisation. The States are gradually surrendering more and more powers to the Centre in the larger interest of the people and the nation. Modern states are undertaking many programmes of social and economic development. The modern state is more positive and it is a welfare state. This has been responsible for the development of centralism. Further, needs of uniform planning and policy have added to the powers of the Central Government. Economic and strategic considerations have also been responsible for the increased power of the Centre. Referring to the development of centralism, Sri C.P. Ramaswami Iyer observed, "What notwithstanding the fiercely avowed intentions and policies of the founders of the American Constitution, has taken place in the United States and what local and provincial patriotism have been unable to prevent in Canada and Australia, has not been statutorily formulated in India."

Relations Between the Union and the States

The constitutional relationship between the Union and States in inherent in a federal system. As the federal system provides two sets of Government - one at the Centre and the other in the periphery—so for the purpose of avoiding possible conflicts of jurisdiction it must provide for the definite relationship between the Government of the Centre and the government of the periphery in their different spheres, namely legislative, administrative and financial. For a proper understanding of the Indian federal system the relations between the Union and the States must be thoroughly examined.

Legislative Relations. The General nature of the distribution of powers by the Indian Constitution has already been discussed. The Union Government has exclusive powers over the subject mentioned in the Union List, and the State Governments over the subjects mentioned in the State List. Over the matters mentioned in the Concurrent List both the Union and the State Governments have concurrent power to make laws, but any Union law will override the State Act in case of a conflict between the two. On matters which are not included in any of the three Lists, the Union Parliament alone can legislative. It means that the residuary powers are vasted in the Union Government. Besides, there are several provisions which empower the Union Parliament to make laws on State matters. They are given below:

(i) If the Council of States passes a resolution by a two-thirds majority of the members present and voting that it is in the national interest that Parliament should make law on a particular subject mentioned in the State List, Parliament acquires that power.

(ii) The Governor of a state has the power to reserve certain bills for the consideration of the President and they become valid only after receiving the assent of the President. However, it may be noted that the President is not bound to give his assent on all such bills reserved by the Governor for his consideration.

(iii) Certain bills cannot be introduced in the State Legislature unless previously sanctioned by the President.

(iv) When the proclamation of emergency is in force, the Parliament has the power to make laws for the whole of India.

(v) If two or more State Legislatures, by a resolution, request the Parliament to make a law for them on any particular matter, the Parliament shall acquire the power to legislate on that subject.

(vi) Parliament has the exclusive power to make laws with respect to entering into treaties and agreements with foreign States. Such a law cannot be invalidated on the ground that it contained provisions relating to the State subjects.

Administrative Relations. The executive power of the Union extends to the matters with respect to which Parliament has power to make laws. Similarly, the executive power of the State extends to those subject with respect to which the States have the power to legislate. In the sphere of Concurrent List, sometimes there are two sets of parallel administration. But to avoid duplicity very often the executive power is vested in the States. Even the laws of the Union, in the concurrent sphere, are administered by the state authorities. Articles 256—263, relating to the administrative relations are intended to secure effective federal control and operation and to minimise friction between the Union and the States which is very common in a dual system of government. The Indian Constitution has provided for special administrative systems for the Union and the States but in this sphere the division of powers is not complete. In the administrative sphere there is the subordination of the State to the Union authority. The following provisions of the Constitution extend the Central executive authority on State matters:

(i) The State are bound by constitutional obligation to comply with the Union laws while exercising their executive power.

(ii) The executive power of the State is to be exercised so as not to impede or prejudice the executive power of the Union.

(iii) The public Acts, records and judicial proceedings of the Union and the States must be given full faith and credit all over the country.

(iv) Parliament can legislate for the adjudication of certain disputes or complaints in respect of the use, distribution and control of any inter-state river or river-vally. The Union Government may also provision for the settlement of such disputes through administrative means.

(v) The Union may order the State Government to construct and maintain certain highway and other means of communication of military or national importance. The Union may also order a State to protect the railways within its borders.

(vi) The I.A.S. and the I.P.S. officers who are recruited and appointed by the Union Government occupy the highest administrative post under the State Governments.

(vii) The President may appoint an inter-state Council to enquire into and advice upon disputes which might have arisen between the States.

(viii) The Union Parliament delegates certain powers and imposes certain duties upon officials serving under a State, in fields of concurrent and exclusive federal jurisdiction. In this connection consent of the State Government is not required.

(ix) The Union Government may ask the officials of the State Governments to perform certain functions of the Union Government, with the consent of the respective States.

(x) The Parliament may impose restrictions on inter-state trade or commerce.

(xi) If any State fails to comply with the orders of the Union Government, the President may declare that the constitutional machinery in the State has failed and he may place all the powers of the State Government under the disposal of the Union Government.

(xii) The Governor, who is the head of the State, is appointed by the President and remains in office during the pleasure of the President.

(xiii) The elections to the State Assemblies or Councils are held under the superintendence, direction and control of the Election Commission appointed by the Union President.

(xiv) The President has the power to appoint and transfer the judges of the High Courts.

In addition to the above powers which are exercised by the Union over the States during normal times, the Constitution vests general powers of direction and control over the States in times of national emergency. During the time of national emergency the federal structure may be converted into a unitary one and the States come under the direct control of the Union in respect of their Legislative and administrative authority. Thus, the Constitution has granted wide authority to the Union Government to exercise administrative control over the State executive.

Financial Relations. The Constitution has provided for independent sources of income and separate heads expenditure for both the Union and the State Governments. But the income of the

States is so meagre that they are never economically self-sufficient. It will not be possible for the States to meet their financial obligations without the economic aid from the Central Government. Due to this reason there is an excessive dependence of the States upon the Central Government, which is considered contrary to the principles of federalism.

In the financial sphere the Centre and the States co-operate with each other. Certain taxes are levied by the Union but they are collected by the Union but given to the States. The Centre also gives financial help to the States in the form of 'grants-in-aid' and 'matching-grants', Terminal taxes on goods or passengers carried by railway, sea or air, taxes on railway fare and freights, taxes on the purchase or sale of newspapers and on advertisements published therein, duties in respect of succession to property other than agricultural land etc. are levied and collected by Government of India but assigned to the States. Income tax (other than agricultural income) shall be levied and collected by the Government of India and distributed between the Union and the States. The Centre also gives grants-in-aid to the States of Bihar, Orissa, Assam and West Bengal in lieu of export duty of jute products. Union duties of excise other than duties on medicinal and toilet preparations are levied and collected by the Government of India but a part of it is distributed among the States in accordance with such principles of distribution as may be provided by the Parliament by law.

The President of India is authorised to appoint a Finance Commission, at intervals of five years, to make recommendations to him in respect of distribution of the net proceeds of taxes which are, or may be, divided between the Union and the States. The Commission also recommends the principles on the basis of which the grants-in-aid to the States are determined.

Further, Article 360, states that if the President is satisfied that a situation has arisen whereby the financial stability or the credit of India or of any part of the territory thereof is threatened he may by a proclamation make a declaration to that effect. Under such a proclamation, the executive authority of the Union extends to the giving of necessary directions to any State to observe such of canons of financial propriety as may be directed by President. The President will have power to issue directions requiring the reduction of salaries and allowances of any class of persons in the service of the State and also any class of persons in the service of the Union Government including the judges of the Supreme Court and the High Courts.

Criticism of Our Federal System

It has been stated earlier that the Indian federal system has been subjected to severe criticism. Due to the prominence of the centripetal forces some critics were not prepared to accept it as a federal Constitution. To analyse the centralism of the Indian federation the unorthodox features of our federal system need to be discussed.

1. The territorial sanctity of the federating units which is a vital principle of a federal government is not allowed by the Indian Constitution. The States can be re-organised and their territorial limits changed, cut short or enlarged by the Parliament unilaterally without the consent of the concerned State or States.

2. As regards the division of powers the Indian Constitution is more akin to the Canadian Constitution than to that of the U.S.A. The Union list and the Concurrent List take away the lion's share for the Union Government. During the times of emergency and at certain other times the Union Parliament also gets the power to legislate on topics in the State List. In India the residuary powers belong to the Parliament. The States are to execute the Union laws in the sphere of residuary powers and for this purpose their civil servants are subordinate to the Union Government.

3. The practice of appointment of the Governors by the President smacks of centralism. The Governor enjoy their office during the pleasure of the President and they are expected to work as the agents of the Union Government in the States. The action of some of the Governors in dissolving the State governments has been severely criticised.

4. The President is empowered to transform the federal Constitution into a unitary one during the time of national emergency. Under such circumstances the Union Parliament shall have the power

to make laws for the whole of India. The entire country will be treated as a single unit for all practical purposes.

5. The Constitution provides that if the President is satisfied on being informed by the Governor that there is breakdown of constitutional machinery in the State, he may assume the executive powers and dissolve the State Legislature. The Parliament may be entrusted with the power to make laws for the State concerned.

6. While in the U.S.A. an individual enjoys dual citizenship, *i.e.*, the citizenship of his State and federal citizenship, in India there is single citizenship throughout the country. Wherever in the country an individual might have been form, he is regarded as an Indian citizen.

7. There is a single integrated judicial saystem in India beginning from the lowest unit of the judiciary upto the Supreme Court at the apex. There is also uniformity of civil and criminal laws all over the country.

8. India has an integrated Constitution covering both the Union and States and thus, the States are not empowered either to frame or change their own Constitution as they are in the U.S.A.

9. The absence of equality of representation of the federating units in the Rajya Sabha is also a flagrant violation of the federal principle. In the American Senate there is equality of representation of all the States irrespective of their size and population.

Rigid division of constitutions into unitary and federal is anomalous because federal constitutions contain unitary feature and under unitary constitutions the local units are granted autonomous status in broader interest of the nation. It has already been stated that there is the development of centralism in every federal constitution of the world. Thus, certain deviations which we notice in the Indian federal system do not take away its federal character. These peculiar features have been incorporated in the Constitution in order to make it suitable to the peculiar circumstances of the country. The framers of the Indian Constitution have valued unity of the country above all other considerations. To maintain the unity of the country a strong centre is indispensable. But at the same time it may be pointed out that the States in India are not just glorified municipalities. The autonomy of the States is not interfered during normal times. Moreover, the Centre is largely dependent upon the States for the implementation of the major national programmes.

Indian Federalism: An Assessment

It is pertinent to discuss the constitutional, arrangement of Centre-State relationship in order to assess the total dependence of States in India on the Centre for their development. Centre-State relations are not independent of political, economic, fiscal and other relations and due to this inter-dependence they are profoundly influenced by one another. Indian federalism departs significantly from the traditional concept of federal government with a rigid division of powers between the federal Government and the Government of component States. The framers of the Constitution provided for a unique flexibility in the division of powers between the Centre and the States as it was thought to be needed by the social, political and economic condition then obtaining in India. In the field of economic and social development, closest collaboration between the Union and State Governments, is contemplated by the Constitution. But this postulate of a high degree of collaboration between the Centre and the States, becomes essentially one sided due to over-bearing powers of the Centre over the States.

The distribution of powers in the Indian Constitution has a pronounced note of centralism. Even though the taxing powers of the Centre and the States have been completely separated, taxes that have an inter-state base are with Centre and those with a local base are with the States. This type of allocation has been responsible for surpluses at the centre and deficits in the States. A study of Centre-State financial relation would show that the balance is rather titled very heavily in favour of the Centre.

In India, all the major resources of revenue have gone to Union Government. The State Governments are not financially self-sufficient. They depend upon the Union Government for financial help in the form of grants-in-aid, and matching grants. A part of the taxes levied and collected by the Union Government is also distributed among the States. The State Governments get loans from the Union Government for matching the obligation of deficit budget. The Indian Constitution provides for the establishment of the Finance Commission within two years from the commencement of the Constitution to make recommendations to the President in regard to the distribution of shareable taxes and payment of grants-in-aid to States after taking into account the needs of each State. It was the desire of the framers of the Constitution that the Finance Commission should act as an independent body and give its recommendations in the most judicious manner without any consideration of fear or favour. This expert Body should play an effective role in the adjustment of the financial relations between the Centre and the States. It should allay the fear of smaller and undeveloped States of partial and unjust distribution. But very often it has not been possible even for the Finance Commission to withstand political pressure from the larger and the most vocal States. The centralised character of the Indian federation does not leave much scope option for the States to plan their own development with their scanty resources. Moreover, through its over bearing financial powers the Union Government gets ample scope to interfere in the day-to-day administration of the State Government. Due to this predominance of the Centre over the States, some critics felt that the State Governments in India are nothing more than 'florified municipalities'. The Planning Commission, the Development Council and the Finance Commission determine the financial relationship between the Union and the States to a very large extent. The Planning Commission works as a super-cabinet and shapes the nature of financial administration and development work of the Union as well as the State Governments. According to B.R. Misra, "The Financial character of the Constitution has made the Centre definitely stronger than it was even under the Act of 1953. Perhaps this was necessary under new political set-up of the country to check the working of separatist tendencies. The States, in view of their limited resources, must always look forward to the Centre for financial aid and thus will be following the dictation of the Union in all important financial and political matters."

The Finance Commission has confined its examination to the non-plan needs of the States after the introduction of planning and the creation of the Planning Commission. It is to be noted that all grants for plan scheme are discretionary grants which are utilised by the Centre and the States for public purposes. These discretionary grants have outstripped the recommended grants by the Finance Commission and have placed the States in the position of supplicants for Centre's assistance. Since the Central assistance to the States is conditional, it tends to circumscribe the freedom of the States in the matter of formulating plans according to their own needs.

The constitutional division of financial resources which consistently produces surpluses at the Centre and deficit in the States has resulted in the increasing reliance of the States on the devolution of taxes, grants and loans from the Centre. In terms of percentage of the total expenditure incurred by the States, resources transferred from the Centre to the States rose from 42% in the first plan to 52% in the third. The percentage of discretionary grants to the total grants from the Centre to the States rose from 62% to 75% during the same period. Thus when the Central component was almost equal to the total plan expenditure of the States in the First plan period, it was exceeded by Rs. 800 crores in the Second and by Rs. 1,600 crores in the Third. It is worth our while to note that the Centre has virtually financed all State plans. State resources on their own have not been enough even to meet all non-plan expenditure. Making the States independent of "the variable munificence or affluence of the Centre", which was the main purpose of the creation of the Finance Commission has been defeated as discretionary grants are outside its purview.

The purpose of the above analysis is to show that the unmistakable trends of comprehensive Central Planning and the predominant financial control of the Union over the States have gone to such an extent in India that no State can think of its planned development independent of Central influence. This makes it imperative on the part of the Centre to make a just and equitious distribution of its resources with a view to removing regional imbalances in the country. The Union Govt. in India has accepted Prof. Gunnar Myrdal's thesis that comprehensive Central Planning is an exiomatic necessity for the developing countries. This means Central control over determination of the composition of most of the economic activity. For Prof.

Myrdal : "To be practical and effective, the plan must be worked out not only as a general frame, but must have this frame filled and concretised by careful segmental planning. And it must contain definite direction on all points, and in addition spellout instructions for the specific inducements and controls by which the realisation of those directives becomes effected." A federal polity provides for a decentralised system of decision making and the centralisation of power as envisaged by comprehensive Central Planning is antithetical to the concept of federalism.

While providing for a strong Centre the founding fathers of the Indian Constitution did not intend to deprive the States from their autonomy in areas marked for them. But under the existing Centre-State financial relations, any meaningful exercise of State autonomy in the sphere of its planned development implies that the Centre must have special considerations for promoting induced socio-economic change in under-developed States. Self-generated change in such under-developed States with their scanty resources is not possible. Regional imbalances cannot be eradicated if induced socio-economic change is not promoted in backward States by means of liberal special grants, discretionary grants and preferential treatment. States can hardly plan their development realistically when resources are limited and they have no idea of the resources that would be made available to them by the Centre. Sometimes schemes sponsored by the Centre and pressed on the States do not accord with the State's view of their own priorities and results in disproportionate growth.

The problems of poverty, inequality and educated unemployment are common national issues. Most Indian States face socio-economic crisis and solid foundations of a viable national economy are yet to be laid. The poverty and misery of the people of these States give a picture of contrast when compared with the high growth rate and development in some of the advanced States in India. Indian planning has a predominantly sectoral approach and essentially normative single-level economic planning. It is due to this sectoral approach Indian planning turns out to be technocratic and normative. Its effectiveness is greatly compromised due to the weakness of the institutional frame required for the implementation of the plan. The lack of an integrated structure in sectoral planning in India has resulted in serious social and human problems such as sectoral and spatial imbalances in the economy, social disintegration and mass poverty in the midst of plenty. Besides, sectoral planning the social contents of which are only peripheral, planning in India is characterized by too much centralization at the national level and the plan formation techniques are technocratic and model-oriented. The State plans are nothing but catelogues of demands. The long-range objective of Indian planning are ill-defined and hazy and there has been excessive emphasis on expenditure rather than on performance.

India's unity depends on its capacity to solve the problems of the poor who form the great majority of our people. The development plans of India should not only aim at increasing the productive capacity of the country and raise the national income, but also to distribute the benefits of development in such a way that the poor people in general and the poor States in particular get most of the benefits. The problems of poverty can be properly tackled only when its institutional and structural characteristics are duly examined and identified. In certain sectors of activity and among some groups of people and regions and localities, poverty is more marked. A multi-pronged attack has to be made for the eradication of poverty. For the development of the Scheduled Caste and the Scheduled Tribe people, there is the need for a variety of legal and social welfare measures at the national level. Similarly for the development of the backward States where poverty is more widespread than other States, national level sectoral plans and welfare measures alone cannot be very effective. The financial assistance given by the Centre will rarely be large enough to counter the negative forces operating within the State. The Centre must have special consideration for the poor States in order to eradicate the regional imbalances. The present system of Indian Planning becomes self-defeating as rich States become richer and poor States become poorer and the gulf of difference becomes further widened. Planning must therefore, be sectoral, economic, social and environmental at the same time so that the benefits of development accrue to the poor States. Eradication of regional imbalances should be one of the primary responsibilities of a federal polity and in case of a backward State, "Where the resource base is poor, the Central assistance has to be of a higher order so as to ensure that the size of the plan becomes viable and economic growth reasonable."

Conclusion

1. At present the Planning Commission is dominated by politicians. The Prime Minister is the ex-Officio Chairman and other Ministers of the Union Government are also associated with it. Decisions are taken at political level and economists are asked to justify them. It is neither an independent agency nor a national body in the real sense of the term. The work of the Commission has to be remodelled so that it can act as an expert body. There should be no coercion on members and they should be allowed to express their opinions freely and function independently.

2. The national plan is prepared in India by the Planning Commission on the advice of the Union Government. The Union Government fixes the priorities of the plan and decides the financial commitments and its strategies of achievement etc. Then the plan goes to the National Development Council for approval. These meetings proved only ritualistic except during the coalition era of 1967-70 and at present of course, some opposition Chief Ministers have started a demand for reording the Centre-State financial relations. The States send their tentative plans for inclusion in the National Plan and these plans are totally sub-ordinated to the discretion of the Union Government. The Central Government decides as to what should be the plan for a particular State, allocates financial resources and even directs the State to raise additional resources to meet plan requirements, irrespective of the fact whether the State can raise the additional resources. This makes the State plan unrealistic and incongruous.

3. There is a need for restructuring the planning machinery at the State level. There should be joint effort and joint responsibility both on the part of the Union and the State Governments to formulate the plans and to implement them with a view to achieving the desired results. The bureaucrats living in ivory towers should not be allowed

to dominate the planning committees. Attempts should be made to include experts and also leaders of the opposition in the planning committees and their views must be properly respected.

4. An objective basis for the allocation of plan assistance acceptable to all States has not so far been evolved.

5. The present overlap of functions of the Finance Commission and Planning Commission should be avoided and an integrated view of plan and non-plan activities should be taken.

6. An objective criteria should be devised for determining the share of taxes, plan assistance and non-plan grants for each State taking into account not only tax efforts, efficiency and the economy in management but alsó the principle of removal of regional imbalances.

7. Just as the State's resources and expenditures are scrutinized so also the resources and expenditures of the Central Government should be scrutinized.

8. The Gadgil formula which provides for distributing major part of the distributable Central assistance among the States on the basis of their population without any regard for its socio-economic characteristics and composition and their relative developmental needs, should be replaced by a suitable formula which takes cognizance of these basic factors.

9. There is a close relation between balanced regional development and dispersal of economic activity. The Central Government must provide the required infrastructure to under developed States to promote growth and diversification of economic activity in these States.

10. At present the principle of Central investment in the States is guided more by the consideration of economic returns to investment than the principle of inter-regional equilibrium and social development. Political pulls and pressures also have a fair measure of their share in securing Central investment in States. In the broader national interest the Central Government must successfully withstand the pressure politics and make sincere efforts in removing regional imbalances by encouraging development activities in under-developed states by

means of location of public sector projects, industrial licensing policy and various incentive measures like tax concessions etc.

"A federation", according to Dicey, "is a political contrivance—intended to reconcile national unity with the maintence of State rights". *Federalism is device to avoid the extremes of centeralisation and decentralisation.* It is intended to bring about a compromise between the centripetal and centrifugal forces. "The problem in every federation", according to Bryce, "is to keep the centrifugal the centripetal forces in equilibrium, so that neither the planet States shall fly off into space nor the sun of the Central Government draw them into its consuming fire." Federalism is thus, an arrangement to strike a balance between the two forces.

The question however arises as to how to strike a balance to achieve a true federation. The basic problem lies in the creation, of balance in relationship between two sets as Government. According to Prof. K.C. Wheare, "There must be a division of powers between general and several regional Governments, each of which in its own sphere is co-ordinate with others, each Government must act directly if the people, each must be limited to its own sphere, of action; and must within that sphere, be independent of the other".

But such a type of federalism has been found impracticable. There cannot be water-tight division between the two sets of Government. A federation can work only in co-operation. Contemporary definition of federation has been given by Birch. He says, "A federal system of Governments is one in which there is a division of powers between one general and several regional authorities, each of which, in its own sphere, is co-ordinated with the others, and each of which act directly on the people through its own administrative agencies".

Different scholars emphasize different things for a true federation. However, almost all the scholars agree that for a federation to exist there should be '*division of powers*' between the general and regional Governments, and the constitutional autonomy of the both. It means that the jurisdictional sphere of both the Governments should be clearly defined. *A Government having no division of powers is not federal.* It can at the most be unitary Government with decentralisation of power.

Wheare makes a distinction between the *Federal Government* and *Federal Constitution*. Even in Federal Constitution, the Government may work as unitary and vice versa. It depends on the political culture of the people. It is the way in which the people put the institutions to work that determines the federal or unitary character of the Government. For example, we find that the Soviet Constitution is federal but the Government it establishes is unitary in working. We find the similar fact in USA also. This is what we term a '*gap between theory and practice of Constitution.*

Nature of Indian Federation. The founding fathers of the Indian Constitution were fully aware of the needs of the new born state and, therefore, took sufficient care to set a federal system that should cater to the peculiar needs of the Indian society. It is worthwhile to remember here that there is no single pattern of federalism in the world. Every country adopts a federal system suiting its own needs. India could not be an exception to this general rule.

The Constitution adheres to the federal system but designates it as "Union of States". It is the use of the word 'Union of States' that has created doubts. Doubts were even expressed in the Constituent Assembly where Dr. B.R. Ambedker, the Chairman of the Drafting Committee of the Indian Constitution declared that India is a Federal State. However, it is advantageous in describe it as a Union of States on the pattern of the Canadian model as it underlines two important factors in the Indian context. First, "Federalism in India was not the result of an agreement between independent states to join a federation, and that federation not being the result of an agreement, no state has a right to ecede from it. The Federation is a union because it is indestructible. Though the country and the people may be divided into different states for convenience of administration, the country is one integral whole, its people a single people living under a single emperium derived from a single source."

Presenting the draft Constitution before the Constituent Assembly, Dr. B.R. Ambedkar, "It establishes a dual polity with the

Union at the Centre and the States at the periphery, each endowed with sovereign power to be exercised in the field assigned to them respectively by the Constitution. The Union is not a League of States united in a loose relationship, nor are the States the agencies of the Union deriving powers from it. Both the Union and the States were created by the Constitution, both derive their respective authority from the Constitution. The one is not subordinate to the other in its own field : The authority of one is co-ordinate with that of the other". He concluded that the *Indian Constitution would be "both unitary as well as federal according to the requirements of time and circumstances"*. K.M. Munshi, a member of the Contituent Assembly, held that the Constitution made India "a quasi-federal Union invested with several important features of a unitary Government". Sir Ivor Jennings worte, "India has a federation, with a strong centralising tendency". P.T. Chacko felt that what the Constituent Assembly created was "in form a federation in substance a unitary Constitution". B.M. Gupta says that under the Constitution, India would be "not a federal State but a decentralised unitary State". Shyamandan Sahay felt that the Constitution is "a kind of fedro-unitary system leaning heavily toware a unitary systems".

Federal Features of the Constitution. Scholars like C.H. Alexandrowics, Paul H. Appleby, D.D. Basu believe that India is a true federal state. T.T. Krishnamachari maintained that, "The concept this Constitution is undoubtedly federal". Similerty did N.V. Gadgil declare: "I doubt whether there is a single individual here or outside, or a partly here or outside, which has stood for or even stands for a completely unitary State". Alexandrowics holds that "India is undoubtedly a federation in which the attributes of sovereignty are shared between the Centre and the States". Paul H. Appleby also calls it "extremely federal".

The following are the federal features of the Constitution:

1. Supremacy of the Constitution. the most important condition of a federation is that the Constitution should be supreme. It has been realised in the Indian Political System. It is the Constitution of India which is the supreme law of the land. Both the Centre and the

States derive their powers from the Constitution. It is very clearly laid down in the Constitution that no organ of State can go beyond its area of authority. The Governments at the State and Central level work within the ambit of powers given to them by the Constitution.

2. Written and Rigid Constitution. The Constitution of India is written and rigid. It is the lenghiest Constitution in the world having 397 Articles with 9 Schedules containing about 90,000 words. The Supreme Court in the case of A. Gopalan V/s The State of Madras (1950), observed, "In contrast to the American Constitution, the Indian Constitution is a very detailed one. The Constitution itself provides in minute details the legislative powers of the Parliament and the States Legislatures".

3. Division of Powers. The very object for which a federation is formed, involves the division powers between the Centre and the States. "The federal principles", according to Prof. Wheare, "implies the method of dividing powers so that the General and Regional Governments are each, within a sphere, co-ordinate and independent". Following the Candian pattern, the Indian federal system incorporates three lists of subjects in Schedule VII for the division of authority between the Centre and States—the Union List, the State List, and the Concurrent List. The Union List has 98 subjects of national importance, such as those of defence, war and peace, atomic energy, currency and coinage, railway, posts and telegraphs, preventive detention, citizenship, foreign trade, inter-State trade and commerce, ports, airways, national industries and highways, etc. The State List has 62 subjects of local importance such as public order, police administration of justice, local self-government, jails, public health and sanitation, land, forests, agriculture, irrigation and fisheries, etc. The Concurrent List has 52 subjects, such as those of marriage, divorce, adoption, succession, civil and criminal law, economic and social planning, trade unions, labour welfare; planning, newspapers and legal and medical professions, education, etc. Both the Centre and States are empowered to make laws on the subjects contained in the Concurrent List.

4. Bicameral Legislature. A federal state, as a rule, provides for bicameral legislature. The Lower House gives reperesentation to the nation while the Upper House protects the interests of the component units of the federal state. The Senate of U.S.A. has on it two representatives from each State. The Constitution of India also establishes bicameral legislature—the Lok Sabha and the Rajya Sabha. The Lok Sabha gives representation to the entire nation. The Rajya Sabha is composed of representatives of the States on the basis of population in each State.

5. Independent and Impartial Judiciary. The basic requirement of federation to work effectively is existence of an independent and impartial Judiciary. The *Judiciary is to work as a watch-dog of the federal structure*. The Judiciary is entrusted with the job of interpreting the Provisions and words of the Constitution and acting as an empire between the national government and Provinces or between the provinces themselves in cases of disputes on cases of constitutional importance. The Constitution of India provides for the Supreme Court with its origional jurisdiction to settle the disputes between the Centre and the States, and the States themselves. It has been empowered to interpret the provision and words of the Constitution and give a decision that is final.

Reasons for Adopting Federal Structure. The founding fathers of the Constitution preferred federal constitutional structure because of the certain factors. These were:

(1) India is a vast country whose different parts are at different stages of development due to different climate and conditions. Kerala has the highest percentage of literacy. Punjab has a network of canals to provide for easy means of irrigation. Rajasthan has not such means. Some States have extremely hot climate while others extremely cold. Still others have temperate climate. Some States produce wheat, others rice, still others sugarcane and so on. Some States have no natural resources while some produce minerals, others different types of natural resources. Naturally different States required different approaches for their development. This could be achieved only in a federal structure where a State Government could promote its own requirements.

(2) Not only this, it would have been very difficult to rule over such a vast country from one Centre. As Justice P.N. Sapru said,

"Our founding fathers wisely did not establish for this country a completely unitary soverignty among various units composing it. Any such attempt would have completely broken down as India is too vast a country to be governed as a completely unitary State.

(3) Another important factor which made India to go for federation was that the foundation of federalism had since been laid down by the Government of India Act, 1935. The new Constitution was thus, obliged to go in for federal structure. The Indian Constitution in its federal aspect is very much influenced by that Act.

(4) Only a federal structure could assure minorities, especially the Muslims, their due place in India. The Muslims in the words of Dr. Mohd. Iqbal, looked upon themselves as '*a distinct political entity*'. Secondly, though in a minority, the Muslims had their majority in certain parts of the country, Only through federalism could they aspire to realise their aspirations. It was only through federalism that the Indian Muslisms could integrate themselves in the Indian polity while enjoying autonomy in areas where they are in majority. According to Sir Mohd. Iqbal, "The Muslims demand federation because it is pre-eminently a solution of India's most difficult problem, the communal problem...... The unity of India must be sought not in the negation but in the harmony and cooperation of the many".

Unitary Features of the Constitution. Even in spite of the fact that the Constitution adopted a federal structure, certain eminent authorities such as Prof Jennings, Allen Gladhil, K.M. Munshi, Prof. Wheare, K. Santhanam etc. argue that Indian Constitution has established a centralised system of government. Even the Supreme Court in the State of West Bengal v/s Union of India observed that the Constitution is "not true to any traditional pattern of federation". Dr. P.P. Gajendragadkar, a former Chief Justice of India, gave the opinion that though the Constitution "partakes of some of the characteristics of federal structure, it cannot be federal in the true sense of the term". K.C. Wheare, an authority on constitutionalism classified our Constitution as quasi-federal. S.P. Aiyar, however, challenges this view. He holds that, "either a Constitution is federal or it is not. It is illogical to speak of degrees of federation". According to him, if there is no constitutional autonomy of the States, it is clearly unitary. He is of the opinion that, "the Indian Constitution which is like that of South Africa, may be described as a 'union Constitution' if necessary, but it should never be called quasi-federal.

The following are the unitary features of the Constitution:

1. Union of States. The founding fathers of the Constitution preferred to use the word 'Union of States' instead of 'Federation'. This explains that the framers of our Constitution were more keen to see India as a Union rather than a federation. However, Dr. Ambedkar, the Chairman of the Draft Committee, while explaining it said, "Nothing turns upon a name". The word *Union* has been used for federal as well as Unitary States. This word has been used to depict U.S.A. But no one can deny that she is a federal country. The word 'Union' has also been used for South Africa which is a unitary country. In this way, the use of the word 'Union' does not have any effect on the federal character of India. Moreover, Dr. Ambedkar pointed out that the word 'Union' reflects two things clearly—the Indian federation has not come into existence as a result of agreement between the federating units, and secondly, the Units have no right to secede.

2. Parliament's Power to Change the Name and Boundary of a State. Article 3, empowers the Union Parliament to alter the boundaries of States or to create new States by splitting or merging existing States or parts of the exising States. Since this action does not imply amendment of the Constitution, a bare majority is needed. For altering the boundaries of States, the Centre has merely to consult the States concerned but is not obliged to obtain their concurrence. The formation of Andhra in 1953, and subsequently of Maharashtra and Gujarat etc. were the result of this power conferred upon the Centre. Article 3, in this way confers a life and death power in the hands of the Centre over the States. In federal countries like the U.S.A., Switzerland, Australia and even U.S.S.R., the boundaries of the components units cannot be changed without their concurrence. It is why Bombwall remarks that while India is, like the United States, an indestructible Union : unlike the latter, it is not composed of indestructible States". But it cannot be denied that the situation that prevailed in India at the time of Independence could only be solved through a provision like the one enshrined in Article 3.

3. Governor as an Agent of Centre. The provision for the appointment of the Governor of a State by the President was introduced with the object of providing a link between the Centre and the States but more with a view to preventing the emergence of separatist tendencies. The members in the Constituent Assembly asserted differently about Governor as the agent of the Centre. So, the precise role he was to play remained undefined. But taken everything into account, Governor is an agent of the Centre. He remains in office during the pleasure of the President and can reserve for the consideration of the President the bills passed by the State legislature. This power has, however, been rarely used and "the States can by speaking in the name of the State list, make it almost impossible as a practical political matter for the President to exercise his power of review to the detriment of State legislation."

However, during the Coalition era, the non-Congress governments alleged that the Governor are furthering the interests of the Congress Party that was in power at the Centre. The conduct of the Governor of Rajasthan (Dr. Sampurnanand) was criticised for inviting Mohan Lal Sukhadia to form Congress ministry when the United Front commanded absolute majority in the Assembly. Similarly, the Governor of West Bengal (Dharam Vira) allowed Dr. P.C. Ghosh (who defected from the United Front Government of 14 Parties) to form a Government on the basis of the support extended to him by the Congress without giving an opportunity to the leader of the United Front (Ajoy Mukherjee) to demonstrate his majority on the floor of the Assembly. Similarly, the Governors in Punjab, U.P. and other States also played the same role. The Governors of West Bengal in this way rewarded the defectors with Chief Ministership because they promoted Congress interests but the Governor of Haryana punished defectors because they opposed the Congress.

4. Intervention in State Subject. Even during normal times, if the Rajya Sabha passes a resolution by 2/3 majority of its members present and voting that a subject in the State List has assumed national importance, the Parliament will become empowered to make law on that subject. This resolution will however, remain in force of one year only. This period can be prolonged for one year at a time by a subsequent resolution and so on. There is no limit on the number of times this resolution may be passed. It may continue for any number of years.

5. Centre as Protector of Constitution. The real nature of our Constitution is quite clear in Article 355. It lays down that the "Government of every State shall be carried on in accordance with the provisions of this Constitution." Centre has as such been made the protector of the Constitution. This spirit is further evidenced in Article 257, which says that : "The executive powers of the State shall be so exercised as not to impede or prejudice the exercise of the executive power of the Union and the executive power of the Union will extend to the giving of directions to a State as may appear to the Government of India to be necessary for the purpose." Every State has in this way to follow the way of the Central Government.

6. Major and Important Legislative Powers with the Centre. The Constitution made the Centre perhaps the strongest in any federal system. Consequently, the Centre has got the major share of the legislative powers. All the important subjects are included in the Central List. It has 98 subjects after the 42nd Amendment. In addition thereto, there are 52 subjects on the Concurrent List. The Parliament is empowered to make laws on subjects enumerated in the Union List and the Concurrent List. Every State Government is under constitutional obligation to give due compliance to these laws. If a State legislature makes any law in regard to any matter in the Concurrent List, which is contrary to the law made by Parliament in the same matter, the State law to the extent of its contravence shall be illegal under Article 254.

7. Emergency Provisions of the Constitutions. Above everything else, the three types of Emergencies envisaged respectively under Articles 352, 356 and 360 demonstrate the over-riding power of the Centre over the autonomy of the State. A proclamation of

Emergency under Article 352, when there is danger to the security of India has the chance of bringing about a virtual cancellation of the federal division of powers. In that event, the executive powers of the Central Government extends over States in all matters and confers upon Parliament the power to make laws on subjects exclusively under the jurisdiction of the States. A proclamation of Emergency at the time of failure of constitutional machinery as provided under Article 356, is far more important. The Union Executive has the power, up to subsequent approval by Parliament, to dismiss the State Council of Ministers and to dissolve or suspend the State legislature. A proclamation of Emergency at the time of financial crisis can be made under Article 360. It empowers the President to limit the fiscal independence of States. Article 360, according to H.N. Kunzru, treats the States "as though they were children and the President a village school-master".

8. Unequal Representation of States in the Rajya Sabha. The Upper House in a federation has equal representation to ensure equality to States. But in India, representation of States in the Rajya Sabha is on the basis of population. This goes against the principle of equality.

9. Absence of Separate Constitutions. In federal countries such as U.S.A., Switzerland and U.S.S.R. the federating units have their own Constitutions. This ensures their independence in local matters. But in India we have only one Constitution for the Centre and the States (J & K is an exception which has its own Constitution). This leads to uniformity in laws.

10. Financial Dependence of States on the Union. In a federation, the resources of revenue are also distributed between the Centre and the federating units in a way to allow the units sufficient amount of autonomy in the financial sphere also. But in India the resources allocated to the States are far from satisfactory. In this way, the States have to depend upon the Centre. One who wields power over the purse, wields power in other respects also. In this way, the Centre is in a position to control the policies and administration of States.

11. Absence of Double Citizenship. A federation confers double citizenship. Accordingly, every American is a citizen of his own State and that of the U.S.A. In India, on the other hand, there is only one citizenship. Whether we are Bengalis or Punjabis, we have only one Indian citizenship. This is against the spirit of federalism where a balance between the local and central interest has to be achieved.

12. United Judiciary. In a federal country like the USA, there is dual system of judiciary—one for the States and the second for the Centre. In India, on the other hand, we have only one unified system of judiciary in which Supreme Court stands at the top. Moreover, there is also a single Civil and Criminal Code for the whole of the country. It clearly establishes the unitary character of our Constitution.

13. Unified Audit and Accounts Services. The finances of the States are accounted and audited by the Comptroller and Auditor General of India. He is appointed by the President. He appoints Accountant General in respect of each State to check and audit their accounts. This also leads to the centralisation.

14. All India Administrative Services. Another provision that goes towards unitary features is the existence of common All India Administrative Services. The important services like the Indian Administrative Service, the Indian Police Service, Indian Forest Service etc. are on the cadre of the Centre but they hold key position in the State administration. Being on the cadre of the Centre, they are appointed by the Centre and are responsible to it. This makes the position of the Centre strong as their men administer matters in the States.

15. Unified Election Commission. Another typical example of the unitary feature of our Constitution is the Unified charactor of the Election Commission. It is appointed by the President. It conducts election to the Parliament and State legislatures also. The State Governments have no say in their appointment.

16. Role of Finance Commission. The Constitution of India provides for the appointment of a Finance Commission by the President after every five years to make suitable recommendations for distribution and allocation of revenues between the Union and the States as also to determine the conditions for giving grants-in-aid to the States out of the Union funds. It is only the Union Government which appoints members of the Commission and no nominee of the State is included in it. Consequently, the interests of the States are not protected. This is indeed a serious lacuna against which the States have been raising their vice from time to time.

17. Role of Constitutional Amendments. The 42nd Amendment upset the federal system and strengthened the hegemony of the Union Government. Certain subjects such as education, forests, protection of wild animals etc. have been transferred from the State List to the Concurrent List upon which Central Government can make laws. Emergency (under Article 352, can be imposed on any State instead of the whole country. This power can be missed to disloged any inconvenient government in the State. Moreover, President, rule under Article 356, could be imposed for one year at a time. However, the 44th Amendment has again provided that it will be imposed only for 6 months as before.

Impact of Federalism. The growth of multiparty system in India affected the working of the Indian political system in may ways.

First, it led to the growth of one-dominant party in India, *i.e.*, the Indian National Congress. The multiplicity of parties led to division in the strength of the Non-Congress voters. Thus, the voters, who wanted not to vote for the Congress, voted for a number of parties, with the result that the parties other than the Congress could not secure the required number of votes to enable their candidates for being returned to the legislature. In this way, the Congress got majority of the Legislators elected even in spite of the fact that it never secured more than 40-45 per cent of the votes.

Secondly, there was no united and effective Opposition in India. Lack of effective Opposition was an obstacle in the ways of good working of parliamentary system of Government. There were not less than 10 Opposition parties at the Centre and equally good number in the States. All these parties had different ideologies and programmes. They could not and did not meet at one table. Their effort in running coalition ministries in various States in 1967, after the Fourth General Elections failed miserably. So, the Opposition remained divided in itself. It was, thus, an Opposition to itself and not to the Congress. This made the Congress rather arrogant.

The establishment of one-dominant party system and the absence of effective Opposition had its impact on the federal structure of Government. It was virtually reduced to that of a unitary system by the dominance of the Congress both at the Centre and the States. In these days of party discipline, every office bearer, rather every humble member of the party has to obey the order of the central leadership. In India, it implied that the central leadership, which was at the top in the Central Government dictated to the Congress leaders at the State level. Whatever in the State was being done, was done on the orders of the Central leadership. *The policy that was to be carried out in the State was not formulated by the State leaders concerned but by the Central leaders. The Central leadership, thus, dictated to the State leadership.*

This is contrary to the spirit of federalism. Federalism implies balance between the Central authority and the State autonomy. According to Freeman, "On the one hand, each of the members of the Union must be wholly independent of those matters which concern each member only. On the other hand, all must be subject to a common power in those matters which concern the whole body of the members collectively......Each member is perfectly independent within its own sphere." Wheare also lays stress on 'perfect independence' of the federating units which means "the method of dividing powers so that the general and regional Governments are each within a sphere, co-ordinate and independent."

Federalism Means Reconciliation Between Two Extremes of Centralisation and Decentralisation. It is in this way an arrangement to satisfy two opposite-moving forces and to strike a balance between the two. According to Wheare, federalism implies that, "there must be a division of powers between one general and several regional Governments, each of which, in its own sphere, is co-ordinate with others, each Government must act directly on the people, each must be limited to its own sphere of action, and each must within that sphere be independent of the others".

Federalism, thus, means that the State leaders should formulate their own policy keeping well in view the particular needs of their State in mind. It does not, however, mean formulation of policy in opposition to the Central Government. But it should be, essentially, State-oriented. Only then can the autonomy of State be maintained in the federal structure. But the dominance of the Congress both at the Centre and the States led to a uniformity of policy-formulation. Even the interests of a State may suffer in such a position. The State leadership had to give unqualified support to the Central leadership for fear of disciplinary action.

In theory, there may be federalism, but in practice there had appeared a unitary type of Government in India. The States acted on orders from the Centre. They had become, for all intents and purposes, as administrative units under a unitary type of Government.

Impact of Party System on Federalism Exaggerated. It is, however, an exaggeration to say that the States became like administrative units of a unitary form of Government under the impact of the non-dominant party system. The reality is just the otherwise. *We Started with a strong Centre, but with the passage of time; the States have continued to assert themselves more and more*. It is even more interesting to note that this tendency started under the towering personality of J.L. Nehru who dominated national scene so well.

The fact, as to how the States exerted more and more pressure on the Central Government, is clear from the following facts :—

1. Central Government Failed to Enforce its Directives Even in Congress-Ruled States. Marcus F. Franda, in his book '*West Bengal and the fedralising Process in India*' writes that it became impossible for the Congress Government at the Centre to enforce its views even on the States which ruled by Congress Governments. *Our view that one dominant party system has gone against the spirit of federalism, is totally unfounded.* There are many instances to show that many Congress Chief Ministers did not accept Central orders. Subhash C. Kashyap is of the view that "No Chief Minister in a State especially if he was a strong leader like Kamraj in Madras, or Chavan in Maharastra, or B.C. Roy in West Bengal, or C.B. Gupta in Uttar Pradesh, or Kairon in Punjab, was prepared merely to act as a tool in the hands of he Congress High Command. Chief Ministers of commanding personalities were able to have their own way." B.C. Roy, Chief Minister of West Bengal who was also a close friend of Nehru, did not agree to implement the land reforms suggested by Nehru.

2. Rejection of Central Orders over Damodar Valley Corporation. The Damodar Valley Project establishes clearly that over the question of power generation, the orders of the Central Government were rejected by the States concerned. The respective States rather pursued their own plans, based on the assessment of their own needs. Not only the Congress Governments of the States concerned, but also the Congress Parties of these States acted against the decision or the Central Government.

3. Unwilling Acceptance Meant no Acceptance. Even in cases, where the orders of the Central Government were accepted unwilling, that meant no acceptance. Those orders were implemented very slowly and half-heartedly. According to Subhash C. Kashyap, "unwilling acceptance amounted to very little in practice, as the State Governments were slow or even unwilling to implement the legislation in accordance with Central Policies."

4. Linguistic Reorganisation of States in Spite of Central Government Opposition. The Central Government was totally against the reorganisation of States on the basis of language. But we find that power-hungary Congressmen in different States pressurised the Central Government into agreeing to form new States. Andhra was created in 1953, because, according to the States Reorganisation Commission: "The Andhra Provincial Congress, the Tamil Nadu Congress and the Madras Government had agreed to it." Bombay was divided into Maharashtra and Gujarat in 1960. Punjab was divided into Himachal Pradesh and Haryana in 1966. Similarly, demands for the creation of new States and giving statehood to certain existing main territories, led to the creation of Nagaland, Meghalya, Himachal Pradesh, Tripura and Manipur.

5. Decisions of Centre Changed Under State Pressure. Not only that, the Centre had to change its decisions as a result of State pressure. According to Marcus F. Franda, in the case of Bihar and West Bengal boundary disputes, "the rumour that the Centre had arrived at a decision without consulting the State leaders, led to a massive opposition within the State....and Central Government and party leaders quickly backed down".

6. Failure of Centre Over the Question of Hindi. The amount of autonomy, which is enjoyed by the States, is also clear from the fact that the Central Government failed to impose Hindi as a compulsory subject of study in non-Hindi States. It is more interesting to point out here that some of these States were governed by the Congress Party. They described the effort of the Central Government as imposition of Hindi imperialism.

7. Gradual Weakening Position of the Central Leadership. One of the factors responsible for the States to assert them selves, was the weakening position of the Central leadership and The Congress High Command. According to R.K. Bombwall, "The High Command has, in fact, become a shaky colossus whose writ runs in State Capitals in inverse ratio to the coherence and stability of the State party units". Bombwall adds that the Congress High Command, with the passage of time, developed a tendency to compromise with the regional forces and to avoid a show-down.

8. Gradual Increase in the Financial Resources of the States. States have been complaining of scarcity of financial resources at their command. Accordingly, they have been putting pressure on the Central Government to increase their share. They have advocated that the vast burden of planning cannot be properly implemented in the absence of financial autonomy. They have succeeded in getting more and more share out of income-tax and excise duties. We find that with the appointment of each Finance Commission, the share of

She States has progressively increased. The Seventh Finance Commission increased State share to a considerable extent.

9. Growth of Regionalism. The growth of regionalism is another factor which led to the weakening the position of the Centre. Regional parties such as the D.M.K., Bhartiya Kranti Dal, Akali Dal and Shiv Sena etc. checked the growth of Central powers. These parties became more prominent after the 1967, Gerneral Elections. Their victory led to a loosening of the centralisation of political authority.

10. Impact of Multi-party System on Federalism during Janata Rule. With the assumption of power by the Janata Party at the Centre in March, 1977, a new chapter was opened in the history of India. The Janata Party was committed to uphold the federal structure as envisaged by the founding fathers. It was determined to decentralise economic and political power. It advocated what is termed as "*Co-operative Federalism*" and tried the create an atmosphere of harmony and co-operation between the Centre and States. Addressing Chief Ministers' Conference at New Delhi on July 31, 1977, the then Prime Minister, Morarji Desai emphatically declared that, "strong Centre is a binding factor. A strong Centre requires strong States. A strong Centre with weak States could lead to dictatorship. I do not see any conflict between the Centre and the States. Both have the common objective of serving the people. Hence, coming of different parties into power in the States should not affect cordial and harmonious Center-State relations".

11. Impact of Multi-party System on Federalism during Congress Rules. It was again in January, 1980 that the Congress under Indira Gandhi came back to power at the Centre. Elections to Nine State Assemblies were also held as a result of which it came to power in States also. At present Tamil Nadu is under the rule of the A.I.A.D.M.K., Jammu and Kashmir under the National Conference, and Kerala, West Bengal and Manipur under the C.P.I. (M). The C.P.I. (M) alleges of undue interference by the Centre. But Mrs. Indira Gandhi has asserted at various occasions not to topple the non-Congress ruled State. However, in spite of these assertions the

Congress (I), is actually engaged in opposing National Conference Rule in J. & K. This is, however, the constitutional right of every political party. There does not appear to be anything to show that the Centre is discriminating against the non-Congress ruled States.

All this clearly shows that federalism, like parliamentary democracy, has come to stay in India. This has been in spite of the fact that one-dominant party system was established by the Congress. The statement of Alexandrowics has not come out true that, "The introduction of multi-party system is likely to affect federal structure and to lead to the establishment of unitary State, undesirable as this may be." Moreover, the multi-party system, referred to by him, was the party system that led to the establishment of one-dominant party system under the Congress rule. Even during that period federal spirit dominated actual working of our political system.

❐

7

Emerging Trends in Centre-State Relations

What should be Centre-State relationship is a very serious problem in India. India is a political democracy and as expected chances have been when the same political party has not remained in power both in the Centre as well as in the States. This happened for the first time after the General Elections of 1967. In that year whereas Congress Party came to power in the Centre anti-Congress governments were in power in the States. D.M.K. came to power in Tamil Nadu and Jansangh in Union Territory of Delhi. Similarly many coalition governments popularly Union as Samyukta Vidhayak Governments were formed in the States. This resulted in serious centre-state relationship in all the fields namely *(a)* Administrative field *(b)* Legislative field and *(c)* Financial field. Though the strains relaxed after 1971, elections, 'yet the problem exists since then. In 1977, when elections were held in the country Janata government come in to power at the centre but in Southern States non-Janata Parties were in power. Similarly when elections were again held after 1980, many non-Congress (I) governments came of power in the states though in that year Congress (I) came back to power at the centre. One salient feature of our political system which effects centre-state relations in that regional political parties are forgoing ahead in many states and national parties are sitting in opposition.

Administrative Relationship between the Centre and the States. According to constitution the subject for the purposes of legislation have been divided into *(a)* Central List *(b)* State List and *(c)* Concurrent List. It has been provided that ordinarily the Centre will enact on the subjects enumerated in the Central List whereas the States will act on the subejcts mentioned in the State list. Both the Centre and States can enact on the subjects mentioned in the concurrent list but in case of a clash it is central law which will prevail over the state law. The residuary powers have also been left to the Centre.

Under the existing arrangements matters connected with subjects like Customs. Income Tax, Railways, Post Offices, Defence, External Affairs, Currency, Civil Aviation etc., are the responsibility of the Centre and that is required to administer them. The State have practically no initiative in their administration.

It has also been provided that the State will so formulate their policies that the execution of central law is neither hampered nor delayed. Under Articles 256 and 257 of the Constitution the centre can give directions to the states for the execution of a law.

One also finds that it is practically the responsibility of the central government to conduct elections in the States. The President is empowered to appoint a Governor in every State and the later will report to the former about the administrative efficiency of the State in which he is posted. The judges of High Courts are posted and transferred by the President of India. Comptroller and Auditor General of India, who is appointed by the President of India, gives directions to the state governments about the maintenance of accounts and getting these audited.

The Central government has special responsibility about development and advancement of scheduled castes and scheduled tribes and can issue directions to the States to administer their affairs in a particular manner and fashion.

The State governments are required to work under the directions of Central government about matters connected with the construction and maintenance of such means of communication which have been declared either the national or of military importance. It is the responsibility of the State governments to protect and save railways in their jurisdictions.

The Parliament is empowered to adjudicate and settle inter-state disputes regarding control of waters of inter-state river vally projects. The President is empowered to appoint inter-state council to advise on disputes between States and also investigate subjects of common interest. Such a council may also suggest measures for better co-ordination of policy between Union and the States.

In the administrative field, the Central government has a hand in the running of State administration by providing All India Administrative and All India Police Service Personnel. The Parliament can also create new All India Service and members of these services are recruited by the Union Government under the rules and regulations framed by it. The personnel of these services hold key posts.

The centre-state relations in the administrative field are also influenced by the absence of economic self-sufficiency of the States. The Centre can give financial assistance to a State provided the administration of such a project is run in a particular direction.

Administrative Relations During Emergencies. Under the constitution if a state government fails to carry out the administration of the State in accordance with the provisions of constitution or if the State fails to run State administration according to constitutional directions of the central government, the President is empowered to declare failure of constitutional machinery in the State. If such a declaration is made and emergency declared, the central government takes over the administration of the State. It will appoint an adviser or team of advisers which will help the central government to run State administration in the desired manner. Administratively the federal structure, for that particular State becomes unitary.

It will thus be observed that in the administrative field the centre can tune state administration in the manner it likes. But normally the centre will allow maximum autonomy to the states within our constitutional framework. In fact, some of the States have been making a demand for more autonomy to the States but that is not being accepted. It is felt that need of the hour not only in India but all over the world is strong and powerful centre which can deal effectively with ever increasing complex problems of present day society.

LEGISLATIVE RELATIONS

In Indian federation there are states as well as Union Territories, each state has a legislature. Some of the states have unicameral, while others have a bicameral legislature. But legislature in every state has a control over the administration. The legislature is very useful forum for the opposition for exposing the weaknesses and drawbacks of the administration.

Legislative Assembly. Lower House of the state legislature is called Legislative Assembly. As compared with the Legislative Council it is far more powerful.

Qualifications. A person for membership to state legislature should be a citizen of India of not less than twenty five years of age; should be hold any office of profit and should posses such other qualifications as may be prescribed in that behalf by Parliament by a law.

Tenure of Office. Every Legislative Assembly is constituted for a period of five years from the date of its first meeting, after which it is dissolved. The assembly can be dissolved earlier also.

Salary and Allowances. All the members of the legislature are paid a monthly salary which varies from state to state. In addition, they get the allowances during the sessional days. They are provided with residential quarters, free travel and medical facilities.

Composition. The Legislative Assembly of each state consists of not more than five hundred and not less that sixty members. These members are chosen by direct election from territorial constituencies in the state. Each person who has attained twenty-one years of age is qualified to vote. If the Governor feels that the Anglo-Indian community has not been properly represented he may nominate two representatives of that community to the Assembly. It may be mentioned that some seats are reserved for the scheduled castes, tribes and other backward classes, but this a temporary phase and will disappear in the course of time.

Presiding Officer. The President Officer of the Legislative Assembly is the Speaker. He presides over the meetings of the assembly. He decides about the resolutions, adjournment motions and points of order. He fixes time limit for the speeches. He certifies whether a bill is money bill or not. The Speaker maintains order and decorum in the assembly. For his assistance he gets the help of Sergeant-at-arm. If any body shows any disrespect to the Speaker or violates the privileges of a member, he may be punished by the Speaker.

The Speaker is elected for a term of five years at the first meeting of the assembly. He can resign his office or can be removed by a notice of fourteen day by a simple majority of votes in the assembly. While the proceedings to remove the Speaker are continuing, he will not preside over the meetings of the assembly. His salary and allowances etc. are determined from time to time. In a word, the Speaker of the State Assembly has exactly the same position in the Legislative Assembly as the Speaker of the Lok Sabha. As and when the office of Speaker is vacated by resignation or removal the Deputy Speaker discharges the duties of the Speaker.

Power and Functions. The powers of Legislative Assembly can be classified under three main heads :

1. Executive Powers. The executive powers of the state legislature are exercised by the Legislative Assembly. The Council of Ministers is controlled by the assembly. It is said that the Legislative Assembly dictates the government. This control of the assembly is exercised in three ways namely :

(a) The members of the assembly can ask questions and put supplementary questions to the ministers relating the department and the minister is supposed to satisfy the members.

(b) They can table ajournment motions.

(c) The constitution provides that the Council of Ministers is responsible to the Legislative Assembly collectively.

(d) They can put short-notice questions.

(e) In the end the assembly can pass a vote of no confidence against the Council of Ministers and in case such a vote is carried, the Council of Ministers will have to resign.

2. Financial Powers. The Legislative Assembly has complete control over the state purse. Removal of old taxes and the levy of new ones is down with the consent of the assembly. Even the money spent by the Governor from the Consolidated Fund of the State is to be approved by the Assembly later. No money can be spent without the consent of the assembly. A money bill can originate only in the Legislative Assembly.

3. Legislative Powers. The state legislature makes laws on the subjects enumerated in the State List and also in the Concurrent List. If there is any conflict on the scope of a law passed by the State on a concurrent subject (on which the Union Parliament also has the right to legislate) and such a law goes against the law of the Union on the same subject, it is the law of the Parliament that prevails over the state law.

LEGISLATIVE COUNCIL

In some states there is bi-cameral system of legislature. In such a system the Upper House is called Legislative Council. The Upper House is a not as powerful as the Legislative Assembly which is the Lower House of the legislature. It is a permanent body and is not dissolved with the dissolution of Legislative Assembly after the expiry of 5 years.

Tenure of Office. The Legislative Council is a permanent body. Its every member elected for six years. One-third of its members retire at the end of two years. The Constitution provides that the Legislative Council of a state is not subject to dissolution.

Composition. The total membership in the Legislative Council of a State shall not exceed one-third of the total membership in the Legislative Assembly of that State. Strength of a Legislative Council will however, in no case be less than forty. The members of the Legislative Council are elected indirectly. The distribution of seats in a Legislative Council is as follows :

(i) One-third of members of Council are elected by electorates consisting of members of municipalities, district boards and such other local authorities in the state as the Parliament may specify by law.

(ii) One-twelfth of the members are elected by the electorates consisting of persons who have been engaged in teaching for a least three years in educational institutions not below the standard of secondary schools.

(iii) One-third of the members are elected by members of the Legislative Assembly of the State from amongst who are not members of the Assembly.

(iv) One-twelfth of the members elected by the electorates consisting of persons residing in the state who have been graduates with a three-year standing.

(v) The remaining one-sixth members are nominated by the state Governor. These nominated members are persons of standing in such fields as literature, science, art, co-operative movement and social service.

Presiding Officer. The Presiding Officer of the Legislative Council is the Chairman. He conducts the proceedings in the Council.He also maintains order in the House and safeguards privileges of the members. He gets salary, allowances and other benefits and privileges as are determined by law.

The Chairman and Deputy Chairman are elected by the members of the Legislative Council. The Chairman of Legislative Council shall vacate his office if he ceases to be a member of the Council. He may also resign his office and can also be removed from his office. In the absence of the Chairman, the Deputy Chairman discharges his functions.

Powers and Functions. Legislative Council is a very weak body. It has more formal functions than real ones. These may be summed up as under :

1. Executive Powers. The Council has practically no executive powers. It is so because the Council of Ministers is not responsible to this House and a vote of no confidence against the Council of Ministers in the Council, does not make it obligatory for the former to resign. Still, the Council can influence the working of the government. If the Council is not satisfied with the performance of the government it can, through questions and adjournment motions, bring the government to disrepute and make it unpopular by exposing its defects. By these methods it can very much lower the prestige of Council of Ministers in the eyes of the people.

2. Legislative Powers. Theoretically the Legislative Council has co-equal powers with the assembly in so far as ordinary bills are concerned. A non-money bill is enacted only when both the Houses approve of it. But in practice there are limitations on the powers of the Council here also. The Legislative Assembly has an upper hand.

3. Financial Powers. In the financial sphere the Council has no control whatsoever. No money bill can originate in the Council. Its opinion or recommendations on money bills do not mean much either. It can only delay a money bills for a period of fourteen days, within which period, if it does not return to bill, it will be deemed to have been passed. it can suggest amendments to money bills but it is for the assembly either to accept or reject these.

Legislature and Administration. An effective and powerful instrument of control in the State over administration is the state legislature. It is a forum where the administration and administrator can be exposed without least danger. Each department of administration is headed by a minister, who is responsible to the legislature for the execution of policies and programmes of his department. A member of legislature can put any questions on the minister about the working of his department and he is obliged to answer that unless such a reply can lead to revealing state secrets. Similarly a member in the legislature can control the administration by moving 'call attention' or 'short notice' question. On such occasions the administration is on its toes to provide information available without any grudge and grumble. Similarly the legislature controls administration at the time of budget.

These are only indirect methods though which a state legislature controls the administration. There are also direct methods when legislature as a whole directly control administration. A legislator can bring to the notice of government, corrupt, under-hand and illegal methods adopted by a public servant. He can allege that a public servant has misused his authority and position. We know that in Punjab, the legislators submitted a memorandum against Late Partap Singh Kairon, the then Chief Minister of Punjab, to the President of India pointing out certain irregularities. The outcome was Das Commission. Similarly in Punjab memorandum was sent to President of India, incorporating irregularities committed by Prakash Singh Badal Ministry. In fact, in India, there is perhaps no states in which charges have not been levied against the government, regarding corrupt and illegal means for amassing wealth, with the help of administration. The legislatures can control administration by means of 'Committee on Assurances' and Estimates Committee' 'Public Accounts Committee' and so on. In these committees the administrator is face to face with the legislator to explain the position of his department. We also find that in the States the constituencies are not as big as parliamentary constituencies. Therefore, a legislator comes into close contact with the constituents.

Thus in the state the legislatures mould the administration. These give guidelines and policies for implementation to the state governments. Thus in a state, legislature is guide and philosopher of administration. Of course the scope of state activity has considerably increased which has resulted in the less time for the legislature to supervise, yet the very fact that the legislatures can take administration to task at any time, is in itself a sufficient guarantee that the administration will not go much wrong.

Legislative Assembly. It is lower house of State legislature and every Indian citizen can become its member. Members of Assembly get monthly salary and other allowances. The tenure of the assembly is 5 years. The members are elected on the basis of universal adult franchise. Seats are however, reserved for the persons belonging to scheduled castes, scheduled tribes and other backward classes. The presiding officer of the Assembly is Speaker who is responsible for maintaining decorum in the house. He conducts the proceedings of the House. The assembly has executive, financial and legislative powers.

Legislative Council. It is upper house of state legislature. Each member is elected for a period of 5 year and 1/3 of its member retire after every two years. It is an indirectly elected House. The House is presided over by a Chairman who performs the same functions as the speaker in the assembly. The Council also exercises executive, legislative and financial powers.

Legislature and Administration. Legislature exercises indirect control over administration by putting questions on the ministers, moving call attention and short notice questions and ultimately by passing a vote of no confidence against the Council of Ministers. Directly an administrator is controlled by the legislature at the time of meetings of committees of the legislature where he is face to face with the legislators.

In a state broad policy guidelines are given by the legislature whereas the administrator is required to implement them. Thus the control is real and effective.

ADMINISTRATIVE RELATIONS

The administrative relations between the Union and the State as envisaged under the Constitution, largely follows the pattern laid down by the Government of India Act, 1935. The arrangement is designed to serve a two-fold purpose : first, to ensure effective federal executive control of matters falling within the legislative jurisdiction of the Union Parliament and second, to minimise the possibilities of conflict between the Union and State administrative machineries.

The General rule is that the executive power in respect of all these matters on which the Union Parliament can legislate, belongs to the Union Government, while the executive power in respect of the matters specified in the State List belongs to the State Government. Now, the existing arrangement is that some of the matters like customs, income-tax, railways, post offices, defence are directly administered by the officers of the Central Government, while the administration of the rest, and the execution of the union laws generally is entrusted to the State authorities. This is particularly evident in the judicial sphere. All the courts, with the exception of the Supreme Court, are State Courts. In this respect there is a striking contrast between the American and Indian federal system. In the United States there is a complete set of federal executive and judicial officers for the executive and interpretation of federal laws. In India it is unlikely that a complete system of Union officers and courts to take exclusive charge of the Union laws will ever be established. Therefore, the Union Government depends largely on State authorities for execution of its laws. However, this administrative coordination between Union and the State is a two-way traffic. If certain federal matters are administered by State authorities, officers of Union Government occupy higher positions in State administration. Thus the administrative systems of the Union and the States though distinct, yet are not altogether separated from each other.

Union Direction of any Control of State Administration. The Union and State administrative relations are so organized in India as to enable the Union Government to exercise considerable control over the administrative machinery of the State. Thus it is clearly provided that the executive power of every State shall be so exercised as to ensure compliance with the laws made by Parliament, and that the executive power of the Union shall extend to the giving of such directions to a State as may appear to the Government of India to be necessary for that purpose—(Articles 256, 257). If the State Government fails to carry out the directions of the Union Government, the President acting under Article 365 may proclaim a breakdown of the constitutional machinery of the State and place all the powers of State Government in the hands of the Union Government. Apart from this drastic action that can be taken against a State Govenrment the Union Government exercises general powers of direction and control in several other matters which concern the Union as well as the States. Thus, the superintendence, direction and control of all elections whether to Union Parliament or to the State Legislatures are vested in the Election Commission appointed by the President. The judges of the High Courts are appointed and can be transferred by the President. The financial accounts of all States are under the supervision and control of the Comptroller and Auditor-General of India. The President has been given special powers in respect of the welfare of schedueld tribes and backward classes. Thus the Constitution has conferred wide authority on the Union Government to exercise control and direction over the State Executive.

Besides, the Union Government may give directions to a State as to the construction and maintenance of the means of communications declared to be of national and military importance and measures to be taken for the protection of the railways in the States. Under Article 253 the President may, with the consent of the State Government, entrust to is functions in relation to any matter to which the executive power of the Union extends.

Mention may also be made of Article, 355 which imposes a duty on the Union to protect every State against external aggression and internal distrubance and to ensure that the Government of every state is carried on in accordance with the provisions of the Constitution. The fulfilment of the obligations may sometimes require Union intervention in purely State matters.

Inter-State Council. Though the federating units are autonomous within their own territorial limits, yet the Constitution of India empowers the Parliament to provide for the adjudication of any dispute or complaint with respect to the use, distribution, or control of the water, or in, any inter-State river or river valley. Parliament may by law also provide that neither the Supreme Court nor any other court shall exercise any jurisdiction in respect of any such dispute or complaint. Provision has also been made for the creation of Inter-State Councils charged with the duty of : *(i)* inquiring into and advising upon disputes between States; *(ii)* investigating and discussing subjects of common interest to some or all States ; and *(iii)* making recommendations on any subject and, in particular, recommendations for the better co-ordination of policy and action with respect to that subject. Parliament also possesses the power to impose restrictions upon inter-State trade and establish such authority as it considers appropriate for enforcing the povisions of the Constitution with regard to such trade and commerce.

In addition to these powers which the Parliament may exercise in regard to the States in normal times, the Constitution vests general powers of direction and control over the States in times of national emergencies. When a Proclamation of Emergency has been issued by the President and is in operation, the Union Government can give directions to any State as to the manner in which the State's executive power should be exercised; during such periods Parliament is also empowered to make laws conferring powers and imposing duties upon the Union or its officers regarding matters which are not enumerated in the Union List. As stated earlier the consequences of the various emergency provisions will be to suspend the legislative and the executive authority of the State even in respect of matters which have been specifically allotted to them by the Constitution. For all practical purposes all the governmental powers will be concentrated in the hands of the Union and the federal government will be transformed into a unitary government for the time being. This clearly establishes that Centre enjoy precedence over States as regards control over State and concurrent subjects are concerned particularly during abnormal times.

FINANCIAL RELATIONS BETWEEN CENTRE AND STATE

An appraisal of the financial relations it may be firstly noted that the Constitution does not enumerate separately the heads of taxation. The power to tax is included in the power to legislate. Thus the subjects which are enumerated in the Union List are within the purview of Central Government for purposes of taxation and similarly the State Governments have the power of taxation in respect of subjects enumerated in the State List. The three lists of powers given in the Seventh Schedule divide the sources of revenue between the Union and the States as follows:

(A) The Union Sources

(a) Taxes on income other than agricultural income.

(b) Custom duties including expert duties.

(c) Estate duty in respect of property except agricultural land.

(d) Taxes on capital value of assets, exclusive of agricultural land of individuals and companies ; taxes on capital of companies.

(e) Terminal taxes on goods or passengers carried by sea, air or railway.

(f) Rates of stamp duty in respect of bills of exchange, cheques, promissory notes, bills of lading, letters of credit, insurance policies, transfer of shares, debentures, proxies and receipts.

(g) Duties of Excise on tabacco and other goods manufactured or produced in India except alcoholic liquors for human consumption and opium, Indian hemp and other narcotic drugs and narcotics.

(h) Corporation tax.

(i) Taxes other than stamp duties on transaction in stock exchanges and future markets.

(j) Taxes on sale or purchase of newspapers and on advertisements published therein.

(k) Fees in respect of any of the matters in the Union List except fees taken in any court.

(B) The State Sources

(a) Land revenue.

(b) Taxes on agricultural income.

(c) Taxes on land and buildings.

(d) Taxes on mineral lights subject to limitations imposed by law.

(e) Excise duties on alcoholic liquors for human consumption, and opium, hemp and other narcotic durgs.

(f) Duties on succession to agricultural land.

(g) Estate duty in respect of agricultural land.

(h) Taxes on the entry of goods into a local area for consumption, use or sale therein.

(i) Taxes on consumption or sale of electricity.

(j) Taxes on sale or purchase of goods other than newspapers.

(k) Tolls.

(l) Taxes on professions, trades, callings and employments.

(m) Capitation taxes.

(n) Taxes on luxuries, entertainments, betting and gambling.

(o) Rates on stamp duty on documents other than those subject to Union stamp duty.

(p) Taxes on advertisements other than those published in the newspapers.

(q) Taxes on goods and passengers carried by road or inland waterways.

(r) Taxes on animals, and boats.

(s) Fees in respect of any of the matters in the State List.

The Concurrent List does not contain any subject in respect of which taxation may be levied.

The division of the resources as given above does not mean that the party to which a tax is assigned is the sole authority to determine it and is entitled to all the proceeds of that tax. So far as the taxes in the State List are concerned, they go entirely to the State but it is different with the Union taxes, the proceeds of many of which are assigned to or shared with the States. The Constitutional distinguish four categories of Union taxes which are available, whole or in part, to the States:

(a) Duties levied by the Union but collected and wholly appropriated by the State : Stamp duties in respect of bills of exchange, cheques, promissory notes, bills of lading, letters of credit, policies of insurance, transfer of shares, debentures, proxies and receipts and excise on medicines and toilet preparations containing alcohol.

(b) Taxes levied and collected by the Union but wholly assigned to the States : duties in respect of succession to property other than agricultural land; terminal taxes on goods and passengers carried by rail, sea or air; taxes on railway fares and freights.

(c) Taxes levied and collected by the Union but whose proceeds are shared between the Union and the States. The tax which comes under this category is income tax.

(d) Taxes which are levied and collected by the Union but whose proceeds may be distributed between the Union and the States if Parliament by law so provide. Union duties of excise other than such duties of excise on medical and toilet preparations fall under this category.

Grants-in-aid. The Constitution also provides for Grants-in-aid to the States. Thus, Assam, Bihar, Orissa and West Bengal receive grants-in-aid in lieu of export duty on jute and jute products. Apart from the Union Government's constitutional obligation to provide grants-in-aid to the States for financing approved schemes for the welfare of the Scheduled Tribes and for improving the standard of administration in Tribal areas. Article 275 of the Constitution makes a general provision for Union grants-in-aid to the States. It is for the Union Government to fix the extent of these grants and lay down the conditions under which they are to be administered. It need not be stated that Grants-in-aid are potent instruments for the extension of Central control and direction of the States

Borrowing Powers. The Constitution also makes certain provisions in respect of the borrowing powers of the States. A State can borrow only within India and it cannot raise a new loan without the consent of the Union Government if there is outstanding any part of a previous loan and guaranteed by the Union or owned to it. The Government of India may, subject to such conditions as may be laid down by or under any law made by Parliament, make loans to any State provided that the limits set by Parliament to Union loans are not exceeded.

During the Proclamation of Financial Emergency the President may empower the Union to give directions controlling State's financial activities and require State Money bills to be reserved for his consideration.

It will be clear from the above description of Union-State relations that every effort has been made to make the Union Government much stronger than what Central Governments are usually found to be in other federations. The emphasis is more on the authority of the Centre than on the autonomy of the State. As a matter of fact interference and dictation by the Centre is not only so prohibited but authorized as a normal procedure of the functioning of the Constitution. The absense of equal representation to the States in the council of States ; the power given to the latter chamber to declare by a two thirds majority any subject to be of national importance, and then to enable the Union to give directions to make a law thereupon; the power of the Union to give direction to the State Government; and the power given to the President practically to suspend the State Constitution in times of emergency—are some of the exceptional features of the Indian Federation which have lead the critics to remark that the Indian Federation is only a quasi-federation or better still as a unitary federation.

DISTRIBUTION OF POWERS

The Constitution of India, as stated already, has established a federal form of Government characterised by a high degree of centralisation. The essence of a federal system in the system is the division of powers between the Central and State Governments by the Constitution. However, the scheme of distribution differs from other federal countries and embodies its peculiar needs. Keeping in view its hoary past which kept India subjugated due to disintegrative and divisive forces. Hitherto the framers of a federal constitution have divided the governmental powers in either of the ways; the specific powers of the Centre are enumerated and the residuary powers are left to the units; or the powers of the unit are specified and the balance is left for the Centre. The former scheme has been adopted in the United States of America and Australia, while the latter in Canada. The word, 'Federation' is not found any where in the Constitution.

Three lists. The Indian Constitution, following the precedent set under the Government of India Act of 1935, divides the governmental powers into three lists—The Union List, the State List and the Concurrent List. The distribution is remarkably elaborated and detailed and attempt has been made to cover the whole field of all possible governmental activity as far as the human mind can visualise at present. If still some powers are left unspecified, they are vested in the Centre. The Union List contains these matters on which the Union Parliament has exclusive right to frame the laws. The State Legislatures have the exclusive powers of making laws with respect the matters enumerated in the State List. As regards the Concurrent List, both the Union Parliament and State Legislature have concurrent powers with the provision that, in case of a conflict, the Central law must, to the extent of repugnancy, prevail over the State law. If, however, the State law has been reserved for and received the assent of the President, it will prevail unless and until Parliament passes a new law overruling the provisions of the State law.

The Union List contains 97 subjects including such subjects as defence; atomic energy; citizenship; railway; posts and telegraphs; foreign affairs; shipping; airways; banking and insurance; currency and coinage; mines and minerals; opium, war, peace and treaties; etc. The State List contains 66 subjects and includes public order; police; jails; local government; education; agriculture and forests; public health and sanitation; roads, bridges, ferries, municipal tramways and traffic therein; ponds and the prevention of cattle tress pass; irrigation and canals of wards; industries; weights and measures except establishment of standards; inns and inn-keepers ; betting and gambling; state public services; etc. The concurrent list contains 47 matters and includes such sub-welfare; price control; factories; electricity; newspapers; legal, medical and other processions; charities and charitable institutions; stamp duties other than judicial stamps etc.

From a perusal of the three lists it is quite clear that the Central Government has been given very many powers. The total number of subjects specified in the Union List is as much as 97 as compared to 66 that are enumerated in the State List. Besides, the Union Parliament has powers to make laws in respect of 47 items included in the Concurrent List. It is true that the State Legislature also is empowered to make laws on matters specified in the Concurrent List, but as told already in case of an inconsistency between the State Law and Union, the latter supersedes the former. It would not be an exaggeration to say that whenever the Union so desires the Concurrent matter can for all practical purposes be converted into Union matters.

FUNCTIONS

The Ministry is responsible for the administration of the finances of the Central Government and for dealing with financial matters affecting the country as a whole. It arranges for raising the resources for developmental and other requirements and regulates the taxation and borrowing policies of Government, It deals with all problems connected with banking and currency and, in consultation with the Ministries concerned, arranges for the proper utilisation of the country's foreign exchange resources. In co-operation with the administrative Ministries, it controls the entire expenditure of the Government of India.

Organization. The Ministry is now organised in four Departments:

(a) The Department of Revenue and Insurance.

(b) The Department of Economic Affairs.

(c) The Department of Co-ordination.

(d) The Department of Expenditure.

Each Department is headed by a Secretary and there are a number of organisations under the control of each of the secretaries. The functions of each of the Department mentioned above are as under :

Functions of the Department of Revenue and Insurance. This Department is responsible for the administration of all direct and indirect Union taxes and for all matters relating to insurance. It advises the Government on fiscal matters, reviews tax structure, examines fresh proposals of taxation, promotes legislation for the modification of tax law and administers Gold Control regulations.

In respect of revenue matter, the Department is assisted by two statutory Boards under it. These Boards are :

(a) The Central Board of Direct Taxes which consists of a Chairman and three other Members.

(b) The Central Board of Excise and Custom which consists of a Chairman and two other members.

The Chairmen of the two Boards hold *ex-officio* status of Additional Secretary to the Government of India while the Members of the Boards are *ex-offico* Joint Secretaries.

The Administration of the Gold Control regulations is entrusted to the Gold Control Administrator who also holds *ex-officio* status of Joint Secretary to the Government of India.

The tax Credit Certificates (Export) Scheme is being administered by a Director appointed in the Department and six zonal and sub-zonal offices have also been set-up for this purpose.

Functions of the Department of Expenditure. The Department consists of following Divisions:

1. Establishment Division. Estabilishment Discussion is responsible mainly for the adminstration of the various financial rules and regulations including those relating to the conditions of service of the Central Government employees. The Head of this Division is also in-charge of the Staff inspection Unit.

2. Civil Expenditure Divisions. There are ten Divisions each headed by an Additional Secretary or a Joint Secretary. In addition to rendering financial advice to the Ministries/Departments of the Government of India, nominated officers of these Divisions also function as financial representatives of Government on Board of Directors of various public sector undertakings and on the governing bodies of autonomous organisations which receive substantial financial assistance from Government.

3. Defence Division. This division is constituted with the Financial Adviser at the head assisted by four Additional Financial Advisers and a number of Deputy Financial Advisers attached to the various Principal Staff Officers of the Army, the Chief of Naval Staff, the Chief of the Air Staff and the Director-General of Ordinance Factories. This Division renders financial advice to the Defence Headquarters, the Defence Ministry and to the Officers directly subordinate to that Ministry. The Financial Adviser (Defence) is also a Member of the Board of the Border Roads Development.

4. Staff Inspection Unit. The function of the Staff Inspection Unit is to keep the staffing position in Ministries/Offices functioning under the jurisdiction of Government of India under constant review in accordance with pre-determined programme of work-measurement studies. The Unit also undertakes *ad hoc* reviews, by special request, of Ministries/Offices not included in the programme as well as of the public sector undertakings. The other aspects of work study, such as procedures and methods etc., are the responsibility of the Department of Administrative Reforms under the Ministry of Home Affairs.

Functions of the Department of Economic Affairs. The Department of Economic Affairs prepares the Government's budget, makes periodic assessments of foreign exchange needs and resources and takes necessary steps to mobilise and allocate resources, both internal and external, in keeping with the country's Plans and development needs. The department works through the following Divisions :

1. Budget Division. It prepares the Central Govenment's Annual Budget (other than that for Railways) and Supplementary and Excess Grants for presentation to Parliament.

2. External Finance and Foreign Aid Division. It deals with all matters relating to foreign exchange and trade agreements with foreign countries.

3. Internal Finance Division. It deals with all matters relating to currency, coinage, banking, industrial finance and control of capital issues.

4. Economic Division. It advises the Department of Economic Affairs on questions of economic policy.

5. Administrative Division. It looks after the administrative matters of the Department as also the work relating to grants to various institutions and councils.

Functions of the Department of Co-ordination. The Department of Co-ordination deals with State Plans and State finances with particular reference to Central financial assistance to the State Government, scrutinises Central and State legislations having financial and economic implications, advises in regard to State Governments proposals for investment in industrial enterprises, irrigation, power and flood control projects, etc., with reference to the available resources, carries out studies in the financial fields of State Governments and is associated with the scrutiny of the proposals of the Central Ministries for large projects involving heavy capital outlays. It also studies specific, economic, industrial and operational problems and bottlenecks in consultation with the Ministries and departments concerned.

The Department was closely associated with the Planning Commission in all phases of the preparation for the Fourth Five Year Plan and the determination of the size of the Central and the State Plans for 1966-67, and the Central assistance for the State Plans, in the light of the resources in sight. The scrutiny and analysis of periodic progress reports from industrial and mineral projects in the public sector also continued to be one of the responsibilities of the Department.

RELATIONSHIP BETWEEN PLANNING COMMISSION AND FINANCE COMMISSION

Article, 280 of the Constitution of India provides for 'an independent, quasi-judicial expert body', termed as the Finance Commission, to recommend the principles and proportions of financial transfers from the Union to the State through the 'built' in balancing techniques. The role of the Finance Commission is regulated by the basic principles of federal finance, which attempts to meet the residuary budgetary requirements of the States, after taking into account the devolution of the proceeds of the Union taxes to the States. The philosophy behind it is that the states, being at different stages of development, are required to be brought upto minimum level thereby aiming at 'equal sacrifice and equal opportunity. In the light of this basic principle, the various Finance Commission evolved their own schemes for determining the quantum of statutory assistance to the States, with common line of emphasis on the need to meet the budgetary gaps of the States.

The process of planned economic development introduced radical changes in the entire fiscal context in the economy since 1951-52. The criterion of 'budgetary needs', inherent in the Finance Commission's recommendations was put into, "insignificance by the impact of Plan expenditure, growing as it did in all these years of economic planning. The formulation of plans at the State level, their incorporation in the National Plans and their implementation at the State level, formed a big charge on the Union exchequer, in fact if not in theory. The tax sources of the States having been relatively narrow and inelastic, their financial resources for putting through the Plan schemes had to be supplemented by increasing assistance from the Union." As a consequence of these changes the criterion of the 'budgetary needs' a concept dealing with the gap in 'current revenues and expenditures for allocation of Union assistance' was replaced by the concept of 'fiscal needs' which is of much wider economic significance, and points out towards the gap in resources in an overall context of gross expenditure of the State.

The approach and thinking of the successive Finance Commissions was influenced deeply by such a gradual change in the Union-States financial relationship in the wake of the planned economic development. The first Finance Commission admitted the need to 'take into account' not only the 'budgetary needs' but also the 'fiscal needs' emerging out the execution of development programmes of the country. The same view was endorsed by the second Finance Commission which recommended Central assistance to the States so as to enable them to put through the Plans but was left to the Third Finance Commission, to embody this view, in quantitative terms, in its recommendations. The Fourth Finance Commission, "guided by its terms of reference to take only non-Plan expenditure into account, calculated the non-Plan revenue gap on the basis of its scrutiny of the estimates submitted by State governments and recommended its complete elimination through Union assistance." Similar changes in the scope of Finance Commission were made just by altering the terms of reference and by any Constitutional amendment. As it has been rightly stated that "otherwise excepting the limitations arising out of the terms of reference, there is nothing to preclude the Finance Commission to take into consideration requirements arising out of Plan expenditures too." Nowhere in these Articles is there an expressed or implied indication that the total revenues of a State should be utilized only revenue expenditure... It is abundantly clear to my mind that the reference in the main part of clause (1) of Article, 275 to grants-in-aid to the revenues of States is not confined to revenue expenditure only... There is no legal warrant for excluding from the scope of the Finance Commission all capital grants; even the capital requirements of a State may be properly met by grants-in-aid under Article, 275 (1), made on the recommendations of the Finance Commission... The legal position, therefore, is that there is nothing in the Constitution to prevent the Finance Commission to take into consideration both capital and revenue requirements of the States in formulating a scheme of devolution and in recommending grants under Article 275 of the Constitution."

The role being played by the Planning Commission regarding the allocation of Union assitance to the States is much wider as well as much more effective and decisive. Precisely speaking, "its role is confined to the needs arising out of additional current outlays and the total expenditure on capital account which is projected while formulating the Five Year Plan. The Planning Commission helps in the formulation of the State Plan, ship-shapes them in overall perspective of the nationwide strategy of economic growth. For the purpose, it considers the budgets of the State governments in their entire including the non-Plan revenue and capital expenditure, and then the quantum and Union assistance of the States is determined.'

The overlapping between the Planning Commission and the Finance Commission is witnessed in the flow of Union assistance since the advent of area of planned economic development. Very often the functions, as discharged these two bodies, 'have resulted in contradictions, disturbing thereby the harmony in the Union-States' financial relations.

Developments Caused by Overlapping

1. The estimates that are placed by the State governments before the two bodies are not consistent because of the fact that 'as the Finance Commission is engaged in filling the 'revenue gap', there is a temptation for the States present figures which underestimate their resources. On the other hand, under pressure to increase their Plan size and show the necessary resources for them in their submissions to the Planning Commission, they consistently overestimate their resource-raising potentialities and capitalities at current rates of taxation and prices and underestimate their non-Plan expenditure liabilities, as the more the undertake to raise, the more they are likely to get.

2. The isolated way of functioning of these two Commissions head led more developed States 'to fudge the figures'. Since according to the provisions, the statutory assistance under the Finance Commission's awards is given to those States which have 'a gap in their non-Plan revenue account', these States seem indifferent to the Finance Commission or 'manouver a gap in the revenue account' but the approach is 'reversed' when they deal with the Planning Commission.

3. State manouver the distinction between Plan expenditure and non Plan expenditure, worked out by the two Commissions for the

purpose of allocation of central assistance. These is a widespread confusion.

4. In the circumstance wherein the Plan expenditure its progressively increasing, "the non-Plan expenditure in so far as it is functionally related to the Plan expenditure, also increases likewise.' It is opined in this regard that 'fast which one body considers as relevant is totally overlooked by the other.' It is further pointed out that 'since it is the total expenditure which is pertinant. It should be the total assistance that must be the concern of the any body charged with the allocation of Central assistance.'

5. The idea behind the grant of staturtory assitance is to bring-up the backward States to a minimum level in comparison to the relatively more developed States. This is also one of the prime objectives of the Union assistance formulated by the Planning Commission. The overlapping occurs when 'in order to aim at balanced regional development, the Planning Commission allows for the relative backwardness of a State or region while formulating the strategy, structure and substance of a development Plan. The Finance Commission ignores, however, the Plan expenditure of the State which is designed to aim at, among levelling the regional economic disparities.' This dichotomy in the functions of the Planning Commission and the Finance Commission in determining the quantum of Union assistance to states have developed many inconsistencies.

It has been pointed out that, "One of the main objectives of Central assistance to State has been to ensure that the States implement effectively those schemes and projects which have a certain rationale in the overall context of national economy. In other words, the pattern of assistance devised was designed to facilitate the use of Central funds in channels predetermined in the Plan. When it was found that these objectives were not achieved on account of lacunae in the procedures underlying the release of central assistance, many reforms were introduced to simplify the procedures. Even then the main objective of ensuring that the funds were used so as to achieve certain results has remained largely unfulfilled. Instead what has achieved is an artificial uniformity in the schemes and projects of different States." This situation necessitates the formulation of a clear policy of plan assistance.

Suggestions for Improvement

1. The Planning Commission has been made responsible for making an 'assessment of the matrial, capital and human resources; framing development Plans for the most effective and balanced growth of the economy; determinating of priorities; and determining the nature of machinery to secure due implementation of the Plans with a view to raise the rate of overall economic development of the country. Planning Commission has been increasing the quantum of assistance in every Five Year Plan. It is suggested that "in a planned economy, its needs and resources will have to be viewed *in toto*. The allocation of resources will have to be consistent with the objectives and utilisation of resources is a point responsibility of the Centre and States. The old federal principle, which regards all the constituent units as independent of each other in their own spheres, has to give place to what may be called the idea of cooperative federalism. All the arrangements for Centre-State transfers of resources will have to be based on the consideration of rapid economic growth without prejudice to the idea of "federal justice."

It is a commonly supported view that in the context of overall economic development, the dominant role played by the Planning Commission should be retained. However, the functions and respective spheres of operation of the Planning Commission and the Finance Commission, relating to the 'Union assistance' should be statutorily defined.

2. The Planning Commission should be made a statutory body to give it 'a position of something more than an advisory body'. "A mere advisory committee of experts can wield but feeble weapons against Central ministries and State governments which are chafing at the restrictions imposed upon them by a Plan, and all trying to go their own ways, often in the genuine conviction that their sectional interests coincide with the national interests. Unless there is a strong countervailing force, these centrifugal pulls can distintegrate a plan very quickly... What the Indian system, with all its faults, avoids is the situation, so dismal to the serious planner, in which the experts sit isolated and neglected it small black rooms, drawning up projections of economic

development and making policy recommendations which few of the politicians read and none feel committed to it."

3. The area of jurisdiction of the Finance Commission and the Planning Commission should be demarcated in clear and definite terms 'by either suitable amendments in the Constitution by conventions'.

4. It is also suggested that the suggestions of the Planning Commission 'in respect of Union Plan-Grants and the Union loans to the States should be accorded a statutory sanction.'

5. The Plan-assistance from the Union to the States must not be specific schemes/projects oriented in the State Plans.

6. There is a need for a well established, sound but flexible institutional framework for Union-State financial relationship under the Constitutional framework.

7. It is further suggested that the Finance Commission is appointed every five year to go into the problems of 'inter-State inequalities of income and other disparties and recommend adequate equalising financial transfers.'

❐

8 Judiciary

SUPREME COURT

The Supreme Court stands at the apex of the Indian Judicial system. It consists of a Chief Justice and 25 other judges. The President appoints the Chief Justice of India after 'consulting' the judges of the Supreme Court. He appoints the judges with the 'consultation' of the Chief Justice of India. The President may appoint *ad hoc* judge or judges at the request of the Chief Justice of India. Only a working judge of some High Court or a retired judge of the Supreme Court can be appointed on *ad hoc* basis. It should be noted that matters relating to the appointment of the judges of the Supreme Court relate to the discretionary power of the President and the provision that he should consult judges of the Supreme Court or of the High Courts, as he may deem necessary, in the event of selection for the post of the Chief Justice of India is of a recommendatory and not of a mandatory character. A person to be appointed as a Judge of the Supreme Court must possess two qualifications. First, he must be a citizen of India. Second, he must have served as a judge in some High Court for at least five years, or practised in a High Court as an advocate for at least ten years, or must be a distinguished jurist in the view of the President. As a matter of practice, one of the judges must be a Muslim so as to ensure secular character of the supreme judiciary.

The judges of the Supreme Court retire on completing the age of 65 years. A judge may resign his post by addressing a letter to the President of India. It is also provided that a judge of the Supreme Court may be removed by the process of impeachment. For this purpose the Parliament may pass a special address by its absolute majority coupled with two-third majority of the members, present and voting, on charging a judge with 'proved misbehaviour' or 'incapacity'. As per the Judges Inquiry Act, 1968 it is necessary that before the matter is taken up for discussion in any House of Parliament, it must be looked into by an inquiry committee consisting of the Chief Justice or a senior judge of the Supreme Court, Chief Justice or a senior Judge of a High Court, and a distinguished jurist of the country.

The jurisdiction of the Supreme Court is of three kinds—original, appellate, and advisory. Its original jurisdiction covers cases of constitutional law or fact between the Centre and the States or between the States. Here it acts as an umpire between the Union and the States. The Matters relating to election disputes of the President and Vice-President may be tried in the Supreme Court alone. The appellate jurisdiction of the Supreme Court covers cases already decided by the High Court. The judgment of a high Court can be taken to the Supreme Court in an appeal in case the High Court itself certifies that the 'case is fit for appeal', or the Supreme Court gives its leave for this purpose. In civil and in constitutional cases, an appeal shall lie to the Supreme Court against the judgment of a High Court if it is satisfied that the case involves a substantial point of law as to the interpretation of the Constitution. In criminal cases, it has to be seen whether the High Court has in appeal reversed the order of acquittal of an accused person delivered by a district court and sentenced him to death, or has withdrawn for trial before itself any case from any court subordinate to its authority and his in such a trial convicted the accused person and sentenced him to death. It shows that a person cannot move the Supreme Court in appeal as a matter of right. The Court may issue prerogative writs for the protection and enforcement of Fundamental Rights. Under Art. 136, the Supreme Court can allow special leave to appeal against the judgment of any court or tribunal in the territory of India. Under Art. 143, the President may refer any matter of law of fact of considerable public importance for taking the opinion of the Court that is not binding, though it his great persuasive value. This is known as advisory jurisdiction of the Supreme Court.

High Courts

The Constitution provides for a High Courts for each State; there may be a common High Court for two or States as well as for a Union Territory. A High Court consists of a Chief Justice and some other judges as the President may determine from time to time. The judges retire at the age of 62 years. It is also provided that the President may appoint additional judges to clear the arrears of work for a term of two years subject to the age limit of 62 years. The President may also appoint temporary judges to fill casual vacancies in the cadre of permanent judges caused by the reason of absence or any other factor. While appointing the Chief Justice or a judge of a High Court, the President may consult the Chief Justice of India, Judges of the Supreme Court, the Chief Justice of the High Court and the Governor of the concerned State. A judge of a High Court must possess two qualifications. First, he must be citizen of India. Second, he must have held a judicial office in the country, or practised as an advocate in some High Court for at least 10 years. A judge resign his post by writing a letter to the President of India; he may be transferred from one High Court to another; he may be appointed as a judge of the Supreme Court; he may be removed by the process of impeachment as applicable to a judge of the Supreme Court discussed above.

The jurisdictional competence of the High Courts still remains as it was before the commencement of the Constitution. As a result, while the High Courts of Calcutta, Bombay and Madras have both original and appellate jurisdictions (in civil cases of the value of more than Rs. 2000 and in criminal cases referred to them by the Presidency magistrates and other cases of revenue), all have limited original jurisdiction in cases relating to admiralty, will, divorce, marriage, company law and contempt of court. All High Courts have appellate jurisdiction in civil and criminal cases. Like the Supreme Court, the High Courts have the power to issue prerogative writs for the protection and enforcement of fundamental rights in the nature of *habeas corpus*, *mandamus*, *prohibition*, *certiorari*, and *quo warranto*. Unlike the Supreme Court, they may also issue such writs 'for any other purpose'. The original jurisdiction of the High Courts also covers election disputes of the members of Parliament and State legislatures. Like Supreme Court, each High Court is a court of record.

The decisions of the district courts can challenged in the High Court. The High Court can call from the subordinate courts returns, issue general rules and forms to regulate their proceedings, prescribe for them account forms and books, and settle the table of fees allowed to the clerks and officers of such courts and to the pleaders practising therein. It has the power of superintendence and control over the lower courts within their areas except military courts. It a High Court is satisfied that a case pending before any subordinate court involves a substanital question of constitutional law, it can take up the case and decide it itself or may send it back to the subordinate court, in question, after deciding the question of law involved therein.

JUDICIAL REVIEW

It may be defined as the power of a court to look into the constitutional validity of an impugned law or executive action and hold it unconstitutional and, for that reason, unenforceable to the extent it is inconsistent with the fundamental law of the land. It is an invention of Chief Justice Marshall of the American Supreme Court and now it has been adopted in the constitutional systems of many countries like Canada, Australis, Switzerland, Germany, Nigeria, Japan and India. The reason behind it is that in a country having a written constitution the ordinary law must be subordinate to the higher (constitutional) law of the land. No organ of government can transgress its area of authority and in case it occurs in the form of a law made by the legislature or some other organ having authority delegated to it or if some administrative active is taken in violation of the doctrine of 'competence,' it may be challenged in the Court and then the Court may declare it null and void to the extent of its being repugnant to the Constitution. Such a unique function of the judiciary stems from a feeling that a system based on a written constitution can hardly be effective in practice without an authoritative, independent and impartial arbiter of constitutional issues and also that it is necessary to restrain government organs from exercising powers which may not be sanctioned by the Constitution."

The source of the power of the judicial review is contained in Art. 13 (2), of the Constitution. It says that "all laws in force in the territory of India immediately before the commencement of his Constitution, in so far as they are inconsistent with the provision of Part III shall, to the extent of such inconsistency, be void. The State shall, not make any law which takes away or abridges the rights conferred by this Part and any law made in contravention of the class, shall to the extent of the contravention, be void. Unless the context otherwise requires, the word 'law' includes any ordinance, order, by-law, rule, regulation, modification, custom or usage having in the territory of India the force of law. It also includes 'laws in force' or laws made by a Legislature or a competent authority in the territory of India before the commencement of this Constitution and not previously repealed, notwithstanding that any such law or any part thereof may not be then in operation either at all or in particular areas."

Weather the word 'law' used in this Article means ordinary law or constitutional law, it is not clear. The Supreme Court in leading case of Sankari Prasad v. The Union of India (1951) and again in the case of Sajjan Singh v. The State of Rajasthan (1965) held the view that the word 'law' occurring in Art. 13, meant ordinary law. But in the case of Golak Nath v. The State of Punjab (1967) it ruled that the world 'law' occurring in Art. 13, and in Art. 368, meant the same. As such, even a law of constitutional amendment could not be valid if it was inconsistent with Part III of the Constitution having fundamental rights. In this case the Supreme Court subscribed to the principle of prospective over-ruling as accepted in the American jurisprudence. It means that a law could remain in operation in spite of being unconstitutional as much work had already been done and that could not be reversed, but in future no such law could be made. In order to demolish this barrier, the Twenty-fourth Constitution Amendment Act came into being in 1971. It provides that the Parliament can amended any part of the Constitution.

The power of judicial review is vested in the High Courts and the Supreme Court. As such, an aggrieved party may challenge a law or any executive order on the ground of its being inconsistent with the provisions or the basic structure of the Constitution. It is true that our Courts cannot invoke the plea of 'due process of law' as it is invoked by the American Supreme Court for the reason that they are specifically bound to follow 'procedure established by law'. It appears that the judiciary is virtually under the sway of the legislature. However, this point should not be understood in a way to minimize the position of the judiciary. The Courts may also look into the fact that the procedure established by law is not a fraud on the Constitution. In the case of Kesavanand Bharati v. The State of Kerala or Fundamental Rights Case (1973) the Supreme Court laid down the doctrine of the 'basic structure of the Constitution'. It is true that the Court did not clearly define the term 'basic framework or structure', but is very clear that it could establish its powerful position vis-a-vis the power of the legislature. The judgment of the Court in this case may be regarded as our Republic's greatest contribution to jurisprudence, and its underlying philosophy as of momentous significance for the survival of democracy in our country.

HIGH COURTS IN INDIA

	Names	*Year of Establish-ment*	*Territorial Jurisdication*	*Seats*	*With Bench or Benches at*
	1	2	3	4	5
1.	Allahabed	1866	Uttar Pradesh	Allahabad	Lucknow
2.	Andhra	1954	Andhra Pradesh	Hyderabed	—
3.	Bombay	1861	Maharashtra, Goa and Daman and Diu	Bombay	Nagpur, Aurangabed and Panaji
4.	Calcutta	1861	West Bengal and Andaman and Nicobar Islands	Calcutta	Port Blair
5.	Delhi	1966	Delhi	New Delhi	—
6.	Guwahati	1948	Assam, Manipur, Nagaland,	Guwahati	Kohima, Aizwal,

Contd.

1	2	3	4	5
		Meghalaya. Tripura, Mizoram and Arunachal Pradesh		Imphal and Agratala, circuit bench at Shillong
7. Gujarat	1960	Gujarat	Ahmedabad	—
8. Himachal	1971	Himachal Pradesh	Shimla	—
9. Juammu-Kashmir	1928	Jammu-Kashmir	Srinagar and Jammu	— —
10. Kerala	1956	Kerala and Lakshadweep	Ernakulam	—
11. Madhya Pradesh	1956	Madhya Pradesh	Jabalpur	Gwalior and Indore
12. Madras	1891	Tamilm Nadu and Pondicharry	Madras	—
13. Myore	1884	Karantaka	Bangalore	—
14. Orissa	1948	Orissa	Cuttack	—
15. Patna	1916	Bihar	Patna	Ranchi
16. Pubjab and Haryana	1947	Chandigarh	Punjab, Haryana and Chandigarh	—
17. Rajasthan	1949	Rajasthan	Jodhpur	Jaipur
18. Sikkem	1975	Sikkim	Gangtok	—

While exercising the power of judicial review, the Courts are guided by certain maxims. For instance, the point of 'competence' is taken into consideration. The Court examines whether the law-making or order-issuing authority has acted within its jurisdiction or not. It is also know as the doctrine of pith and substance. The Court also distinguishes between the good and bad parts of an impugned law and, as such, it may declare only its bad part void. The Court may declare a law void in case is transgresses the authority of the legislature or of the Supreme Court invalidated a decree of the

President (1970), that derecognised all former rules of the princely State and thereby made them ineligible for privy purses and privileges. The Court may also see whether a law or decree is bad in part and may then strike it down as it invalidated some parts of the law whereby 14 banks were nationalised in 1969. In case the Parliament makes an amendment in the Constitution, or it makes a change in a law in rectification of a mistake for which the Court had invalidated a particular law, then the Court will not strike down an impugned law or administrative action. Moreover, the Court may change its view from time to time in the light of new conditions of circumstances.

The position of the Courts with regard to the exercise of the power of judicial review, as it obtains in our country, is well evident from the observation of Justice S.K. Das in the case of A.K. Gopalan v. The State of Madras (1950); "In India the function of the judiciary is somewhat between the Courts in England and the United States. While, in the main, leaving our Parliament and State legislatures supreme in their respective legislative fields, our Constitution has, by some of its Articles, put upon the Legislature certain specified limitations. The point to be noted, however, is that in so far as there is any limitation on the legislative power, the Court must on a complaint being made to it, scrutinise and ascertain whether such limitation has been transgressed and if there has been any transgression the Court will courageously declare the law unconstitutional, for the Court is bound by its oath to uphold the Constitution. But outside the limitation imposed on the legislative powers, our Parliament and State legislatures are supreme in their respective legislative fields and the Court has no authority to question the wisdom or policy of the law duly made by appropriate legislature. Our Constitution, unlike the English Constitution, recognises the Court's supremacy over legislative authority, but such supremacy is a limited one, for it is confined to the field where the legislative power is circumscribed by limitations upon it by the Constitution itself.

The power of judicial review, as exercised by the Supreme Court and the High Courts, has been criticised as well as defended by the writers on constitutional law and politics. It is said that judicial review opens the flood-gates for more and more judicial debate signifying a "lawyers' paradise". It leads to judicial despotism that virtually results in a hostile confrontation between the executive and the judicial departments of the state. It is also commented that judicial review becomes an effective instrument in the hands of the vested interests owing to the highly conservative attitude of the Courts. Further, the Courts, in stead of giving stability to judicial thought, tamper it with their shifty stands as a result of which uncertainty prevails in the realm of law and justice. Above all, it elevates the position of the courts to act like the 'powerful third chambers' or the 'super-master of the legislature.' As a learned writer remarks : What is distinctive to the Indian experiment...is the fact that the Indian Supreme Court has functioned largely in an inapposite Westminister model of Parliamentary democracy."

However, viewed in a correct perspective, judicial review looks like an essential instrument in the hands of the judges to work as the protectors of our democratic system as enshrined in the provisions of the constitution. It is by virtue of this power that the judiciary can save the ordinary people from the onslaught of executive of legislative despotism. What is really needed is that the custodians of the Constitution must not exercise their power in a way that would lead to the intrusion of their personal philosophy into the social philosophy of the nation and thereby cause a sort of hostile confrontation between the two organs of the political system.

INDEPENDENCE OF JUDICIARY

We may now enumerate some provisions of the Constitution which ensure independence of the judges of the Supreme Court and the High Courts as under:

1. Though made by the President on the advice of the Ministers, the appointments of the Judges are regarded as' constitutional'; they are governed by specific high qualifications pertaining to the realm of law and justice which a person must possess.

   The Judges are paid a salary and allowances as determined by a law of the Parliament and, until it is done, as specified in Second Schedule of the Constitution. It also includes their right to leave and pension. These cannot be varied to their disadvantage after appointment. The provision of Art. 360, is an exception when during financial emergency the President may reduce the salaries and allowances of all public servants, including the Judges. It is also given that the salaries, allowances and pensions of the Judges and all administrative expenses of the Supreme Court shall be charged on the Consolidated Fund of India and of the Judges of the High Courts on the Consolidated Fund of the concerned State.

3. It is also given that a Judge may be removed on the Charge of 'proved misbehaviour' or 'incapacity' or both if the resolution of impeachment is passed by both the Houses of Parliament by special majority. The Judges Inquiry Act makes it binding that the matter must first be investigated by a high-powered inquiry committee. The process of impeachment of the Judges is quite tedious.
4. Art 220, puts restriction on private legal practice by a person who retires from service in the Supreme Court. But a retired Chief Justice or a Judge of any High Court excluding the High Court or High Courts where he had served in a permanent capacity.
5. The constitution and jurisdiction of the Supreme Court and the High Courts is a Union subject. As explained by Sir Alladi Krishnaswami Ayyar, the placement of the High Courts under the control of the Union in certain important matters had been done in order to keep them outside the range of 'provincial politics.'
6. The conduct of the Judges cannot be discussed in any State Legislature; it can be discussed in the Parliament only when a substantive motion for the removal of a Judge is under consideration.

SUBORDINATE COURTS

Chapter VI of Part VI of the Constitution has provisions for the subordinate courts of a State. Art. 233, says that appointments of persons to be, and the posting and promotion of, district judges in any State shall be made by the governor of a State in consultation with the High Court exercising jurisdiction in relation to such State. A person not already in the service of the Union or of the State shall only be eligible to be appointed a district judge if he had been for not less than seven years in advocate or a pleader and is recommended by the High Court for appointment. Art. 233A, provides for the validation of appointments and judgments etc. delivered by district judges in certain cases. It lays down: "Notwithstanding any judgment, decree or order of any court:

(a) *(i)* no appointment of any person already in the judicial service of a State or of any person who has not been for less than seven years an advocate or a pleader, to be a district judge in that State, and *(ii)* no posting, promotion or transfer of any such person as a district judge made at any time before the commencement of this Constitution (Twentieth Amendment Act, 1966), otherwise than in accordance with the provision of Article 233, or Article 235, shall be deemed to be illegal or void or ever to have become illegal or void by reason only of the fact that such appointment, posting, promotion or transfer was not made in accordance with the said provisions;

(b) no jurisdiction exercised, no judgment, decree, sentence or order passed or made, and no other act or proceeding done or taken, before the commencement of Constitution (Twentieth Amendment Act, 1966) by or before any person appointed, posted, promoted, or transferred as a district judge in any State otherwise than in accordance with the provision of Article 233, or Article 235, shall be deemed to be illegal or invalid or ever to have become illegal or invalid by reason only of the fact that such appointment, posting, promotion or transfer was not made in accordance with the said provision."

Art. 234, provides for recruitment of persons other than district judges to the judicial service of the State. It says that the appointment of persons other than district judges to the judicial service of a State shall be made by the Governor of the State in accordance with rules made by him in that behalf after consultation with the State Public Service Commission and with the High Court exercising jurisdiction in relation to such State. Finally, Art. 235, says about the control over subordinate courts. The control over district courts and other courts subordinate thereto, including the posting and promotion of persons belonging to the judicial service of a State and holding any post inferior to the post of a district judge, shall be vested in the High Court, but nothing in this Article shall be construed as taking away from any such person any right of appeal which he may have under the law regulating the conditions of his service or as authorising the High Court to deal with him otherwise than in accordance with the condition of his service prescribed under such law.

The object of these provisions is to secure the independence of subordinate judiciary from the executive and to that extent to effect separation of powers. Since the Governor has to exercise his powers in consultation with the High Court, it has been held by the Supreme Court that it must be 'effective' as it is mandatory. In the context, the High Court means full court of all the Judges. Consultation with a sub-committee of the High Court or of some other body would be invalid in case of any appointment made by the Governor. But the judgment delivered by a district judge whose appointment is subsequently held invalid would not be taken invalid. Moreover, the Governor cannot make any rule in this regard that is violative of the provisions of the Constitution.

ADMINISTRATIVE TRIBUNALS AND LOK ADALATS

Part XIV A, of the Constitution inserted by the Forty-second Amendment of 1976 "opens a new chapter in Indian constitutional and administrative law by substantially excluding judicial review of administrative decisions." In pursuance of Art. 323A, (which provides for adjudication or trial by the Administrative Tribunals of disputes and complaints relating to recruitment and conditions of service of persons appointed to public services and posts in connection with affairs of the Union and State government), the Administrative

Tribunal Act, 1985 came into effect. (It was amended in the following year.) It sets-up Central Administrative Tribunal to provide speedy and inexpensive justice to the employees of the Central Government in respect of their service matters. The principal bench of the CAT is a New Delhi. It has 16 other regular benches at the principal seats of the High Courts; namely, Ahmedabed, Allahabed, Bangalore, Bombay, Calcutta, Chandigarh, Cuttack, Ernakulum, Guwhati, Hyderabed, Jabalpur Jaipur, Jodhpur, Lucknow, Madras and Patan. These benches also hold circuit sittings at other seats of High Courts where wrokload for the tribunal is less.

Sec. 4(2), of this Act provides for the setting-up of Administrative Tribunals in States by the Union Government in respect of specific requests made by the State governments. Accordingly, such tribunals have been set-up in Himachal Pradesh, Orissa, Maharashtra, Karnataka, Madhya Pradesh, TamilNadu and Andhra Pradesh. Like CAT, the State administrative tribunals have the power of all courts except that of Supreme Court in regard to service matters of the employees of State governments.

However, the important point to be noted is that these tribunals have got the jurisdiction to settle disputes relating to service matters of the government employees and thereby deprived the civil courts and the High Courts of their jurisdiction in such matters. What the civil courts and the High Courts could do, has new been given to the tribunals. They may grant relief to aggrieved party as well. The decisions of the CAT can be taken to the Supreme Court in appeal.

Lok Adalats (People's Courts) are voluntary agencies at present monitored by the State Legal Aid and Advice Boards. They have proved to be successful alternative forums for resolution of disputes through conciliatory methods. The Legal Service Authorities Act of 1987, has been put into effect for this purpose. It provides statutory status to the legal and movement and it also provides for setting-up of Legal Service Authorities at the Central, State and district levels. These authorities will have their own funds. Further, Lok Adalats which are at present informal agencies will acquire statutory status. The award of the Lok Adalats shall be deemed to be a decree of a civil court or an order of a tribunal and shall be final and binding on the parties to the dispute. It also provides that in respect of all cases decided in the Lok Adalats, court fee paid by the parties will be refunded.

Critical Appreciation

It is true that the provisions of the Constitution have made effective arrangements for keeping the judges independent so that they may perform their duties fairly and impartially. But some deficiencies may also be pointed out. Since the judges are appointed, transferred and promoted by the President and since he invariably acts on the advice of his Ministers, one may easily diagnose the fact that politics in injected into the process of the appointment, transfer and promotion of the Judges of the High Courts. The Law Commission of India in its XIV Report (1958), regretted that "communalism, regionalism and political patronage have in a considerable measure influenced appointments to the High Court judiciary." It expressed its distress over the fact that the judgeship of a High Court "has become a post to be worked and canvassed for." Unfortunately, the policy of reservations in favour of certain castes, tribes and classes in the name of 'social justice' has its own deleterious effect on the functioning of judiciary where nothing but the consideration of merit and ability should prevail.

One important point that applies to the Judges of the Supreme Court but not to the Judges of the High Courts should also be taken into account. It is related to doing practice of law after retirement. The judges of the High Courts should have been placed in the same category as we find in the case of the judges of the Supreme Court. That is, they should not have been allowed to practise law after retirement in as much as they may take an unfair advantage of their high connections made in the past. It is also a fact that the standards of the integrity of the judges are not as high at the lower level as they may be seen at the higher level of the judicial structure. Quite often we come across the allegations of rampant corruption in the judiciary at the lower levels. The bar associations often make agitations and demonstrations for the removal of a judge on some charge of nepotism or corruption. The practising advocates go on strike continuing for many days as a result of which the work of the courts remains paralysed, Unfortunately what is at the top of judicial hierarchy is not available at its lower strata in the country.

However, on certain occasions, the role of an over-active judiciary has been a matter of concern. The growing trend of judicial assertiveness had not been appreciated by those who desire to see that all organs of a political organisation should remain in a state of, what the Americans call, 'chacks and balances'. The Supreme Court has been very sensitive in respect of protecting its area of authority. As such it invalidated the provision of the Forty-second Amendment of 1976, laying down that a law of constitutional amendment could not be challenged in the Courts. It invalidated Sec. 7, of the anti-defection law that empowers the Presiding Officer of a House of Parliament or State Legislature to disqualify a person from the membership of the House on the ground of being a defector and also says that such a decision can not be challenged in a Court. It forced the Speaker of the Manipur Legislative Assembly (Dr. Borababu Singh) to appear before it in a contempt of court case as he had not followed its directives. In the Bommai Case it went to the length of holding that Art. 356, was justiciable and that the advice tendered by the ministers to the President before the invocation of this provision of the constitution could be demanded in the Court, and that the Presidential proclamation issued under Art. 356, could be put into effect after its approval by the Parliament. It certainly amounted to the circumvention of the provisions of the Constitution.

The range of subjects on which the Supreme Court has pronounced over the last few years "is mind-boggling; it decided whether Speakers have acted properly in applying the anti-defection provisions; whether the Central Government acted rightly in taking over State Legislatures; whether contracts have been properly awarded; how and when foreigners should be permitted to adopt Indian infants; when prisoners should be hand-cuffed; which quarries should be permitted in the Doon valley; whether decisions of the Election Commission are valid." Why has it come to occur? The same writer well answers: "Disillusionment with politicians, disgust with government apathy and the ability of the courts to respond, have all led to the acceptance of an enormous *de facto* enlargement of the powers of the courts and almost constitution courts into a super-legislature and a super-executive. A working democracy no doubt requires an independent judiciary; it also requires an effective executive and a responsive legislature. The legislature and the executive represent the people who periodically elect them; Judges are appointed and are thus not representatives."

The Union Judiciary

The existence of an independent and impartial judiciary is an essential pie-requisite of a federal form of government. It holds the balance between the Central Government and the governments of the federating units. It acts as the custodian of democracy and the guardian of the rights and liberties of the people. The Supreme Court of India which stands at the apex of the judicial system has been provided to play this role in the Indian federation.

The Supreme Court

Its Constitution. The Supreme Court of India consists of the Chief Justice and 25 other judges. A quorum of 5 judges is required to enable the Court to hear constitutional cases or to give advisory opinion to the President. The number of judges may, however; be varied by Parliament by law and no formal amendment of the Constitution is required for this purpose.

To be eligible for appointment as a judge of the Supreme Court a candidate must be a citizen of India, and *(a)* have been at least for five years judge of a High Court or of two or more such courts in succession, or *(b)* have been at least for 10 years an advocate of a High Court or of two or more such courts in quick succession, or *(c)* is in the opinion of the President a distinguished jurist.

The judges of the Supreme Court are appointed by the President according to the Constitution, after consulting with such judges of the Supreme Court or High Courts as he may deem necessary. In the case of the appointment of a judge other than the Chief Justice, the Chief Justice must be consulted. The Judges of the Supreme Court are to retire at the age of 65 years. It is specifically laid down in the

Constitution that a person who has held office as a Judge of the Supreme Court cannot plead or act in any court or before any authority within the Indian territory. This provision has been incorporated to ensure impartial justice.

The salary of the Chief Justice will be Rs. 5,000 per month and that of other Judges Rs. 4,000 per month. The Constitution (54th) Amendment Bill has enhanced the pay of the Chief Justice of the Supreme Court to Rs. 10,000 and that of the other Judges to Rs. 9,000 per month. The salary of the Judges is charged upon the Consolidated Fund of India. The salary and the other privileges enjoyed by the Judges cannot be varied in a manner which may adversely affect them during the tenure of their office. By this constitutional the independence of the judges is guaranteed by keeping them free from the executive.

The security of office of the Judges as guaranteed by the Constitution is also vital factor which promotes the independence and the impartiality of the supreme judiciary of the country. Regarding the removal of a judge from office Article 124(4), lays down: "A judge of the Supreme Court shall not be removed from his office except by an order of the President after an address by each House of Parliament supported by a majority of the total membership of the House of Parliament supported by a majority of the total membership of that House and by a majority of not less than 2/3rd of the members of that House present and voting has been presented to the President in the same session for such removal on ground of proved misbehaviour or in capacity."

The Supreme Court of India is a court of record and has all the powers of such a court, including the powers to punish for the contempt of itself.

The Supreme Court will sit in Delhi or in any such place as the Chief Justice will the decide with the approval of the President.

Jurisdiction

The jurisdiction of the Supreme Court can be discussed under the following heads:

Original Jurisdiction. The Supreme Court has original jurisdiction to the exclusion of any other court in any dispute *(a)* between the Government of India and one or more States, *(b)* between the Government of India and any State or States on one side and one or more States on the other, and *(c)* between two or more States. In all such matters the Supreme Court plays the role of federal court.

Appellate Jurisdiction. The Supreme Court has also appellate jurisdiction in all cases from every High Court involving questions of law as to the interpretation of the Constitution. An appeal shall lie to the Supreme Court from any judgement, decree of final order of a High Court, whether in a civil, criminal or other proceeding, if the High Court certifies that the case involves a substantial question of law as to the interpretation of the Constitution. It may be pointed out that the Supreme Court has the power to grant special leave to appeal to it.

The Supreme Court will exercise its appellate jurisdiction both in civil and criminal cases. In civil cases, an appeal may be made to the Supreme Court from the judgement of a High Court provided the latter certifies that: *(a)* the amount or value of the subject matter in dispute is not less than Rs. 20,000 or such other sum as may be specified by Parliament, or *(b)* the judgement, decree or final order involves directly or indirectly some claim or question respecting property of the like amount or value, or *(c)* that the case is a fit one for appeal to the Supreme Court, and where the judgement appealed from affirms the decision of the court immediately below; in any case other than a case referred to in item, *(d)* if the High Court further certifies that the appeal involves some substantial question of law. The Constitution provides that no appeal shall lie to the Supreme Court from the judgement, decree or final order of one judge of a High Court.

In criminal cases, an appeal shall lie to the Supreme Court from any order, judgement or sentence in criminal proceedings of a High Court in the territory of India, if the High Court: *(a)* has on appeal reversed an order of acquittal of a convicted person and has sentenced him to death, or *(b)* has withdrawn for trial before itself and case from any court and has sentenced the accused to death, or *(c)* certifies that the case is a fit one for appeal to the Supreme Court. Parliament has been authorised to enlarge the appellate jurisdiction of the Supreme Court in criminal cases.

Application of Article, 136. As per Article 136, the Supreme Court of India enjoys the power to allow a case to be taken in appeal to its own jurisdiction even if no such recommendation is made by the High Court. This is popularly known as the Supreme Court's power of Special Appeal. But this power is to be utilised by the Court judiciously and sparingly.

In the case of Pritam Singh Vs. The State (1950), it was observed that restricted and sparing use of Article 136, is to be made by the Supreme Court.

In the case of Dhakeswari Cotton Mills Vs. The Commissioner of Income Tax (West Bengal) 1955, it was observed that there could be no more fetters on the powers of the Supreme Court as vested by Article 136, than that it should be sparingly used.

The Supreme Court's power as per Article 136, also extends to decisions of Election Tribunals. In the case of Raj Krishna Vs. Vinod (1954), the Supreme Court set aside the decision of the Election Tribunal which was made final by an Act of the State Legislature.

Article 136, also extends to the decisions of Industrial Tribunals. In the Calcutta Tramways Company's case it was observed that the Supreme Court can interfere in the following circumstances:

(a) When Tribunals act in excess of their powers.

(b) Where there is an apparent error in the judgement.

(c) Where there is erroneous application of well established principles of jurisdiction.

In the case of Bharat Bank Vs. Employees of Bharat Bank, the Supreme Court gave the verdict that Industrial Tribunals discharge judicial functions and have all the attributes of a court. Hence against lapses in their decisions or awards, the Supreme Court has the power to allow leave for Special Appeal as per Article 136.

The Supreme Court, in the case of Muir Mills Vs. Suit Mills Mazdoor Union, gave the verdict that it has got exceptional powers to interfere where justice is denied or no fair deal is allowed to a litigant.

As per Article 136, the Supreme Court shall interfere in the following circumstances:

(i) Where there is violation of natural justice or disregard for forms of legal process.

(ii) Supreme Court shall not interfere merely on the ground that on the basis of evidence in the case, perhaps there could be different inference.

(iii) Where the Court of First Instance and Court of Appeal have given concurrent decision, the Supreme Court may interfere only in exceptional cases.

Advisory Role. The Supreme Court of India enjoys the power to give advisory opinion on all such matters which may be referred to it by the President of India on important question of law and fact. It is obligatory on the part of the Supreme Court to give its opinion on all such questions referred to it by the President. The judgements and opinions of the Supreme Court must be declared in open court. The advice given by the Supreme Court, however, is not binding upon the President.

Guardianship of Fundamental Rights. The Supreme Court has been empowered by the Constitution to act as the guardian of the Fundamental Rights enjoyed by the citizens. If any law passed by any State Legislature or the Union Parliament violates the Fundamental Rights, the Supreme Court can declare it as unconstitutional or *ultra vires*. On the same ground it can also nullify any executive order. For this purpose the Supreme Court has concurrent jurisdiction with the High. Courts.

Guardianship of the Constitution. The Supreme Court of India also acts as the guardian of the Indian Constitution. It is also an essential pre-requisite of a federal system of Government. The Court has the power to interpret the provisions of the Constitution and its interpretation shall be final. The law declared by the Supreme Court is binding upon all other courts. But is not binding upon itself as it has got the power to review its own judgements. Like the American Supreme Court, the Indian Supreme Court enjoys the power of judicial review.

Power of Judicial Review. The Supreme Court's role as the guardian of the Constitution and the Fundamental Rights of the citizens makes judicial review by the court necessary. The Supreme Court has been empowered to declare a law passed by Parliament unconstitutional or *ultra vires* on he ground that it contravenes the provisions of the Constitution. When compared with the power of judicial review of the American Supreme Court, the Indian Supreme Court enjoys limited powers of judicial review. The scope of judicial review has been limited because the Constitution makes an exhaustive enumeration of the powers of the Union and the States. The comparatively easier method of enlarging the powers of the Union government, specially during the emergencies, also acts as a check upon the Court's power of judicial review.

The Supreme Court of the U.S.A. extends its jurisdiction over both matters of procedure and also matters of substantive law in accordance with the "due process of law" clause. It can nullify a law on the ground that it does not conform to the standards of natural justice. Due to this extraordinary power the American Supreme Court plays the role of a 'super legislature'. It is also considered as the third chamber of legislation. The Supreme Court interprets the Constitution and the law and in the guise of interpretation, it can very well determine the social and economic policy of the state.

The 'due process of law' clause has been deliberately avoided by the framers of the Indian Constitution and in its place they have "according to the procedure established by law". The Indian Supreme Court can, therefore, declare any law null and void only if it is repugnant to any provision of the Constitution. It has no power to question the fairness or natural justice of Parliamentary legislation.

The framers of the Constitution did not intend to make the Supreme Court as powerful as the American Supreme Court because it would have impeded the growth of socialist legislation. They intended to make it a powerful body designed more to act as a check on arbitrariness of the executive and violation of the Constitution, than on the legislative enactments. It can only play the role of an interpreter of the Constitution. The judges are not to make laws, that is the work of the legislatures. They are only to interpret the Constitution, they are not to add anything of their own.

According to the Forty-second Amendment Act, 1976, Art. 32A, has been inserted saying: "Notwithstanding anything in Art. 32, the Supreme Court shall not consider the constitutional validity of any State law in any proceedings under that Article unless the constitutional validity of any Central law is also in issue in such proceeding." Article 131A, has been inserted saying: "Notwithstanding anything contained, in any provision of this constitution, the Supreme Court shall, to the exclusion of any other court, have jurisdiction to determine all questions relating to the constitutional validity of any Central law. When the High Court is satisfied that a case pending before a court subordinate to it involves questions as to the constitutional validity of any Central law, or as the case may be, of both Central and State laws and that the determination of such questions is necessary for the disposal of the case, it shall refer the questions for the decisions of the Supreme Court. The Supreme Court, if it deems it expedient so to do for the ends of justice, may transfer any case, appeal or any other proceedings pending before any High Court to any other High Court. The minimum number of the judges of the Supreme Court, who shall sit for the purpose of determining any question as to the constitutional validity of any Central law will be seven. A Central law or a State law shall not be declared to be constitutionally invalid by the Supreme Court unless a majority of not less than two-thirds of the judges sitting for the purpose of determining the question as to the constitutional validity of any such law hold it to be constitutionally invalid."

❒

9

Political Parties and Pressure Groups

A study of political parties and pressure groups in one chapter is informed by a certain reason. A modem democratic system cannot operate without the role of political parties. A pluralistic social order has a number of organised interest groups that play a part of their own in the political process of the country in alliance, open or secret, with political parties" A two-way traffic can be noted in that while the political parties need followers and resources which groups provide, the groups require leadership and direction which is provided by the parties. The groups articulate their interests and the parties aggregate them. Thus, interaction takes place that has its visible form in the role of political parties and its invisible form in the role of organised (catalyst) groups. Since India has a pluralistic society and a democratic welfare state, the role of political parties and pressure groups deserves a particular study.

Party System

The critics of the Indian political system comment that India has parties but no party system. The crux of their argument is that while there are several political parties, big and small, in the country, there is nothing like emotional or psychological attachment of the people with a particular party or some parties on the basis of which some concrete rules of political behaviour may be formulated. Moreover, frequent fragmentation of political parties and, at the same time, a movement for the polarisation of like-minded parties creates another baffling problem. Facts indicate that many political parties come into being as a result of either splits in their ranks or an alliance of various contending factions. The 'charismatic' personality of a particular leader has its own place. A leader of national or regional importance may carry with him a large number of followers and fioat his private political party that loses its identity with the death or eclipse of the leader or its merger with another party. The panorama of Indian party system is also vitiated by rampant factionalism operating in every political party. For all these reasons, a neat picture of the Indian stasiological scenario cannot be drawn.

Characteristics. In order to make an empirical study of the Indian party system, we may enumerate its characteristics as under:

1. India has neither a single party system as prevailing in a communist or a fascist country, nor does it have a bi-party system as prevailing in Britain and the United States. Here operates a multi-party system as prevailing in many countries of the world. If a complete catalogue of Indian political parties is prepared, the number many exceed the astonishing figure of 50. At the national level, we may mention the names of Indian National Congress, Janata Dal, Bharatiya Janata Party, Communist Party of India and Communist Party of India-Marxist. At the regional level we may refer to National Conference in Jammu-Kashmir, Shiromani Akali Dal in Punjab, Telugu Desam in Andhra Pradesh, Dravida Munnetra Kazhagam and Anna-DMK in Tamilnadu, Forward Bloc and Forward Bloc-Marxist in West Bengal, Mizo National Front in Mizoram, Sikkim Sangram Parishad, Assom Gana Parishad in Assam, Samajvadi Party in U.P. and Bahujan Samaj Party in U.P. and M.P. etc. Besides, there are many parties like *ad hoc* and fringe organisations.

2. A multi-party system is one in which different parties have the chance to be in power. Power alternates from one party to another. We may take note of the multi-party system at the regional level. But the situation is somewhat different when the examine the case of political parties at the national level. In other words, India's mult-party system is different from the multi-party system of countries like France or Italy. Leading writers on the Indian party system like Myron Weiner, Rajni Kothari and Giovanni Sartori have preferred to call it 'single-dominant-party system.' It means that one party is so powerful that all other parties put together may make no match and

may be thus, in no position to pose a serious or meaningful challenge to its sway. This position was enjoyed by the Indian National Congress that had been in power at the Centre and in most of the States since independence. Now this system looks like broken down.

3. Recently a new development has taken place that may be visualised in the formation of some loose organisations within or outside a political party which may, and also may not, be identified with a political party. Since the anti-defection law of 1985, prohibits leaving a political party voluntarily on whose ticket a person is elected to any House of Parliament or State Legislature, the way out has been discovered in the formation of a para-political party so as to avoid the penalty of the said law. In 1988, some members of the Parliament (V.P. Singh, Arun Nehru, Arif Muhammed Khan, V.C. Shukla, Ram Dhan etc.) left the Congress party and formed Jan Morcha (People's Front) for this purpose. It is also possible that a shrewd dissident leader may float a Manch (Forum) inside the party to work as a ginger group. A Vikas Manch (Development Forum) floated by Dr. Jagannath Mishra in Bihar and another by Bansilal in Haryana or a Forum for Action floated in the Congress by V. Patil are its instances.

4. Ideology plays an important part in the organisation and working of political parties. But the element of ideology cannot be traced in many political parties of India. Leaving aside the BJP on the right and the two Communist Parties on the left, all parties are like ideologically neutral organisations. Their commitments to the principles of social, economic and political significance are so flexible that they may be termed non-ideological organisations. It is a different matter that someone may characterise it as a typical case of ideology and therefore coin a term like 'Congress ideology.' Moreover, with the making of an amendment in the Representation of the People Act in 1988, every political party is required to have its faith in and allegiance to the Constitution of India and endorse its commitment to democracy, secularism and socialism. As such, rightism, leftism and centrism have lost their sanctity; expediency and pragmatism have taken the place of commitment to certain principles.

5. The factor of 'personality' has a place of its own in the operation of Indian party system. The Indian National Congress lived

like an organisation of Mahatma Gandhi, then of Nehru, then of Indira Gandhi and then it was identified with the name of Rajiv Gandhi. An influential leader of U.P. like Chaudhry Charan Singh left the Congress in 1967, and then floated his own political parties like Bharatiya Kranti Dal, Janata (S) and Lok Dal. In Tamil Nadu M.G. Ramachandran left the DMK and floated his Anna-DMK, in Sikkim Nar Bahadur Bhandari floated his Sikkim Sangram Parishad in Andhra Pradesh Telugu Desam is the party of N.T. Rama Rao for many years the National Conference of Jammu and Kashmir worked like an organisation of Sheikh Abdullah. Same thing can be said about Laldenga's Mizo National Front and Subhash Gheishing's Gorkha League. Such organisations generally eclipse after the death or fall of their 'charismatic' leader.

6. Above all, we may take note of the perplexing fact of frequent disintegration and polarisation of political parties. There are two Congresses, two Communist parties, two Janata Dals, two DMKs, three Akali Dais, three Muslim Leagues, about half a dozen socialist parties etc. Most of these parties are sustained by the factor of anti-Congressism. Politics means struggle for power and struggle for power requires combination of strange partners. Thus, *ad hoc* alliances are formed. Such experiments were made during the period of politics of fragmentation and individuation (1967—71) which eclipsed with the re-emergence of Congress under the leadership of Indira Gandhi. The Janata experiment (l977—79) was a model of the same when five parties (Congress (O), Bharatiya Jana Sangh, Bharatiya Lok Dal, Socialists and lately the Congress Defectors) joined hands. Its latest example is the formation of the Janata Dal of V.P. Singh being the biggest constituent of the National Front formed on the even of Lok Sabha polls in 1989, under the Chairmanship of N. T. Rama Rao. The success of such pragmatic alliances may be attributed to the downfall of the Indian National Congress.

Fall of the Single-Dominant Party System

We have taken note of the fact that India's party system hitherto pertained to a peculiar variety of the multi-party system. Here one party operated in the midst of many parties in a way like a giant operating in the midst of the pygmies. It was different from one-plus part system of Japan where one party (Liberal Democratic Party) has been in power since 1955, but on some occasions it has formed a coalition with a very small party like Sokka Gakkai (Buddhist organisation). The dominance of the Congress party had sometimes blurred the distinction between the party and the country, between the party and the government and, above all, between the party and party system three important characteristics of this system may be pointed out:

1. The system was democratic and pluralistic. It permitted freedom of thought and action that amounted to the making and unmaking of any political party playing its role in the political process by constitutional means. At the same time, it was pluralistic which meant that every party and group, including faction, had the freedom to fight for the protection and promotion of its specific interest. Hence, all segments of the society had their representation in the party system. The Congress party enjoyed the position of dominance by virtue of being an alliance or federation of diverse interests. It accommodated persons from rank rightists to rank leftists, from secularists and nationalists to communalists and regionalists and the like. Rajni Kothari called it 'Congress System.' It had two prominent characteristics; firstly, plurality within the dominant party making it more representative, providing it flexibility and sustaining internal competition; secondly, absorbing groups and movements from outside so as to prevent other parties and groups from gaining strength.

2. The party in power never tried to create the condition of party singularism. Its aim was to keep the foes in disarray and not to send them into oblivion. Other parties were allowed to exist and operate as legal and legitimate organisations, though they would be in the position of playing a really effective role in the game of struggle for power. It could have some sort of open or concealed alliance with a small or regional party for sharing the fruits of power without placing itself in the capacity of a meek and junior partner. The alliance of the Congress with Anna-DMK in Tamil Nadu, with National Conference in Jammu-Kashmir, and with Muslim League in Kerala

may be referred to here. It forced all other parties to live in a state of dilemma. Sometimes, they sought to come closer so as to offer an effective opposition to the Congress; sometimes they ran in different directions when it tried to dismantle their fort of unity by showering favours in an open or clandestine manner. Consequently, mono-partyism in the midst of multi-partyism assumed a peculiar form showing 'dominant' but by no means 'hyper-dominant' position of the Congress party.

3. However, this single-dominant-party system exhibiting the hold of the Congress party could not continue as a permanent and immutable feature of the Indian stasiological phenomenon. The electorate took a critical view of its performance and then showed its preference for some viable alternative as happened in 1977, when the Janata Party replaced the Congress but in 1980, the electorate once again placed the Congress in the position of power. The wheel turned back again in 1989, when the Janata Dal replaced the Congress. Now the BJP has its government in some States and Janata Dal in some other States. Obviously, such a system was just a type and not a class by itself in so far as the study of our party system is concerned.

Credit goes to Nehru and his great comrades of the days of the freedom movement that party system could have an institutionalised form after the advent of independence. The leaders of the first generation of the post-independence era had a commitment to operate the political system within the framework of rules and conventions of the Westerly democratic countries. As a result of this, the democratic traditions of the West could have their transplantation in a slightly modified form owing to the peculiar conditions of our country. The Congress could establish its 'dominance' in the Indian stasiological system. Under the leadership of Nehru it developed a highly institutionalised character that is measurable in terms of its effective adaptation with the changing times and contexts, its structural and functional complexity and its autonomous and coherent performance despite social pressures and factionalism."

RECOGNISED POLITICAL PARTIES, (1999)

Parties	*Status*	*Area of Operation*
	National	All-India
1. Indian National Congress (I)	"	"
2. Bharatiya Janata Party	"	"
3. Janata Dal	"	"
4. Samata Party	"	"
5. Communist Party of India	"	"
6. Communist Party of India—Marxist	"	"
7. Telugu Desam	State/Regional	Andhra Pradesh
8. Telugu Desam (Naidu)	"	
9. Assam Gana Parishad	"	Assam
10. Autonomous State Demand Committee	"	"
11. Jharkhand Mukti Morcha	"	"
12. Maharashtrawadi-Gomanatak Party	"	Goa
13. Haryana Vikas Party	"	Haryana
14. J.K. National Conference	"	Jarnmu-Kashmir
15. J.K. Panthers Party	"	"
16. Muslim League	"	Kerala
17. Kerala Congress (M)	"	"
18. Shiv gena	"	Maharashtra
19. Kuki National Assembly	"	Manipur
20. Manipur People's Party	"	"
21. All-Parties Hill Leaders Conference	"	Meghalaya
22. Hill People's Union	"	"
23. Hill State People's mocratic Party	"	"
24. Public Demands Implementation Convention	"	"

Contd.

	Parties	Status	Area of Operation
25.	Mizo National Front	"	Mizoram
26.	Nagaland People's Council.	"	Nagaland
27	Shiromani Akali Dal	"	Punjab
28.	Bahujan Samaj Party	"	Punjab and U.P.
29.	Rising Sun Party	"	Sikkim
30.	Sikkim Sangram Parishad	"	"
31.	All-India Anna Dravida Munnetra Kazhgam	"	Tamil Nadu
32.	Tamil Maanali Congress	"	"
33.	Dravida Munnetra Kazhgam	"	"
34.	Revolutionary Socialist Party	"	Tripura and West Bengal
35.	Tripura Upjati Juba Samiti	"	Tripura
36.	All-India Forward Bloc	"	West Bengal

The single-dominant-party system had a set-back in the elections of 1967 when the Congress party had no stalwart of the stature of Nehru. But after an interlude of some five years, it managed to restore the earlier position. The disastrous consequences of the 'split' (1969), could be averted when Indira Gandhi became the arch-leader of the new Congress party that managed to be in power at the Centre and in most of the States of the Indian Union. However, the events of 1971-72, may be treated as a dividing line between the constructive and destructive roles of Mrs. Gandhi. Whereas she managed to restore the Congress system, she also played instrumental in eroding its foundations. Gradually, the National Congress was converted into the private political organisation of the 'supreme leader.' Loyalty to her became the solid test. Not only this, an extra-constitutional centre of power came up under the leadership of her younger son (Sanjay Gandhi) that reduced all office-bearers of the party and all important Congressmen to the position of 'palace guards.'

The excesses of mother-son dominance made the orgnisation highly unpopular. The Congress of Indira Gandhi and her younger son had a lesson in the elections of 1977. But the Janata experiment failed and once again the single-dominant-party system of the Congress came into being in 1980. And yet, like the Bourbons of France, Indira and Sanjay failed to take any lesson from the events of history. Things deteriorated more and more and by the time of Sanjay's untimely death in June, 1980, the process of 'deinstitutionalisation' of the Congress system had seen its completion. "He (Sanjay) died as he lived. Daring, impetuous, contemptuous of the rules, a danger to himself and others... The effect of Sanjay's leadership on the Congress was to deinstitutionalise it further by increasing its patrimonial features. By the time of his death, the party had become his and his mother's bailiwick."

The people had hopes when the leadership of Congress came into the hands of Rajiv Gandhi, not when he worked as the General-Secretary of the Congress but when he became the Prime Minister of the country and the President of the Party after the assassination of his mother in 1984. In violation of the rules of the constitution of the Congress party he, in the fashion of his mother, managed to hold the offices of the Prime Minister as well as of the President of the party, deferred organisational elections again and again, convened the meetings of the Congress Working Committee as per his convenience, paid casual regard to the status of his Cabinet ministers as well as the Chief Ministers of States, and did a host of other things that consolidated the process of deinstitutionalisation more and more. The result of all this appeared in the form of defeat of the Congress in the Lok Sabha elections of 1989, and State Assembly elections of 1989-90. The democratic principle of 'from the bottom up' was substituted by the fascist principle of 'from the top down.' The Rudolphs comment thus on Rajiv's style of functioning. "The emphasis was on the top down rather than bottom up communications and authority. Rajiv's managerial ideology and professional style took the form of training camps, public relations campaign, and information gathering and analysis by his computer boys all instruments of central control and coordination. Under Rajiv's party stewardship, one heard or saw little of service and mass contact."

As a matter of fact, party system constitutes real arena for the operation of democratic political process. But unfortunately not so much in the 1970s as in the 1980s, it witnessed its systematic erosion on account of its gradual but irresistible displacement by personalised caucuses. Since Rajiv could demonstrate his position as an all-India leader by virtue of being the son and natural successor of Mrs. Indira Gandhi, it appeared that "the structural shell of one-party dominance has persisted in the midst of sea changes in its environment, but the giant internal tortoise has undergone a substantial transformation." But as coming events showed, he failed to prove his mettle like his mother and that caused the dismantling of the Congress system in the year of Nehru's centenary celebrations. The inner coalitional Congress system now stands replaced by another system of outer coalitions without the existence of a towering leader. Unless such a towering personality emerges, the single-dominant-party system of the days of Nehru and Mrs. Gandhi would not be restored. One may, or may not, endorse the view that, "the greatest cause for pessimism today is the poor quality of leadership. People in power, whether at the district or at the national level, seem incapable of measuring up to the enormity of the tasks that face them."

INDIAN NATIONAL CONGRESS

It is the oldest party of India. It was founded in 1885, to organise constructive and sane nationalism in the country. It became the vehicle of national movement under the leadership of Mahatma Gandhi, who converted it into a mass organisation of all 'hues' of people. The Congress became like a huge umbrella under whose cover people of diverse backgrounds and different 'ideologies' could come to pray their part in the freedom struggle of the country.

The leadership of the Congress fell into the hands of Nehru after independence. He sought to make it a socialist organisation without giving to it the name of a socialist party. In 1948, his critics like Narayan, Dev and Lohia left the Congress party. After the death of Patel in December, 1950, he had no peer to challenge his ideological stand. As such, for some time he assumed the office of the party President while working as the Prime Minister of the country. In 1955, the Congress adopted the goal of 'socialist pattern of society' at its Avadi session. The Second Five Year Plan drafted in 1956, incorporated the same ideal and thus, it became clear that Nehru wanted to implement his socialistic programme through the process of democratic planning.

Due to this, the Congress stole the thunder of the socialist parties. On the occasion of the requisitioned meeting of the AICC (N) in New Delhi in November, 1969, Mrs. Gandhi declared: "The Congress party must continue to be the instrument of India's revolution, her massive thrust into the future. Economic policy will demand urgent attention. It is of immense concern to every man and child. We shall take steps to revive the faith of the people in the party and its socialist programme. In so doing, we shall also take a.' total view of our revolution-secularism, toleration and inter-national understanding."

As a matter of fact, the Congress cannot be designated as a socialist organisation for the obvious reason that its socialistic professions are too vague and, more than that, different factions operating within its fold try to pull things in different directions. These factions have different approaches to the matters of social and economic significance and they "interact in a continuous process of pressure, adjustment and accommodation to provide an in-built opposition."

We may thus, describe the Congress as a party of the parties having various competitive factions within its fold; we may also describe it as a party of the Prime Minister controlling the federal constitutional system of the country through the mechanism of his party at the Union and State levels. The Prime Minister and his loyal lieutenants have all the powers and resources; they may attract any number of careerists by the charm of their 'patronage,' who are not swayed by ideological considerations and who are in the Congress because it brings them additional power and prestige. The underlying current of the entire politics of the Congress leaders hinges on the point of reaping the fruits of influence by living in power through the mechanism of party.

What is the ideology of the Congress party? We may say that it is an ideologically neutral organisation. It subscribes to certain policies and programmes of social, economic and political significance that display a curious blending of three different currents—Gandhism with its emphasis on rural reconstruction on the lines of decentralisation of power and economic self-sufficiency; Liberalism recognising the right of free enterprise in a mixed economy; and Socialism with its emphasis on State ownership and control of the means of production and distribution. It is the radicalism of the Congress that has had its manifestation in the nationalisation of some major private establishments and that attributed to this party the label of a left-of-centre organisation.

The Congress leaders have been of the view that the strength of this party lies in its lack of ideological clarity. Jagjivan Ram preferred to call it 'Congress culture' and SadiqAli cautioned that the Congress ideology 'must not be interpreted as any rigid and unaltered system of ideas whose acceptance is obligatory on all Congressmen.' Thus, the leaders of the Congress make use of the term 'ideology' in a particular sense so that the amorphous character of the organisation is maintained. Its ideology stands on the pillars of parliamentary democracy, democratic socialism and enlightened secularism. The Election Manifesto issued on the eve of the General Elections in 1989, revealed four ingredients of the Congress ideology—*(1)* Independence of thought and action in the face of external challenge to our freedom and internal subversion of our integrity; *(2)* Democracy, to translate independence for the nation into the freedom of the individual; *(3)* National integration, to preserve the emotional integrity of the country while celebrating its glorious diversity; and *(4)* Equal respect for all religions.

The single-dominant party system as established by the Congress saw its rapid fall, after, the death of Indira Gandhi for the reason that it had no queen of its own on the chess-board of Indian party politics, Rajiv proved a misfit for the role he inherited by virtue of the norm of dynastic rule. The pace of deterioration became more rapid under the leadership of Rao who failed in keeping all parts together as a result of which first Arjun Singh left the party and then the disgruntled elements formed their own Congress under the leadership of N.D. Tiwari in May, 1995. As things stand now, never before was this party so discredited, never before has it been so deeply divided. Its causes may be noted as under:

1. Indian National Congress had the tendency of operating under the leadership of a single 'hero' as Mahatma Gandhi in the pre-independence and Jawaharlal Nehru in the post-independence periods. Indira Gandhi sought to follow this tradition by drifting the current in a way of her own. She lacked the sense of conviction and commitments what was the peculiar quality of Gandhi and Nehru. In stead she reduced the values of tolerance and dissent and thereby killed the tradition of intra-party democracy. Her leadership style "was characterised by intolerance of party bosses, impatience with factions, greater reliance on populist slogans and mass mobilisation techniques than on the instrument of the, party and, finally, a preparedness to teach out to the Indian people over-arching the party, to seek from them a kind of plebiscitary endorsement for her policies and her leadership. To her the party was no more than a tool' at best and an inconvenience at worst. This brought handsome electoral returns and Indira Gandhi emerged as the single-most valuable resource of the party. Everything else became secondary only to be manipullated to strengthen the asset. Thirteen years of hegemonic leadership inevitably produced organisational decay as vital organs of the party lay in disuse."

2. After the exit of Rajiv Gandhi, more particularly after the exit of the dynatstic tradition, the Congress could not be like a party of the masses. It lost its popular credentials by finishing inner-party democracy; it lost its mass base by compromising on the basic tenets of secularism. Rajiv Gandhi appeased the Muslims by circumventing the judgment of the Supreme Court in the Shah Bano Case of 1985, but Narsimha Rao annoyed them by vicariously permitting the demolition of the Babri Mosque in 1992. As a veteran Congress leader frankly puts: "In the Directive Principles, we proclaimed that we will go in for a common civil code. But in stead of developing a common understanding among our citizens to move in this direction, we went in for softer option, compromising with the fundamentalist and obscurantist urges of the extremist elements of different religious communities. We did this when we changed the law of the land to please a section of the extremists among the Muslims. When we saw that this was having a reaction on a section of the Hindu community,

we thought that we could please these elements by opening the lock of the Babri structure. We kept on wavering on this issue and even allowed *shilanyas* (foundation-stone laying ceremony) to the performed in the hope that this will placate the obscurantist elements in Hindu society. All these gestures were influenced by our desire to retain the vote banks."

3. Above all, the Congress lost its base among the poor and weaker sections of the people by abandoning its socialistic affirmations. The merits of the move towards privatisation of national economy could not be brought home to the common people. The rising tide of corruption and inflation could not be checked and a broker of Bombay caught in securities scam case could go to the extent of publicly declaring that he had given a huge sum of money to Prime Minister Rao. As a result, other parties like the Janata Dal, Samajvadi Party and Bahujan Samaj Party could capture the attention of the voters in general. It is well agrued: "The point is how can a set of policies like the ones promulgated by Mr. Narsimha Rao's government take on a human face when its actual impact is so inhuman and corrosive of the lives and dignity of the poor, the minorities and in fact the people at large including sections of the middle class." So says Bidwai : "The plain truth is that in large parts of the country the Congress is seen as mainly an upper caste, upper or middle class party with an elitist economic and social policy, which is communally thoroughly compromised, and which has wilfully wrecked the broad coalition once furnished by 'what was called the 'core minorities'—Dalits, Muslims, tribals and other plebian groups."

The fate of the Congress, under these conditions, looks as sealed at any rate for the next many years. The dissident sections of the party have lost faith in the resolve of the Tirupati Congress (1991), that 'Rao being a father figure could restore harmony between the wavering brothers of a single family.'

JANATA DAL

We may have a brief study of other national and secular political parties as well. On 11 October, 1988, (birthday of Jayaprakash Narayan) a new party came into being with the merger of three parties (Janata Party, Jan Morcha and Lok Dal) under the leadership of V.P. Singh. Its name is Janata Dal. Shortly before the Ninth General Election (1989), it had an alliance with Congress (S), Telugu Desam, Dravida Munnetra Kazhagam and Assom Gana Parishad that assumed the name of 'National Front' under the Chairmanship of N.T. Rama Rao. The policies and programmes of this party cover social, economic and political spheres and they look like based on the foundations of democracy, secularism and socialism. In the political sphere, it desires restoration of civil liberties and extension of the rights of the people, era dication of corruption, revitalisation of parliamentary institutions, reversal of over-centralisation process, more autonomy to the States, and decentralisation of powers, solution of national problems through the process of national consensus and reconciliation, social justice to the weaker sections of the community, incorporation of right to work in the list of Fundamental Rights, curbs on the use of Art. 356, sanctioning President's rule in the States, reorganisation of Panchayati Raj, establishment of a responsive administrative structure etc.

In the economic sphere, it desires prevention of concentration of wealth in the hands of the few encouragement to small-scale and cottage industries, more production of basic consumer goods, land reforms, crop insurance system, maximisation of employment opportunities, alleviation of poverty and indebtedness, rationalisation of tax system etc. In the social sphere it desires preferential opportunities and concessions to Scheduled Castes and Scheduled Tribes, improvement of the status of women, social security for the physically handicapped people, vocation oriented education etc. In the words of the then leader of this party (Chandra Shekhar): "Mending of broken hearts and propping up human dignity and self-respect is the essence of the policy of the new party."

BHARATIYA JANATA PARTY

The Bharatiya Jana Sangh founded by Shyama Prasad Mukherji in 1951, lost its identity when it merged with the Janata Party in 1977. But after the failure of the Janata experiment it had its revival in 1979, under the leadership of Atal Behari Vajpayee with the name of Bharatiya Janata Party. It expresses its commitment to five ideals-nationalism and national integration, democracy, positive secularism,

Gandhian socialism, and value-based politics. It shows its faith in democratic norms with the hope that it would attempt to create a consensus on all major issues and compete with others where situations of conflict arise. However, as national consensus cannot be built on mere struggle for power, it must be based on certain principles and national objectives. The people of different faiths and ideologies should be able to coexist in peace and harmony, but those who have extra-territorial loyalties or engage in anti-national activities cannot be expected to contribute to national consensus and, for this reason, would have to be kept out.

As a believer in democracy, the BJP would fight against all trends of fascism and authoritarianism. Its commitment to positive secularism implies a rejection of what the Congress has been advocating so far. It rejects the case of appeasement towards any community and instead supports the idea of full protection to the life and property of the minorities. It desires distillation of common moral values whether derived from different religions or from other historical and civilisational experiences and approaches, which always remained integral to Indian nationalism. While accepting the doctrine of Gandhian socialism, it seeks to replace both capitalism and statism by the principle of a cooperative system arid a form of trusteeship in all fields of economic activity. Finally, it desires value-based politics. It means that social and political life should be guided by a set of norms and values the abridgement of which should bring forth social sanctions and punishment. It successfully contested the elections of 1989 and 1990. Under the Presidentship of L.K. Advani it managed to secure 117 seats in the Lok Sabha in 1990. Its performance became more spectiacular in the Assembly elections of 1990, 1991, 1993 and 1995, as a result of which it could have its governments in the States of U.P., Himachal Pradesh, Madhya Pradesh and Rajasthan. In 1995, it formed its government in Gujarat and with Shiv Sena in Maharashtra.

COMMUNIST PARTIES

Both Communist Parties claim Marxism-Leninism as the foundation of their ideology. According to its constitution, the Communist Party of India is the political party of the Indian working class, its vanguard, its highest form of class organisation. It is a voluntary organtsation of workers, peasants and toiling people in general, devoted to the cause of socialism and communism." The policies and programmes of the CPI cover political, economic and social spheres. In the political sphere, it desires restructuring of the federal system in a way so as to ensure autonomy of the States, abrogation of Art. 356, sanctioning President's rule, abolition of the office of Governor, introduction of proportional representation with list system, enlargement of democratic rights of the people, making justice inexpensive and easily available, ensuring freedom of the press and repeal of all 'black' laws, pursuance of the policy of peace and friendship with socialist countries.

In the economic sphere, the CPI desires curbs on monopolies and transnational giants, nationalisation of major industries (sugar, textile, steel, jute and vanaspati) and foreign trade, State take-over of trade in foodgrains, strengthening the network of public distribution system, need-based minimum wage for low paid factory workers, encouragement to cottage and small-scale industries, protection of the trade union rights of the workers, participation of workers in the management of industry, employment programme for rural workers and educated youth including unemployment allowance ete. Finally, in the social sphere, it, desires free education of all children upto secondary stage, economic assistance in matters of education for low income groups, security of the person and honour of the people belonging to weaker sections, social insurance in the event of accident or disability, ban on communal and obscurantist organisations, secularisation of the polity etc.

The Communist Party of India-Marxist (CPM) claims itself as the genuine leftist party based on the ideology of Marxism-Leninism. It frankly accuses the CPI of being a gathering of opportunists and class collaborationists working in alliance with the feudal-bourgeois elements having their place in the Indian National Congress. As such, it desires end of the Congress rule and instead establishment of 'people's democracy.' Its social, economic and political commitments are more or less the same as espoused by the CPI. However, what is striking about the CPM's ideology is that it denounces the CPI as body of Dangeite revisionists and seeks to keep itself in equidistance from the 'rightism' of the BJP, 'centrism of the Congress' and so-called 'leftism' of the CPI. When formed in 1964, it adopted a frankly pro-China line and lauded Mao as the real source of revolutionary inspiration. Thus, it could be described as a pro-China and anti-USSR Communist Party, but after some time it left its pro-China stance and thereby could improve its relations with the CPSU, Under the leadership of Jyoti Basu and E.M.S, Namboodiripad, it adopted an independent line and thereby followed the course of equidistance from the Communist Parties of China and the USSR. It is for this reason that the CPM was critical of the *glasnost* and *perestroika* policies of the USSR under the leadership of Gorbachov; so it criticised the action of the Chinese government in suppressing the movement for democracy by means of force in June, 1989,

As a result of the disintegration of the Soviet Union and China's patent moves towards the system of 'state capitalism,' the movement of the leftist parties has declined all over the world. It would not be wrong to say that now the left is in an unprecedented state of quandary. So is the case with the two Communist Parties of our country. While both are still critical of each other on account of smarting under the shadow of the past, the way out of the present impasse has been found out by them in supporting any national or regional organisation, or any alliance of this sort, that declares its resolve to improve the lot of the poor and backward sections of the people. The trend of globalisation of economy has overtaken them. It is a fact which they cannot deny. The Marxist Chief Minister of West Bengal (Jyoti Basu) has desired investment of foreign capital in his State so as to solve the problem of economic development. The Communists know that the Nehruvian strategy of development has lost its relevance. And since the Centre has frankly taken to the course of 'privatisation,' it is now better to remould their ideology than to curse and took at the boons of a capitalist system with a coloured eye.

REGIONAL POLITICAL PARTIES

We may also have a brief study of the regional political parties in India. Since most of these parties operate in a particular State, Morris-Jones has preferred to call them "One-State parties." In this connection reference may be made to National Conference in Jammu Kashmir, Shiromani Akali Dal in Punjab, DMK and Anna-DMK in Tamil Nadu, Telugu Desam in Andhra Pradesh, Assom Gana Parishad in Assam, Sikkim Sangram Parishad in Sikkim, Jharkhand Mukti Morcha in Bihar, Maharashtravadi Gomantak Party in Goa, Naga National Party in Nagaland, People's Party in Arunachal Pradesh, Manipur People's Party in Manipur etc. In some parts of the States sub-regional political parties may be referred to as Gorkha League in West Bengal, Jharkhand Party in Bihar, Utarakhand Kranti Dal in Uttar Pradesh etc. A study of these regional and sub-regional organisations shows that they have now become a force to reckon with in the political system of our country. It is well pointed out: "No academic endeavour to analyse or evaluate the dynamics of Indian politics today can be valid if it ignores what may be described as the regional perspective and fails to take adequate account of the increasingly critical role played by the regional political parties.

The emergence and the increasingly important role of these political parties may be said to be a consequence of these reasons. First, India is virtually a land of many regions. The fact of diversity may be noted in respects of languages, customs, cultures and, above all, levels of social and economic development. A powerful national party like the Indian National Congress could give a setback to the destructive forces of regionalism by preaching as well as sincerely sticking to the way of 'unity in diversity.' But as a result of the decline of this party, regional organisations naturally raised their head and managed to defeat the Congress in various States of the Indian Union. Second, these regional organisations could successfully exploit the fact of local, regional and parochial grievances. The leaders of these organisations could well thrive on the propaganda of 'regional imbalance' in respect of economic development caused by the negligent attitude of the Centre. Last, the rise and growth of such parties is also sustained by the existence of primordial loyalties exploited by communal and ethnic forces. It is for this reason that the regional leaders fail to broaden their area of operation to other parts of the country. Such regional parties thrive on exploitation of the regional issues and 'local' grievances with the result that the charismatic element of the personality of a leader like N.T. Rama Rao of Andhra Pradesh, Laldenga of Mizoram, Subhash Gheishing of West Bengal and the like remains confined to the areas inhabited by the people of the same stock. An effort made by N.T. Rama Rao to convert his Telugu Desam into Bharat Desam failed to make any headway.

It is a patent fact that the identity of a regional political party is marked by its area of operation. But in the case of some parties we may also take note of their eagerness to improve their image by establishing links with an all-India party either for the sake of bettering their electoral prospects or for having a mark of national recognition. For instance, the Anna-DMK of M.G. Ramachandran and the National Conference of Dr. Farooq Abdullah had an alliance with the Congress (I) and thereby they managed to remain in power safely and comfortably. In 1989, the Telugu Desam, the DMK and the Assom Gana Parishad joined the 'National Front' and subsequently became partners in its government of the Janata Dal headed by V.P. Singh.

The regional political parties may be called 'grievance groups,' for their aim is to thrive on the exploitation of local and parochial discontent of the people. Very often they demand amendments in various provisions of the Constitution particularly those making a strong Centre in our federal system. Since politics means struggle for power, even national and secular parties try to establish links with these regional organisations by espousing their cause in an indirect or covert manner. The leaders of the Janata Dal, BJP, CPI and CPM often make sophisticated expressions to usher in a true or genuine federal system in the country ensuring 'autonomy' to the States. They may also lend their support to the demands of regional parties like incorporation of a particular language (as Nepali or Manipuri) into the VIII Schedule of the Constitution or implementation of special measures to bring about development, for instance, in the areas inhabited by the Gorkhas in Darjeeling region or by the tribals living in the belt of Chhota Nagpur and Santhal Parganas.

However, the role of regional parties should not be studied with a sense of undue apprehension in each and every case. There is nothing wrong if a particular party fights for the interest of its own people without endangering the unity and integrity of the nation. In case a regional political party can give a better and stable administration to the people of a particular State by working within the framework of the Constitution of India (as we may see in the case of the role of the DMK and Anna-DMK, Telugu Desam, Assom Gana Parishad, Sikkim Sangram Parishad etc.), it should be appreciated as a development in the direction of a healthy and viable federal system. On the other hand, in case a regional political party distorts the provisions of the Constitution and fails in suppressing anti-national elements (as Akali Dal in Punjab or National Conference in Jammu-Kashmir), its role should be denounced. Only in the latter direction, the role of regional political parties should be seen with a sense of apprehension. One thing is, however, certain that regional political parties have come to stay like "a prominent and durable feature of India's political landscape."

Criticism

A critical study of the Indian party system shows that it suffers from certain weaknesses. First, the fact of ideological orientation is missing in most of the parties operating of the national and regional levels. Leaving aside the BJP on the rightist and the two Communist Parties on the leftist spectrums, all other parties are ideologically neutral organisations more concerned with their attitude towards 'personalities' than with a clear-cut commitment to some particular type of social and economic philosophy. The requirement of the amended Representation of the People Act (that every political party seeking its registration with the Election Commission must have a constitution of its own expressing its commitment to Democracy, Secularism and Socialism) has made the line of distinction between parties further blurred. Second, frequent events of fragmentation of parties and then moves for polarisation of like-minded parties disturb the stasiological map of the country from time to time. One faces difficulty in preparing a list of all kinds of 'socialist' parties in the country, for instance.

Above all, each party is ridden with rampant factionalism and even the Indian National Congress has failed to manage its internal dissensions. Consequently, the opportunists and careerists have been able to establish their hold over the organisation. In recent years a more pernicious trend may be noted in the growing nexus between the politicians and the criminals. The sanctity of elections has been vitiated by the criminalisation of politics to a great extent. These developments stand as powerful barriers in the growth of a healthy party system in the country. This view of an American writer may be appreciated with some reservation that the general outlines of the party system in India "are relatively clear, although they present some very contradictory tendencies. A healthy party system has not emerged, and there seems little likelihood that it will emerge in the foreseeable future."

PRESSURE GROUPS

A number of organised groups play their own part in the political process of the country. Since these groups are organised on the basis of some 'interest,' they are known as 'interest groups' and since they adopt pressure tactics to protect and promote their specific interests, they are generally taken as 'pressure groups.' Here we have to see the role of numerous associations of the businessmen, industrialists, workers, peasants, engineers, technicians, lawyers, teachers etc. Arthur Bentley of the United States discovered this field in his work. The Process of Government, (1908) and since then a number of leading writers (as D.B. Truman, V.O. Key, Jr., G.A. Almond, Harry S. Eckstein, Josephla Palombara, Myron Weiner, S. A. Kochanek etc.) have made their own contributions to highlight the role of these groups in the political process of various countries of the world. In view of the importance of the role of these groups they have been nicknamed as 'invisible government' and 'unofficial government.' S.E. Finer has coined the meaningful title of 'anonymous empire.'

General Characteristics. Through some broad features of the nature of pressure group politics having its universal application may be enumerated, it should be done in the light of typical conditions of each country. As such, we may enumerate these characteristics of pressure group politics in our political system:

1. As we have a loose, disorganised and fragmented multi-party system, we have numerous groups, big and small with long as well

as ephemeral durations, living in conflict with one another, appearing and disappearing in response to the prevailing conditions and, above all, riven with shifting political allegiances. It presents a very confusing as well as a perplexing spectacle. Though we may make a list of such groups for the sake of a convenient study, it is quite a tedious job to prepare their taxonomic illustration as most of them may be found cutting across the boundaries of their real political character. In addition to that, the shifting affiliations of the groups with political parties and the penetration of the influence of the political leaders into the functioning of these groups further adds to our difficulty.

2. The organised groups, like political parties, lack definite political commitments. Their political loyalties are shifting and that contributes to their unstable political culture. Their attitudes towards political parties as well as their faith in the strategies and techniques lack definite commitments in respect of which rigid norms cannot be laid down. For instance, if we take up the case of the business groups, we may take note of the fact that they "are divided politically and have conflicting views about strategy towards particular parties and also about the potential consequences of the support that they give to any of the major parties." The Birlas alone are known for invariably being pro-Congress, others criticise the policy of 'socialism' openly. As Kochanek affirms : "The relationship between the business and the Congress party has fluctuated according to shifts in emphasis of Congress policy from qualified support to political affiliation." About the groups of the workers it can be said that there is no unanimity on the means to be adopted. "While the moderate leader tries to adjust his followers to reality, the militant calls for the overthrow of the system which has not been able to satisfy his impossible demands."

3. Owing to the absence of clear-cut ideological commitments, most of the groups feel interested in creating conditions of anarchy and lawlessness. They have less, rather very little, faith in the use of constitutional methods as adopted in democratic countries. It appears that they have no hesitation in indulging in activities of an extra-constitutional and unconstitutional nature. Strike is a favourite weapon in their hands that sometimes assumes the form of *bandh* (complete

closure); demonstrations and long marches are undertaken. The groups may unhesitatingly take to the ways of arson and violence causing great damage to people's life and property. More than this, the path of rank militancy may display overtones of anti-nationalism. It may, therefore, be admitted that violence has come to occupy a special place in the political process of our country."

4. The point of 'bi-culturalism' may also be discovered in the political behaviour of groups. That is, while they try to operate on modern lines, they cannot give up their traditional mores or primordial loyalties. They may have their registered offices; they may openly or clandestinely finance political parties and try to induct men of their favour into the legislative and executive organs of the government, or they may adopt the way of keeping the bureaucrats in good humour by paying them in cash or kind. And yet they may not make themselves totally free from religious, communal, communitarian, regional, sub-regional or parochial attachments. Thus, the elements of tradition as well as modernity may be traced in the political behaviour of most of the groups playing their part in the political process of the country.

5. Above all, the role of the groups can be termed non-autonomous. They prefer to work under the leadership of some political party and be guided by its directions. The fear psychosis has its indelible effect so mush so that while playing their definite role in the politics of the country they not only pretend to be natural in political matters, they try to change the label of their political affiliations in response to the requirements of a rank opportunistic policy. It enables the ruling party to set the parameters within which the groups in loyalty towards the parties in opposition have to operate.

Leading Interest Groups. As already pointed out, organised groups may be horizontally classified as business groups, labour groups, peasant groups, professional groups and the like. Almond has classified them as associational, non-associational, institutional and anomic groups. Some groups may also be termed as religious, communal, tribal, ethnic, linguistic, cultural and the like. For the sake of a convenient study, we may put them under these broad heads:

First of all, we may refer to a number of business groups or the organisations of the industrialists and capitalists that came into being in the pre-independence period like Indian Merchants Chamber of Bombay, Southern Indian Chamber of Commerce of Madras, the Bharat Chamber of Commerce (originally Marwari Chamber of Commerce) of Calcutta, Bengal National Chamber of Clacutta and Oriental Chamber of Commerce (originally Mauslim Chamber of Commerce) of Calcutta. In the post-independence period we have three great organisations of the business class—Federation of the Indian Chambers of Commerce and Industry with its major constituents like Indian Merchants Chamber of Bombay, Indian Merchants Chamber of Calcutta and Southern Indian Chamber of Commerce of Madras; Associated Chamber of Commerce having its major constituents in Bengal Chamber of Commerce of Calcutta and its lobby. (Central Commercial Organisation in Delhi), and All-India Manufacturers Organisation with its headquarters in Delhi and branches in Calcutta and Bombay.

It is a paradox that while all business groups detest 'socialism,' they have to support this or that political party frankly subscribing to it as a matter of compulsion. Socialism is an instrument of mass appeal and, for this reason, every political party feels bound to invoke its name in order to collect the votes of the hungry millions. And yet every party knows that elections cannot be fought without financial resources that may come from big business houses. On the other hand, the business houses understand that Indian socialism permits the system of 'mixed economy' in which their interests may remain safe. They preferred to support the Indian National Congress owing to their conviction that "the socialist bark of government was louder than its bite and that at certain points critical to individual business the government did not yield to ideology."

The business groups contribute to the funds of the political parties with the hope of getting their support when they are in power. Pragmatism may be termed as the ideology of the Indian business groups. Most of the business groups support the party in power as their policy is to salute the rising sun. They also try to have good relations with important ministers and bureaucrats with obvious motives. They have their lobbies for this purpose in the Central and State legislatures. They also use press as an instrument for protecting and promoting their interests. In the last resort, they prefer to move the judiciary for this purpose. Any law or executive order going to harm their interests is challenged in the courts and then best legal brains are engaged to have it struck down in the name of being unconstitutional. In the main, they rely upon the support of the influential members of the ministry and bureaucracy. As Weiner says: "Since they have no effective influence on law-makers, Indian businessmen establish high particularistic relationships with individual administrators, who are appealed to on the basis of blood relationship (when it exists), personal friendship, or most often financial rewards."

The trade unions play the part of pressure groups of the working class. Here two points are noticeable. First, such organisations act like the labour wings of different political parties and, for this reason, the relationship between a trade union and a political party is invariably static. For instance, the Indian National Trade Union Congress is the labour wing of the Indian National Congress; the All-India Trade Union Congress is the labour wing of the CPI; the United Trade Union Congress is the labour wing of the CPM; the Hind Mazdoor Parishad is the labour wing of the BJP; and the Socialists have their Hind Mazdoor Sabha. Second, the labour groups adopt the methods of strike, *gherao* (encirclement of the officer concerned for compelling him to meet their demands), *bandh* (complete strike), demonstrations, marches etc. and may go to the extreme of damaging public property by violent means. They fight for the security of employment, better emoluments, more bonus, housing and medical facilities, adequate compensation in the event of death or physical disability of a worker etc.

The trade union movement in our country is marked by rivalry and factionalism as a result of which labour groups often fail to have what they struggle for. Weiner rightly points out : "The Indian Trade Union Movement is one of the most maligned in the world. Unions are poorly organised, membership turn-over is great, dues-paying is limited to a few and is irregular, and union activities are limited to strikes, demonstrations and election work. Only rarely does a union provide services for its members. Rival unionism is rampant, unions are led by outsiders, and control of the unions is often in the hands of political parties seeking to use them for their own ends. Employers, political parties, trade union leaders (with the exception of communists), and government officials all lament the politicisation of trade unions; but the trend has been towards a more fragmented trade union movement paralleling the fragmented party system of India."

Then, we may look at the role of peasant groups or farmers' organisations. The Indian National Congress established its peasant wing (All-India Kisan Congress) that after some time became All-India Kisan Sabha. The Socialists set-up their Hind Kisan Panchayat and the Communists their United Kisan Sabha. All-India Kisan Sammelan was organised under the leadership of Chaudhry Charan Singh in 1978. Recently some more organisations have come up as Shetkari Sanghathan under Sharad Joshi and Barartiya Kiasn Union under Mahendra Singh Tikait. These peasant groups fight for their own interests like availability of seeds and fertiliser at a cheap rate, remunerative price for agricultural products, development of irrigation and agriculture, rural credit scheme, insurance of crops, supply of electricity at cheaper rates, representation of the farmers in all decision-making bodies of the government, waiver of loans given to small farmers, implementation of the scheme of land reforms etc. However, like the groups of workers, these groups of the farmers have not been able to assert effectively due to mass ignorance, casteiet rivalries, inadequate financial resources, rampant factionalism etc.

Finally, we may refer to a very large number of professional and anomic groups. The lawyers have their bar associations. The medical practitioners have their Indian Medical Association and also a large number of subsidiary organisations. The teachers have their own groups. So is the case with other professionals like engineers, technicians, artists etc. The students unions may also be included in this category. The Hindus have their religious organisations like Arya Samaj and Vishwa Hindu Parishad, the Muslims have their Jamaat-i-Islami; the Christians have their Roman Catholic Association; the Parsis have their Anjuman; the Shiromani Gurdwara Prabandhak

Committee protects the interests of the Sikhs; the Republican Party of India fights for the interests of the depressed classes; the Jharkhand Mukti Morcha is an organisation of the tribals of Bihar.

Here two points are noteworthy. First, in some cases a political party looks like a pressure group or a pressure group becomes like a political party. The line of distinction between the two is blurred as the membership of the organisation is open to the people of the same stock and the range of their interests is confined to the parochial interest of its members. For instance, the Akali Dal of the Sikhs and the Dravida Munnetra Kazhagam of the Dravidians are primarily concerned with their communal interests. Second most of such organisation are 'anomic' in the sense that they often take to the ways of unexpected and unwarranted violence and extremism touching the verge of anti-nationalism. The groups of the Khalistanis and Jammu-Kashmir Liberation Front may be referred to in this direction.

In fine, Indian political system provides considerable freedom to different sectors of society to make demands upon its operators. The groups articulate their 'specific' interests and the political parties manage to aggregate them so that the process of accommodation of diverse interests remains undisturbed. But the unfortunate thing is that the decision-makers do not understand the gravity of the situation until the groups take matters to the streets and public peace is disturbed. A noted Indian sociologist, M.N. Srinivas, has correctly evaluated that in India a grievance has to mature into a street riot in order to attract the attention of those in power. It would not be an exaggeration to say that all classes of Indians everywhere have come to realise that the only way they can convince their rulers about the strength of their feeling is by resorting to the politics of street violence. However, it is the role of political elites whereby the problem of crisis management is solved. It is well said by Y.K. Malik: "Indeed, agitational methods have become an accepted part of the political process. Tension generated by the use of such agitational methods is often diffused by the politics of accommodation practised by the Indian elites."

❐

10

Elections and Electoral Behaviour

At the time of Independence of India in 1947, most of the people of India had no experience in the electoral process. Indians are illiterate and were seemingly unprepared to play a responsible role as free citizens in a democratic society. The decision of the Constituent Assembly and the Government of India to give every adult Indian, male or female, the privilege of franchise under a system of universal and direct suffrage was "*an act of faith in the common man of India and in his practical commonsense*." The Constitution of India provides for adult suffrage. It means that every citizen who is not less than 21 years of age, except those who are mentally unsound or who have been found guilty of criminal or corrupt practices, has the right to vote. Thus, for the first time in the history of elections, "India became the greatest testing ground of the adaptability and workability of universal adult suffrage in free and secret elections in under-developed countries, whose people are mostly illiterate, tradition-bound, unaccustomed to the idea as well as the practice of voting, and unfamiliar with the way and tenets of democracy."

Universal Adult Franchise. The decision of the Constituent Assembly to give every adult Indian the privilege of franchise was truly momentous. Most of the people of India not only had no experience in the electoral process, but also were seemingly unprepared to play a responsible role as free citizens in a democratic society. The pernicious system of separate electorate was abolished. Article 235, of the Constitution states that no person shall be ineligible for inclusion.....in any special electoral roll......on grounds of any religion, race, caste, sex or any of them." However, Articles 330 and 332, provide for reservation of seats in the Lok Sabha and in every Vidhan Sabha of the constituent State for Secheduled Castes, and Scheduled Tribes. These seats are to be filled by representatives of the 'backward' groups. The only other special arrangement for particular groups in the Constitution relates to the Anglo-Indian Community. Article 331, empowers the President of India to nominate not more than two members to the Lok Sabha if he feels that his community has not been properly represented. According to the Constitution, both the provisions for reserved seats for the Scheduled Castes and Tribes and for nomination of representatives of the Anglo-Indians of "cease to have effect" after ten years of the promulgation of the Constitution. These provisions have, however, been renewed in 1960, again in late 1969, and again in 1979.

Having reposed faith in the unprepared people, India bacame a great testing ground of the adaptability and workability of universal adult suffrage in free and secret elections in under-developed and developing countries. In most of the newly independent countries such as Burma, Pakistan, Indonesia etc. universal adult suffrage has not been given a fair trial. In India, on the other hand, nationwide General Elections have been held in 1951-52, 1957, 1962, 1967, 1972, 1977 and 1980. In 1969, a mini election or midterm elections was held in five Indian States—West Bengal, Uttar Pradesh, Bihar, Punjab and Nagaland.

Role of Election Commission. The gigantic task of organising election in India has been entrusted to the Election Commission. It is charged with "the superintendence, direction and control of the preparation of electoral rolls," and the conduct of all elections to Parliament and to the Legislature of every state and of elections to the offices of the President and Vice-President held under the Constitution. The Election Commission consists of the Chief Election Commissioner and such number of other Election Commissioners as the President may from time to time fix. The appointment of the Chief Election Commissioner and other Election Commissioners is made by the President subject to the provisions of law made in that behalf by Parliament. When any other Election Commissioner is so appointed, the Chief Election Commissioner shall act as the Chairman of the

Commission. The President may also appoint after consultation with the Election Commissioner such Regional Commissioners as he may consider necessary to assist the Election Commission in the performance of its functions. The conditions of service and tenure of office of the Election Commissioners and the Regional Commissioners shall be such as the President may be rule determine. The conditions of service of the Chief Election Commissioner shall not be changed to his disadvantage after his appointment. He can be removed from office in the same manner as a Judge of the Supreme Court. This means his removal is not any easy affair. The President or the Governor of a State shall, when so requested by the Election Commission, make available such staff as may be necessary for the discharge of its function.

Ballotting System of Voting Stopped After 2nd General Election. The tremendous task of holding first General Election was undertaken under the able guidance of Sukumar Sen, the Chief Election Commissioner. Over 173 million voters were registered. As many as 3,772 constituencies were democrated, 489 for the Lok Sabha and 3,283 for the Vidhan Sabha. To make the procedure of voting as simple as possible and to instruct the voters in this procedure, a great deal of advance preparation was done. Some 9 lakh government employees, including thousands of teachers, were used as election officials. To avoid some of the problems created by the illiteracy of over 80 per cent of the voters symbols and the multiple ballot box scheme were employed. The balloting system of voting was used in the first two elections. It was felt that this system was the simplest possible one and would be most suitable for a vast, inexperienced and largely illiterate electorate system. But there were certain disadvantages also. It was slow, cumbersome and expensive. It gave rise to many difficulties and allegations of fraudulent practices. As such, after the Second General Election, the Election Commission abandoned this system, except for a few more backward or isolated constituencies.

Secret Ballot System. The allegation of fake equality has been solved by adopting secret ballot system and by the requirement that ballots shared not be counted at the level of Polling Station. The repression of various forms of fraud has also been attempted. The permanent electoral register with the provision to include newly eligible voters is aimed at curbing fraud, in particular impersonation or double voting. A kind of indelible ink is used to see that the same person does not get the chance to vote twice within the voting days. Attempts have also been made to prevent outright bribery, threats or blackmail. But success in this respect is not complete.

Rules for Deposits and Forfeiture. The positive requirement to achieve real equality and to avoid wasted votes, there are rules for deposit and its forfeiture in case the candidate fails to secure a prescribed minimum number of votes cast. There are limitations on the amount to be spent by a candidate seeking election. The candidate is required to submit an account of the expenditure to the election authorities. But it cannot be denied that the candidates file figures of expenditure prescribed by law. Election laws have been amended to the effect that funds provided by the Party are not counted. The political parties raise funds through donations, from industrial houses and commercial concerns. In this way, the party in power has definitely an advantage over the opposition parties because of immense patronage at its disposal in the form of licences, permits and quotas.

Single-Member Constituencies. The electoral system in India allocates seats on the basis of single-member constituencies. This has been done on account of its simplicity. This was considered highly desirable in a country like India where vast majority of voters was not only illiterate but had no prior experience of the exercise of vote. The single-member constituencies are so distributed that the number of voters, as far as possible, are equal. But on account of variation in population over time, redistribution becomes necessary. This redistribution called delimitation is also undertaken by the Election Commission.

ELECTORAL BEHAVIOUR

Studies of Indian elections can be broadly classified into three parts. The first deals with process of election. The second deals with the investigation of factors which determing voting behaviour. The third deals with Government. It is indeed difficult to analyse the voting behaviour of the electorate. Prof Mavo remarks that the individual may cast his vote to protect his personal interests or that of a group to which he is loyal. It may be that he may merely express his preference for the candidate. Still, there are instances when the voter may be exercising his right to vote just for the sake of the ritual that he has to perform after every five years. He may exercise it to express his faith in democracy and his country. He may pass in judgement on the government's record. He may get an opportunity to study carefully the party programmes and the personality of the candidate seeking election. All voting is an emotional experience for the illiterate voter and the scholar alike.

Factors Affecting Voting Behaviour in India. Thus, there are certain factors which determine voting behaviour of the electorate in India. These factors are:

1. Caste. India is traditionally a caste-ridden country. Even in politics caste plays a dominant role. Caste is rather the first and major factor which influences the behaviour of voters to a considerable extent. So much important is caste to politics that Morris-Jones writes: "...politics is more important to castes and castes are more important to politics than before." The major consideration for giving a seat to a candidate with a party weight on the basis of the fact as to what caste dominates in a particular constituency. When one party allows a particular contestant, the other party sees to it that it also allows the contestant of the same caste. Caste appeal works miracles on the sentiments of the electorate.

In most of the constituencies, it is nearly possible to predict the result of the election by keeping in view the caste of the candidate seeking election and the majority caste resident in that constituency. It has been noticed that generally the people of the caste group vote en bloc for a candidate of their own caste. This naturally obliges the political parties to put up candidates keeping in view the caste considerations above everything else. It is why Salig Harison has said, "The political role of caste is widely conceded in the Indian press, and invariably the most perplexing election surprises become crystal clear when the caste factors in a constituency come to light."

There is no exaggeration to say that nowhere else as in Haryana the caste system is so dominant. The election result can with certainty be predicted keeping only this factor in view.

Like Haryana, Andhra has displayed a leading role of caste in politics. The whole of Andhra politics has been a sort of cock-fight between the Kammas and the Reddys. The Kammas joined the Communists and the Reddys the Congress. The Congress was in fact alarmed at the Kammas supporting the Communists in the First General Elections. So, on the eve of the Second General Elections, the Congress deputed S.K. Patil to get the support of the Kammas. Ultimately, Prof. N.G. Ranga, a Kamma leader, agreed to support Congress. The Congress was as such able to match caste with caste in the choice of candidates and thereby ensure that communities were not able to have the advantage of caste. Harison said, "As an example of Hindu caste discipline in political motion, the post-war decade in Andhra merits special attention. Caste has played a fundamental role during this period that this examination becomes in effect caste history in the impact of caste on India's representative institutions."

In Maharashtra there are three important castes—Marathas, Brahmins and Mahars (untouchables), which have played an important role in state politics.' The Brahmins are numerically smaller but their advancement partly due to their western education, led them to play the dominant role in politics. The Marathas also small in number, nearly 23 per cent, have enjoyed a position of dominance. The Mahars constitute majority of the population and have been won over by the Congress. The Congress has accordingly consolidated its position on their strength. Miss Patterson says, "All along in various ways caste has exerted an important though at times, subtle effect on the Congress organisation in Maharashtra."

Certain sociologists are, however, of the opinion that castes is on its last legs. But Prof. Srinivas holds that this wrong impression. Caste has not lost its appeal. Caste was no doubt on the decrease. But politics has exploited caste feelings. They appeal to caste sentiments just with a view to gaining majority. In this way majority of the sociologists are now veering round to the point that caste is now manipulating politics. Rather it is politics which is manipulating caste loyalties. In caste they find a source of support.

2. Religion. Religion plays an important role in elections. The rise of religious parties like the Hindu Mahasabha, Akali Dal and Muslim League is all due to this fact. Certain people are still swayed by the religious slogans rased by the communal parties for their selfish ends. The Hindu Mahasabha stands for the revival of ancient Indian culture and civilisation relating only to the Hindu religion. Similarly does the Akali Dal appeal to the Sikh masses by raising the bogey of "Panth in danger". The Muslim League has again been revived only due to the fact that certain Muslims in India went to vote for a party which can safeguard their religion.

The Hindu Mahasabha has been wiped out of existence. But it does not mean that the voters have become to conscious as not to listen to religious appeal. The place of Hindu Mahasabha was taken over by the Jan Sangh. The Jan Sangh considered itself to be a secular party. But the Hindu communalist voters voted for the Jan Sangh only. The communalists among the Sikhs vote for the Akali Dal. It has big appeal mostly in villages and in some Pockets in the cities in Punjab. Muslim League has again raised its head. It has won success particularly in Kearla and is spreading its influence in other States also. All this clearly shows that people in India are still influenced by religious considerations.

3. Regionalism. If communalism means love of the community in preference to the nation, regionalism means love of a particular region in preference to the country. Communalism is limited mainly to the two communities but regionalism is a country-wide phenomenon. The most prominent manifestation of regionalism appeared in the DMK party which originated from the Justice Party in Madras, standing for the rights of non-Brahmins against the monopolistic hold of Brahmins on the administrative and political positions. The more militant among the members of the Justice Party from Dravida Kazhagam (DK) which called upon the Dravidian people of South India "to guard agaomst a transfer of power from the British to the

Aryans." It demanded a separate South Indian state—Dravidstan. On the event of Kamraj succeeding as Chief Minister in 1954, the DK gave its support to the Congress ministry on the consideration that Kamraj was a non-Brahmin. This divided the DK and the splinter group named itself as DMK (Dravida Munnetra Kazhagam) which pleaged again for the attainment of Dravidstan. The appeal of DMK on the voters in Tamil Nadu became so powerful that the DMK formed ministry in 1962. It continued to hold this ministry even in 1967, and 1972, elections until 1976, when the Central Government had to take over the administration of the state due to misrule. In the General Elections held in 1977, it is the All India Anna-DMK which has come into power. It is also a regional party.

In Punjab, during the struggle for independence. Master Tara Singh demanded Khalistan, Then on November 2, 1949, "he demanded a "Sikh Province" in East Pakistan on the plea that the Hindus had become narrow minded communalists". He further pleaded that the Sikhs could not "hope to get a fair deal at their hands." This demand was then given the shape of 'Punjabi Suba' for which agitations were launched. The demand was met in November, 1966. This made the Sikh masses future realise that their future is bright only under the Akali Dal. In 1967, General Elections, the Akali Dal was returned in big numbers to the State Legislature. The Akali Dal formed coalition ministry. The coalition failed to deliver goods to the people. The Akali Dal in collaboration with the Janata Party came to power in Punjab in 1977, General Elections. But certain section in the Sikhs still feel that their interests can be safeguarded only by the Akali Dal. The AKali Dal has started claiming something like autonomous Punjab.

4. Class. There is no denying the fact that the Indian political parties "....appeal to and secure support from all major social sectors." But there is some evidence to show that certain sections of society are more active in politics than others. In rural areas, for instance, the middle peasantry whose interests are greatly affected by what the Government does, is more active then either the rich peasants or the agriculture labourer.

The Communist Party appeals to the working classes—the labour in factories and land. It appeals to the have-nots as against the haves. How the class appeal works miracles is evident from the result of every election held so far in the Chheharta (Amritsar) constituency where the majority of the voters are labour. This seat has always gone to the Communist candidate who is also a labour leader in all the General Elections.

5. Kinship. Kinship is by no means a less important factor that determines voting behaviour in India. Kinship so often pervades over party affialations. A voter may be committed to the ideology of a particularly party but he will always vote for a candidate who is related to him irrespective of the fact that he belongs to some different party. This is particularly so in rural areas where the poeple are mostly illiterate.

6. Factions. One of the most distressing features of voting behaviour in India is factionalism. The voters are swayed not so much by the Party ideology and programme as by the faction. Those committed to a particular person would always vote for the candidate of their own faction within the party. This has sometimes bewildered the Congress Party. This Congress Party allows a candidate to seek election but finds it defeated by the intrigues a particular faction within their own party. One faction works against the other leading thereby to the defeat of the candidate of their own political party. This happens more so in the ruling party and it is but natural for factionalism to exist more manifestly in the Congress when it was in power. This factionalism displayed itself so clearly in the Janata Party also when it came to power. To quotean example, the official candidate of the Janata Party was defeated in the Narnaul bye-election because the ruling section of the Party in Haryana favoured an independent.

7. Community. This is a big factor in voting behaviour. A Jat will invariably vote for a candidate of the Jat community caring little for the political party to which he belongs.

8. Party Programme. Party programme has an important effect on the minds of the voters. Leaving aside the committed voters, the other voters are generally attracted by the party programme. Taking into consideration the fact that majority of people in India are poor, all the political parties resort to politics of poverty. Every political party prepares its programme in such a way as to allure the poor masses. Even such parties as the Jan Sangh come forward with economic programme aimed at ameliorating the condition of the poor.

9. Party Organisation. However, charming the programme of a party might be, it cannot have much impact upon the voters so long as it does not have a well-knit organisation. The most disciplined and organised party in India was Bhartiya Jan Sangh. Its organisation on the shoulders of dedicated workers was one of the major causes that brought it success after its formation. Only a sound organisation can reach every home for the making appeal to the voters. The voter is interested not so much in the ideology of a particular party as in its capacity to get things done. Things can be got done only if the party organisation is strong enough.

There is an explanation why the Bhartiya Janata Party (erstwhile Jana Sangh) is losing ground is that the R.S.S. cadre has independence from its leadership to vote for a candidate that protects and promotes the interest of our motherland. And, at present, they find this element in the Congress and the B.P.J. Previously, there were clear instructions for the R.S.S. to work for he Jana Sangh candidates.

10. Economic Status. The economic status of a candidate seeking election also affects the voting behaviour. Certain people vote only for a man of wealth. They have the inclination to think that a poor legislator wields no power and no influences. It is why big landlords, big industrialists and ex-rulers get elected in India. One of the reasons why Scindhia won against Atal Behari Vajpayee was that he belonged to the royal family.

11. Political Issues. The support a party enjoys depends largely upon the nature of political issues it espouses. The Congress has taken up the cause of Socialism and Secularism. The Jan Sangh took the cause of revivlism while the Communist Party that of bringing in communism. The voter invariably votes for the party which espouses the cause of those political issues which is dear to him.

12. Personality of the Candidate. The personality of the candidate seeking election is of great importance. A resourceful candidate has definitely an edge over a candidate having no resources. Magnetic appeal of personality definitely counts much more in India.

That is why film starts such as Rama Chandran and N.T. Rama Rao not only became Chief Ministers of their respective States but also wield considerable influences over the masses. It was on this amount that Congress (I) fielded film starts such as Amitabh Bachchan, Sunil Datt and Vyjantimala Bali against the stalwarts of the opposition parties, and won with considerable margins.

13. Party Loyalty. Party loyalty weighs with many voters. Party loyalty means commitment to the party under every circumstances. The explains as to why some voters are deadly committed. We find that every party has committed voters. Those people who are loyal to their party will always vote for their own party regardless of its omissions and commissions.

14. Demagogic Slogans. With few exceptions, all the voters are influenced by demagogic slogans. Demagogic slogans appeal more to sentiments than to commonsense. The voters become emotional and are enslaved by catchy slogans. This explains how the Congress got majority of the votes in the 1971, election to the parliament when Mrs. Indira Gandhi raised the slogan of '*Garibi Hatao*'. Everyone in India felt elated that they have found their messiah in Mrs. Indira Gandhi. The people were tired of other parties. They voted en mass for the Congress Party. To realise this slogan, decades are required. Poverty cannot be removed by a magic wand. It has to be fought and eradicated. Then, the slogan of 'Government that Works' raised by Indira Gandhi paid heavy dividends.

15. Local Power Structure. Voting behaviour depends also on the factor of local power structure. Local power structure implies the dominance of a particular party over the local self-government institutions. If the Congress wields authority in Gram Panchayat it will mean definitely that majority of the voters are influenced by the Congress. It is because of the fact that the Congress by virtue of its holding power wields the power of patronage.

16. Money. Money is also a great factor that determines the behaviour of the Indian voter. Money is spent lavishly just to please the voters. Money is distributed among the voters. The leaders among the voters are bought through money. The voters are thus, allured by money.

17. Party Performance in Running Government. The Indian voter has become very much conscious from the political angle. He has shown that the major consideration with him is the performance of the party in running government when it becomes the ruling party. If the ruling party fails to deliver goods to the people, the Indian voter uses the instrument of *negative vote* to dislodge that party from office. Congress was voted out of office in many states in 1967, on this consideration. The non-Congress parties gave a bad account of themselves and were voted out of office. Similarly, the Congress was again voted out of office in 1977, due to the blunders it committed during Emergency. The Janata Party that made a very poor show of themselves, were voted out of power in 1980, elections.

18. Government Role. The sincerity and the role of government also determines noting behaviour in the following manners.

1. While demarcating constituencies the government can indulge in or avoid gerrymandering of areas to the benefit of particular group. Gerrymendering is done in a number of ways:
   (a) By separating different groups into exclusive constituencies. The reorganisation of states and districts was an effort in this direction.
   (b) By clubbing two religious communities or those having opposed political outlooks adjust in a constituency in a way to allow one group have an ourwhelming majority. This is almost invariably done by the party in power at the time of demarcation.
2. The party in power something leaves out chunks of population opposed to it at the time of preparation of electoral rolls. The voters, particularly the illiterate ones,

cannot afford to get their names entered at the eleventh hours.

3. The policy of rejection of nominations materially affect's the opposition parties and the election behaviour. It has been alleged that the nomination papers of various opposition candidates were rejected in Jammu and Kashmir in the May, 1977 election.
4. Invalidation of votes also serves as a big handle to tilt result in favour or against a particular candidate.
5. The timing of election is always chosen by the ruling party by keeping in view only its advantage.
6. The opposition parties are also put to great disadvantage by the ruling party through intimidation. The supporters of the opposition parties are intimidated through governmental machinary.
7. The candidates of the ruling party can be declared elected through false counting or recounting of votes. In the 1962, elections at Tarn Taran in Amritsar District, Partap Singh Karon, the then Chief Minister, was declared elected through recounting and showing a majority of 34 votes although he was lagging far behind when a meddle was created by switching off lights.

None of the factors listed above is the sole reason that determines voting behaviour. But it is a fact that some of them taken together determine the behaviour of a particular voter. Some factors are bound to have effect upon every voter but certain factors like money, caste, religion, regional affiliations and the like should be discouraged. They are bound to have a bad effect upon our political system.

ELECTION COMMISSION

As pointed out above, the Election Commission of India is the central body entrusted with the task relating to superintendence, direction and control of elections. Art. 324, lays down:

"1. The superintendence, direction and control of the preparation of the electoral rolls for, and the conduct of all elections to,

Parliament and to the Legislature of every State and of elections to the office of President and Vice-President held under this Constitution shall be vested in a Commission referred to in this Constitution as the Election Commission.

2. The Election Commission shall consist of the Chief Election Commissioner and such number of other Election Commissioners, if any, as the President may from time to time fix and the appointment of the Chief Election Commissioner and other Election Commissioners shall, subject to the provisions of any law made by Parliament, be made by the President.
3. When any other Election Commissioner is appointed, the Chief Election Commissioner shall act as the Chairman of the Election Commission.
4. Before each General Election to the House of People and to the Legislative Assembly of each State, and before the first General Election and thereafter before each biennial election to the Legislature Council of each State having such Council, the President may also appoint after consultation with the Election Commission, such Regional Commissioners as he may consider necessary to assist the Election Commission in the performance of the functions conferred on the Commission by Clause (1) .
5. Subject to the provisions of any law made by President, the conditions of service and tenure of office of the Election Commissioners and the Regional Commissioners shall be such as the President may be rule determine. Provided that the Chief Election Commissioner shall not be removed from his office except in the manner and on the like grounds as a Judge of the Supreme Court and the conditions of service of the Chief Election Commissioner shall not be varied to his disadvantages after his appointment. Provided further that any other Election Commissioner or a Regional Commissioner shall not be removed from office except on the recommendation of the Chief Election Commissioner.

6. The President or the Governor of a State shall, when so requested by the Election Commission, make available to the Election Commission or to a Regional Commissioner such staff as may be necessary for the discharge of the functions conferred on the Election Commission by Clause (1)."

This provision is very comprehensive. It says about the appointment of the Chief Election Commissioner by the President and also of other Election Commissioner by him. Thus, the Election Commission may be a multi-member body under the headship of the Chief Election Commissioner. He may be removed on some charge by the process of impeachment as applicable to the removal of a judge of the Supreme Court. That is, a resolution to this effect must be passed, after at least 14 days' notice given to him of this intent, by both the Houses of Parliament by absolute majority of the whole House coupled with two-thirds majority of the members present and voting. Though the Parliament may regulate the scope of functions of the Chief Election Commissioner, he may act on his own in any contingency not provided for by law and to issue necessary orders for the conduct of elections including repoll in a constituency or some of its polling stations. He also empowered to settle disputes relating to the allotment of symbols to political parties and to recognise or derecognise any political party for such a purpose. This is in addition to the powers given to him under the Representation of the People Act, 1950 and of 1951. In such quasi-judicial matters the Election Commission is like a 'tribunal' and hence its decision is subject to the jurisdiction of the Supreme Court in appellate matters.

The main functions of the Election Commission may be enumerated as under:

1. To prepare electoral rolls for the elections and suitably revise them after every decennial census and before every General Election to the Union and State Legislatures;
2. To supervise the machinery of elections throughout the country so that elections are held in a free and fair manner;

3. To notify the dates and schedules of elections so that nomination papers are filed and properly scrutinised before elections take place;
4. To appoint officers for inquiring into disputes relating to electoral arrangements;
5. To request the President of India or the Governor of the State for requisitioning the staff necessary for conducting elections;
6. To cancel polls in the event of mass-scale rigging or other irregularities;
7. To act like a court for settling matters as giving recognition to a political party or allotting a symbol for electoral purposes, including derecognition of a party or withdrawal of its symbol;
8. To advise the President on a matter relating to the disqualification of a members of Parliament and to the Governor about the disqualification of a member of the State legislature; and
9. To advise the Government whether elections can be held in a State under President's rule in order to extend the duration of emergency there after a year.

Seshanism

It is rightly held that the nature of an office is determined by the personality of the wielder himself, not merely by the rules written in the Constitution or elsewhere. For the first time, Chief Election Commissioner T.N. Seshan could make a meaningful exercise of the powers given to him under Art. 324, relating to the superintendence, direction and control of the preparation of the electoral rolls for, and the conduct of all elections to Parliament and to the Legislatures of the States, including the offices of the President and Vice-President. With a solemn determination to hold the elections in a free and fair manner, as far as possible, he, like his predecessors; issued guidelines on the eve of elections, but also saw to it that these were followed strictly by the Union and State Governments. Not only this, on receiving the complaints of rigging and booth-capturing, he either ordered for the cancellation of polls in some constituencies or repolling there. He took strong exceptions to the official declarations regarding introduction of schemes or works of public welfare so as to bribe the voters. Most important of all, his decision to cancel by-elections throughout the country was the turning point. "The action was so sudden and drastic that he lost all appreciation and support. He was dubbed as a halter of the democratic process on flimsy grounds."

What, however, came as a source of unstinted activism on the part of Seshan was his opposition to the appointment of two Election Commissioners (S.S. Dhanoa and V.S. Sehgal) whose posts were abolished by the Central Government after some time. But the scene was re-enacted when the President issued an ordinance in October, 1993, and thereby appointed G.V.G. Krishnamurthy and M.S. Gill as Election Commissioners. The Chief Election Commissioner did not bother to allot them work and other facilities befitting their posts. Nor did he express his willingness to be the head of a body in which all decisions should be taken by the majority of votes. Despite clear verdict of the Supreme Court, he issued orders to stop counting in the Calcutta Assembly by-election. His order was stayed by the Calcutta High Court; when he challenged it in the Supreme Court, he lost his case. And yet he went ahead in his own manner. He issued directions to the States of U.P. and Mizoram after unilaterally declaring the schedule of elections. In U.P. an advertisement in a newspaper, issued at the cost of public exchequer by the Chief Secretary of the State, was taken by the Chief Election Commissioner as 'a gross violation of the model code of conduct for the guidance of political parties and candidates.' In Mizoram the transfer of the Chief Secretary was viewed by the Commission as a violation of its order directing that all actions relating to transfer of officers connected in any way with elections should not be undertaken without prior approval of the Commission as the elections had become imminent. Seshan also made it clear on certain occassions that government servants would be given suitable punishment in case they were found guilty of dereliction of duty in conducting elections.

Seshan created a very awkward situation by appointing the Secretary of the Election Commission (Bagga) to officiate him during his absence when he left for the United States in June 1995, on a month's leave. This was patent violation of the rules as the charge ought to have been given to one of the Election Commissioners. This action of Seshan was widely criticised in view of the fact that he had acted not from ignorance but from arrogance and that too under the firm impression that any amount of wrong done by him would do him no harm. Any sensible person could accuse him of violating the norms of propriety when he himself was so sensitive in seeing others to follow the rules and norms of the Constitution and laws of the country. In July, 1995 the Supreme Court delivered a long-awaited judgment in a case in which it ruled that the position of the CEC in a multi-member body was like that of the 'first among equals.' The verdict underscored the principle that no constitutional authority could safely by vested in a single individual and that some checks and balances were also necessary to ensure that the individual concerned could not, in the name of being a constitutional authority, extend his power beyond that given to him. The Court ruled that the CEC "is merely the creature of the institution, he can exist only if the institution exists. To project the individual as mightier than the institution would be a grave mistake."

It appears that the Chief Election Commissioner followed the path of assertiveness in reinterpreting and exercising powers given to him under the provisions of the Constitution and the Representation of People Acts of 1950, and 1951. By settling disputes relating to the allotment of symbcls at the time of elections or recognising and derecognising political parties, he has assumed quasi-judicial powers. Though the Supreme Court has put a check on the powers of the Election Commission in some cases, it has held the action of the CEC valid in several other matters. He knows that annoyed executive cannot do anything that puts him in a state of disadvantage in terms of his salary, emoluments, jurisdiction etc. While the Election Commissioners may be removed by the President only on his recommendation, he can be removed by the process of impeachment applicable to a judge of the Supreme Court. This is the reason that while some Union and State Ministers and Legislators, on some occasions, loosely talked of his removal by impeachment, nothing could be done in this regard. In fine, Seshanism stands for an active and assertive role of the Chief Election Commissioner in the fashion of the Secretary of State for India who had the power to 'superintend, direct and control' the administration of this country under the Government of India Act, 1858, and as also known by the nickname of 'Grand Vizier' or 'Mughal-e-Azam of India.'

Critical Appreciation

Democracy is sustained by free and fair elections that take place periodically and afford the people a chance to choose and change their rulers. The Constitution of India has, indeed, elaborate mechanism for this purpose. Apart form this, we have a system of laws that cover the entire work of elections as Representation of the People Act of 1950, and of 1951, and the Delimitation Commission Act of 1962, as amended in 1972. From what we have seen above, some fundamental principles underlying them may be inferred as under:

1. There is one general electoral role for every territorial constituency. The Constitution has abolished the system of communal or separate representation introduced under the Acts of 1909, 1919, and 1935.
2. Equality has been accorded to each citizen in the matter of franchise and the electoral roll is prepared on a secular basis.
3. Elections are held on the basis of adult suffrage and every person who is a citizen of India, is above 18 years of age, and is not otherwise disqualified is a voter. A voter may be disqualified on any ground as of non-residence, unsoundness of mind, undischarged insolvency, commission of a criminal wrong, doing of a corrupt or illegal practice etc. A person found guilty of adopting illegal or corrupt practices may be debarred for 6 years by the Courts, but the Election Commission may reduce or waive it after giving reasons for it in writing.

4. Seats may be reserved in elections to Parliament and State Legislatures for the Scheduled Castes and Scheduled Tribes.
5. Only Supreme Court can decide a dispute relating to the election of President and Vice-President. Other election disputes covering Members of Parliament and State Legislatures can be decided by the appropriate High Courts, but their decisions may be taken to the Supreme Court in appeal. This matter can be assigned to the Administrative Tribunals by a law made by the Union or State Legislatures.

Though the Constitution has sought to ensure independence and impartiality of the Election Commission, some flaws in its composition and working may also be pointed out. First, the Constitution says nothing about the qualifications and term of the Chief Election Commissioner. Every matter in this connection has been let to the jurisdiction of the President pending a proper enactment by the Union Legislature. It may be feared that the President, while acting on the advice of his Council of Ministers, may appoint a person purely on the basis of political consideration. The unofficial Tarkunde Committee in its Report on Electoral Reforms (1975), had proposed the constitution of a multi-member Election Commission and the appointment of the Chief Election Commissioner and other Election Commissioners to be made by the President on the advice of the Prime Minister, the Leader of the Opposition in the Lok Sabha, and the Chief Justice of India. Last, the Election Commission, though entrusted with the august responsibility of conducting elections to the Union and State Legislatures, including the offices of the President and Vice-President, "has been denied the right to recruit and regulate the conditions of service of its secretariat staff—a right available to some organs of State, viz., the two Houses of Parliament, the Supreme Court, the Union Public Service Commission, and the Comptroller and Auditor-General of India."

EMERGING TRENDS IN ELECTIONS

1. Understanding Intricacies of Elections. In India, the common citizen has grown used to the mechanics of elections. A degree of expertise has developed and the awkwardness that characterized the attitudes of the voters in the earlier elections has largely disappeared. Thus, on one side elections cause less and less commotion for they seem to be taken in the stride. Excessive publicity by candidate and parties is, therefore, necessary and may soon begain to produce counter-results. On the other hand, there is appearently some grasp of what the elections can deliver.

2. Exploitation of Personal Popularity. Much of the drama of elections is the exploitation of personal popularity. There are glamorous Maharanis, Cinema stars; aging giants and young giant killers. The cinema stars have in particular great attraction for the people. M.G. Ramachandran of A.I.A.D.M.K. came to power in Tamil Nadu on account of his popularity as a film star. Similar drama has been enacted in Andhra Pradesh where N.T. Rama Rao, a vetern film star has become Chief Minister. His party, Telegu Desam, has won more than two-thirds of the Assembly seats—all due to his personal charm as a film star. His role as a herevolent character in films endeared him to the masses. People wonder, on that very analogy, why should not Amitabh Bachchan become Prime Minister as a hero of the Hindi Cinema when the heroes of regional films can become Chief Ministers. Wandering around the country at election time one comes to recognize the fact that personal drama is linked inextricably with electoral politics and perhaps with general politics. There is the cycle-rickshaw driver moved to tears because a princess has come to ask his vote Aware of the charm of film, artists, the Congress put-up Amitabh Bachchan, Sunil Dutt and Vyjayanti Mala against the formidable candidates of opposition parties such as Bahuguna, Jethmalani etc There is no wonder that all the film artists won with thumping majority.

3. Rise of Young Blood. There is another new development in the elections: the rise of young-blood. One of the consequences of the pattern of human reproduction is that every twenty to twenty-five years there is a new generation on the scene. Whatever the virtues and sins of the other generation, there is at least a chance that the new generation would start with a relatively clean slate. In many parts of the world men and women in the age bracket of fifteen to thirty sow a marked inclination to take a fresh look at the affairs of their societies and governments. They are not impressed by the shibboleths of their elders, whether these be religious or ideological fanaticism such as anti-communalism or racism, or the cult of the golden calf. This generation has lightly rejected, like a swan shedding water from its feathers, the hypocritical morality of its procreators.

In India also there are beginnings of the generational renewal and the youth is making its impact for the first time in the political history of the post-indepenence period. We heard of the youth taking a hand in politics in the mid-term election in Kerala for the first time. The return of Sanjay Gandhi to power with an unprecedented majority is a proof of the fact that youth has asserted itself in the political field of India. Vote for Rajiv is indeed a vote for *change and continuity*—change to young leadership and continuity of the Congress culture. There is no wonder that more than 60% of the voters are below 40. Only 232 out of the total members of 508 returned to Parliament for which elections were held on December, 1984, are old hands. A big majority of them hail from youth.

4. Feminine Role. Women were becoming less conspicuous in the political scene of India. Touring the country, one does gain the impression of a faminine decrease in politics. If the impression is valid, the reason may be the increasing professionalisation of politics. If business firms and political parties are investing a great deal of money and effort in fighting the elections, and the campaign is likely to be rough, women may not be desirable candidates from the viewpoint of the party bosses. It cannot be denied that the number of women contestants has increased, the number of successful women has all along been on the decrease.

This trend has, however, been reversed in the elections to the Eighth Lok Sabha held in December, 1984. The number of successful women candidates has risen to 43 in a total tally of 508. The previous record was at 33 in 1962 while in 1980 elections the number stood at 20.

5. Elections getting Professionalised. With the increase role of money elections appear to be getting professionalised. Only a few big people who can afford to spend, have professionalised elections.

A new entrant into the field knows not the intricacies of this game. He is sure to be defeated although being supported by an influential party. Rather, the trend in the parties has grown that only few selected persons allowed to contest on their ticket. Elections are thus being monopolised in India.

6. Secular Trend. There is the rise of a secular trend. For the first time after independence, secular-minded Muslim thinkers are coming forward to express their views and stake a claim for leadership. The major critique of their more conservative correligionists is that the latter are lagging too far behind the times. If the traditional leadership continues to pursue a communal political line, argue the secularists, it will remain an isolated and relatively insignificant group in all-India politics. The thinking of the communalist Muslims is still caught in the mould of the pre-partition and pre-independence politics whereas the country has moved a great distance ahead. If Muslims do not march step-in-step with the rest of India, they will remain condemned to backwardness nor will they gain the respect of other communities.

The more orthodox Muslims, who in South India are organised politically in the resurgent Muslim League, have a simple and effective answer to the secularist which, ironically, is irrefutable in a democracy. It is that the masses of he Muslims in India do not support progressive or secular minded Muslim leaders. The conservative leaders want to maintain the communal and social distinctiveness of the Muslims in India—their traditional personal law, their language (Urdu), and their social cohesion. It is obvious that the economic and educational backwardness of a large proportion of the Muslims in India generates a circle of isolation, engendering a sense of neglect, much resentment at being left behind by the other communities.

7. Big Role of Money. Elections appear to be getting increasingly influenced by Money. One hears frequently from the ward-level political workers, who are the foot soldiers of election battles, that they need a wealthy candidate who can pay his own election expenses. The jeep for the election has become the watch-word; the more the jeeps the better the campaign. One party worker estimated that there may be as many as seven hundred polling booths in a parliamentary constituency and a candidate has to spend at least one hundred rupees per booth, making a total expense of seventy thousand rupees for their work alone. What India seems to be heading towards is the Americanization of the elections, where the sky is the limit for campaign expenditure. Considering that even in the U.S.A. only wealthy candidates have a chance of success, and even they become indebted to the business-houses who help to pay their expense, the consequences of increasing cost of fighting an election for Indian democracy are nothing but baneful. There must be a way in which this extravagance is curbed.

8. Political Consciousness. It is quite heartening to find that the voter in India has by and large gained political consciousness. He now makes free choice. He is not swayed by petty considerations. He has grown conscious to the extent that it is not possible to predict in whose favour he will cast his vote. He accepts money from someone, promises somebody else but still votes yet another person. This clearly establishes that he has become aware of the value of this vote.

This became manifestly clear in the General Elections held since 1967. The voters in India voted non-Congress parties in power in more than half of the States in 1967, General Elections due to the failure of the Congress to better their lot. But when the voter found that the non-Congress parties have failed to deliver good to them they voted en masse for the Congress. The voter in India came to realise that stability in administration can be brought only by the Congress. This fact induced them to vote for the Congress. The excesses committed by the Congress during the Emergency made the Indian voter vote Congress out of office and instal the Janata Party in office. They found the Janata Party incapable of ruling over the country and brought the Congress back to power. At the time of 1984, elections when India was faced with national stake, the electorate voted for Unity and Integrity of India with unprecedented majority. This is indeed a great testimony to the political consciousness of the Indian voter.

9. Unfair Advantage. The ruling party enjoys unfair advantages in many respects. In the first place, the ruling party is allowed use of are helicopter which is denied to the others. In the beginning, even the electioneering Prime Minister had to use special trains, engaged by the Congress.

Secondly, the time allowed to the ruling party at the A.I.R. and Doordarshan is more than allowed to other parties. All parties should have equal chances of access to the people through national media. They are the media of not one party but of the nation as a whole.

10. Separation of Assembly and Parliament Elections. The separation of elections to the State Assemblies from the elections to the Lok-Sabha, as it has developed, is one of the most undemocratic developments. At the time, elections were held simultaneously, all parties in office or out of office were simultaneously and equally engaged in all constituencies all over the country. At present, whichever party is in power at the centre, has advantage in fighting isolate elections. The Centre can pick-up two or three States, concentrate all its resources in them, and try to secure them. It can then pick-up a batch of two or three other States, and thus, consolidate its base in as many States as possible before it will call for elections to the Lok Sabha.

11. Rigging. Elections are becoming more and more subject to rigging. It makes difficult to dig out the party in power. The fact that Ministers are defeated in election after election has increased the faith of the voter in the fairness of elections, though there are deliberate violations of freedom and fairness by authorities or mobs.

12. Declining Role of the Election Commission. The date for holding elections is gradually passing on to the Central Government to decide. The Election Commission appears to be losing ground in this respect, especially after Trivedi, the present Chief Election Commission took over. It is the centre which has decided elections to State Assemblies in Andhra, Karnataka and Tripura, not the Election Commission or the local Government. Again, it was the Centre which decided on the elections to Assam, Meghalya and Metropolitan Council in Delhi, It does not seem that the constitution makers envisaged this kind of situation.

13. Emergence of Regional Parties. The use of whims by the ruling party at the Centre has given rise to the emergence of regional parties such as D.M.K. and All India Anna-D.M.K. in Tamil Nadu, Telegu Desam in Andhra Pradesh and helped consolidate the position of already existing regional parties such as the national Conference in Jammu and Kashmir and Akali Dal in Panjab. The growth of regional parties under such centralised pressure is but natural. With the establishment of Governments by regional parties in the States, they would be able to control a week centre to adjust itself to their moods. The United States has reduced the urges of regionalism in a vast sub-continent by the four-year Presidential elections and the two year elections to the House of Representatives. It is indeed difficult to derive a system on the American pattern at this stage in India. But it should not be difficult to approximate the elections to the State Assemblies to the elections to the Lok Sabha. It would certainly be one way of encouraging evolution of two or three national parties with regional branches.

ELECTORAL REFORMS

Free and fair elections are an integral part of democracy. Without a periodic vote of approval or disapproval of the legislatures, political parties and governments, there can be no democratic government. In democracy, it is the elections that are ultimate sources of power and if the springs are poisoned at the very source, it is unrealistic to expect a clean and clear stream to emerge. The working of the Indian electoral system so far has been marked by a number of disturbing factors. Because of these disturbing factors, talk of change in our electoral system is being talked about. Eminent people like J.P. Narayan, B. Shiva Rao, G.D. Sethi, Subhash C. Kashyap and A.J. Singh came forward with a strong plea for reforms in electoral system. No less a person than S.L. Shakdher, the previous Chief Election Commissioner, whose responsibility it was under the Constitution to conduct Elections, had on several occasions made certain far reaching suggestions with regard to what needs to be done. They have often urged the need for reforms as pressing. Yet, it is surprising that no systematic case for electoral reforms has been made so far. The talk, by and large borders on gossip. It is so because the reasons advanced in favour of effecting electoral reforms are generally more negative than positive. None of the major political parties have followed matter this matter to its logical conclusion.

Electoral Defects and their Reform. The need for electoral reforms has been urged on account of the fact that there are various defects in our electoral system. These defect have come to light during the course of the various elections held in India so far. These defects are:

1. Discrepancy in Representation. India has opted for majoritarian system of elections as prevalent in England and America. Under this system, the country is divided into single-member constituencies, which elect their representatives not by an absolute majority but by a relative majority. It means the candidate getting the highest percentage of votes in relation to votes secured by any other candidate singly gets elected. So, the number of votes polled by the successful candidate may come to less than the total number of votes polled by other candidates taken together. Often a candidate polling just 30 to 35 per cent votes in the constituency get elected. Sometimes, this discrepancy between the percentage of votes polled and the percentage of seats won entirely perverts the results. The Congress stood to gain by this system. In 1952, the Congress poll percentage for the Lok Sabha was 44.99; in 1957, it was 44-78; in 1962, it was 44.73; and in 1967, it was 40.82. Nevertheless, the Congress succeeded in getting some 60% seat in the first three elections and a clear majority even in the fourth. In Delhi, the Congress secured in 1962, fifty per cent of the total votes polled but bagged all the Lok Sabha seats. But in 1967, with its vote percentage down to 38, it could win only one out of the seven Lok-Sabha seats. Even in the 1971 election, the Congress's popular support was 43.68% but it got about 0 per cent of seats.

Another glaring example of such defect is provided by West Bengal where in 1967, elections, in terms of popular support, both the Congress with its 41.1 voting percentage and the United Front with 41.36 voting percentage were more or less evenly balanced. But in respect of seats, the Congress was badly mauled. In the mid-term polls of 1969, the relotive position regarding poll percentage changed but slightly. The Congress actually improved it voting percentage from 41.1 to 41.31. The United Front percentage also improved slightly from 41.36 to 41.98. But in terms of seats, the results were shocking for the Congress. Its legislative strength fell steeply from 127 to 55. Such examples can be multiplied. Thus, under majoritarian System, election often becomes a pure gamble. The horse that goes past the victory post first of all is the winner, be it just a hair-breadth or a head of second. Hence, the majoritarian system of elections is also called first past the Past System.

In the 1977, elections to the Lok Sabha, the Congress got 34% of the votes. But got not even a single seat in the Lok Sabha from U.P., Bihar, Madhya Pradesh, Punjab etc.

Thus, Elections often become a gamble. While discussing the ailments of the existing system of elections, that is, single-member constituency, one elector one vote, and election by simple majority, C.P. Bhambri has pointed out the following defects:

(a) The existing system of elections gives importance to the individual candidates than the political party. The result is that these important individuals dictate their terms for remaining in the party.

(b) Elections are not an exercise in choice among various party programmes. The so-called merits of the candidate assume a decisive role in elections. All sorts of primordial loyalties and ethnic instincts work in the mind of the voter at the time of elections. Elections become personality oriented instead of being issue-oriented.

(c) Political parties, instead of selling their programmes and policies try to measure the constituency in terms of religions or caste arithmetic and search for candidates who qualify in that arithmetic. Its result is that the parties tend to be a collection of individual who can walk in or walk out of the party at their convenience.

(d) Not only the existing system of elections dilutes party programme or ideology, it leads to all sorts of nepotism in the body politic. The candidate who wins on the basis of "local qualification". keeps himself busy in bringing public resources for his constituency...

(e) Another serious defect of the present electoral system is that there is little relationship between the electoral performance of a party and its strength in the Assembly or Parliament. A serious point of public debate in India was that the Congress party obtained more seats in the Lok Sabha than the percentage of votes secured by it, during the first four General Elections.

Defect in Single-Member Constituency System. Election on the basis of a single member constituency system results in tension and bitterness among different sections of the populations. In a single-member constituency, there are just two alternatives before the Campaigners; complete victory or defeat. After the polls, therefore, supporters of the defeated candidates feel sore and frustrated.

Bandwagen Phenomenon. This is yet another feature of Majority System. The voter is reluctant to waste his vote on a party sure to be defeated even though that party may be the best in that particular election view.

Caste Factor. Another lamentable defect of our Majority System is that in most rural constituencies caste is the largest factor that affects election result.

Instability in Politics. From 1947 to 1967, the composition of the legislatures made India polity a single party set-up. Politics was not stable but stagnant from 1967 to 1971. We witnessed a phase of multi-party politics, with Coalition Government in which each major partner felt tempted now and there to break from the coalition, force a fresh poll and gamble for a superior position. This resulted in a sort of instability in politics.

2. Influence of Money in Elections. The second important aspect of electoral reforms that needs to be paid to reduce and control urgent attention is the growing influence of money in elections. The expenses incurred on election are so huge that parties tend to give ticket only to a millionaire. One of the questions almost all political parties put to candidates seeking their ticket is: how much are you willing to spend on this election? And a major factor influencing a party's choice is the ticket-seeker's capacity to spend. The limited resources of parties make it inevitable. Where parties are in a position to supplement the candidatess' resources, they do. In exceptional cases, they may even entirely finance a certain candidate's election. But as a rule, every candidate has to finance himself.

The sharp rise in a candidate's election expenses has for some time been the subject of considerable concern. It is generally admitted that the statutory ceilings on expenses are seldom observed in practice. The actual expenditure incurred by a candidate does not bear any relation to the maximum limits laid down. Even the Election Commission in its report on the Fourth General Elections conceded the growing influence of money in elections. The Commission has repeated its earlier recommendations made in its third report as to how to lessen the influence of money. It suggested that:

(a) a limit be imposed on the number of vehicles that may be used for elections;

(b) processions and demonstrations be banned during elections;

(c) the use of peripatetic loud-speakers on roads be prohibited;

(d) no paid canvassers be allowed;

(e) The period of accounting be not confined, as at present, to the period between the date of election notification and the date of result, be extended further back; and

(f) parties be made to account for expenses incurred by them in promoting the election of particular candidates.

The Election Commission, in its report on the 1962, elections had also expressed the view that the legal provisions relating to election expenses now in force were of no use and called for drastic amendments. The report mentioned and extreme case in which a candidate had rendered his account of election expenses by means of a single entry, namely, the payment of a lump sum to the party sponsoring his candidature.

In a recent case, the Supreme Court upheld the view that it is not necessary to include in a candidate's election expenses the money spent by a political party. In its report on the 1967, elections, the Election Commission suggested a provision on the lines Section 63 of the British Representation of the People Act of 1949, which prohibits election expenses being incurred by any other person except the candidate. In India, the electoral laws, on the other hand, have been amended to lay down that the expenses incurred by the party shall not be included in the expenses allowed to the incurred by a candidate.

Eradication of Money Factor in Elections. A solution to the problem can be found only if it is accepted in principle that all election expenses be charged from the governments funds. Even in the Constituent Assembly, Prof. K.T. Shah introduced as amendment to this effect. The amendment reads:

"All expenses in connection with election to Parliament of all candidates, whether at the time of General Election or a bye-election shall be defrayed but the Public treasury in accordance with a scale prescribed by Parliament; provided that any candidate securring less than 10 per cent of the votes cast at the election shall not be entitled to claim such expenses."

The only argument given against this amendment was that the country was not rich enough to undertake so huge an expenditure. It is estimated that the total amount so incurred would be Rs. 10 crores. According to the Election Commission's report on the 1967, elections, the total expenditure incurred by the Government on the elections was about Rs. 22 crores. An additional sum of Rs. 10 crores would not matter much to eradicate the bad influence of money of elections.

S. L. Shakdhar, the previous Chief Election Commissioner, had suggested that the state should be responsible for financing election expenses. He said: "I believe that if an election fund of Rs. 100 crore for a period of five years is created initially it will take care not only of government expenses on elections but also of the expenses incurred by the candidates and parties."

Of course, the implementation of such a scheme would have to be carefully worked out. A certain percentage of votes would have to be fixed to entitle a candidate for reimbursement. There was a time when, in England, even the fees of Returning Officers, the cost of constructing poll booths, etc. had to be paid by the candidates. It was only in 1918, that a law was enacted transferring to the State the burden of paying Returning Officers and running the official election machinery. This trend has grown. Today, every candidate is entitled :o send one election address, postage-free, to every single voter is his constituency.

3. Eight Forms of Electoral Corruption. The electoral law as it stands today regards eight kinds of practices as corruption. There are:

1. Bribery,
2. Undue influence,
3. Exploitation of religion, caste, community etc. for electoral purposes,
4. Preaching Communalism, Consterism, linguist racist hatred,
5. Slander,
6. Providing transport to voters,
7. Exceeding ceiling on election expenses,
8. Using Government employees for electoral ends.

As things stand today, almost all corrupt practices are used in election. "It is indeed a matter of shame," said Sh. S.P. Sen Verma a former Chief Election Commissioner, while addressing the All-India Conference of Chief Electoral Officers in September, 1968, "that even after more than twenty years of political independence and four country wide General Elections in the second half of the twentieth century, when we take pride in our intellectual achievements in many spheres, corrupt practices in our elections are not showing any signs of abatement or diminution."

After the 1967, General Elections, as many as 397 election petitions were filed. A majority of them were based on the charges of corrupt practices.

(a) Abuse of Official Machinery. Abuse of official machinery is included in the list of corrupt practices. In 1971, the ruling party's election campaign opened with press conference arranged by the Press Information Bureau at Vigyan Bhawan duly broadcast and televised by the AIR. Early in 1974, the U.P. and Orissa elections were held. During the three months immediately preceding the poll, Prime Minister Mrs. Gandhi went round launching one project after another most of them without even proper financial sanction. These so-called inaugurals arranged at government expenses were nothing else but election rallies. Often the Ministers disburse money from the dicretionary funds at their disposal on the eve of elections to the voters.

The governments servants only take part in elections to help the rulling party. This is inspite of the law that: "The obtaining or procuring, or abetting, or attempting to obtain or procure, any assistance for the furtherance of a candidate's election from any Government servant." Clearly, this provision covers only such abuses in which individual Government employees are deployed for election purposes.

(b) Abuse be Checked Through Law. Steps should be taken to make election laws more clear and stringent to cover any case of corrupt practice in which the Government servants take part to help any candidate. Not only should the election be declared invalid, the government servant concerned should be dismissed from service.

(c) Abuse of Public Media. It was alleged by the opposition parties that the Radio and Television are used only the Congress which is in power. The opposition parties were promised to be given some time but they have not been given. This thing has gone a long way in helping the party in power by protecting its image. There public media have thus been abused.

Use of Public Media be Made Open to All. The only way to eradicate this evil is that all the parties be given equal time to put their programme before the public. It is not at all justified to give time to a party proportionate to its representation. When the representation figure is itself based on wrong electoral system, how can the time proportionate to representation be justified?

The Joint Parliamentary Committee on Amendments to election law unanimously recommended that during election campaigns all recognised parties should be allowed equal time on the AIR. In areas covered by T.V. a similar arrangement should be made on T.V. also preference worked out to enable, individual candidate to make brief appearances.

The aforesaid committee also suggested that instead of separate public meeting by parties and of candidates joint meetings should be organised by the Election Commission at key points in the constituency and candidates or their spokesman should be invited to address these meetings. This proposal had been practically accepted by the Janata Govt.

There should be a limit on the number of posters, pamphlets, newspaper advertisement, etc. a candidates should be permitted to display during an election. The use of loud-speakers and the organising of processions should be banned.

(d) Cenveyance for Voters. A corrupt practice extremely spread is the use of vehicles on polling day to provide free conveyance to voters to and from a polling station. Station 123 of the Representation of the People Act, 1951, defines this as a corrupt practice. But this practice is resorted to indiscriminately.

Abolition of Conveyance on Polling Day. More than a hundred years ago, J.S. Mill observed: "The polling places should be so numerous as to be within the easy reach of every voter; and no expenses of conveyance at the cost of the candidates should be tolerated under any pretext."

In its report on the Fourth General Elections, the Election Commission recommended that "the number of motor vehicles that may *i.e.* used for electioneering purposes should be limited to three in an Assembly Constituency, and to six in a Parliamentary Constituency."

In fact, the plying of all vehicles on polling day, except those connected with official election arrangements, police, hospital etc. should be completely prohibited. Passes should be issued to such authorised vehicles on the lines of curfew passes.

(e) Problem of Impersonation. This problem is quite common among the urban voters. Impersonation does not directly come under the election law. It is an offence under the Indian Penal Code, punishable with one year imprisonment, or with fine or with both. But it is generally found that the Presiding Officer avoids legal proceedings against the offender. This is so simply because he wants to save himself from the botheration of criminal proceedings. The provision is certainly useful. But this practice of impersonation is not on the decrease. In its report on the 1967, elections, the Election Commission questioned the allegation that the indelible ink is not really indelible. It has reiterated that the device of putting an indelible ink mark on the left fore-finger of every voter at the time he receives the ballot paper is a fool-proof guarantee against bogus voting. It has been alleged by many opposition leaders that the so-called indelible ink is delible and the device is not fool-proof.

4. Role of Defections. The greatest malady needing immediate reform is the role of defections in our electoral system. People getting elected to Parliament or State Legislature on the ticket of a party, defect to another party to get monetary benefits and so on. This practice has gone a long way against the democratic practices. S.L. Shakdhar, the former Chief Election Commissioner of India suggested that the defections can be stopped merely by an amendment to the Representation of the People Act, 1951. However, certain legal experts are of the view that such an amendment will be against the provisions of the Constitution which does not recognise any party of Party affiliations.

This is clear from Articles 81(1), and 170(1), Article 81(1), says: "Subject to the provisions of Art. 331, the House of People shall consist of, *(a)* not more than 525 members chosen by direct election from territorial constituencies in the States, and *(b)* not more than 20 members shall represent the Union Territories, chosen in such manner as Parliament way by law provide." Art, 170(1), repeats what is contained in Art, 81(1).

Again Rule 5, of the conduct of Election Rules, 1961, framed under the powers conferred by Section 169, of the Representation of

People Act provides for the recognition of parties merely for the purpose of reserving election symbols. On these grounds, the Chavan Committee on Deflections ruled out the possibility of making deflection a penal offence Law curbing defection would also be violating Art, 19 (1) (c), which reads: "All citizens shall have the right to freedom of speech and expression and to form associations or unions."

However, R.K. Trivedi, the former Chief Election Commissioner has also agreed with Shakdhar and suggested that defection should result in the reaction of seat in Parliament or State Legislature.

5. Higher Voting Age in India. The question of an appropriate voting age has in recent years assumed considerable significance. The fathers of the Indian Constitution established a representative democracy in which all adults of twenty-one years and above, male or female, without any distinction of caste, creed, colour, region or race have been given the right to vote. This brought about a great social revolution by enabling the dumb millions and giving them for the first time in centuries, a voice in their affairs. It is these millions whose vested interest in democracy has today become the greatest sheet- anchor of the system. The constitution, however, deprived the youth in the age group of 18—21 of the right to vote. This group of blooming youth thus feels completely estranged, alienated, and ignored. It has become the weakest link in our democratic apparatus. The members falling within this age group feel completely outside the current politico socio-economic culture of our country. They remain uninvolved.

6. Counting Procedure is Defective. Before 1971, counting of votes used to taken place polling station wise. In 1971, this procedure was changed. Now ballot papers of all polling stations in a single Assembly constituency are mixed-up and then counted. The argument that this system of mixing voters prevents intimidations and harassment of small polling areas with about 1000 electorate on an average is wrong. Even on this patterns it should not be difficult for the political parties, if they were so bent to find out broadly how a particular area voted. The idea is again gaining ground that we should revert to the original system.

Voting Age be Lowered. These member of the youth became either nihilists, drug-addicts or hippi-imitators. Sometimes they become rebels demanding a role in vital decision-making. The student unrest to much taken about in India is confined to this group of the youth. There is no denying the fact that there is a close relationship between the problem of youth unrest and the question of lowering the voting age. These is a general desire among the youth to secure full participation and a decisive voice in administering their affairs. Denial of franchise to about 5 crores people mean lack of faith in our youth. The youth may, in turn, lose all faith in democracy.

7. Election Commission's Role. *(a)* The Election Commission should be a multi-membered body and not a single membered body as it has been till now. *(b)* The practice of nominating retired secretaries to the Government of India for the office of Chief Election Commissioner should be given up. Only persons who are qualified to become judges of the Supreme Court should be appointed. *(c)* Retiring members of the Election Commission should be reappointed to any other office. *(d)* The Election Commissioner must revive its practise of convening frequent all party meetings to discuss election matters.

8. No Age Limit for Contestants. It is indeed very painful to see that contesting elections has been professionalised. Only those very few persons who are professional, continue to contest election even when they are very old. This is harmful in the sense that it leads to frustration among the young who are otherwise capable but do not find accommodation. Moreover, the old people become naturally rigid and are not so accommodating resulting in inflexibility in approach. Certain people are of the view that a person having attained the age of 60 should not be eligible for election either to Parliament or State Legislative. Dr. Karan Singh, however, in his Article published in The 'Tribune' of March 5, 1981, suggest 65 as the maximum age. This means that if a person contest before completing 65, he can continue up to 70.

9. Election to Local Bodies Out of the Purview of Election Commission. Still another glaring drawback of out election system that need reform is that election of local bodies is not conducted by the Election Commission with the result that a number of seats in the Legislative Councils have been lying vacant for many years because the local bodies, which form electoral college for those seats, have not been constituted. Very often Panchayats and other local bodies continue to be suspended, thereby negating elections to Legislative Councils in various State. S.L. Shakdhar, the previous Chief Election Commissioner of India, was of the view that elections to local bodies should also be entrusted to the Election Commission so that this situation is remedied.

10. Right to Exercise Voting. Dr. Karan Singh is of the view that voting should not be left to the whims and conveniences of individual citizens. If we line in a democratic system, it should be required of us to fulfil our responsibility on the voting day. It should be made compulsory. These are many instances of constituencies where less than fifty per cent of the people have taken the trouble to vote. It is true that the citizens should be obliged to fulfil their responsibility in this regard. Not only will this enable the election results to reflect more accurately the public mind, it will also ensure that no action of society is allowed to be bullied or bulldozed into abstaing from voting, and at the same time, place a responsibility upon many members of our urban elite who seem to consider it below their dignity to stand in the quence and cast their vote in elections.

❐